T0353662

SUDDENLY WHITE DREAM!

DURIME P. ZHERKA

authorHOUSE

AuthorHouse™
1663 Liberty Drive
Bloomington, IN 47403
www.authorhouse.com
Phone: 833-262-8899

Published by AuthorHouse   04/11/2025

ISBN: 979-8-8230-4412-7 (sc)
ISBN: 979-8-8230-4411-0 (e)

Library of Congress Control Number: 2025903588

Print information available on the last page.

Any people depicted in stock imagery provided by Getty Images are models,
and such images are being used for illustrative purposes only.
Certain stock imagery © Getty Images.

This book is printed on acid-free paper.

Teenagers On The Beach

It was one beautiful afternoon time when the Summer, season was leaving with something with desperate its place to autumn season. Really looked that summer season wanted to extend her existence and some days more while the children to take by its days not by autumn.

Also, summer season cannot afford the pride of Autumn season that children were happy to go in school with happiness in first week of its time. The Summer season, in hidden way was keeping its big jealousy about Autumn season when it was showing so much pride about yellow color that was spreading all around environment.

The Autumn season was appeared in bold way, with yellow color on garden and sidewalk by the leaves of trees and wanted to dominates everywhere. It was overdue by Autumn season when wanted to show up with mixer color, like yellow to orange close to open read color on the hills with different trees and this situation was making so much nervous the summer season.

This was another strong reason that during this afternoon the summer time was pleasing the golden hot Sun to stay more longer on the beach above sand and blue, ocean's water and to dismiss in gentle way the weak wind that Autumn season was sending before time only to be provocative to the summer time.

Summer time was thinking that its season is beautiful with hot sun with different color flowers, with different birds that were coming from the cold weather, so people loved Summer, season more than others seasons plus they were going to the beach during this time. Summer season, whispered calmer that she is more worth than Autumn season.

In this hidden fighting of Summer, season that with pain was leaving its place to Autumn season were one crew of younger teenager boys and girl that were playing with ball on the yellow sand. At that time one woman from another crew of adult people that were sitting on the sand and were talking with each other, called her children and said get prepared you with your friends because we are going now. After that the teenagers that gave created one circle and were playing with ball while they were thrown with their hand to each other, left their game with ball and started, to run from the sand to blue water of ocean.

They were laughing and talking loudly and entered to ocean while were splashing the face of each other with water after started to swim all together, while seeing each other who was swimming faster.

Their enthusiasm and loudly talking with happiness, got attention of some people that were sitting on the sand in crew and were talking and were seeing this group of teenagers.

After some minutes one younger man said to the other people that were his friends, let's go to swim in ocean. So, they started to walk slowly, all of them and entered in ocean.

From the distance the lady made with sign with her hand to her children and all others to come out of ocean and called them in foreign language. She did not want that teenagers to deal with stranger people, so she was persistent and was repeating her calling and her sign with hand to come out of water her children and their friends too.

So, after her calling so many times teenagers decided to go out of water of ocean. At the moment one younger man Zeeshan that was with his friends, was in front of this crew of teenagers and was seeing and listening their conversation.

Close to him came one very good looking, younger boy with very white face, that was covered with one very open pink to red color, while his nose has bold red color, by the hot gold sun on the beach, looked that they were not so longer on this beach.

At that time another very beautiful younger girl was thrown water with her elegant very white hand to face of this younger boy that he was closing his eyes and was blocking his mouth with his hand, while she was laughing loudly.

She was talking in foreign language, with another younger beautiful girl and another younger good looking, boy and was laughing, they laughed too, and all other were laughing with the younger boy with his close eye and his mouth blocked by his hand.

2

The younger man did not understand that foreign language and said hello in English language in front of younger boy that the girl was playing with water with him. The younger boy when heard his voice opened his eyes that were so beautiful with mixer color between green open to blue color, and put down his hand that has blocked his mouth.

The younger boy said to this younger man: Hello!

The younger man asked his do you speak English language? The younger boy said to him: I speak but my English language is weak language now but am studying hard so much and I will have progress in future.

Okay, very good said the younger man, but what language are talking your friends? The younger boy said they are speaking Albanian language. We are Albanian, people with ethnicity but we all are living to one village named "Lunaria", that is in border between Croatia and Slovenia. So really. we are speaking two languages, Slave language that is official and in school too, and Albanian language in our family.

So, all of you are friend for same village and country, asked the younger man. The younger boy started enthusiast to tell that:

We all are Albanian people we are living, really in big village but this village is separated by one bridge and longer river in two places, one is Lunaria where I am living with my sister and my family and with that boy that is my friend and his sister too.

At that time, he showed with his hand the beautiful younger girl that was playing with water with him, he was continuing her name is Agneza and my name is Gentius, also this friend of mine, is living to my village "Lunaria" with his sister, his name is Dalmet, and his sister's name is Armina.

They were staying in water close to Agneza and were listening, also all others teenagers, friends were listening with silence so and the younger man's friends were listening with attention.

The other part of this big village has name "Kauntia", and over there are all Albanian community, but to "Lunaria" is administrative village with office of local Government or "Comuna" as we named, where are working and our parents of me and Agneza. "Lunaria" has with medical center, with shopping center, with so many stores, for different repairs and with culture center's building too. Also, to "Lunaria "village is and our beautiful big building of school that is servicing, since first grade of elementary school until to the fourth grade of "High school".

All children from "Lunaria", village and "Kauntia" village are coming to this school. The names of those villages are Albanian names too.

So, all of you are Albanian as I understood while he was watching Agneza, he shocked with her beautiful eyes with mixer color like green bold and green open to open blue too.

Her longer eyelashes were creating on frame like crown around her eyes and were giving more dark color like shadow that were doing her eyes more intrigues. Her face was so white but has got some easy pink to red color by the hot golden sun.

When she was smiling with her brother during his explanation with enthusiasm her beautiful lips that were natural red color like cheery, were showing inside very beautiful white teeth like beautiful white pearls inside their shelves.

Her brown longer heavy hair was covering her shoulder, while her body was so white normal taller and so much elegant.

At that time Gentius said with strong voice: Yes, we are Albanian people, and was continuing, and in those two villages are Albanian community too.

Our parent are, over there while he showed the group of adult people on the yellow sand that were prepared to go but they were waiting their children. We came all together some friends and our parents for five days' vacation, here because our parents, found tickets with discount and hotel's rooms with discounts too.

Our Ancestors are Ilirian, our King at that time had name Agron and our Queen at that time has name Teuta, our country was Illyria at that time.

They were very brave and were protecting all the beach of Adriatic, sea, from others and from pirates too. After the death of King Agron, Queen Teuta got leadership, and was leading Ilirian people while was doing business with Venedicas.

Our queen Teuta was very smart and brave woman too. He spoke in bold way and all laughed with his explanation

She protected so much our country and all Ilirian people that today are Albanian people. Really after Ilirian era our Albanian people named Arbers and the country named "Arberia" that today is Albania.

The younger man loved the enthusiasm and smart mind of Gentius but all the time he was watching the younger girl Agneza. When time by time he was crossing his watching with Agneza's watching, he felt sweet feelings and hot inside him and shiver and why he was staying inside cold water of ocean at the end of Summer, season and beginning of the Autumn, season.

After Gentius asked the younger man,

What is your name?

and without interruption asked another question,

Are you off today with your friends by your job or business that all off you are on beach now? Younger man laughed loudly and all his friends laughed too, after he said to Gentius:

My Name is Zeeshan, and we did not have off day, today, but we had some jobs to do in this area about my business and came now later to the beach with my friends to enjoy this afternoon.

So, you are businessman? asked Gentius

Yes, I am businessman answered the younger man.

But you look very younger for big business. In my country businessman are older.

Why you think that younger people are not able to do business?

Some younger are doing business but they have small business.

While you have so many people today with you and I think you have big business, for his I think you are younger.

You are right said the younger man Zeeshan, I have a big business and I am working with those people friends of mine days and night without interruption.

Gentius, made one cheer: Ooooouuuu, it is good that you are younger, I am happy that I saw one younger man with big business.

All laughed loudly friends of Gentius his sister Agneza, his very close friend Dalmet and his sister Armina, and friends of the younger man Zeeshan.

At that moment the younger man Zeeshan said to Gentius:

With your full explanation you made me to fly tomorrow to see your big village with two parts "Lunaria", and "Kauntia" in border of Croatia and Slovenia, also to see that big and beautiful school that is servicing from elementary school until to the end of high school.

Gentius listen me carefully I loved that fact that you speak fluently slave and Albanian language but you are treasure because you are speaking and English Language.

Gentius said: Oooo My English language spoken, needs so much hard job to improve but I will do in future I will study hard. The younger man Zeeshan said to Gentius:

I believe to you that you will study hard and you will speak fluently English language in future.

I promise to you and all of you that I will come with my friend to see your big village with its two parts "Lunaria" and "Kauntia". He gave his hand and hugged Gentius.

Gentius asked his very fast:

Really you are coming to our village and to our country that we are living. Really replied the younger man Zeeshan.

After he gave hand to younger beautiful girl Agneza, at that moment he felt hot inside his body when he touched her elegant white hand and was seeing her very wonderful sweet smile through her very white beautiful teeth.

He felt that her chest and beautiful small breast that showed a little bit by suit bath were moving like with hard breath. He understood that she had emotion.

He felt his really his shiver and stronger, hot inside his body this time, so the cold water of ocean cannot influence to give fresh to him about this situation. He felt happiness to himself when he saw her emotion, but she was so younger and her beautiful face looked so innocent.

After he gave his hand to Dalmet and Armina and the teenagers got out of the water of ocean and went to their parents, after some minutes all they went to one minibus that was to the road and left that place while the children were greeting with their hand the younger man Zeeshan.

During their driving to their home the younger man Zeeshan started to talk with his friend Emin, leader of secret service. I got so much wondering by those teenagers, boys and girls about their enthusiasm, and specific about Gentius how smart he was.

He knew three languages, does not matter that he said for weak of his English language but he was able to communicate anyway. So, we must to do something for children of our city and our country too, about those foreign languages.

His friend Emin replied you are very right the central government of our country and our local government must to do many progressive things for children and specific for foreign language.

The younger man Zeeshan continued his speech it is very interesting, about their happiness and they were living in village in simple life but they were so much smart and they were not shy to speak they were speaking freely with full confidence. They were so lovely youngest people too. They, were so proud for their native story in centuries, like Albanian people. Really the teenager Gentius gave me so much enthusiasm and so many ideas in my head about our children in our city and our country.

He gave me so much inspiration about education of youngest children also he gave me so much happiness this afternoon. We did very good job that we came this afternoon on this beach: Thank You "Allah" for this beautiful afternoon with those very lovely teenagers, boy and girls. Amen.

His friend leader of secret service said: Amen and continued: Really it was one unexpected occasion today. They gave to all of us so many fresh ideas like fresh air that was coming from blue water of ocean.

After that Prince Zeeshan was thinking about this beautiful younger Albanian girl Agneza. He was whispering with himself she was so beautiful and so lovely girl and she loved so much her brother too.

I do not know why am thinking now for her, something I felt when she was watching me during conversation with her brother Gentius. Aaahhh Agneza, Agneza, he repeated her name two times. His friend heard him and smiled, while asked what is about her.

The younger man Zeeshan smiled and said, I do not know what is, but I think it is something unexpected that is giving me one new feeling of happiness after a long time. His friend laughed loudly while he was happy that his younger boss was happy, really, he loved his boss younger man Zeeshan.

It was a longer time that he was seeing his younger boss Zeeshan in deep thought so much serious, with different conversation without feelings, when he was talking with different people in business, he was strict but was missing ingredient, of happiness in his eyes and his speech.

So, people when they seeing the younger man Zeeshan's strict serious conversation without feelings, they were something, withdraw to express freely their different ideas because with this kind of conversation the younger man was creating one beautiful transparent wall between him and them, really transparent wall, but anyway it was wall.

So, his leader of secret service felt happiness inside him for this changing that, was coming to his younger boss Zeeshan during this conversation, while he whispered to himself" "Allah" bless the younger Zeeshan and bless those teenagers children and specific Gentius that influenced to him.

After some days the younger man Zeeshan decided to go with his friends of security team to the place that was in border with desert land. They wanted to see over there relieve for one new idea that the younger man Zeeshan has to build one new modern highway like bridge through the desert so the sand with its "Duna" not to cover in different place the highway.

At the moment the leader of security Emin, with his younger boss Zeeshan saw behind one bush plant one adult couple that were staying in hidden way behind the bush plant while they asked them what is the problem?!

In distance from behind one tropical tree, they saw one very elegant taller girl with longer curls black hair, with blue eyes and brown color of her face, while her beautiful red lips were like frame of very white and beautiful form of teeth. Her eyelashes were so longer in half circle that looked so beautiful when she was seeing down to the ground.

The couple said that she is their daughter Samira. Her mother called her. She came closer, she was scared and shy girl. When she came in front of them, her watching crossed with the eyes 's watching of the younger man Zeeshan.

He shocked with her beauty, while she got wondering with the beautiful eyes of the younger man Zeeshan. Time by time she was watching him, she can not stop her eyes to see him. The younger man Zeeshan was smiling. The adult couple the parents of Samira told to them that they came from Morocco, to hidden in Dubai because one richer lazy boy was not leaving quiet their daughter Samira.

His family is very rich but they never got in consideration this poor family. They wanted to protect their only child that they have this girl, Samira. When they came in Dubai, they closed their small house that they have in Morocco and left one their cousin to take care for their house.

This boy got new where we are and he came with some the others younger boys that are his cousins. We came here but we see that is not any road through the desert, so it is very danger for us, so we thought to turn back in Dubai city.

They all are following us everywhere that we are going. At that time the younger man Zeeshan and his security team's leader Emin heard one big noise that was coming from desert. The sound was, like hihajaja, while one heave cloud yellow color by sand of desert was lifting up. When the cloud by desert's sand was opening, they saw 6 (six) younger boys that were riding 6 (six) beautiful horses.

The Father of Samira, to the younger man Zeeshan, this is the richer boy with his cousins. They came wild in front of the crew of the younger man Zeeshan, and one handsome boy went with his horse close to Samira while started to speak nervous and was yelling.

This is my fiancé. I love her. Really, he did no and not care for her parents at all, about their presence over there while they were speech less and were watching with fear. All the younger boys Moroccan had in their hand big knife. At that time all the members of the security crew of the younger man Zeeshan got out their gun and were ready, all got position for trigger to them.

The boys stopped. The leader of security team said to his younger boss Zeeshan, I will take in my home this family until tomorrow we to decide where to establish. After he asked the boys in which hotel they were established. They told to him the name of hotel. Emin, the leader of security team of the younger man Zeeshan said to those Moroccan boys that he will go to their hotel to meet them and to talk with them that evening.

The younger man Zeeshan with his friend Emin, got this family to their car, the others members of security team came behind with the other car, while the Moroccan boys were riding with their horses until to, place where they have left one minibus that they have got with rent.

The younger man Zeeshan was watching time by time this Moroccan girl Samira, while was whispering: How beautiful is this girl! When they arrived to his palace he said to his friend Emin, I will come to your home later after noon to talk together for this family. He gave greeting to them and left to go to his palace.

Samir with her parents got shocked when they saw this huge, luxury and very beautiful palace, they opened their eyes saw each other but did not speak anything. Emin the leader of security team got this family to his home while he told his wife for those guests during driving the car.

While they arrived to the Emin's home, his wife waited them with smile and big welcome. Their student son Jetmir was with his mother Semiha, to the door of their home and he got shocked with beauty of Samira.

His mother said to him: Jetmir, go to your room because you need to study you have exam tomorrow. Her son went to his room right away. Firs she told them two bathrooms to take shower, because they were very tired and were out close to desert a longer time.

They got shower to those luxury bathrooms with big mirror, with luxury thick cotton big towels and so many different shampoos and different perfumes for younger for adult for women and men too.

After she prepared in dining room, the table, while she put different meals in table, so she said to them to come to table and to eat. They ate and they said to Semiha that was really beautiful lady: "Allah", bless you and your family too. she told them that they have two children one girl Saida, and one boy Jetmir, both are students.

Their daughter Saidas, is studying for chemistry industrial engineering, while their son Jetmir is studying for architecture engineer. Their daughter that day is to another town with her class for externship to one chemical – factory, they have project and need to stay over there one week.

Needed to do that before to give exam. My girl Saida, is finishing university this year, while Jetmir has and two years to finish, both are excellent students too. we are very proud for our children she finished her speech.

After some minutes came the younger man Zeeshan that time by time was crossing his watching with Samira, while was talking with his friend Emin, and his beautiful wife Semiha. At that time Semiha said to the parents of Samira: You were lucky today that my husband Emin and our lovely Prince Zeeshan found you over there. They spoke with one voice parents and their daughter Samira, prince Zeeshan of Dubai? Yes, said Semiha while was smiling he is Prince Zeeshan our leader of Dubai. I am very sure that he will help you for everything. After that Prince Zeeshan laughed and got out with his friend Emin, he to go to his palace while Emin to go to hotel to meet the Moroccan boys, because he promised to them.

Prince Zeeshan said to his friend Emin to get every information for parents of this boy Aludin was his name, because he wants to contact with them. We need to help this family and to make calm situation, because the father of Samira told me that he wanted to go back to Morocco, he said that in Dubai life is so much expensive.

The leader of security team Emin went to hotel and found and met all boys. He talked with them he got full information of the rich boy Aludin 's parents and after he invited them to come next day to play friendly food ball game with his son Jetmir and all his friends that are student in university for architecture engineer. The Moroccan boys hesitated first but after they said yes.

After Emin left hotel while said to them, I see you tomorrow to the field of game and have a good night, he called his younger boss Zeeshan and gave full information to him for this rich Moroccan family parents of Aludin, because he said that he will put connection with them tomorrow.

Dream In Desert

THE YOUNGER MAN THAT NIGHT DID NOT SLEEP QUIET, HE WAS NOT IN mood and to talk with his wife but he said to her, that he is very tired and is taking some rest to other room because he had headache.

Really, he was thinking so much for that big story that he faced to land close to border of desert area. He thought for Aludin, that rich Moroccan boy, that he was in deep love with this very beautiful brunet girl with blue eyes Samira.

He did not care for her parents but said in front of all of us: I love her. She is my fiancé. He did all this way from Morocco here in United Arab Emirates (UAE) in Dubai to find her and he found her. He was very handsome boy and so much courage- person. He has loyal friends and cousins too.

I think he will be great in future with his persistence whatever he to study in university he will be success. After the younger man was thinking with himself: What is doing love for people. Love is making people to make impossible possible. People in deep love can escape rivers hills mountains in easy way for their lover.

With those thoughts the younger man Zeeshan, that has opened the window of this room and the breeze of blue ocean was giving fresh air to his face suddenly fell in sleep. Strangely he was enjoying one very interesting dream. He saw himself in desert under one Palma trees that was one in desert, he was with Albanian girl Agneza, she has dressed white Nailon, transparent pants and shirt while her lace underwear and lace bra was showing it selves through this Nailon dress.

While one red wide belt was around her very elegant body. Her brown longer hair, were covering her shoulder and she was standing up in front to younger man Zeeshan, he was sitting to one mattress, with design bold wide green strips and wide beige color strips too. He has dressed white pants and shirt with longer sleeves and one white scarf to is head while around his elegant body he had one wide gold color belt.

Close to him to the bottom of the Palmas tree was one tank pottery red color with water. The beautiful silver moon, was giving light to desert while the stars that decorating, during this night the sky were creating light and shadow to sand of the desert.

Friends of the younger man Zeeshan, were sitting above one wool carpet in few distance to the bottom of their big car, and were talking with each other. At that time, they saw in distance in light and shadow by the moon and stars in desert one caravan with camels.

There were four men with four camels, while camels have heavy staff to their "xhidavia". They stood in distance while one taller older man came to the Palma tree, when was staying the younger man Zeeshan and Agneza, at that time the friends of the younger man Zeeshan got alert they stood up with their gun ready to shoot.

The leader of caravan one older man came to the trees after he said greeting, he said that they wanted water, they have done a longer trip in desert and their water is finished. The younger man Zeeshan, gave to him this red pottery with water and got to his car one bottle with milk and gave to him.

He said: "Allah" bless you with your beautiful wife and gave greeting to his friends and left. He was walking slowly, slowly, while was weighting on his shoulder so many years and hard job of his life. He went to his friend sand gave water, after they continuing their walking with their camels too.

The younger man Zeeshan, said: Thank You, and "Amen" to the older man.

The night was so beautiful and the younger man wanted to huge his girl Agneza and he stand up and touched her hair that were like soft silk textile while got her close to his body.

At the moment the younger man Zeeshan heard one longer, loudly sound of horn came from faraway. He got shocked and this sound was coking closer, all got shocked and all stand up to see what is this in this evening close to desert. The younger man Zeeshan got shocked because this sound came more stronger in this silence of this beautiful night.

All his members of security team got alert and prepared their gun for shooting. But happened the strange phenomenon, all around was spreading folk Albanian music with one megaphone that was installed to the top of the first car of this caravan of so many cars.

There were some small cars in caravan. The cars stopped in road aside the Palam tree where was the younger man Zeeshan with his lovely Albanian girl Agneza. From every car came out two couple so were five cars and came out ten younger people.

They said in distance: we are Albanian people we, are tourists. We got news that Prince Zeeshan will come here close to desert area, this evening. We thought will be secure for us while he is over there so let's go to enjoy with him this beautiful night close to desert area, so we came here.

Really was older road to the land close to desert area. They came all together while were speaking loudly in their native Albanian language while they got from their car some big boxes with some food.

When they came and meet the younger man Zeeshan with his lovely girl Agneza they were happy when got news that she was Albanian girl that was living in Croatia, after they meet friend of the Prince Zeeshan. they brought big flesh light with battery, they brought meat, hotdogs, beers and started to speak English with those people, Prince Zeeshan and his friends too, it was created one happy environment under the silver moon and stars above the sky.

All Albanian younger people were seating direct on sand of desert and were talking loudly while the megaphone was giving with high voice folk Albanian music to the top of the first car, and was spreading all around area.

All were happy for this Albanian crew of people. The night with beautiful silver moon and stars on desert was wonderful with noise of this crew. At that time the younger man Zeeshan saw happiness to the face of Agneza and he whispered: Thank You, "Allah". After he thought: Everywhere I have Albanian people, when he opened his eyes, he understood that he was seeing one very interesting dream. He opened his eyes it was middle night. He got out of the bed went to kitchen to drink water and go after to his bed room to sleep.

Next day in the morning the younger man Zeeshan, when he arrived to his office, ordered one his official man to call that family in Morocco, to speak with parent of the richer boy Aludin. The man called this family and told, about their son Aludin, they got shocked and they were happy because they said we are reaching for him all around those days.

After they promised to him that they will come with emergency that day afternoon until to the evening for their son Aludin to Dubai and they said one big thank you to official of the younger man Zeeshan.

After lunch Emin in his home, told to Samira and her parents that they will go to their home next day maybe afternoon because parents of Aludin will come to Dubai they said apologies to you what happened.

..While Prince Zeeshan will meet them tomorrow and he is doing arrangement for tickets for you also he called one his friend business man in Morocco that has cement factory. He promised to prince Zeeshan, that your father will work in his factory and your mother will work for cleaning offices in his big building of his business, so you will continue quiet your school.

They got wondering and were very happy while Semiha said to them: I told you, our prince Zeeshan will help you, because he has big and golden heart for people.

Later afternoon Emin and his younger boss Zeeshan went to field of football where was game between students of Dubai and Moroccan boys. They found over there Jetmir with his friends, students and Moroccan boys.

The game started wild and the younger man Zeeshan entered to the field and said to student crew of Dubai, do not play wild because they are our guests from Morocco.

When they saw the younger man Zeeshan they started to speak loudly with happiness they screamed: uauaua Prince Zeeshan and went to meet him, the Moroccan boys got wondering when they listen name the Prince Zeeshan of Dubai, they said to each other this is Prince Zeeshan of Dubai, they went to meet him with happiness.

When the game finished Prince Zeeshan got pictures with all of them and his friend Emin. The Moroccan boys went to Emin and said to him, Thank You, very much for your invitation and for this occasion to meet Prince Zeeshan.

We hesitated for your invitation because what happened yesterday in the morning, we thought something else, but your persistence gave to us this happiness to see this prince, your son Jetmir and his good friends, students too Thank You, very much. They meet each other and said good night too. the Moroccan boys went to hotel, while others students went to their homes.

Next the younger man Zeeshan and his friend Emin met the parent of Aludin they discussed so many things. The parents of Aludin promised to Prince Zeeshan that never anymore this girl will have problem by their son Aludin because he will start university and will be busy with his studying.

The younger man Zeeshan told them for his friend that will hire in Cement 's factory father of Samira and her mother to clean offices in his business 's building while Samira will continue quiet her school.

They said Okay very good. He said that he will pay their tickets and will give to them some money until them to start job next week. This speech and arrangement by Prince Zeeshan touched the heart of parent of Aludin and they were seeing him with full attention while said to him:

May "Allah" Bless You Prince Zeeshan. He said Thank You and Amen.

After prince Zeeshan went to his friend home Emin and talked with family of Samira, he told them about job that they will start to his friend to Cement' factory next week. Samira's father will work in factory, his wife will clean offices in business's building, while Samira will continue quiet her school without problem by this rich boy Aludin.

Prince Zeeshan, told them that he paid tickets for them and he gave money dollars to them to have for that week for food or something else, until they to start job, next week. He said to them: Later afternoon you will travel to your country, while my friends will send you to airport.

Prince Zeeshan promised to them when he will come to Morocco for business, he will go to visit them while he was seeing Samira to her beautiful eyes she was shocked by his action and his speech. She was seeing him in lovely way.

After ten days Samira 's parents called Prince Zeeshan in his office and told that they started job to his friend to Cement 's factory, and Samira is continuing school and is preparing herself to go to college next year. They said: Thank You to him and at the end they said we are waiting you to Morocco. Prince Zeeshan laughed with happiness.

-So, with the time and days that were going on so fast, this big changing of the younger man Zeeshan got attention of so many people around him and all his people that were working with him. Really were two sides opposite of his big and good changing.

One reason was that, they were happy because with his good mood they will feel freely to speak to him about every problem, and about any new good idea that they have in their mind.

The other reason was the curiosity what was the source of this big changing of him and if is another woman who is this woman and what she will be for him and them in future. So, the curiosity escaped the border of ethic and so many people started to make rumors and to make so many questions of investigation.

So, whispers were spreading and existing all around in building, in different office in different level of people of business and of course inside his family too, that they were more interested of him more than any one in his world.

Strangely those days that were going so fast, the younger man Zeeshan was feeling himself so good, he was so much active to work was so happy every day. He was feelings something changed inside him, he was doing so many conversations with so many leaders of education institution and different school and universities, and some of the different culture's institutions and nonprofit organizations.

He has and some new ideas that was not ready to express, but strangely he was thinking so much for those teenagers and this beautiful Albanian younger girl Agneza from "Lunaria" village of Croatia really between Croatia and Slovenia in border between them.

Those days were full activities while he was thinking so much about this "Lunaria" village and was so much curious and full wish to visit this place and those three countries Slovenia, Croatia and Montenegro of the Western Balkan.

Really, he never was keeping attention to those countries in serious way so this occasion will be very good to see those two countries Slovenia and Croatia and to see those teenagers and this younger girl Agneza. This idea was coming every day bigger was growing up and was hitting everyday his head to do that.

One day he went with his secretary lady and his secret service crew to one elementary school of this city, to see environment of the school and level of knowledge of pupils.

All pupils were lovely and their class was so beautiful and all environment all around was so good luxury for level of one school. He started his conversation with the teacher of this class and the director woman of this school, and asked them about program about level of knowledge of pupils and about practicing foreign language.

The director lady explained to him that needed so much to improve about knowledge but it is very important if you will put more budget to our school to hire more teachers and to practice foreign language since elementary school.

... Also, to have program for teaching music's instruments, two hours in week, like piano, violine, phisarmonic, that is very important but maybe and trumpet, oboy, etc, so to hire and teacher of music.

The younger children will be so much professional about teaching since youngest time music 's instrument and we will develop those pupils who have talents too for music. So, we will create one great foundation for their future life.

The younger man Zeeshan, said he will discuss with his people in his office and will give answer very soon, but he promised that something he will give to this school anyway. Whatever you to make addition of budget of money to our school, it will be so much beneficiary for our pupils here.

After the younger man left this school with his people and went to his office while his secretary called some people of different departments and they discussed about those topics, that they discussed in school. The account lady Adara, said I will calculate, everything how we can make addition of money to budget of this school so they will be able to hire some more teachers. So, at the end of this meeting all were agreed, and the younger man Zeeshan was very happy about those ideas of the teacher and director of this school also he loved so much his "flesh – fast" meeting like light on the sky during raining day.

After that he decided to go to his luxury big palace. The leader of secret security's crew got prepared with his people after his meeting and they sent him to his palace. He went to his studio and was watching the map of Western Balkan while made some calculation about expenses that he will do over there during this new trip with his crew.

He was thinking to take the account lady Adara, also one journalist Hamad, of his business and one cameraman Jassim, also all his crew of people of secret service. All his people, were discussing about the younger man Zeeshan that he is so much strict about expenses and why he is very rich.

He does not like to spent so much money for ordinary things but he is spending so much about investing so to have big profit in future, for himself for his family and for society of course.

At that evening he was continuing that tradition about calculation about everything and to give so much pleasure to his people that will be with him in that trip to those three countries in Slovenia, and Montenegro, of Western Balkan. He was writing to one notebook with beautiful cover leather open brown color.

After he went to room of his two children and spent some times with them while was playing with them and was laughing too. He felt so much pleasure with his children while the lady Farrah, that was taking care for his children was laughing and was watching him in silence to the door of the room of his children.

She said sorry, dear Zeeshan but now is time children to get sleep. He laughed said: You are right and left his children with that lady to take care for them. He went to one room and lied to one luxury sofa with silk cover with beautiful design int with some flowers open different colors.

He got one small book started to read but slowly, his eyes got closed and he was in kingdom of dream. Suddenly in front of him appeared one beautiful white angel, and was flying around his head, while angel left in other direction, he was watching this angel and in distance, some hills and mountain appeared, while white angel disappeared, he saw one very beautiful younger lady, that was greeting him and was doing sign like come here.

She has in her head one crown with white flowers, very white face like porcelain Chinese – doll, while her dresses were so much transparent more transparent that Nailon. Her hair was so longer with curler, her smile was magical.

She was like beautiful serena of lakes in ancient time's history. At that time that the younger man was enjoying this beautiful dream, he felt some body was touching to his shoulder, and he open his eyes while was listening sir Zeeshan, sir Zeeshan.

He heard the lady Aasma, that was servicing to his kitchen. She said I went to see you in studio to ask if you want something to drink and I did not find you, I came here and I found you sleeping here what is going on?!

He said to her ooo sorry I came here to read something but I was tired and I got sleep. After the lady asked him if he want something to drink. The younger man Zeeshan said: I need to drink one hot lemon tea. She smiled and said now I am bringing here.

She loved so much the younger man Zeeshan, like her son, because she serviced to him since childhood. She was so much confident to him; she was so much loyal person to him and to all his family and his parents and siblings too.

She has more power to him that all others ladies that were working in his big luxury palace. When the younger man got out of sofa and went to small table to drink the tea that lady brought with some small package of sugar, he was thinking.

"Allah" bless me this dream is one sign, this white angel gave me direction to go somewhere in distance to escape hills and mountain to see this beautiful girl that was appear like serena and was doing with her hand to go to her. This is "Suddenly White Dream" for me. She is thinking for me, she is waiting for me.

I will do this trip to Western Balkan. I will go to see this very beautiful younger Albanian girl Agneza, this is sign, for me. Something is happening with me, I do not know myself anymore, why I am thinking so much for this younger girl. Maybe is fiction, or maybe is something new that is giving warm to my heart and happiness to my life. I want to know what is about me and definitely I must to do this trip to West Balkan and to Slovenia, Croatia and Lunaria village and to Montenegro too. After he finished his tea, he went to sleep in his bed room.

Restaurant Close To Field!

NEXT DAY IN THE MORNING, THE YOUNGER MAN ZEESHAN, WAS THINKING for this dream, when arrived to his office 's building he got out of his car that was with Emin, the leader of secret service while others were in other car, after went to his office he felt empty himself while was drinking his morning's coffee with big cup. After he finished his coffee, he called his secretary lady Adara, and ordered her to call and bring some other people in his office.

She went and came fast to his office with some other people. He gave instruction to them about daily – duty and said that he will go out for some other matters. So, when his officials left, he was thinking that was missing something to him, he called the leader of security crew and told him to be ready because they will go to field of animals.

The younger man Zeeshan, got out of the office and went out to his black Mercedes Benz car. His security crew's leader entered to his car the others men got another car and started their driving to field of animals. During their riding was so much traffic in longer highway while all high buildings look, that wanted to kiss the blue sky. All different very high buildings were in race who will arrive the blue sky to play with white clouds, while some top of them were hidden inside those white clouds.

While one super high beautiful modern tower looks that was smiling and playing with other buildings with irony while was breaking the golden sun's rays to its beautiful blue glass wall, was sending those rays like specter to others buildings. Of course, the other buildings were staying skeptical and pedant, with their cement wall for those rays that was sending the super modern beautiful, blue glass wall super high tower.

In line were continuing different buildings some with cement wall different colors and some with glass wall, grey, green, blue, or pink color, but all those were showing their very high height proudly.

The younger man was seeing all of those building in line and was thinking that the hand of human being is doing super great job while was driving in this beautiful super highway that different luxury colorful cars were creating with their driving like one colorful water river that is happening sometimes in fall (autumn) season.

After they got out of highway between this very beautiful modern city, they got out to rural area that modern highway was continuing to the field of animals.

They escaped the field and went first to desert area while all of them were watching over there and started to discuss for future project in desert. Some of them showed their skeptical behave and feeling, some of them were wondering what will build in desert but younger man Zeeshan, said with optimism will build very interesting thing.

After the younger man their boss said with smile are you hungry because I need to eat to restaurant one good lunch and all of them approved him while they laughed all with happiness. Their boss was showing so much friendly by his side.

They went to restaurant that was close to field of animals, they ordered their preferred food while they started to speak for the beach of day before and for teenager that were playing over there. They started to laugh and to discuss comments and knowledge of younger boy Gentius while said that he was so much energize boy.

One of those men said that this beach is so beautiful but so lonely and needed some people at last younger people to spend time over there and to give some enthusiasm to this beautiful lonely beach. The other man said that those boys, girls, and their parents were so happy and why they were doing simple life in their small and beautiful village as they were describing.

At that time their boss younger man Zeeshan, interrupted this loudly enthusiast discussion by all and said in strict way. Do you like to make one tour to see their village. They saw him in shocked way after some seconds with one voice they said of course we want to make this tour, and started to laugh, but they were not sure that their boss was serious with this question or was doing jokes with them. After that question the younger man said Okay, I promise you that we will go soon to see their village.

All then did one strong loudly expression like uuuaauaua and were very happy. They finished their lunch and went to their car to go to field of animals

When they arrived over there, they stopped the car and dropped out. When the younger man Zeeshan, was ready to get out the car came with speed two beautiful Camels with beige color to cream color of their body, and they put their head to window of car while younger men Zeeshan gave to them seed of herbs and started to kiss them.

The leader of security crew Emin, started to take picture about this very beautiful and humanity moment of younger man with those soft animals. In front of them appeared one huge very beautiful field covered with green grass and all around was white wood fence.

Aside the field was one section with some huge flat building with red roof. Those were servicing like shelter for Horses, Camels, Giraffes and others animals plus those were using to make maintenance and feed animals.

The younger man Zeeshan, went to white wood fence and started to hit with his hands the wood – fence suddenly in distance started to ride fast like were running in race, in crew some beautiful horses.

One horse of this crew, was red with very shining black hair to his head until to his body (xhidavia), the other horse, was very white color, another horse was red open color, while in front of his head has one longer sign white color and to four his bottom legs has very white hair like rings all around legs above hits feet.

Really this horse was so beautiful, another horse was gray color and the other was very black shining color. All horses were beautiful.

Behind this beautiful crew of horses were running three ponies, one pony was white color, other pony was red color, and the other pony was half of the body red color, from head to middle body and other part of the body was white was so beautiful and his tale was very shining white color.

When horses came close to fence were was staying younger man Zeeshan three horses, horse with red color, horse with white color and horse with open red color with white longer sign in front of his head and white color like ring to his legs came, in front of him and they put their head to his face.

Younger man Zeeshan, started to touch in gentle way their head and started to kiss in easy way. After in line came horse with grey color and horse with shining black color to play with younger man.

When came time of beautiful ponies they did not left space to each other but wanted in same time to touch the face of younger men with their head. It was one beautiful view and that time Emin, the leader of security crew was taking so much pictures. At that time that came to fence three beautiful giraffes that were looking like confuse all around.

During this time came one of the workers that were taking care about maintenance of animals. The younger man Zeeshan, discussed with him and gave some order for his job to do. After that the younger men Zeeshan, with his security crew decided to go to cars while to drive to their home.

At that moment that younger men Zeeshan started engine came fast and jumped one dog with white color, with some sign grey to purple through his body and jumped from window entered inside the car and was staying on the legs of younger men Zeeshan, inf front of the wheel. Of course, younger men Zeeshan were so lovely with his animals and was taking care so much for them

During this trip he said to his security crew leader Emin, that he will take some rest to his home at the evening they will go to one meeting for business. The man said to him yes sir we will be ready to get you to this meeting.

He entered to his big luxury palace, when he opened the door that was honey color good quality Oak wood with beautiful design in itself the younger man Zeeshan felt one fresh air that came through three open big windows that were with beautiful crystal glass that were going until to the ground of the floor. Windows were covered with beautiful transparent curtains, cream merchandise mixer with Nailon, while aside them were thick silver green color merchandise curtains with design in itself like some very thin branches green with very small white and open eggs colors flowers. In space between windows with those very luxury curtains were two big paints with nature's image, also to others walls were two big paintings with view of his city.

Some heavy sofas with silk merchandise with milk color and design some colorful flowers through it while standing with pride above one huge colorful carpet with wool, and silk mixer, with red blood color space while so many beautiful big colorful flowers were like design and some green branches with their big green leaves through this red blood color field of carpet.

The huge carpet was covering the middle of this huge hall while very beautiful mermer, (quality marble) floor was staying cold to carpet with its white color with some gray line thought it.

One very big crystal chandelier with some different level of circles with very bright crystals that has created one shape like pyramid, in the middle of this huge hall was breaking the rays of the hot golden sun and was giving one big reflection to the floor and to one big mirror that was close to the door.

Those sofas curtains and this colorful carpet combined with painting in wall were giving one magnificence view to this huge hall.

The younger man saw all this hall this time very carefully, while thought so many people dream to have that and are working very hard, while I have but what I am doing for really unusual for my name and for my country too?!

At that time, he was climbing stairs so fast to go to the second floor, while the beautiful floral multicolor carpet while red color was dominating through field of this carpet, was covering the middle of the wide mermer stairs.

During walking to stairs, he was watching all the pictures aside the wall that were pictures of his paternal grandfather that started project for modernize of his city but died early, of his paternal grandmother, of his father, and some of his siblings. He was watching very carefully, while whispered this is history of the family of my father side this is history of my great and beautiful city.

He entered straight to his studio while after some seconds came his lady Aasma that was servicing in kitchen. She asked what he wanted to eat. He said:

I ate out with my friends, but I want only one big cup with hot chocolate and full cream milk to the top and bring to my studio, because I have something to work now. He went right away to his table of job and started to see his telephone while the lady brought the big cup with hot chocolate and full cream milk to the top and left with one beautiful luxury silver ashtray to his table and said to him: Enjoy it. After he said to her Thank You very much, she got out of his office in this studio.

Next day he went to his office and gave so many instructions to his secretary lady and to the others his different specialists that were working to his office 's building.

Also, he called to his office the account lady Adara, one journalist Hamad one cameraman Jassim, while did one short meeting to them and told them that they will travel all together with his secret service people to Western Balkan next Monday.

He said to them: You have all this week to prepare yourselves to make arrangement about everything that you have scheduled about different activity for, your family and about your job here.

I think that this trip maybe will take one-week days for us because we will see three different countries, Slovenia, Croatia and Montenegro, for business first about future investment if it is going to happen and for culture too.

So, you have time to get supplies or different equipment specific you cameraman Jassim, because I want to register in video camera everything that we will see over there and to take different pictures too.

Also, I need by you some information in general way, about those three countries, about their tradition their culture, education and their economy too.

I will do arrangement for all my schedule with different directors of different departments, while I will continue to do as much as I can about my schedule for different appointments that I have with different group of business in our city.

So, I hope all of you will do same thing so we will not be out of our schedule during our trip in Western Balkan, in Slovenia, Croatia and Montenegro too. After he finished his meeting and called his leader of secret service Emin, and told to him that they will go to some center of business and to one restaurant that owner is one Albanian man from Kosovo.

So, they got the car and all together went first to restaurant where owner was Albanian man Besnik, from Kosovo. He got shocked for this unusual visit and waited them with full welcome.

He asked them what they wanted but the younger man Zeeshan, said we have not time to stay longer here and to eat but we will prefer one coffee and I want to ask you for something.

After waiter brought coffee to their table the owner Albanian man Besnik took sit close to the younger man Zeeshan and asked quietly: About what you wanted to ask me? The younger man Zeeshan said to him:

I need one dictionary book in Arabic – and Albanian language or English and Albanian language if is not possible in Arabic and English language.

The Albanian man was seeing him with full attention and smile, while the younger, man Zeeshan, explained to him that he will go to visit Western Balkan specific to Slovenia, Croatia and Montenegro, but I am going to one village that has only Albanian community so I need to learn some simple words in Albanian language.

Yes, I know that are so many Albanian community in different Slavic cities in Wester Balkan, but main body of Albanian ethnicity are Albania and Kosovo. I have visited so many countries of Western Balkan.

Now to enter to the matter that you are interested: Really you are lucky because I have one dictionary book in Albanian language and Arabic language. This dictionary book was prepared by one Albanian professor of theology that study for religion in Saudi Arabia and now is using those for youngest people to learn Arabic language.

After the Albanian man Besnik, went to his office of business and when he came out was holding one book in his hand. He came to table where was the younger man Zeeshan, with his leader of secret service, and said to him:

Okay this is the book and you have gift by me this book while I am wishing you to learn Albanian language and congratulation too. The younger man Zeeshan said to him, Thank You very much, and I will come to visit you when I am coming back from this trip.

They said the greetings to each other "Have a Nice Day" and the younger man Zeeshan with his bodyguard got out of this restaurant to go to the other business center to meet some the others people, while the others bodyguards were waiting to other car outside.

This week was full schedule for the younger man Zeeshan before he to go to this trip in Western Balkan with his people. He was so much enthusiast for this trip but inside him he was a little anxious and was thinking how will wait the beautiful younger Albanian girl Agneza, his visit surprise.

He was thinking so much about this matter and this surprise meeting that he will do for her and to her and to her brother too. Really, he did not have patience until to travel and to find the true of his emotions and his feelings that were not leaving quite him since that day that he saw this beautiful younger girl Agneza.

Japan's Project!

AFTER HE GOT OUT WITH HIS SECURITY CREW 'S LEADER TO GET HIS CAR while the others people were waiting over there and got the other car. During this trip the younger men Zeeshan, in deep thought was seeing the different color advertises to different residence building, or hotels and some business buildings, through this highway that were creating one beautiful specter in this beautiful city.

When they arrived to place of meeting it was one luxury building, they got elevator to go the room of meeting.

When they entered to the huge room that was one big oval table with wood design with open brown color while so many chairs with wood design in itself covered with blue castor merchandise, and big window that was sending shining by gold sun's rays to room and to people to give light to their mind during this meeting, they (he and his security crew's leader) saw one crew of Asian businessmen from Tokio of Japan.

After that moment the leader of security crew's leader spoke with low voice something to his boss and left this room of meeting

All those Asian businessmen were dressed with official suits with ties, while they black and brown bag were on the top of table. The younger man Zeeshan, gave his hand to those businessmen from Tokio of Japan and got seat to top of table, to the other side was younger man's crew people of business.

One of the representatives of Asian crew started to explain and to make full presentation of the project that they have prepared for city Dubai, of the younger man Zeeshan. He started with eloquence to speak English language for one new idea to connect two different small islands in blue ocean with special iron bridge with each other and after one longer iron bridge to connect those two small islands with top of the hill.

To the top of hill, we think to build one big room by special iron and glass while inside will have so many electronic equipment and electronic for game that will be able to play every kind of age of people children younger and adult people. Those electronic machineries are the last word of science.

Near to this huge room will have one luxury glass cafeteria that will service and soda drink and sweets.

He explained in artistic way that the bridge by iron will be light by led lamps while during night their colorful shining with create one beautiful view while the fresh air of water of blue ocean with noise of that are creating one easy sound, like symphony, will gave impact to the brain of people and will create one peaceful and fresh thinking to them.

So, people will come to enjoy their evening in this section. During the line of iron bridge will have some iron glass luxury cafeterias and restaurants that people will enjoy those during day time and night.

So, this will be one very beautiful project for your beautiful city, also we have another project for desert outside of this city. At that time the younger man said it is true that our city Dubai, is so beautiful. It is better to study and to decide for one project first, and I like this new idea for our beautiful city, but about desert project we have time plus I have some other projects.

So, there are some other options, about desert project but that does not mean that I will not think about that project desert anyway I will give notice to your corporation but first to finish with this project of iron - bridge.

I want to discuss with my business specialists of my office about this project of connection with iron bridge to different islands and with, top of the hill plus this room for using those electronic machineries for different game.

At that time the younger man saw his people to the other side of table in front of Asian people, his officials of business gave to him one sweet smile, so the younger man understood that that they were very happy for his answer.

The younger man gave one diplomatic answer to representative of Japan, so both sides were happy. The Asian businessmen were happy that this younger, leader accepted their project of iron bridge to connect two islands and top of the hill.

The younger man Zeeshan, was happy that gave diplomatic answer with smile about desert project, he saved this desert for another project of his best friend, while was thinking that he did not want to betray his best friend because he was religion person, and thought that he did not want to do this unfaith action while he believes to "Allah" – "God", and why his best friend was not religion believer.

He whispered to himself, that he never will sell for nothing this desert of his country and his people of Dubai of United Arab Emirates, (UAE) never will sell this desert to foreign never ever.

He thought that his people must to study and work and to build this project – desert, also he thought that and other leaders behind him will continue this rule never ever to sell their country desert land or to give with concession to foreign people or company or corporation whatever they are.

After that the younger man Zeeshan, gave his hand to member of Japan business 's crew and went to discuss with his people about this meeting that were staying stand up and quiet in front of table.

They were very happy with their boss 's answer and were speaking so much enthusiast while promised to him that they will work very hard to achieve this goal with good result.

When they left the younger man Zeeshan, was seeing from the window the beautiful colorful view created by different lights through this night with so many bright stars up to the sky. He whispered with himself very beautiful night and was quiet and beautiful evening with good meeting with full and good understanding.

Suddenly his thought interrupted by Emin, leader of security crew that asked him with smile how was your meetings with those Asian businessmen. The younger man replied so much enthusiast was very good meeting with good result with one very good, interesting new idea for our beautiful city Dubai, and for our people here.

-*When they were driving to his palace, he was watching very carefully with calmer all the advertise that were creating one colorful river by different led lamps, while those lights were moving in intercalary way, they were creating image like moving of this colorful river's water through different buildings and thrown to the bottom of building to touch the ground.

The time that Prince Zeeshan entered to his beautiful garden in front of his luxury and big Palace, he smelt the scent of different white, pink, yellow, red roses. He was feeling the fresh air that was coming by ocean and was moving all the branches of the trees in this garden.

The colorful of different flowers like red Fire flowers, Lily flowers, Orchid flowers, all different color Snowball flowers like pink, blue open, lily open, and white color, that he has planted last summer those Snowball flowers, to remember one his best friend - lady in Europe that loved those flowers so much.

His best friend - lady from Europe, told him, that she has nostalgia for her mother that was planted all the time all colors those Snowball flowers in their garden around their home, when she was child and younger girl. She told him that really those Snowball flowers are so beautiful and are giving magnificence to the garden between other colorful flowers too.

Also, she told him to plant so much different colors roses, like, pink, yellow, white and red color, and very beautiful low, Red Fire Flowers. So, he ordered his landscape person to plant those different colorful Snowball flowers, different colorful roses and low Red Fire flowers.

Also, he made addition and some pink and white Orchid flowers, Lily flowers, Lavender flowers, different paths with green grass and some Tropical trees that were blooming with their red and orange flowers in their circle crown.

These garden, looked like one wonderful colorful carpet like Universe has thrown all the beautiful colors to the ground. In right side when people entered to this garden they saw that specialist of the stone, have created one small waterfall with some small white marble sculpture around.

During holidays time, they were putting to swim some very beautiful colorful Mandarin ducks, while children were playing around and were happy with those beautiful ducks too. During holiday the landscape man is opening waterfall with music so with interval of music the water is going up and down. This is the most wonderful pleasure of children of Prince Zeeshan.

In this wonderful environment his children are playing around with their small lovely and beautiful beige color body and open egg color of his tale, dog that, they and their father Prince Zeeshan, are calling Zoros.

So, Prince Zeeshan was walking through this beautiful garden that he with his landscape good man has created so much beautiful and colorful while under the light of beautiful silver moon, that on ground was campaigning by small phosphor light of firelight insects.

31

During this walking through this night Prince Zeeshan, was listening the noise of some white Flamingos birds, Crau Crau, Crau, Crau, that were flying from Ocean, while Gjinkalla big insects that were flying through the garden with their noice Zhu, Zhu, Zhu, Zhu, wanted to be rivals with those capricious white big Flamingos that were flying night.

Really night, is for small firelight insects to fly around and to give their small beautiful elegant phosphor light around the plants, also Gjinkallas more big insects with their very beautiful brown color mixer with orange color to their transparent wings, with their Zhu, Zhu, Zhu. Zhu beautiful easy noise is to give to silence night one sound like easy symphony.

At that time Prince Zeeshan said: What wonderful night. Thank You, "Allah".

He was thinking at this moment that he wants to see his two children in their room now and was walking faster. When he entered inside the big very luxury hall, he was running to stairs up and went to second floor while entered right, away to the room of his lovely beautiful small children.

They were sleeping he was watching them some minutes after kissed them and entered to his studio. Suddenly, Aasma, the lady that was servicing later night to kitchen came and asked him what he wanted to eat.

He said to her, I do not want to eat, only I want one big cup with coffee with cream milk at the top. Bring it to balcony of my room. She said yes to him. Prince Zeeshan went to balcony he did not go to his bed room, he got sitting to the chair, while the lady brought to him with ashtray one big cup with coffee and some small sweet and said to him enjoy while he replied Thank You! *

Travel To Slovenia

MONDAY.

Day of this week were going so fast and came the day that he with his friends and employees will travel to Slovenia, Croatia and Montenegro on Western Balkan. Monday, they started their trip early in the morning with one average plane of the younger man Zeeshan. Their trip was nonstop so took only five hours and fifty seven minutes (5 hours and fifty-seven minutes) from their city Dubai, of United Arab Emirates (UAE) to Ljubljana of Slovenia. In normal way this distance with 4,280 km is going to six hours and twenty minutes (6 hours and 20 minutes Before to enter in space of Slovenia they saw the greyer, weather, were so much grey clouds up to the sky so pilot was flying carefully.

When they arrived in airport of Slovenia, they got one minibus where they established their luggage and all equipment like big video cameras and some supplies of cameraman.

When they arrived to hotel of Ljubljana that they have done arrangement one week before, they found over there two very handsome younger people one girl and one boy that they said with beautiful smile one sweet welcome.

Both of them were speaking fluently English during time of registration. When they finished registration, they got keys of their rooms and one another younger boy got luggage of the younger man Zeeshan to send to his room in second floor, while Emin, his leader of body guards was campaigning him too.

He entered to his suit and saw one very cleaning and big room with balcony, in front of one park with heavy trees. Everything was okay the place to eat and drink coffee also television was on the wall and one king size bed was in middle room plus others furniture like big closed small table etc.

Bathroom was bigger with one big mirror with silver beautiful frame around he saw everything and kept his luggage inside big closet, and got out with his leader of bodyguards. All other people they left their luggage in their room and were waiting to the hall of this hotel with architecture Austro- Hungarian.

They saw the beautiful restaurant of this hotel that was so much elegant inside all the table were with open honey color wood with design in it, cover with luxury, shining white table clothes, that has elegant design in itself, and chairs too, but they decided to eat outside and to see the center of old city that was close with hotel.

They got their minibus and went to eat to one restaurant in center of old city that was not far away, as told them those younger people to receptionist place.

When they went to restaurant that were full with people in middle day they ordered meal and after some minutes they asked with some curiosities one younger girl waiter about Dubrovnik of Croatia, because they wanted to go next day.

She said to them: I am sure that you know that is only one hour with plane to go to Dubrovnik, while to Zagreb is only maybe 30- 40 minutes. They started with this waiter girl to speak in English and she said that and Ljubljana is beautiful, but they said that they wanted to spend more time to Ljubljana before to go back to their country.

They ate tradition meal of Slovenia in this simple but cleaning restaurant, with cotton cover table with colorful and design in it with squares shape. After they ordered coffee and decided to go right away to airport and to go that day afternoon to Dubrovnik in Croatia.

All together they went to hotel they spoke with those younger people and said they need to go that day to Croatia in Dubrovnik. So, they changed the schedule but they will come again within two or three days and they wanted those rooms too.

The younger boy said that he will do good management that they to have those room again but they need to call when they are coming. So, they did this arrangement and went to get their luggage while got their minibus and went to airport of Ljubljana of Slovenia.

Travel To Dubrovnik, Of Croatia

MONDAY EVENING.

THEY STARTED WITH THE PRIVATE PLANE OF THE YOUNGER MAN Zeeshan flying to Dubrovnik later afternoon, but the day was short as are generally days of later fall and they started to see the different place while light of the electric towers, started to show up.

When they arrived in Dubrovnik they understood because they saw so much light in the evening in this city after some village that they were flying through. They arrived in airport of Dubrovnik and they got again one minibus with rent over there and started their trip to Dubrovnik's hotel that they called from Ljubljana of Slovenia.

Employees of hotel knew for their coming but not for that day. So, when they went over there the youngest people that were doing registration were ready to service to them while they were speaking fluently English language and French language with some others tourists.

They finished their registration and some younger people helped all of them to get their luggage to send to their room, while with younger man Zeeshan was and Emin, his leader of bodyguards that was campaigning him in second floor to his suit. He said to his people that they will eat to the restaurant of this hotel with colonial architecture, with three floors but longer building. Inside hotel was so much luxury with floral carpet and heavy dark brown wood sofa and chairs in hall.

While to his suit all furniture king size bed big closet were by wood with honey open color with design in it. Also, the table and chairs were so beautiful oak wood open honey color with design in it-selves.

The room was big with the other part to sit and eat or to drink coffee. One balcony with big glass was in front of room and was seeing outside to one beautiful park with very taller trees, some trees with circle crown of branches and some very elegant (Italian Cyprus trees).

Curtains were white Nailon with two other part thick silk merchandise textile dark green color. The bathroom was bigger with one big mirror with beautiful silver color frame. The younger man Zeeshan, got out to the balcony and felt the fresh air by one easy wind was coming from Adriatic Sea.

He got fresh water to his face to sink of bathroom and got out fast of the room to go to restaurant in first floor. Emin, the leader of bodyguards that was waiting him in room went with him to restaurant too.

They meet the other people in restaurant and ordered dinner. Restaurant was bigger like parallelogram shape with big window, with some oil painting with easy open color of nature.

Table and chairs were with oak wood with open honey color and beautiful design in it, and some small cabinets were with walnut wood with more dark color with design in it, where were different white dishes, forks spoons and glass.

Tables have table- clothes white silk with design in it, while the chairs were cover with silk thick merchandise with some strip white, blue, red color, French merchandise.

Four beautiful crystal chandeliers were through this luxury hall of restaurant, while one low volume classic music was spreading around this restaurant with peaceful situation while people, to the other tables were eating drinking and speaking with low voice like their whispering. All this environment was creating one pleasure of serenity.

Everything was close to perfect, while the younger man Zeeshan, saw the waiter, with very good looking with hair cut so short, that came with full sweet smile, with his uniform white shirt with longer sleeves and black pants and asked them what they wanted for dinner.

They ordered the dinner and all have pleasure for this beautiful environment and luxury situation and so much cleaning inside. Between three longer lines of tables and four chairs to each table, while in two corners of the hall, were two big tables with eight chairs for group of people, through this hall were longer rouges with red color in middle and some blue open and milk open color in two sides of rogue.

The younger man Zeeshan got table in corner with his people where were eight chairs. They ordered and started to discuss enthusiast for next day about their visiting the historic older city Dubrovnik.

After dinner they went to their rooms. When the younger man Zeeshan entered to his big suit, he changed his dress got shower to the big bathroom with bigger beautiful crystal mirror and dressed his silk pajamas, with red blood color and some milk color small squares design through it.

When he went to his king, size bed he felt the wind that was touching his face and he wanted to stay some minutes like that while he was thinking about this visit also about this younger beautiful Albanian girl Agneza.

He was thinking with himself while he was whispering: I do not know why I am thinking so much for this younger girl, something is happening with me, I am not knowing myself. It is really one unexpected sweet feeling that is born and grow up inside me for her.

So many times, I am doing analyze with myself for different problems and I am putting logic above feelings but in this case I am not able to put down my pressure of this feeling so this new feeling is winning inside me about my logic, this is very strange situation that is happening with me now.

While he started to pray and whispered: "Allah" give me light and clarity about this feeling and give me courage to about this new situation. "Allah" bless me, whatever to be this new feeling inside me: "Amen". After that he went to balcony, to close its doors but he felt the fresh air of this wind that was coming from Adriatic Sea, and said to himself. Look and beautiful silver moon and all stars, up know my situation.

Really, he wanted to find the bright star Procyon to make wish but that night some capricious white clouds were moving slowly and were covering time by time, so many starts so he did not see the Procyon star.

After he whispered with himself: I am blessed by "Allah" that my friends are with me here in this trip.

TUESDAY MORNING.

Next day in the morning the younger man Zeeshan, got awake and did shave elegant shave of his beard, washed his face and his teeth and used, his perfume, while dressed up at that time, he heard the knock to the door of his suite that came Emin, his leader of body guards.

He opened the balcony and both of them felt the fresh and something cold air of the morning in Dubrovnik while they said beautiful fresh weather and beautiful environment outside that they saw from balcony.

They went to restuarant where all other people were waiting them. They ordered breakfast while were talking for their trip around this touristic older city.

The account lady Adara, explained in short way about Dubrovnik and where they must to start their visit. She said that this city is fortress city with great story but I will tell you during drive. They ate breakfast and got out while got their minibus and started their driving right away to center of older town of Dubrovnik.

During the trip Adara, the account lady started her speech like "ciceron" while all others were listening very carefully and full silence.

Dubrovnik is a city in southern Croatia in front Adriatic Sea. It is known for its distinctive old town that is surrounded or encircled with massive, stonewalls completed in 16 Century.

Its buildings are ranged in line from Baroque St. Blaise church, continue to Renaissance Sponza Palace that is and Gothic rector's palace, that now is history museum paved with limestone.

The pedestrian place "Stradum" of Plaza" is in two sides with shops and restaurants. Dubrovnik has 42, 615 people with good weather.

Dubrovnik has Mediterranean weather with four seasons with fresh and cold spring time, short hot summer, short cold autumn, longer winter wet, wind, cold. So many sunny days spring and summer time.

Dubrovnik is called "pearl of "Adriatic Sea". This beautiful city in south coast of Croatia is one of the most popular travel destinations, on the mediterranean sea. Dubrovnik is well known for its rich history and culture and culture stunning architecture and very picturesque landscape.

Dubrovnik historically is known like "Ragusa" (Italian language) is city in southern Dalmatia of Croatia by Adriatic Sea. In 1979 city of Dubrovnik was added to UNESCO list of the world heritage sites in the recognition of its outstanding medieval architecture and fortified old town.

The history of Dubrovnik started back since in 7 century, when known by refugees from Epidaurum ("Ragusa Vecchita"), that it was at that time protection by Byzantine Empire and later under the sovereignly of the Republic of Venecia (Venice at that time).

Strangely but fact is that Dubrovnik during the century 14 until 19 century, ruled itself a free state. So, during this time the prosperity of this state free came by "Maritime" trade and Dubrovnik came capital of maritime, of Republic of Ragusa.

During this time achieved a very high level, development, particularly during the 15th and 16th centuries as it became notable for its wealth and about skilled of Diplomacy. At that time Dubrovnik became cradle of literature of Croatia.

One big damage or tragedy happened during 1667 that Dubrovnik was destroyed totally by devastating of Earthquake.

During the Napoleon wars, Dubrovnik was occupied by the French empire forces, after the Republic Ragusa was demolished and incorporated into Napoleonic Kingdom of Italy and later into the Famous "Illyrian" provinces that are ancestor of Albanian people e today.

In later time on early the 19th century to early 20th Dubrovnik was part of Kingdom of Dalmatia while with Austria empire Dubrovnik became part of the Kingdom of Yugoslavia upon of his creation and became incorporated into "Zeta Banovina" 1929- 1939 before become "Banovina of Croatia".

Also Croatia has some other grey dark points, during world war the second (WWII) that it was part of "AXIS" ("AXIS" 's member were Italy, Germany, Japan) state puppet of "AXIS" like puppet state independent of state of Croatia. All this story was before Croatia or "Hrvatia" to become SR Croatia (Republic Socialist of Croatia) in SFR Yugoslavia (Republic Federal Socialist of Yugoslavia).

In 1991 during the Croatian war for independence, from Yugoslavia Federal Republic, the Dubrovnik was be sieged by Yugoslavia People Army for seven months and suffered so much and significant damage from shelling.

After this time from 1991 until 2000 Dubrovnik made very great job of repair and restoration while it remerged as one the most mediterranean top tourist destinations from all around the world also as popular filming location.

By statistical information according to it Dubrovnik, is the most over touristed destination in Europe, with 36 tourists for each resident. Account person was continuing strict her explanation:

There are some palaces to visit in Dubrovnik, like old historic town with its "Stradum" or walking place that we are going now, Fort Lovrijence, is famous church of Dubrovnik, there are some rastuarants like "Nautika" Restaurant and "European – Croatian" seafood, Mostar and Kravicde waterfalls tours also "Locrum" island etc.

Really there so many to see in this city but I am not sure how time we will spend in this city while she was seeing the younger man Zeeshan.

The younger man Zeeshan, said if all of you want to go first to this famous church of Dubrovnik and after to center of the older town and shopping too it is up to all of you. All of them said let's go to this church first.

So, they went to the church. This famous church of Dubrovnik it is the assumption Cathedral Croatian. Cathedral Velike Gospe, Cathedral Marijina Uznesenja) is a Roman Catholic Catedral in Dubrovnik of Croatia. It is the seat of diocese of Dubrovnik.

The Account lady Adara, started with full inspiration her explanation about this church. The assumption Cathedral is built in site of so many other cathedrals before that were built in 7th, 10th, 11th centuries and the other cathedral built in 12th century, successor in Romanesque style.

The money to build the basilica of this cathedral was partially contributed by the English King Richard "The Lion Heart". This donation has one very interesting story was continuing her explanation the count lady Adara.

This donation was given by this English King Richard the Lion Heart because as votive for having survive in 1192 a shipwreck near the island of "Lokrum" in Dubrovnik, of his return from "The Third Crusade". This building was damaged by earthquake of 1667.

The senate of Dubrovnik at that time appealed to Italian architect, Andrea Bufalini of Urbino who sent a model for new building of church in "Baroque" style with a nave two aisles and a cupola.

Several others Italian architects including Francesco Cortese, from 1667 until 1678 until his death, Pier Antonio Bazzi of Genoa, from 1667 until 1674, and friar Tommaso Napoli of Palermo from 1689 until 1700, all they worked with local Government and imported Stonemasons, and they finished building of this Cathedral for three decades. So was very hard job to completed this Cathedral and got more next than three decades.

Tommaso Napoli of Palermo made so many crucial changes to origin plans including the use of cross, vault and open a large, thermal windows, at upper level that give to the whole interior so much lighter and brighter feel.

The style of this cathedral is in keeping with esthetics of Roman Baroque architecture as practiced by Bermini, Carlo Fontana and their 17th century Contemporaries. Construction of this cathedral started on 1673 by while the building was finished in 1713, by Dubrovnik Architect Ilia Katicic.

The building of this beautiful Cathedral that were working so much famous architect for so longer time got damaged by 1979 Montenegro's earthquake. This Cathedral to repair got so many years.

Another damage happened to this cathedral during siege of Dubrovnik in 1991 at least one shell was damaged. Inside the cathedral on the main altar holds a polyptych by Titian, portraying a version of "The Assumption of Virgin". The painting probably dates from 1551 while the side of altars hold painting of Italian and Dalmatia's masters of later centuries. This is known and like Cathedrale of "Assumption of Virgin Mary".

This Cathedral of the assumption of Virgin Mary is placed to UL. Kneza Damjana Jude 1. Dubrovnik. at that time the younger man Zeeshan was seeing very carefully the account lady Adara, with deep thoughts and said it is very interesting story let's go to see this famous Cathedral.

The account lady Adara, make addition and some other explanation; that there are and some other churches like Church of "Saint, Ignatus", church of "Saint Salvation" and so others.

At that time the younger man Zeeshan said we need to see this famous Cathedrale, "The Assumption of Virgin Mary" because for others we do not have time, because we need to see center of older town of Dubrovnik, also their shopping center, business center and we need to see the beach of Dubrovnik that all are on behalf of our investment in future for this place and generally of Western Balkan countries.

They went to this cathedral and the host of this cathedral did not have to be tired because they have so many explanations by their friend account lady Adara, but they did some questions about this cathedral. During this time the journalist Hamad, was taking picture, of cathedral and his people too, and was writing so fast in his note book what was explained the man to Cathedral.

While the cameraman man Yassim, was registering in camera everything and all this group of people.

After that all were driving to shopping center of old town. They parked their minibus and started to walk to "Stradum" old town of Dubrovnik. They saw shopping "Minceta", "Gruz" market, with very fresh vegetable and fruits, "Dubrovacka Kuca" with food and different beautiful gift souvenir while all they bought some small souvenir for gift for their families.

After they went to "Life According to Kawa" with homeware boutique artisan Croatian charm product for home with its contemporary interior design good. They decided to go to "Nautica" restaurant to eat seafood it was European Croatian restaurant for later lunch.

In the restaurant they started to discus with enthusiasm about what they saw during this time in this antic old stone town. After their delicious lunch and very good service by waiters and others staff of the restaurant that was full with tourists and so much enthusiast was inside it, the younger man Zeeshan said, let's go to see the beach, later afternoon.

All were happy and very enthusiast, they got shocked that younger people that servicing in restaurant were speaking some different languages English, French and Croatian and generally Slavic, languages. Tourists did not have hard time to communicate with them like in hotel and in stores or in restaurants.

After their lunch they got their minibus and went to the beach. In front of them appeared one very beautiful view. Aside the beach that were so many white solid stone and small space with white sand, that was getting cover by the white waves of the very blue water of Adriatic Sea.

The water that in distance was so blue but when was coming close to the sand was getting white color and was telling to the sand that was lovely sweet water, while allow through itself that the beautiful small different stones to enjoy the rays of golden sun. so many white small and bigger yacht and cruise, was showing beauty of it-selves, like they were in race who was more big and more beautiful.

The white color and blue open dominated to their metallic body, with different flag symbols of different countries that was giving so much pride to Dubrovnik city for its beauty and its attraction of tourists from all around the world.

In some places the blue water of Adriatic Sea, waves were coming with speed with color blue and full happiness while was changing to white color when the water's waves were kissing the cold white stone, but when was feeling this cold solid stone were going again inside the sea with disappointing and were hiding it selves inside the blue water of Adriatic Sea.

The younger man Zeeshan, was seeing that phenomenon and whispered very right who wants to deal with cold object like those solid white big stone aside the beach same and for people who wants to deal with cold people without feelings.

He with his friends were staying in silent and were enjoying this beautiful view while the orange to pink color of the sunset was leaving slowly, slowly its place with some hesitation to the huge of grey cloud of the evening that will bring later the beautiful dark night above the Adriatic Sea.

The easy fresh wind from Adriatic Sea was touching the face of the younger man Zeeshan and lifted his hair up while awaked him for one imagination inside his mind. He whispered with himself how beautiful peaceful view that is giving inside me so much love for life.

At that time, he thought about his small children and said: I wish to have them here now with me to enjoy and to play to this white sand while to make fresh their small hands and legs to this very blue water that is turning to white water close, to white sand of Adriatic Sea.

I wish them to be here with me and to play with those small stone that looked so beautiful under this water like crystal while to collect some shelves with different colors. At that time, he though it is very stranger I have only on night and two days faraway and I miss them so much maybe is concept of distance that I am faraway, not concept of time in my current trip, and felt that tears were feeling his eyes.

He thought to change his plan and told to his crew: I have one meeting in the evening with some business men in hotel, but I think that we can go tomorrow to Montenegro what do you think?

The Account lady Adara said: We can go because distance from Dubrovnik, to Podgorica of Montenegro is only 61 miles or 99 km so driving, is only two hours and 30minutes while flying is going, 37 minutes but with very speed can happen and for 8 - 10 minutes. So, they decided to travel next day to Podgorica of Montenegro.

They left the beach and return to hotel they got coffee to restaurant all of them after the younger man Zeeshan went to his room to take shower to change his dresses, and to prepare for his meeting in 6:00 P.M.

He prepared himself so fast while wore one beautiful blue open shirt quality material with some very thin white stripes, through it. Strangely he did not want to put tie. He dressed classic pants grey color while put his favorite perfume got his black bag and got out of his room with his leader of bodyguards, Emin, that was waiting him in his suite balcony.

Meeting

TUESDAY EVENING.

WHEN HE ENTERED TO BIG HALL OF THE HOTEL WHERE PEOPLE WERE waiting him for meeting, he saw the big beautiful, hall with some big crystal chandeliers and huge carpet with modern design like geometric, figure with green, blue and milk color.

There were big circle big tables with white table clothes with six chairs with cover silk merchandise with bold blue color. The wood of tables and chairs was dark color oak wood quality with beautiful design in itself.

People were dressed classic were men and women and some tourists all were working in business. Were some people that came from Zagreb too. Meeting was going so good smooth with so many questions and answers with so many interventions, to each other in good way and so many reactions.

Sometime, meeting was continuing with smile and laughing for different ideas when they were comparing their city and town with the younger man Zeeshan 's super modern and beautiful city Dubai of United Arab Emirates, (UAE) build for so short time compare with older historic cities in Western Balkan.

They have pleasure during this meeting and they expressed so many curiosities to the younger businessman Zeeshan. All were taking notes in their note books and so many were registering in their iPhone, the speech of the younger man Zeeshan.

At the end of the meeting all wanted to take picture with the younger man Zeeshan, while the cameraman Jassim, was registering in video camera and the journalist Hamad was taking pictures and was concentrated to his writing all the time to his notebook.

Time by time and account lady Adara, was giving some facts, about account by some information of their city, because the younger man Zeeshan was giving opportunity to her to explain, during his speech.

When they finished the meeting and got out of this hall, all people, were enthusiast and no one of them wanted to leave the hotel but were continuing to ask the younger man Zeeshan, to the hall in front of restaurant.

They were happy for friendly, speech by the younger man Zeeshan so they felt themselves freely to express their ideas. This enthusiasm got attention of others foreign tourists in the hall of this hotel and outside it. They started to ask about him and so many of them came to take picture with him.

Also, and staff of the restaurant were coming outside and inside restaurant while was seeing this enthusiasm. After all of that situation, the younger man Zeeshan, with his people went to restaurant and some younger waiters, boys and girls pleased him in English to give permission to take picture with him. The younger man Zeeshan, smiled and got pictures with group of that staff of the restaurant and main manager too.

All were happy, and the younger man with his people got the big table to the corner of restaurant while was enjoying the beautiful colorful marble like "mermer" of the floor aside the rouge while the wind was coming inside through the longer Nailon white curtains through windows.

They ate dinner while were discussing for next day travel, they decided to start flying around 9:00 A.M. in the morning so they need to take rest and to awake early to eat breakfast and to fly. Really all the day was so heavy with schedule but they performed so good that day. He changed the schedule because so many jobs he left behind to his home city, but he thought this trip will lead to the other trip in future to those countries in Western Ballkan.

When they left restaurant while they, said good night to each other, the younger man Zeshan, went to their rooms. The younger man Zeeshan was with his friend Emin, leader of bodyguards and went to his room, when his friend left him with greeting good night, the younger man Zeeshan got out to balcony and was watching the stars up to the sky while started to make wish for his "Suddenly White Dream".

After was watching the trees and in distance lights around environment while was thinking this historic city who knows how many romantic stories has inside it. He changed his dresses pajamas while was staying to the bed, he cannot close his eyes by his deep thoughts.

He was thinking for the Albanian younger girl Agneza how she will wait this surprise of him and how she will react.

He was thinking with himself and whispered:

I do not know why I am thinking so much for this younger girl. I am not sure what is this feeling?! It is fiction?! It is curiosity or is something strong feeling inside me that is a long time I did not have after so much turbulent time in my family. I did very good with this trip to see myself in what point I am with my life.

I see here that people are working very hard for good life, while they do not have so much good condition or equipment or supplies in different business but their enthusiasm and their action with logo: "That We Can Do" is giving me so much inspiration.

All those that we saw and we are seeing and those others days in Dubrovnik Croatia, in Podgorica of Montenegro and Ljubljana Slovenia, are experience of people to give us different ideas and to adopt those ideas with our good condition in our very rich country United Arab Emirates (UAE) and specific in our very beautiful city Dubai.

One phenomenon is for sure that in Western Balkan the education is very high and so much important is for those people learning of foreign languages. We need to adopt and practice this method in our country United Arab Emirates, (UAE) education 's system for our children and youth people in every level in elementary school middle school high school and university too.

But for one thing I am sure I cannot live without my children in every situation I miss them so much this time. With those thoughts he felt tired and cannot keep open his eyes anymore but sleeping was dominated to his brain, while was sending him in this longer night in beautiful dream for future.

Travel To Montenegro!

WEDNESDAY. MORNING.

NEXT MORNING ALL WERE TOGETHER IN RESTAURANT TO EAT FAST breakfast and were driving with their minibus with all their luggage and equipment and supplies of media. They arrived in Airport of Dubrovnik while the pilot got the private plane of the younger man Zeeshan and all together started their flying to Podgorica of Montenegro.

During this flying they were watching very carefully all the beach side of Dalmatia that was most of the line coast with stone and blue water of Adriatic Sea, not so much space with sand was most of the line with difficult relieve. So much hills and so much green space between Dubrovnik of Croatia and Podgorica of Montenegro.

During this flying the younger man Zeeshan asked the account lady during this trip can we go for some hours to Albania that is very close with Montenegro is about one hour from border to North West city Shkodra of Albania.

Account lady Adara explained very fast to him. It is true because Albania really is very close to Montenegro and to go from Podgorica to Tirana of Albania is taking driving maybe three hours while with plane not more than 30 - 40 minutes let's say.

Problem is that Albania has a very beautiful longer coast with so many beautiful beaches from northwest to southwest and south. Albania's beach is between two seas, Adriatic Sea and Jonian, sea.

Albania needs so much time because has big relieve and more important has so much historic and very interesting cities and older towns with history dates back to 1400 that has proof so many castles. Really history of Albania is older like Hellen people of Greece, ancestors of Albania were Illyrian with 2000 years history.

Their king was Agron and their queen was Teuta after death of the king Agron that was her husband, Teuta queen was leader of Illyrian with great history and was dealing with Venecia at that time with Venedicas.

Albania has so beautiful relieve with high mountains, with hills with huge fields and so much longer line of beach. Albania has some older cities with great history like Shkodra, that has great and hug Rozafa castle, that is controlling from top of the hill the lake of Shkodra that is between Albania and Montenegro, the beach of Velipoja of Adriatic sea, and big wide Buna river that people has so many resources for fishing in those three water places, plus river Buna boat can riding.

Shkodra city has older tradition shopping center also has one very beautiful modern mosque that is gift by Arab organization also has so many other beautiful catholic churches

Shkodra has so much fields aside the line of hills from border of Montenegro, until to another historic city of Lezha that is only 40 minutes driving from Shkodra. Shkodra is very beautiful city with lovely and very friendly people and with so much humor.

Also, Lezha has one big castle up to the hill and very beautiful beach too. Also has catholic older churches too.

It is another historic city Kruja with one very beautiful castle on high hill and all city is built, on hills. Kruja is before to go to Tirana capital of Albania.

Another historic city is Berat that is beautiful and very tourists. This city has big castle on top of the hill, also has one very older bridge Gorica bridge, plus is famous for all houses since ottoman time built on hills.

All homes are one above one, so their roofs are above each other from bottom of the hills until to the top of the hills. This area Magalem I believe is I am not doing mistake its name like area of windows one above one.

All city is built in two sides of Osum river and houses in old city separates with this bridge of Gorica has homes since ottomans time and so they are now with very good esthetics and saved their originality. So definitely is very important and interesting to visit. There are so many older statues inside the castle too.

Another historic city is in south with big castle that named Gjirokastra, all city is old with his street inside cover with stones "Kalldrem" as they named in Albania language is all on hills built.

Another interesting with older and great history is one place named Butrint has stone amphitheater since Hellenic time. Butrint can name like small Amphitheater of Athina, like "ACROPOLI".

Butrint is in south and close with very south beautiful city of Saranda. The beach of Saranda is so beautiful and is going in line until to very beautiful place Ksamil name. This city Saranda is close with Corfue (Corfuse are calling Albanian people) of Greece country.

Tirana is capital of Albania center of administrative, also big center of education with so many universities private and public and foreign universities like New York university and Europa university with so many colleges and professional institutes and high schools general and professional.

Tirana is center of art and culture with opera, theater etc. Really Albania has to so many cities' universities from north to south of Albania. Tirana has so many research institutes of science and medical is big center of medical field with so many modern hospitals plus American Hospital.

Tirana has becoming modern city has so many beautiful catholic and orthodox churches, has one older mosque in center of Tirana also one modern and very beautiful mosque is building in center of Tirana by Arab organization.

Generally, people in Tirana and all-around Albania are in full harmony with different religions like catholic, orthodox and majority of muslim, people.

Durresi, is beautiful city with very modern beautiful beach of Adriatic sea and big main port of Albania so and Vlora in south Albania is very beautiful city with longer beach this is coordinated between Adriatic sea and Jonian sea too. also has airport now and big main port sea too.

It is another city Elbasan with one more small castle in center of city with older history all those cities are with Byzantine architecture, their older home, while another beautiful city in south east of Albania is Korca with occidental architecture of its houses because they had so immigrants sine 1912 in the United States of America and in South America in Argjentina, als and in mediterranean, in Greece too.

So many people before since 1900 and now immigrated from Korca in Greece because this city is close with border of Greece in his rural area. They have one very interesting Walley or field in Korca that they named "The Field of Tears" because in this field they were separated with their family's members that were going to emigrate outside of Albania.

Korca has so beautiful Cathedrale in center of city and so many other beautiful Orthodox churches too.

Another city close with Korca and before to go to Korca is Pogradec with his very beautiful lake that is divided by Albania and North Macedonia. Pogradec is very beautiful with wonderful view It is in border with Struga town of North Macedonia.

Albania has so many beautiful places for ski in North, or North East and in Korca to Dardha village, also Voskopja village that last years are so much frequented by German tourists. While so much tourists are coming from Italy and more than 25.000.00 Italian businessmen are working and living in Albania.

So, Albania has so much potential for future investment in future so needed more time to visit it.

Really Albania it is so beautiful with nature and with historic center.

The younger man Zeeshan and all others were listening the account lady Adara, very carefully and he said; Very interesting, we need to come next time and to spend more time to visit Albania.

After he asked her: How do you know so much about Albania and those countries in Western Balkan. She smiled and said:

I worked hard with research all the week after you told us that we will travel to Western Balkan to Slovenia, Croatia and Montenegro. So, I got notice by internet and I am well prepared.

The younger man Zeeshan, said to his account lady Adara, of his office:

You did one wonderful job for really, plus you save our time about information during our visit in Dubrovnik, I hope and to Slovenia too, in near future. Definitely I need to read about the countries of Western Balkan before we to do another trip in those countries to see any opportunity for investment.

All other people in plane said to account lady Adara, you did great job. With this conversation they never understood how fast they arrived to Podgorica airport of Montenegro.

After the younger man Zeeshan asked the account lady Adara:

How hours are taking flying with plane from Podgorica of Montenegro to Ljubljana of Slovenia. She answered so fast:

Distance form Podgorica of Montenegro to Ljubljana of Slovenia is 578 km or 358 miles, so to make driving is taking 10 hours and 23 minutes while flying by plane is taking 1 hour and five minutes.

The younger man Zeeshan said to all:

Better we to spend all the day visit Podgorica and some places around and at the evening to go tonight to Ljubljana so we will win in time, to visit Ljubljana and Zagreb and those two villages "Lunaria" and "Knautia" where are living those Albanian teenagers.

Next trip to see for investment and to visit Albania we will have more time. So, all were agreed and all were happy for another trip in Western Balkan. Now they were preparing with their curiosity to see Podgorica of Montenegro.

After her strict explanation, the younger man Zeeshan gave hope to them in future to visit Albania.

When they arrived above the space of the Podgorica of Montenegro, they saw from up the beautiful city with no so much high buildings. They got in airport one minibus and all their equipment of Media but they did not get their luggage.

They went in center of Podgorica and they saw this beautiful city very cleaning with very good street and roads inside different area. They saw one the "Independence Square" close to sport palace, also was the National library and "Art Gallery" that bordered this center that is so much live. In this center has a lot Palmas trees and so much benches while one sparkling Fountain is in center. At the night, Independence square is lit up in bright colors and filled with people socializing in surrounding bars and cafes.

So many concerts and performances are regularly hosted in this center plus they have beautiful Christmas market, while different buildings where not so much high only to one street they saw five high buildings in line.

Really name of Podgorica has meaning of its name "Under the Hills". Podgorica is the capital and the largest city of Montenegro.

Podgorica is in north of the beautiful and big lake "Skadar" and close to coastal of Adriatic Sea. Position of Podgorica influenced by two rivers "Ribnica" that is going through this city and river "Moraca" that is going in center of the city and most of the time in summer is dry.

Both of those rivers are influencing to its weather or air and the meeting point of Fertile Zeta Plain (Zeta means Harvest of grain so it is field of grain) and Bjellopavlici Valley while is surrounding with landscape that is dominated by mountains terrain. During their driving through this city they saw the old bridge of "Ribnica" river. After they saw the clock tower a century - old time keeper.

This clock tower is 16 meter tall it is 300 years old it is like monument that remains relics of Ottoman Empire. It is iconic monument and testament to Islamic architecture, and can be found to old Town. This clock tower is providing the interesting, contrast to the modern architecture of this city.

After that they saw, "Dajbabe Monastery" is built in 19[th]century while in beneath of this monastery it is one secret cave contain of Orthodox church, covered in religious frescoes painted by the founder of Monastery.

There are so many frescoes of different prophets, religious figures and different local saint cover the cave. Following the natural shape of stone. In the dome there, are so many a fine painting of Christ and Virgin Mary. This church has so others icons that are since 10[th]century. It is very interesting place.

They saw the "Waterfall Niagara of Podgorica" that is out of Podgorica and is surrounded by farmland and landscape of vineyards which produce red wine called "Vranac" that is famous in Montenegro. This area is very peaceful, while this waterfall is most sensational in spring time.

They saw Cathedral of Resurrection of Christ in short time. This cathedral is Serbian Orthodox church that got 20 years to be build. It is very interesting inside and outside with provocative imagery while it is one provocative painting showing Karl Marx burning in hell!?

During their driving they saw from outside the Mall of Podgorica that inside of circular building there are all from local and international brands, also and one huge supermarket with fresh product market.

After saw this Mall of Podgorica they spent some minutes to Center of "Contemporary Art" that was created to floor of one mansion that was royal palace before.

There were so many collections to this gallery by local artists and from other countries like Africa, Asia, Latin America and Europe. This center is located to park that is close to the "Union" bridge that is short walk from old town while is free to enter.

After they were going through to "Njegosev Park" that is overlooking to Moraca River, where early in the morning people can take tranquility of Podgorica. This park is located between three main rivers crossings and through so many pines trees people can find one in the middle of park one store of strong coffee.

They stopped their minibus in middle of this park and wen to drink coffee to one cafeteria. During this time the account lady Adara, said to the younger man Zeeshan; we need to go to see "National Park" of Podgorica Montenegro that is closed to the most beautiful and big blue "Skadar" Lake, that is house of hundreds different colorful birds.

We can see one touristic beautiful village "Virpazar" is over there that we can eat good lunch with tradition meal that is famous in that area, and so much preferred by foreign tourists all around the world.

The younger man smiled and he was shocked by her full information and more he liked her passion about explanation, while at the moment he heard one strong applause by all other people in minibus so he got enthusiast and said with happiness let's go to see this national park and this interesting beautiful touristic "Virpazar" village. At that moment the account lady Adara, said:

We have time until later evening to travel to Ljubljana because it is only one hour and five minutes but we can do faster maybe. All were agreed with her and all were happy to see this "National Park with this famous "Skadar" Lake and "Virpazar" village.

"National Park" Of Podgorica
Of Montenegro

When they were driving to national park and "Virpazar" tourist village the journalist Hamad, said to the younger man Zeeshan:

Now is my time to explain everything for that area and for Ulcinj too, because I did research, about Podgorica and Montenegro too so let' leave our friend account lady Adara, to take a little break not to be tired with so much explanation. All people laughed while the younger man Zeeshan said to journalist man Hamad, continue your explanation while was smiling.

As we saw that Podgorica the capital of Montenegro is in distance by Jaz Beach only 42 km by different road 66, 2km, In Podgorica as all around Montenegro, is Montenegrin language, also is Croatian, Sloven, Serbian, Bosnian and Albanian Languages recognized like official.

Albanian people in Montenegro are doing 4,2% of population of Montenegro. Specific Montenegro has people very friendly also is very safe country between other countries in Western Balkan that is very important for tourists. The meaning of name Montengro, is the "Black Mountain"

The younger man Zeeshan was listening quietly and with attention while said: This is very interesting and very good for people and for investing of business too.

The journalist man Hamad, was continuing, there are so many national parks in Montenegro so beautiful but this that we are going now is the most beautiful because is close to "Skadar" lake and to village "Virpazar". In this National Park, we will see so many interesting things, like hills with green cover, wine yards all around some old fortress, older bridge etc. so many green space close to bold blue water of "Skadar" lake. While they were driving through this park they saw between old trees one small store cafeteria by wood so they decide to go to drink coffee.

When they went over there, they got sitting on the chair to one wood table outside under one big old tree with heavy big crown of her branches and were discussing. One crew of students listened them and they did not understand their language one of them asked them what is your language. The journalist man Hamad, answered: Our language is Arabic language.

So, they started their conversation about the national park and "Virpazar" and "Skadar" lake. One of those students said to them did you see Ulcinj?

The journalist Hamad, answered no yet. Okay, I like to be with you to go over there is not more than one hour to go over there or more less also I have my uncle that has small restaurant over there so we will enjoy his restaurant too and all of you will be my guests. All were agreed because the younger man said to them you never can leave Montenegro without seeing Ulcinj.

The younger student said to them that Ulcinj is with majority Albanian people, also I am Albanian boy too and said his name Arber, while my friends are different Montenegron, Croatian, Bosnian etc.

I am studying for architecture and two others of my friends, while two the other are studying for law they are becoming Lawyer. Today we had off day because is one tradition religion local holiday, so we decided to come to this national park.

After this conversation, they finished their coffee, while all got driving to "Virpazar", touristic village, the younger man Zeeshan with his people in minibus while the Albanian student with his friend with two others small cars behind them.

"Virpazar" Village

"Virpazar" pronounced Yirpaza:v (Serbian cyrilik).........
Bhprazar)? is a village in the municipality a Bar, Montenegro. "Virpazar" is a
famous vacation area and in the past, it was a transitory station for the cruise
over lake "Skadar". In front of them showed up one very beautiful view with
green space so many hills some boat and yacht on water blue of lake.

Virpazar standing up pride with old houses built by stone or new modern
architecture, houses that all of them have their red roof that was creating one
magnificence view with green and of blue color of nature and white color
of boats or yachts.

They saw winery and beautiful vineyard of Masanovic, while in distance
they saw vineyard of Kapitovica and Zavjet.

To Masanovic winery they saw inside beautiful wood big table with
crystal glass and they tried a little bit wine that is famous in Virpazar.

They saw Besac fortress built in 15th that is military fortress and is
separating the Turkish land from Slavic land, now this fortress is value
historic monument on Balkan.

They saw in short time from outside the Monastery of Verkhnie Brchely
built on hills 100 meter above level of the sea. The complex of monastery has
four building during the reign of Balsic, church itself that historian argued
that is dated back of 18th century, the bell tower, the school the cells where
monks live. All the building are with different shape and they are fenced
with a large stone wall.

They saw in old town in short time, super market and market with so
many beautiful artisan items produced by local artisans, professionals, that
were selling for tourists

They saw the castle in distance after they went to old bridge where people were going to get boat or yacht, suddenly in front of them appeared one magnificence view that all made one uauauaua.

In front of them was showing up with it beautiful with its bold blue water decorated by some water flowers on water suddenly one big crew of colorful birds started to fly above the water and so many white pelicans around that was famous "Skadar" lake, while some beautiful small wood boat, big wood boat, luxury yacht were anchored around and some in front of some houses.

"Skadar" Lake

THE "SKADAR" LAKE IS THE LARGEST LAKE ON THE BALKAN AND THE second lake in Europe. Skadar lake has more than 200 various birds' species started his explanation with full enthusiasm the journalist man Hamad.

Really the account lady Adara, was seeing with one expression that no one can understand him, maybe with jealousy that he decided for this beautiful place to show his art's explanation or maybe that she wanted to send until to the end during all this trip in Slovenia and Croatia her information.

Suddenly the younger man Zeeshan, understood her situation and said you was so great in your information but you have Ljubljana of Slovenia, Zagreb, "Lunaria" and "Knautia" village to give information too, while all others laughed, she laughed and journalist man Hamad, laughed too.

So many tourists are watching those birds with binoculars so it is the most beautiful and attractive view for all, while all those various birds are flying above the blue "Skadar" Lake in crew. "Skadar" lake is the biggest settlement Pelicans on Europe. There are 12 kinds of snipes, 3 kinds of ducks, and more than 160 specific unusual birds and 28 different kind of general birds.

Tourists can see to the blue water of this big "Skadar" lake different ducks, gooses and pheasants. Often they can see stork, herons (white, yellow and gray) grebes and other birds that are rare around the world but are often found here.

Also, to "Skadar" lake are birds: "Cormorans" and "Gulls"

In the "Skadar" lake fishing is frequent most frequent are carps and eels.

Driving the "Skadar" lake, tourists can see so many interesting and beautiful Flora. If tourists have wish, the captain of the boat can slow down the speed for the moment and tourists can touch or can pick the water Lily flower or a beautiful Lotus flower that can be found all over the "Skadar" lake.

All people and students were watching this wonderful view of "Skadar" lake while the younger man Zeeshan said this is one "Magnificience" view for really. All agreed with him while were watching the blue water of "Skadar" lake.

While the journalist Hamad, was explaining and was taking so many pictures and was writing same times too, and the cameraman Yassim, was registering with video camera everything around

The journalist man Hamad, was continued his explanation with full passion, while all were listening him

Also tourists can visit the beach of "Murici" while they can refresh in water of "Skadar" lake and to take rest under the hundred years old trees. In this area are fruit like "Kasoranja" that is black irregularly, shaped bristled fruit that they are calling "Sea Walnut"

Tourists when they are staying to Hotel "July 13" and to Motel "Pelican" and are comfortably are accommodated over there, they quickly will leave hotel or motel room because the call of "Skadar" lake and his different numerous monuments around will draw then and will make them to go to their Cruise or boat or yacht to drive around and to enjoy this miracle view.

In the motel "Pelikan" it is an unusually interesting place that tourist will enjoy while the host of the motel will take them in one hidden place called "Odzaklija" (Chimmey house) an old house that is in the attic of the motel. About this place tourists will reveal only that much that beside the past of Montenegro.

They will see tools, weapons and folk costumes and some others old items that some of them are even several centuries old. The others things tourists, will find out by their experience and they will enjoy their trip too.

When they seeing all of those very interesting things in national park, and "Virpazar" and "Skadar" lake, the account lady Adara, asked the younger man Zeeshan,:

Are we going to Ulcinj?, because is taking one hour and 12 minutes it is 66 km to go from here over there and one hour and 18 minutes because is 78 km, from Ulcinj to go back to Podgorica we must to calculate that we are traveling night to Ljubljana of Slovenia.

The younger man Zeeshan, said to account lady Adara: you are very right, I am calling the hotel to Ljubljana of Slovenia but we must to call them yesterday anyway let's try, if the room are not free we must to stay tonight here and to go early in the morning to Ljubljana of Slovenia.

So, at the moment the younger man Zeeshan, called the hotel in Ljubljana of Slovenia, while he heard the voice of the younger man Zeeshan, that show so much happiness to hear the voice of the younger man Zeeshan. He explained to him that his suite they did not give to anyone, but for the others people they will give others rooms they have free some the others rooms not what they had before so at the end he said you very welcome.

The younger man Zeeshan, replied with one strong Thank You, and with full smile while explained to the account lady Adara, that we have rooms to this hotel so definitely we will travel in the evening to Slovenia so we are wining one day more to go more early to our home city (....) and to our country (....).

Really the account lady Adara, was so happy for this answer that they will travel to Ljubljana that evening. So, they prepared themselves to travel to Ulcinj. The students were going behind them with their two cars too.

"Ulcinj Town"

THEY TRAVELED FOR ONE HOUR TO ONE VERY GOOD STREET, AND THEY arrived to this beautiful old town Ulcinj. They parked their minibus and students parked their car in one place close to one park and started to walk around.

The Albanian student Arber, said to the younger man Zeeshan, we will see all around the old town of Ulcinj we will see the beach, but we are going to visit and to eat something to restaurant of my uncle.

The younger man Zeeshan, saw his passion and said with smile yes, we are going to visit your uncle to his restaurant and to eat over there to give him a small business today.

Ulcinj is a town on the southern coast of Montenegro and the capital of Ulcinj municipality. This town has an urban population 10. 707 people the majority being Albanian people.

As the one of the oldest settlements in Adriatic coast Ulcinj it was founded in the 5th century B.C. It was captured by the Romans in 163 B.C. from Illyrian with division of the Roman Empire. Ulcinj later was part of the Byzantine empire and Serbian Kingdom in the Middle Ages, until the Republic of Venice captured it in 1405. It was known as a base of piracy.

In 1571, Ulcinj was conquered by the Ottoman Empire with the aid of the North African corsairs, after the battle of "Lepanto". The battle of "it was "Leponto" it was Naval engagement that took place on October 7, 1571.

This Naval engagement it was between collation of Catholic states arranged, by Pope Pius, comprising, Spain- Italian territories, several independent Italian states and the sovereign military order of Malta, that inflicted a major defeat, on the fleet of Ottoman Empire in Gulf of Patras in Greece.

In this battle the Empire Ottoman forces were sailing westward from their Naval Station, in "Lepanto" Venetian name, when they met the fleet of the "Holy League" which was sailing from eats form Mesina of Sicily. (Gulf of Patras in "Jonian" sea, in Greece and "Holy League" is coalition of catholic state), Catholic states of Southern Europe, (Iberian Peninsula and Italian Peninsula.

Their power based to the Spanish Empire as well as the Italian Maritime power too that break the Ottoman Empire, (really was intended to break Ottoman Empire) that control the Eastern Mediterranean Sea and was formally concluded on May 25, 1571.

So, after that the town of Ulcinj gradually become a Muslim majority settlement. During this time under the Ottomans numerous oriental styles hammams, Mosques, and clock towers were built.

Ulcinj town was remained like place of piracy until this put to the end by Mehmet Pasha Bushati in 1673. Also, the self-proclaimed, Jewish Messiah, Sabbati Zevi, was exiled here by Istanbul. Definitely Ulcinj town remained as Ottoman town for more than 300 years until become part of the Principality of Montenegro in 1878. Montenegro It is a former medieval Catholic bishopric and remains Latin titular.

Ulcinj is a destination for tourists because of its long beach, Lake Sas, Ada, the beautiful "Bojana" island for its two millennia – old castles.

There are 26 (twenty-six) Mosques on Ulcinj town and surrounding country sides. Ulcinj is the center of Albanian community in Montenegro. Ulcinj is an old town. It is typically settlement near to Adriatic – sea, a fortress, small streets while everything is made by stones.

The younger man Zeeshan was seeing with full attention this older historic town.

All around Ulcinj were beautiful houses built with stones and some modern houses and villas but all with red ceramic roof. Old town has in center one long line of different cafeteria, small and big restaurants with tradition meal.

All around people were speaking Albanian language. They entered to one of so many others store, with souvenirs for gift that tourist were buying. Those stores or boutique as they named had a lot art figurine, souvenirs, hand - made prepare by artisan people of Ulcinj.

There were so many Albanian flags red and black eagle design, and so many colorful by wool handmade socks for winter so beautiful, and wool scarfs colorful, with design in it, handmade by artisan Albanian people, that tourists liked so much.

There were, so many art's figurine by shells of Adriatic Sea, so many potteries by earthenware or baked clay, with some colorful design in surface and so many others artisan items.

They saw some item with product of "Alabaster" some product by copper like small copper knife with design, sword copper with design also some dishes copper with design.

They saw in those small stores full with items like folk tradition colorful dresses for men and women, old fashion, like lace handmade also they saw some silk scarfs colorful, handmade too.

They wondered for that, the younger man Zeeshan, asked the owner of the store how they are doing, but the owner of the store said to them that some families are cultivating in one area butterflies and are producing in artisan way small natural silk and are doing in artisan primitive "Tezgja by wood" wood machine, silk scarf to sell.

There were in store different size of bottles with Raki, strong alcohol, Albanian tradition products by grape or prunus. Also were so many postcards colorful with very beautiful view from Ulcinj's environment, by Podgorica, "Skadar" lake, different National parks of Montenegro, different cities and towns of Montenegro.

There were so many post cards with different view of environment of mountains, hills, fields, rivers, lakes, and Adriatic Sea beach from Montenegro, from neighbor city in border of Albania, city of Shkodra.

There were, so many post - cards and from different beautiful and historic cities of Albania, like Lezha, Kruja, Durres, Elbasan, Berat, Gjirokastra, Berat, Korca, Pogradec, Vlora, most of them have older, with huge dimension with stone Castles with great older history inside it.

Also, so many post card with image of capital of Albania beautiful city Tirana. There were and some post card by different cities of Kosova like Prishtina and Gakovo but more important were from historic city of Prizren, of Kosovo.

Beach Ulcinj. Montenegro

THEY WENT ALL AROUND, AFTER THEY WENT AND STAYED SOME TIMES to the beach. In front of them appeared the Adriatic Sea with its very clear blue color. While some luxury yachts and some others white boats were driving all around the water blue.

Some of those yachts were stationary in front of some big modern villas close to the beach, that were some stones and wild plants and not so much sand, while to the other places of the beach was white sand that people were frequenting. In distance looked pride two old stone castles.

At that time Albanian student Arber, said to the younger man Zeeshan, that was staying quiet and was shocked by this beauty of this corner of the beach of Adriatic Sea.

We need to go now to my uncle's small restaurant, because all of you will travel this evening and hours are going fast. The younger man Zeeshan, answered to this young student:

You are very right we are going now to your uncle's restaurant. So, all of them, got their car and were going to old town of Ulcinj to visit the restaurant of uncle of Arber the Albanian student.

Albanian Man's Restaurant. Ulcinj

WHEN THEY ARRIVED OVER THERE, THEY SAW SO MANY OTHERS STORES and cafeteria close to his restaurant also some people were drinking Turkish coffee, in very small cup, out of this restaurant, to some table in front of this restaurant to one small sidewalk.

They were talking with so much happiness. In front of the restaurant close to the roof they saw one Albanian flag was moving slowly by the wind that was coming from the Adriatic Sea.

They entered inside the restaurant while one taller white man with gray hair waited them with full smile and with big "Welcome". He Shaked, hand with all of them, while he introduced himself with name Bekim, while all they got sit to two tables, that the owner Bekim has made together for them and ten chairs were around.

The younger man Zeeshan, with his people took sit to those two tables, while other students, friends of Arber, the Albanian student got another big table in corner of the restaurant too. The younger man Zeeshan, understood that the owner of the restaurant got news by Arber, the Albanian student.

They ordered some tradition meal, but really the owner has prepared for them delicious Albanian meal with meat, big tank with green salat with tomatoes and cucumber. Also, so many soda' s bottle in front of them. One big dish with pica with vegetables and two big dishes with some part of "Byrek", Albanian meal too.

They started to eat and do conversation. At that time came the owner Bekim, Albanian man and asked them if they wanted something else. He said to them I know that you do not want to drink alcohol so if you need something else tell to the waiter.

The waiter one good looking younger boy, was staying in front of them and was asking them in English language also Arber, the Albanian student was helping too, about translating from English language in Albanian language too.

After twenty minutes that they were eating and talking came inside the restaurant two younger taller men, that they wanted to talk with the owner of the restaurant. They entered to one small room that was like office of this restaurant.

After some minutes they got out and the owner Bekim, was seeing the younger man Zeeshan, with very attention while Arber, the Albanian student got wondering about those two men that came and got out silently.

At that time the owner Bekim, called the waiter to his office and after some minutes the waiter got out so fast. He came after some minutes with one big paper bag in one hand and some others small bags in the other hand. He entered in restaurant and went to office while left those bags and came to the floor to service to people.

When they finished the later lunch, they wanted to pay and they called the waiter but, in this time, they saw some people in front of the door with their camera and small video cameras.

They were taking pictures and were registering inside with video camera in direction of table where was the younger man Zeeshan, with his people, but the owner Bekim got out of the kitchen of the restaurant and said to them to go and to wait out.

When they were ready to pay to go out of the restaurant the owner Bekim, came and said the lunch is present by me to all of you. Also, he ordered the waiter to bring the big paper bag and some others small paper.

The waiter brought those bags on the table. The owner Bekim, said to the younger man Zeeshan: Those bags are with gifts for you. There are some souvenirs artisan hand- made by Albanian people of our old city with great history so you will enjoy those

Also, I have some small bottles with raki strong alcohol Albanian product by the grape, for you and your friends like gift. Now I have one request with your permission I want to take one picture with all of you.

The younger man Zeeshan, said "Thank You" to him and all did one picture with him.

Bekim, the owner of the restaurant said to them: This is the beginning to visit my restaurant that to lead this visit in so many others visit in future. The younger man Zeeshan, said: I wish and I hope so.

When they got out so many people were staying in front of the restaurant while two younger journalists one girl and one boy started to ask the younger man Zeeshan, in English: They asked with his honor title Prince Zeeshan, what do you think about this trip of Ulcinj of Montenegro?

At that time Arber, the Albanian student and others students got shock and they started to speak with each other about Prince Zeeshan. After one short interview by those two journalists and answers by the Prince Zeeshan, people around pleased Prince Zeeshan to get picture with him. So, he did picture with all of them in crew in front of this restaurant.

After that they got their minibus and students got their car to go straight to Podgorica. During the driving all were happy and they said that Bekim, the owner of the restaurant was so good person and all others people were so much friendly.

They arrived to the Podgorica at 6. P.M. (six) a clock, they stopped to meet the students that were very happy and they gave their number of telephones, to the younger man Zeeshan, while Arber, Albanian student said: I hope you will call me.

The younger man Zeeshan said to him: You did one very good job that you sent us, to your uncle Bekim, I am very happy and I will be in touch with you. After that they were driving to Podgorica's Airport.

They left their minibus to the center of the rent car, of Airport and spoke with representative or this office and they went to the private plane of the younger man Zeeshan. They established everything supplies and equipment, of media inside.

They started their flying in 7:30 P.M (seven and thirty minutes) at the evening to go to Ljubljana of Slovenia. This trip will take for them 1hour and 10 minutes, (one hour and ten minutes) because was night and pilot was driving carefully not with so much speed. During their flying they were seeing from the window so rare in different towns and some villages light in distance

Travel To Ljubljana Of Slovenia

WEDNESDAY EVENING.

WHEN THEY ARRIVED CLOSE TO BORDER OF SLOVENIA, THEY SAW THAT light were stronger and they understood that they were flying above Ljubljana of Slovenia. They arrived in Ljubljana of Slovenia at 8: 40 P.M. (Eight and forty minutes. P. M.) in the evening.

They went to airport and after left the plane over there they got again minibus to go to Ljubljana capital of Slovenia.

During the modern highway that was full with light, they saw so many advertise colorful for different restaurants, some factories and some motels too.

They arrived in center of Ljubljana Capital of Slovenia, while journalist Hamad, said to the younger man Zeeshan, will be better to eat dinner to any small restaurant with tradition meal of Slovenia before to go to hotel. The younger man Zeeshan, asked all others and they were agreed with idea of journalist Hamad.

So, they went to one, beautiful small restuarant in old town where were in line different stores and restaurants too. The evening was so beautiful with wind and so many people were walking around, was lively night.

The light on two sides of boulevard were giving light to trees that were creating one light, and shadow by their branches above the sidewalk, while so many colorful small and bigger advertises, were giving in light the name of the object store restaurants and some small cafeteria and bars too.

They were very enthusiast and they ordered the traditional meal for dinner while the waiter younger boy, serviced to them so fast because they explained to him that they came from Montenegro, they have one short trip to Dubrovnik of Croatia and Montenegro to different towns and city.

The younger boy waiters that loved his home city Ljubljana said fast in English and our city is very beautiful and lovely too with so many historic objects too. while with smile he said we are more with western standard life.

At that time the account lady Adara smiled and said of course because your country Slovenia, is in border with Trieste of Italy and Austria too. All laughed for her interruption him.

After that conversation the younger man Zeeshan said to all his friends about schedule for next day. I think tomorrow we must to go to Croatia in Zagreb, after, to village "Lunaria" and "Kauntia" we will spend all the day over there and will come in the evening. I know that is heavy schedule but we need to win time and turn soon to our home city Dubai and our country United Arab Emirates (UAE) too

After one day that we will spend to Zagreb of Croatia and those two villages "Lunaria" and "Kauntia" we will start to visit around some institutions and object historic also we will go to one University of Slovenia to see because we need that experience for our education system in our country. I think we will spend two days in Slovenia, but second day we will travel at the evening to our country.

Also, for those days in Croatia and Slovenia information will give us and schedule will do in line what to visit our friend the account lady Adara. All laughed and were agreed while the cameraman Jassim, said to journalist Hamad, so you got out from your position like person to give information like "Ciceron".

The journalist Hamad, said with smile; Yes you are right happened now she will lead us and all others people laughed loudly so they spent that evening in this restaurant with full happiness and enthusiasm.

After dinner they went with their minibus in hotel where one boy, that has that shift that night gave to them the card to open the door of their room and to the younger man Zeeshan the card to open the door of his suite too, and all were going to their room while to others younger boys helped them for their equipment and supplies of media to send to their rooms and their luggage too.

The leader of guardian Emin, was campaigning the younger man Zeeshan until to his suite. When they entered over there the younger man Zeeshan, said good night to his friend and went to open the door of balcony, while the wind that was coming through from one park full with different trees touched his face and gave fresh air.

In small distance was one beautiful hill with trees while in distance was coming the noise grr, grr, grr, of the water of river. The younger man Zeeshan, started to see all around and to the other corner of the balcony he saw some people that were walking down to sidewalk slowly, slowly, he thought they want to take fresh air too.

The younger man Zeeshan thought, that people in Ljubljana of Slovenia were quiet and friendly too, also they like nature and environment and want to enjoy it with their walking in the evening.

At that moment he thought for his children, what they were doing maybe they are sleeping and he felt that he missed them. While was seeing all around the park from balcony he thought about the younger Albanian girl Agneza, what she will react? How she will wait this surprise for her? while he was feeling something warm inside him and said like whisper: I do not know what is going with me now?! What is this new strange feeling inside me. I will discover what kind of feeling I have for this younger beautiful Albanian girl tomorrow when I will meet her. And after some seconds he said with low voice:

Aaaahhhh, Agneza, Agneza. He thought that because of her he was visiting those three countries of the Western Balkan, like Slovenia, Croatia and Montenegro, so one trip and so many jobs performance too. He was seeing up to the sky and started to do wish to the stars for his new romantic story.

He was seeing with curiosity the stars and was watching to find the bright "Procyon" star, and why some white clouds were covering time by time different stars in distance.

The beautiful silver moon that was so clear in her surface, looked that did not want to open way to the younger man Zeeshan for this new unknown romantic story, so time by time was appeared and was hiding itself inside the clouds.

The younger man Zeeshan smiled and said:

I see tonight that silver moon and stars are not ready to fill full my wish, maybe they are doubting like me, so I need to give time to them in their constellation to think about my new love story too.

He got out his dresses and went to take shower. When he went to the bed it was around 12 A.M (twelve. A.M.) time in middle night. He lied on the bed while with is thoughts the beautiful night sent him with his brain in beautiful dream.

Travel To Zagreb

THURSDAY MORNING.

NEXT OF THE MORNING THE YOUNGER MAN ZEESHAN, PREPARED himself for those visiting, after he washed his face, washing his teeth, with one new product of toothpaste, and used his official perfume he was waiting the leader of bodyguards.

At the moment he heard the knock to the door and he opened the door that saw his friend Emin, leader of bodyguards while both went to the first floor in restaurant. They were waiting all the others people with their equipment and supplies of media. It was 7:30. A.M. (seven and thirty minutes) and they ordered their breakfast, while two waiters one girl and one boy with their uniform, the boy with black pants and white shirt while the girl with black skirt and white shirt both with very good looking, were servicing them.

They ordered milk with biscuits and strawberry jam, while the younger man Zeeshan, ordered and white cheese, when he ordered he smiled and the waiter got is order. The younger man Zeeshan, was thinking with himself while whispered:

I do not know why I am thinking my friend woman from Europe that she liked white cheese with everything and I am continuing her tradition now in Western Balkan. At that time his friend Emin, leader of body guard saw him because all the time he had his attention to him, asked him right away:

It is anything that you need? because I saw you were whispering. The younger man Zeeshan, smiled and said, I have no problem, but everything is very Okay and this breakfast is so wonderful, while all the others agreed with him.

The restaurant was so much cleaning and all around was peaceful environment with those white tables' clothes and all crystal glasses and white dishes, European Poland's faience's products.

They finished their breakfast and they got out while they got their minibus to go to the airport. They arrived in airport in 8:00 A.M. (Eight a clock in the morning) they left the minibus over there and entered to airplane, while pilot started flying in 8:30 A.M. (Eight and thirty minutes, A.M.).

The flying from Ljubljana of Slovenia to Zagreb of Croatia got only 40 minutes (forty minutes) because distance from Ljubljana to Zagreb, it is 116,9 km or 73 miles, by car driving it is 1 hour and 51 minutes (One hour and fifty one minutes).

When they arrived above space of Zagreb, they saw from the window so many red roofs of the building or of the big houses between so many trees that looked, weak like half naked by leaves or brown dry leaves some trees with yellow leaves but some with green bold leaves that were resisting the fall time and welcoming the winter time.

They went to the airport of Zagreb while they did same routine, they dropped by the plane while left it to airport and rented one minibus over there. After they established all their equipment and supplies of media, they started their driving through the modern highway with good maintains, while entered in Zagreb city, very cleaning and beautiful city with so many gothic architecture buildings, with so many trees in every area and street inside the city.

The account lady Adara, started her general explanation about Zagreb city, Capital of Croatia, while she was seeing some notices to one beautiful with leather cover luxury notebook, where she has writing information by her research to it pages that were easy colorful inside with some green branches tree design inside.

All understood that she was taking care about notices in her luxury note - book and so she was in her daily life job about keeping in order all documents in her office that was keeping in elegance in shelves with different color to her office. She was doing with perfect her document in "scedar", (in order her document) like archive in order.

It was the second time that the younger man Zeeshan, was smiling while was listening her and whispered again:

Like my friend from Europe, she liked to put in order documents and her books. The leader of bodyguards asked him again:

What is about her information? The younger man Zeeshan, answered right away: Everything is excellent about her information but I see her beautiful, colorful, elegant, luxury, with leather cover notebook and notices writing and I remember friend of mine from Europe that is taking care for luxury notebooks and putting books and documents in order.

She is using so many colorful pages and white paper for her notices. For this I am smiling, so good experience by different people or ethnicities, and different countries too, but that have one common things, to keep in beautiful their supplies that they are working.

Account lady Adara, smiled and continued her explanation:

Zagreb is the capital of Croatia in Northwest of Croatia location it is distinguished by 18th and 19th century, with Austro – Hungarian architecture most of the buildings in city.

At the center Upper town is the site of the gothic, twin- spired Cathedral and 13th century, Saint Mark's Church with colorful tiled roof, while near is pedestrian – friendly "Tkalciceva" street, lined with outdoor cafes. The Lower Town has the main square "Ban Jelacic", also many shops, museums and different beautiful parks too.

Standard language of the Croatia is Croatian. Population of Croatia is 3, 899 million in 2021, while population of Zagreb is 806, 341 in 2019. Zagreb is in North West of Croatia along the "Sava" river at the southern slopes of "Medvenica" mountain.

Zagreb stands near to international border between Slovenia and Croatia, also it is 158 meters, (518 FT.{Feets}) above the sea's level. Density of population is 1,271, 150 inhabitant/ square km, in 2021, between quarter or third of population of Croatia.

While at the 2021 census city itself has population of 767, 131 people so more of than before maybe of immigration or other reasons moving people to different area town or another city too.

Zagreb has diverse economy, high quality of living, museums, sporting and so many entertainment events.

Saint Mark Church located in Saint Mark square, that is it one oldest church with architectural monuments in Zagreb. This Saint Mark church, has colorful tiled roof and those are added on 1880. Those tiles of roof are laid and painted with figure symbol that represent the coat of arms and emblem of Zagreb making it am iconic and memorable sight

The "Eponymous" square on which its sits is also worth a wonder being home to a number of Zagreb's others important and historical building such as Croatia Parliament, and the old city too. Cathedral of Zagreb it is the most spiritually important building in Croatia. As one of Zagreb most iconic and well visited attraction, the cathedral is prized for its Gothic architecture, with impressive spires than can be spotted from afar, almost no matter where tourists are in Zagreb.

The structure of this Cathedral dated back to 11th century but it was partially reconstructed after suffering damage the Zagreb 's Earthquake in 1880, that's those famous spires were added on.

The Cathedral also houses the grave of Archbishop Cardinal Stepinac in memory, of his instrumental role in Croatia achieving independence. In Zagreb is main square, "Dolac" Market also upper and low town. Zagreb city it is with rich history dating form Roman time.

The older settlement in the vicinity of the city was roman "Andautonia" in today Scitanjevo. The historic record of the Zagreb dated from 1134 in reference to the foundation of the settlement of Kaptol in 1094. Zagreb became a free royal city in 1242. In 1851 Janko Kamaul became first Zagreb first mayor.

Zagreb divided in 17 (seventheen) city districts. Mos of those districts lie at low elevation along the valley of the river "Sava". But the northern and northeastern city districts such "Podsjeleme" and "Sesvete" districts are situated in the foothill of the "Medvenica" mountain making the city of Zagreb's geographical image quite diverse.

City of Zagreb extends over 30 (thirty)km 19 (nineteen) miles east to west and around 20 km 12 (Twelve) miles north to south. Zagreb ranks as a global city with a "Beta – rating from the globalization and the world Cities Research Network,

In Zagreb are two statues of the Saint George one at the Republic Croatia Square the other at the stone Gate where the image of "Virgin Mary" is said to be the only thing that did not burn in 17[th]century fire. Also, it is an art installation starting in the "Bogoviceva" street called "Nine Views".

Zagreb is famous for its award winning, like Christmas market that has been made the one in the Europe for three years in row (2015, 2016, 2017) by European Best Destination. Zagreb is well known for its best restaurants that offer than more than traditional Croatian food and classic dishes.

At that time one man interrupted the account lady Adara, speech while he said this is good information for best restaurants that we need to eat good special food, while all others laughed loudly. The Account lady Adara, continued her speech.

The historic part of the city to the North to the "Ban Jelacic" square is composed as Gornji Grad and Kaptol a medieval urban complex, of churches, palaces, museums, galleries and government 's buildings that are popular with tourists on sightseeing tours.

People are walking to this center until to "Tomiceva "street. Each Saturday from April until September, tourists can meet members of the order of the "Silver Dragon" (Red Srebrnog Zmaja) who reenact the famous historical conflicts between Gradec and Kaptol.

There are more than 14 (fourteen) big shopping centers in Zagreb that are offering crystal China ceramic, top quality wine Croatian, gastronomic products diversity of quality clothes. Many Zagreb restaurants offer various specialties, of National and International cuisine.

Domestic products which deserves to be tested because are so specific include Turkey, duck or goose with mlinci (a kind of pasta and, strukli, strudel cottage cheese) also siri vrhnje (cottage cheese with cream), kremsnite (custard sices in flaky pastry) and orehnjaca (traditional walnut roll).

That is the Archeological Museum with collection today about 450 varies archeological artefacts and the monuments that have been gathered for so many years from different sources.

Also, it is the Natural History Museum that holds one of the world most important collections of Neanderthal with 250.000 specimens. In Zagreb it is and technical museum that is founded in 1954 maintains the oldest preserved machine in the area dating from 1830 that still operation.

This museum has car, machinery, art craft, coal, iron, ferror of mine. It is another museum in Zagreb that named museum of "Art and Craft Museum". It another "Ethnographic Museum" with 80.000 items ethnographic from Croatia. This museum is founded in 1919.

Classified in three cultura zones:

1- The" Ponnonian" center trade Hall in 1903.
2 – "Dinaric and Adriatic" has 3750 work of various

technique in "Mimara" museum, Croatian museum of
"Naïve Art", Museum of Contemporary.
In Zagreb is "The Stross Mayer Gallery of Old Master
has painting 14th Century until 19th."

Ivan Mestrovic studio also so many others museum and Galleries.
Zagreb has 136 primary schools 100 secondary schools including 30
Gymnazia. This city has 5 public high education institution, 9 private
professional higher education schools and 4 International schools.

Zagreb's university is founded in 1669 it is the oldest and the largest
university in Southeast Europe where more than 2,00,000 students got
Bachelor's degree, 18,000 master degree, and 8000 Doctor's degree. this
university is ranked among the 500 Best Universities of the world.

Zagreb has and to private Universities, Catholic University of Croatia,
and the Libertas (International University) also so many polytechnics
public and private colleges and high education school. Zagreb has theater,
opera, and so many festivals by famous artists.

The account lady Adara, finished her speech and gave suggestion we
need to see the Cathedral and center with park of Zagreb City maybe to
visit one museum or "Natural History Museum" or "Art and Craft" museum,
because of restriction time that we will go to those two villages "Lunaria
"and "Kauntia".

At that time the younger man Zeeshan that was anxious about that visit
in "Lunaria" said to all his friends in minibus:

I think to visit only this Cathedral, "Saint Mark" and to go to those
villages, before to go to villages we can eat something in any restaurant of
highway, because is taking around 1hour to go to those villages. All agreed
with him, when he said that we will come and another time to visit Croatia,
Slovenia and Montenegro for investing in business but we will have more
time and strict schedule.

So, let's finish this visit today and tomorrow in Ljubljana of Slovenia,
while the second day to Ljubljana of Slovenia we will spend all the day and
in the evening we will fly to our home city Dubai and our lovely country
United Arab EmirateS, (UAE). All were happy and they did one uauauau.

The younger man Zeeshan laughed and said to them so you miss your
home city, they said loudly: Yes, we miss it, and we miss our families too,

after all laughed. They continued their driving straight tot "Saint Mark Church" so they finished visiting to this church where the host explained to them in strict short way the history of this church but they were prepared by information of the account lady Adara.

After the "Saint Mark, Church ", they went in center of Zagreb that has same architecture like Ljubljana, Austro – Hungarian architecture and gothic architecture of different cathedrals. at 11: A.M.

Through that way as they saw the center of Zagreb, they started to drive in direction of "Lunaria" village the younger man Zeeshan said: we are in good time because we will go to the school before to finish the class so we will use their short break between hours. they stopped to one restaurant in highway to eat one short lunch, over there they asked about: "Lunaria" village.

The owner of the restaurant, told them you are very close to this village only ten minutes now to go over there. The owner was one white blond lady so much energize and friendly, restaurant was like for working people in that area and was so much cleaning.

Tables were covered with cotton merchandise table's clothes colorful with square design. They saw that so many people of construction looked by their uniform, entered in that restaurant while they were parking their car to parking aside the highway.

They ate tradition meal while were drinking only water and left restaurant with happiness and gave big thanks to the owner of the restaurant, that was smiling all the time. they arrived to school before 12 (twelve a clock) P.M.

"Lunaria" And "Kauntia" Villages! Travel To "Lunaria" And "Kauntia"

THURSDAY.

DURING THEIR DRIVING IN HIGHWAY, THEY TURNED TO ONE CORNER and entered to the village street, they saw so taller trees in two sides of the street, they stopped in corner of the street that in front appeared one solid bridge above the river, and asked one farmer man, for school he told them with his hand the school that was to one smooth hill.

They went to the school and the younger man send the leader of bodyguards to ask for Gentius and Agneza because they saw that students were going inside after short break.

School was three floor brand new building with big window and wide stairs in front, with one big square in front of school too, and was fence all around the

The leader of bodyguards Emin, asked for Agneza and Gentius, one man to the door that was like guardian of the school.

He said to him wait some minutes I am calling someone to find those in their class. At that time came in front of the leader of crew of secret service of the younger man Zeeshan one beautiful younger lady very white with brown hair, and said Hello to him. She introduced herself with her name Vanesa and told to him she is teacher to that school. She knows to speak English language:

He asked for Gentius and Agneza and she said: Okay I am taking now them to come to meet you and your friends. After some minutes he saw that Gentius was dropping stairs inside school two of two so fast and when he saw

78

him smiled and meet him but when he saw the younger man Zeeshan he run fast and went to him and hugged with so much love while said:

Ooouuu what surprise! While he never wanted to get out his arms by the younger man Zeeshan. All were laughing. After some minutes came Agneza behind her was another lady taller, blond short hair with beautiful face she was walking fact.

The younger man Zeeshan, understood that the first teacher told to her about some foreign people were waiting out in front of the school, so she wanted to take care for her students.

When they came in front of the younger man Zeeshan, Agneza expressed so much happiness and gave her hand to him and after hugged him but her face got one pink to easy red color. She looked so beautiful with uniform of the school after those came and the other younger teacher. The taller lady introduced herself. I am director of the school, my name is Ljubica, and is my responsibility to know about my students.

The younger man Zeeshan, smiled and said to her: You are very right is delicate job with so much responsibility. After the younger man Zeeshan explained to her that he with his friends were introduced with Agneza, her brother Gentius and two others brother and sister Dalmet, and Armina and some the other friends of them, on the beach in their city of Dubai in their country United Arab Emirate (UAE) when they were with their family with vacation.

The director lady Ljubica, said ooo yes I know there were some families with my school's students to that beach ooo so good. The younger man Zeeshan, continued I promised to them that I will come to visit your village and your school because Gentius was so much enthusiast to explain everything about this village and this school.

Gentius was smiling and was holding strong the hand of the younger man Zeeshan. The younger man Zeeshan said to the director lady Ljubica:

We came to visit some countries of Western Balkan and to see for any possibility, of investing about business. During this conversation the cameraman Jassim, started to take in video camera and journalist Hamad, started to write notices in notes book and to take some pictures with camera of those people their, same thing was doing and account lady Adara.

At that time some students saw those from window and came out like running some of them were happy when saw the younger man Zeeshan and went and gave their hand.

Suddenly the director got wondering, and asked all those know you. The younger man Zeeshan, said we were talking inside the sea with Gentius and all those younger people, were around, it was one very beautiful with full happiness conversation and some questions and answer with fun by Gentius and his friends.

The director lady Ljubica, was so happy when saw this atmosphere, while show to her face more peace expression. Maybe she was speaking with polite but she was something anxious for those foreign people, but when she saw and other students with happiness that met the younger man Zeeshan she became calmer.

After they did some pictures and registered with video camera with all students and two teachers and friends of the younger man Zeeshan. The director lady Ljubica, said I am giving permission to come with you now Agneza and Gentius.

The younger man Zeeshan, said no it is not necessary they will finish their class and they will take and their cousins and friends Dalmet and Armina while we will see around the center of the village "Lunaria" and we will wait for them.

We will come to pick up them because is very close center of village with your new beautiful and big school. The director Ljubica said:

Okay very good. after she explained that the school is build brand new and is servicing for elementary, middle school and high school too.

We are working with two shifts, but high school is only day time, so and middle school, while so many classes of elementary school are doing afternoon. School is bigger is in form U because are coming here pupils of elementary and middle school, of "Lunaria" village and students of high school of "Lunaria and "Kauntia" village too.

"Kauntia" village is to the other side of the bridge but they have elementary and middle school. High school is only here for two villages, but "Lunaria" and "Kauntia" are so closer in distance.

The school has bus for students and pupils but sometimes students of high school can walk form "Kauntia". Really our villages are so beautiful with very good calmer and friendly people too, finished her speech the director lady Ljubica.

After the younger man said to Gentius all of you can go to finish your school today and we are coming to pick up you at 1:30. P.M. So, you can wait us here in front of school. After that the director lady Ljubica, gave her hand and the other teacher gave her hand to the younger man Zeeshan, with smile and both of them said with smile:

We wish to see you next time in our school too!

The younger man Zeeshan, said to them:

I promise that I will come to visit next time with my friends your school.

The younger man Zeeshan, left the school with his friends and went in center of "Lunaria" village. This village was so beautiful with so many older and big houses some with stones and some with red brick, while all roofs were with red tiles.

So many very taller trees were around houses and in two sides of main street of village that was connecting the residential area with center of village. In the center of village were in line stores, medical center, one library, one big restaurant, one cultural center and office of commune, local government for those two villages "Lunaria" and "Kauntia" and some others villages in distance.

When was going the time, they went to school and got over there Gentius, Agneza, Dalmet and Armina in their car while they said to them that they are going together to see "Kauntia" village.

When they were going straight to the street, Gentius told to the younger man his house that was aside the street and he said to his sister too, look our cousin is going to our home. The younger man Zeeshan asked Gentius:

Do you want to call her and to take with us, we can stop here you to meet her. Gentius with Agneza said in same time: Yes, we want to take her with us. So, they stopped their car and Gentius drop out the car and was running while was calling his cousin, Ardita.

They came together and enter in car. She said hello to everyone was very simpatico girl, when she spoke her face got one easy red color. Gentius started to explain to the younger man that was in front of the minibus. Our cousin Ardita, is studying in Ljubljana of Slovenia for Law, she will become lawyer in future, she is claiming to become famous lawyer. At that time the younger man was listening Gentius and time by time was watching Agneza.

Agneza was feeling something warm inside her chest, while was liking his lovely watching. When the younger man Zeeshan, was asking her cousin Ardita, for her university and her major of law, Agneza was seeing very carefully reaction of her beautiful cousin.

Agneza, started to be something uncomfortable with that situation so she understood that some feelings of jealousy were growing up inside her heart and were creating one unstable situation, so she was not concentrated when the younger man Zeeshan, was asking Agneza about her cousin too.

The younger man Zeeshan, understood her distraction and smiled so after that he was watching only Agneza and was not talking anymore with her cousin Ardita.

They were driving through the bridge and saw in distance "Kauntia" village with so many big houses with red tiles roof. They entered in center of the "Kauntia" village, and they saw in center of it one big school that was elementary school and middle school too.

They got so many pictures in center of villages and to some beautiful big houses, also they got pictures to one historic statue too. All the time the cameraman, Jassim, was doing register with his video camera and journalist Hamad, was taking picture while was writing some short notice.

Village has more green space and so plantation with vineyard, because big center was in "Lunaria" with so many social objects. While "Kauntia" was more residential village with so many stones and red brick houses.

In front of every house was garden with flowers and fruits trees. All this groups got pictures to some specific flowers with those green leaves resistant to fall and winter. When they decided to go back to "Lunaria" village, the younger man said if you want we can buy something to eat to this store that was close to the bridge, but Gentius said: We can go to another small restaurant in corner of the highway and the street of our village to eat good food cover there.

Gentius continued his speech:

I have one idea if you have time to go to our small town is not far away, 15, (fifteen) minutes with car, and we can see over there to shopping center one beautiful library and one big aquarium with all kind of fishes of our river and some fishes by Adriatic see.

It is so beautiful has so much collection of different fishes, (Pisces) and some of them, are colorful. The younger man Zeeshan, said to Gentius we are going to this small restaurant to eat something and after to go to this small town.

They went to the store where were making hotdog and meat ball that were so bigger with so many other ingredients.

This small restaurant was longer like building very cleaning inside while the tables were cover with white good quality textile tables' clothes. The younger boy waiter came with full smile while was speaking with Gentius and was laughing with him, while got order by all of them.

The waiter was speaking English, language with them, with accent and with some simple English phrases, but it worked out. So, they ate hot dog and some of them got big meatball that were smelling so good while were drinking water with gas.

When they finished that short lunch later afternoon, they got out of the restaurant and started driving to the small town. When they arrived over there, they saw one beautiful town with so many private houses and some building three four floors.

They entered through one very beautiful square with so much trees around and was cover with big grey and white marble and some benches were around. They went straight to library.

They entered to one big older stone building while inside was one big library that has in order so many books very interesting books and some books were put in order as they have color. There were so many kinds of books science, historic, archeologic, novellas, dictionary etc.

Library inside was so beautiful and to corner of this big hall were some shelves with different colorful advertises with view about those two villages "Lunaria" and "Kauntia", about Zagreb, Dubrovnik and all around, Croatia.

The younger man and all his friends liked this library while they were losing themselves inside it. All the time the younger man was staying close to Agneza and time by time was asking her, but her cousin Ardita, was more energize and was giving answer so fast.

During this time about her intervention the younger man Zeeshan and Agneza started not to feel comfortable themselves, while the younger man wanted to speak only with Agneza.

So, he created one minor scenario and called his account lady Adara, to find one book while she said that this lady Ardita, cousin of Agneza knows so good English so she can help her. Really Agneza's cousin Ardita, was so happy to help her so they left the younger man and Agneza to that section of library.

The younger man Zeeshan, got her hand fast and he got courage too, to speak with her fast. He said to Agneza, I created this trip with my friends only to see you, while he saw her very sweet smile and her face got one bold pink color. At that time the younger man Zeeshan, felt that all the world was in his hand.

Agneza stared to speak freely with her melodious voice. I know that, I can say to you Thank You very much. I was thinking for you so much but I did not believe, that you really will come, and never I imagined that you will come so fast.

I was discussing with my brother Gentius time by time, but really, he was so much optimist and he said all the time:

He will come to meet us. He will come I am sure for that because he promised me my dear sister, do you understand me, while I laughed with him and I was happy for his optimism about you. His optimism was giving so much hope to me about you.

The younger man Zeeshan was seeing her straight in her very beautiful eyes and he forget to leave her hand in this magical moment, while so many people were around and some of them were watching them. He moved with her more inside to that corner of this section and they were continued their conversation.

He was very happy.

He was spreading his happiness to her face and to her eyes too, while he felt inside his chest so much warm too, and he whispered with himself:

I am really in love with this beautiful Albanian girl Agneza.

They were going around this section of library, why they saw so many others people in line in silence were waiting to enter inside this section and some they were waiting outside, but strangely all of them were whispering with each other and were seeing with big attention the younger man Zeeshan.

They got out and meet all others people outside while were going to get the minibus and to drive to big aquarium, that was not so much far away. The building were big glass aquarium was in corner to one field that they had plant the corn and the dry body and dry leaves of corn still over there after they gathered the fruit of corn.

Really inside to one section like big hall was one huge glass aquarium, with so many beautiful with different shape fishes, with different colors. Some fishes have shape like wide flat with some small spoil white through the orange color of their body.

Some other fishes were with same shape but with blue open color with some yellow, and pink color stripes through the body, while to the other section another hall were in line two big glass aquarium and two small aquariums.

To two big aquariums, were two huge fishes, grey mixer with white and blue open color, while to the other big aquarium were so many small fishes, some were with orange color, some were with yellow color and some were with blue color, they were very beautiful fishes really.

While to the other section were creating one environment like creek with small stones and some turtles, were inside the water. Also, one big glass aquarium was above one big marble table there were some really longer linguino fishes.

Inside this big aquarium in enter door was one small cafeteria.

They wanted to drink coffee over there but Gentius as energies boy he was told them to go to another cafeteria, that really it is small store with books for selling.

Gentius continues his explanation: To this small store that is servicing café and like store for selling books most of them are school's books and children's books but they have and for adult's books, there are some books and in English language.

So, they decided to go over there, to drink coffee. they entered in store and they ordered coffee. The younger man Zeeshan, was sitting in table with his leader of bodyguards, Emin, also with Gentius and Agneza. The younger man Zeeshan was very happy when he was crossing his eyes with Agneza eyes, while both of them were expressing so much happiness.

At that time Gentius, stand up and was walking to book section, he got one book and came to the table while was showing to the younger man Zeeshan that historic book of Croatia in English language, while inside the book in front was one big map that was fold in elegance way that looks like page of book.

This book has one colorful cover. Really the younger man Zeeshan, was laughing loudly with explanation, so much enthusiast by Gentius that got attention of all others his friends and some others people that were inside.

When they saw that scenario with happiness between the younger man Zeeshan, and Gentius, his cousins and friends too, Dalmet, and Armina, came to their table while their cousin Ardita, that was student in Ljubljana of Slovenia, for law was staying to one table with account lady Adara, with journalist man Hamad, and cameraman Jassim, too.

They were talking while they were laughing with this student Ardita, that was trying to explain in English Language, as she can but with something weak English, while was said sorry but I will improve my English language when you will come next time.

All were happy, while all others bodyguards they were sitting in corner of this store and were talking calm with happiness.

In this cafeteria and books 'store, too was creating one enthusiasm for really. After some minutes the younger man Zeeshan got Gentius and went to books' section.

They were seeing over there while Gentius that was perfection about those books to this store, he explained to the younger man Zeeshan, he knows everything about this store, because he was coming all the time, to buy any book that he needed for school or for summer time that he wanted to read during vacation in his home.

So, the younger man Zeeshan, got one book in English with information for all countries of Western Balkan, while for every country has big map colorful that were folder, that looked like pages of the book.

The cover book was so beautiful colorful with view from Dubrovnik and Adriatic sea, with very blue water and image of Western Balkan, with information inside. He got two beautiful colorful books with animals for children and five dictionary books in English and Croatian language.

He went to pay to cashier girl, also he paid all coffee for people and students that were with him. The cashier one younger beautiful very elegant girl, wanted to put the books in beautiful colorful paper bag but the younger man when she saw her big preoccupation about those colorful paper bag, while was smiling said to her:

Do not spend so much paper bags put two books in one bag, two to other bag and one to another paper bag too. While those three books put to one another colorful paper bag. So, she did, while was smiling with Gentius and said to him:

Gentius, you did good job today, you brought to us today good clients, it was surprise for us. Gentius laughed, while she explained in English language to the younger man Zeeshan, that Gentius is coming often to our store, to see for new books that are coming.

Gentius is our permanent client and buyer too. The younger man Zeeshan and Gentius laughed. After they went to their table where were waiting the leader of bodyguards, Emin, Agneza, Armina and Dalmet.

They got sit and the younger man Zeeshan said to Gentius help me now. Gentius did not know about what he need help but he said yes; I will help you with full smile to his very white nice face. The younger man, gave one colorful paper bag to Gentius and said give to your cousins this bag with those two books.

Gentius got shocked and said: Okay I am giving to them. He got the bag and gave to Dalmet, while the younger man Zeeshan said to them, those are two books dictionary in English and Croation language for both of you Dalmet, and your sister Armina. They were very happy and said: Thank You Very much, to the younger man Zeeshan.

After he gave another colorful bag with two books dictionary to Gentius and said serious this bag you must to give, to your sister Agneza, those two dictionary books are for you and your sister too.

All laughed because Agneza was sitting, aside the younger man Zeeshan, and Gentius hugged him, and said: Ooouuuu. He gave to Agneza that colorful bag with two books. While she said with full smile and happiness: Thank You very much!

After that the younger man gave to Gentius, the last colorful bag with book, and said give that to your other cousin, Ardita, student of Ljubljana of Slovenia, that is sitting over there to the other table with my business 's people.

Gentius said to him: Yes, sir I will do and smiled all were laughing with his action and his full energize and happiness. He went over there and told to his cousins Ardita, that this colorful bag with one dictionary book English – Croatian, inside is gift for you, by our lovely guest, really my lover guest he made addition, the younger man Zeeshan.

All laughed at that table, the account lady Adara the journalist Hamad and the cameraman, Jassim too, also and his cousin Ardita, that she got out of the chair, got the colorful bag with dictionary book inside and went with Gentius to the table where was the younger man Zeeshan.

She gave her hand to him and said: Thank you very much, while she got one easy red color in her very beautiful white face, with mixer, green to blue color eyes, and after she hugged him again.

This action of her got attention of Agneza that she was watching very carefully the younger man Zeeshan. He understood situation, and got the hand of Agneza and asked her: Do you think that she liked this present? So he wanted to make smooth that situation.

His sweet action of touching her hand gave so much happiness to Agneza, that she understood that he has Agneza priority not her beautiful cousins Ardita student.

He was holding her hand some minutes, during those minutes both of them felt warm inside their chest, that was magical moment for both of them, that was giving to them big hope for beginning of one beautiful romantic story.

The leader of the bodyguards Emin, saw action of the younger man Zeeshan and sweet reaction and beautiful lovely expression of face of the younger beautiful Albanian girl Agneza and he smiled.

Really, he was happy that his younger boss Zeeshan, was happy, really he was his good loyal and good friend and he loved the younger man Zeeshan for really while was taking care for him about everything.

During this time, the owner lady that was taller with short black hair with beautiful face, when saw that he bought so many books and paid coffee, she came to his table when the younger man Zeeshan and Gentius came back and got sit. She gave to the younger man Zeeshan, one small box with red color cover shining paper, that have one colorful, and beautiful advertise with small circle and square chocolates.

She said to the younger man: Thank you very much. Really, she never knew, who he was, but wanted to honor him. The younger man said to her. I liked your store I found one very interesting book and we had a beautiful time this afternoon here that was surprise for me for this town.

Thank you very much to you and your staff for good service too. The owner lady said; My younger people that are working in my store are servicing so good they know English and French language because in our small town are coming so many tourists.

During their driving through this small town to go to "Lunaria" village, they were going aside the building of library, suddenly aside to library to one boutique the younger man Zeeshan saw one colorful advertise "Fashion Clothes". He said to the driver to stop the car.

All got wondering about his order to stop. He got out the minibus and said to Agneza and Gentius come with me, while he said to others: If you want to come to see this store of clothes, come with us. So, the driver turned to parking the minibus and all dropped by the minibus and went to see this store with "Fashion Clothes".

They entered inside and they got shocked for really, when they saw in beautiful, modern shelves with metallic frame and glass, that were organize in beautiful way shirts, pants, wool sweater, that were "Cashmeres" - wool, "Angora" – wool, acrylic, cotton quality etc.

They saw, luxury women dresses in crystal hanger and suits men too. To the other section they saw winter clothes like "Astragan" coats and women - suits. There were on those luxury metallic and glass shelves trend jeans pants for youth and for adult female and male too.

To the other section they saw different kind of shoes for youth and for adult female and male. So many of them were "Ferragamy" firm, all were with quality leather, also and boots too. During this time this store kept in shelves most of all winter time, while for spring and summer time's they were changed after January month.

In this store after January month were putting in order shoes for those seasons. Same operation they were doing and for clothes because this time they have put clothes for autumn and winter season.

Close to cashier they saw one small metallic – glass shelve with different perfume and creams. Most of them were perfume "Dior", "Channel 5" for men and women also "Nivea" cream and some other products of Croation's cosmetic too, some luxury lingerie.

They were seeing every section and the younger man did not say anything but was continuing his walking through store with Agneza and Gentius aside. The others people were all around seeing for different items.

When they were going close to cashier that was one younger girl with very beautiful white face with blue eyes and natural golden color of hair, the younger man asked her if they have cotton pajamas or sportive suit.

She said; Yes is one corner to the hall that have pajamas, cotton products and wool product but they are average quality not very luxury but for using daily life. The cashier girl explained to the younger man Zeeshan, that in this store are coming so much tourists for this reason are those high-quality merchandise to those section that you saw before.

She continued her explanation, so many people and tourists are buying those other products for using daily life. She tried to help him and to convince his mind to buy and those products because are good too, really, she did not know with whom she was speaking.

So, they went to this section and they saw over there, thick cotton pajamas, thick cotton night gown and this cotton sportive suit also and cotton underwear and shirt with longer sleeves.

The younger man said to Gentius and Agneza that were not speaking but were seeing all products. At that time the younger man smiled and thought that Gentius is not speaking now but he liked to see all around, when they got out of this section they saw to one table some boots for youth and some sneaker shoes for winter with advertise of big orange ball on the side.

At the time Gentius screamed Oooo how beautiful those sportive sneaker shoes and he called with his telephone right away his father and was explained to him. When they were going to other section and were in front of the cashier younger girl, Gentius said to her:

Please can you put in save one par sneaker sportive shoes with orange ball because, I will come with my father tomorrow and he told the size to her, while she wrote to one small letter that, and said: I am going now to get those shoes and put in save here in this shelve of the cashier.

All laughed but the younger man Zeeshan, laughed loudly. He thought that this very good looking and very lovely boy never know why we are here. He hugged Gentius while he put his arm above his shoulder and said let see again those sections.

They went to "Cashmeres" – wool products and he said to Agneza chose what color you want and size from those sweater and blouses. She got red in her face and she said:

No thank you. He said Okay: What size you are buying blouses or sweater? Gentius smiled while answered, I know because I am going with my mother in shopping and she is buying for my sister. She has small or to petit middle size.

After that the younger man got three "Cashmer – wool, blouses with three different color, one blue open, one grey open and one bold pink color. They went to another section that found thick wool blouses, and he got one bold red color wool blouses middle size for Agneza, and three thick wool blouses for Gentius that he wanted middle size because he was a little fat, and the younger man said to him: You will wear those with cotton shirts inside.

Gentius was very happy and said: Oooo, Thank You, Okay I will do as you said. The younger man laughed loudly, he started to love so much the younger lovely good-looking boy and so many energize.

After that he said to Agneza is Okay this size for you cousin Ardita student, and your cousin friend Armina. She said: Yes. So, the younger man Zeeshan, got two others thick wool sweater one blue open color one green open color and said let's have different color, while he asked Gentius about size of Dalmat for blouses, while Gentius answered fast, he is taller and he is fatter than me so, it good for him to have large size for youth people. So, the younger man Zeeshan got one thick wool bold green blouse for Dalmet too.

They were continued to the section of jeans pants and they said the size when the younger man Zeeshan asked them as always Agneza was speaking like shy girl she was, also they told him and for their cousin – student Ardita, also for Armina and Dalmet.

So, the younger man got three par jeans pants for Agneza and three par jeans for Gentius while one par jeans pants for Armina, Dalmet and their cousin student Ardita. He said to them let's go now to the section with cotton product after we are coming again here.

They went over there and he said to Agneza get what you want now pajamas or sportive suit. Agneza said Oooo no, Thank You, very much there are so much and those that we choose to the other section.

After that the younger man Zeeshan, did not speak anymore but went to shelves and got two par thick cotton pajamas with different design with square and circle figure colorful, two thick cotton gown pink and green color and one thick cotton, open grey color sportive suit.

He got for Gentius two thick cotton par pajamas with different color grey, and white and blue and white with stripes for Gentius, one thick bold blue color, sportive suit, and two cotton white longer sleeves shirts.

Also, he got one big package with socks for Agneza and one big packet with socks for Gentius. While he said to Gentius find your size of underwear. He found and got those items. While he said to Agneza you can get what you want. She got cotton underwear to this section and said Thank You.

The younger man Zeeshan, thought: This is very good girl, I thought she will take luxury lingerie and underwear, to the other section but not, she did not do that. She is very good simple girl in life. At that time, she said to the younger man Zeeshan, that he is going to ask the cashier for big bag or to get one cart.

During this time the younger man got the hand of Agneza and said I want to help you to have those clothes and for the next year that you are going student in Ljubljana of Slovenia, because is very longer and cold winter in Croatia and Slovenia so you need those clothes.

She felt warm inside her chest sand so much happiness. Her very beautiful eyes with mixer color green to blue, were sparkling brightly why her chest were showing moving up and down in ritual like, she has difficult breath and her face got red color while through her natural bold red lips were coming words of Thank You, and her white beautiful teeth like pearls were showing up.

She was so much impressed by his action and was so emotional also she was really very happy she was feeling this magnificence feeling of love for him. At that time came with one cart of shopping Gentius and they went to the section of shoes, where he got two par winter shoes one par with black color and one par with bold blue, color and one par black color boots for Agneza.

He got another par sneaker sportive shoes with blue ball for Gentius, two par winter shoes with different color one par shoes dark brown and one par shoes black color, for Gentius and one par black color boots. But Gentius said in strong way the cashier got one par sneaker shoes with orange ball she has over there.

The younger man Zeeshan, laughed and touched the top of his head with his hand and said I know but you need two par sportive sneaker shoes because you are playing football with friends in school.

That time the younger very good-looking lovely boy, Gentius, screamed with happiness with his expression, Ooooo, and he put his hand up to his head, after he kissed the hand of the younger man Zeeshan with full happiness

Really it was magical moment with those two younger people for the younger man Zeeshan. He saw so much happiness to them and to their innocent shy beautiful younger face.

At the moment the younger man Zeeshan said to Gentius get three par of winter shoes one par for Armina one par for Dalmet and one par for your cousins student Ardita. Gentius said ooo will be big beautiful surprises for them.

They went to cashier younger girl, and were taking in order to pay all the items. over there the younger man Zeeshan asked cashier - girl, if they have school's bag or student bag classical shape.

She answered very fast: Yes, we have so beautiful and quality, but I need to go to storage because we did not advertise yes, because we will do reorganize of the shelves and will put and those bags that came this week.

She went to storage and came fast with three kind of bags with thick leather with design in itself so beautiful one was bold red cherry to little dark color,(like Burgundy color) looks like those two colors interfere to each other in harmony, it was so beautiful, one was brown color and one was black color. Those bags have classical shape, were to put so many books and notebooks and were to hold by hand.

He asked Agneza which color she liked. She saw him and was seeing and the bags too, really the bag with bold red cherry to little dark color (like Burgundy color) it was so much intrigues so much beautiful, that attracted the beautiful eyes of Agneza and she said I like that. The younger man Zeeshan, said to her get it.

The younger man Zeeshan, asked again the cashier beautiful younger girl if they have for pupils' bag? She asked: What kind of shape want? The younger man Zeeshan, while laughed loudly, said to cashier girl ask this boy Gentius, because he is my boss today about shopping. He knows everything in this town for books and for clothes shoes or whatever. All they laughed.

Gentius, said to girl I want bag thick leather of course but to hold behind to my shoulder, so hanger bag. the cashier girl explained to Gentius that hanger leather bag maybe is heavy for you because is this leather, the others people, prefers and are taking special textile hanger bags. Gentius said:

I know that fact, but I loved the design of those leather bag are unusual and beautiful but if is expensive this kind of bag do not bring, I will take textile hanger bag, and he was watching the younger man Zeeshan.

The younger man Zeeshan laughed loudly and said this kind of bag is not expensive you will get that. He said to cashier – girl, please go and find one with unusual design in itself of leather and beautiful color.

She went to storage and came with one bag that was covered with one elegant not transparent white paper. All were curious what its color and design was, the cashier girl laughed she knows but wanted to make surprise to young lovely boy Gentius.

She said to Gentius open I am sure you will like that. Gentius opened so fast that cover of bag white not transparent paper and when he saw the most beautiful bag with open brown color with some nuance orange interfere to brown color and with design in itself with green color Dinosaur.

He screamed from happiness and got attention of all people in store. Some people came and some tourists, to see what happened, after them were gathering friends of the younger man Zeeshan.

He lifted that bag up and said to all of them look how beautiful hanger bag is this, and was doing his expression Oooooo. All laughed and they said congratulation, enjoyed it. At that time one younger lady with one child that was holding with her hand, suddenly creamed with happiness and said Oooo My God this Prince Zeeshan from Dubai of the United Arab Emirates. (UAE).

The younger man Zeeshan, smiled while she said please may take one picture with you and with small boy. The younger man Zeeshan, said to her of course, and she got picture with him and got out fast. After some seconds came her husband and some her friends, tourists that she talked about Prince Zeeshan.

They wanted picture and some other tourists inside the store pleased him to take picture with him. Gentius, Agneza, Armina that came at that time, her brother Dalmet and their cousin student Ardita got shocked, while Gentius spoke with high voice:

You are Prince?, you are Prince? and got his hand again and was holding strong. Gentius said:

Oooo, this is my lovely Prince Zeeshan, my very lovely friend all laughed, while he said to Gentius let's pay now and we will do some pictures outside to park before to get car to drive to "Lunaria". Gentius said Okay.

Really enthusiasm of Gentius did not finish yet when the younger man Zeeshan was paying all were seeing all those staff, while the younger girl cashier was putting in different paper bags, Gentius said to Armina and Dalmet come here. They said you need help?

Gentius said, no I do not need help I am strong boy but take those two bags with wool blouses and this bag with jeans pants because are yours that my lovely prince Zeeshan bought for you.

All people present laughed loudly, while Armina and Dalmet got shocked, both of them got red color in their face and smiled and they gave their hand to the younger man Zeeshan, hugged him and said: Thank You. after that Gentius called his cousin student Ardita, that she was talking with account lady Adara, while they laughed with action of Gentius. She asked him what do you need Gentius, because i am talking with this lady.

I do not need you and I am working here, you need to come here now. She came and he gave to her two big bags one with jeans pants and one with wool blouses, while said to her this is gift for you by my very dear Prince Zeeshan, so take those bags and go out leave us quiet to finish this job.

All people laughed loudly with words of Gentius, while his cousin student girl Ardita, got emotion, and felt that tears were filling her eyes, she came and hugged the younger man Zeeshan and said:

Thank you very much.

After that the younger man asked Agneza:

What kind of perfume you need? She did not speak was shy girl, he got for her one Croatian perfume for youth people, but when he asked Gentius, he laughed and said, I am not girl and I do not need those crazy perfumes and if they are for boys too, and was laughing. All people laughed.

Gentius, was so much sincere boy and with full enthusiasm and humor. The younger man Zeeshan, paid and got pictures with Gentius Agneza, Armina, Dalmet, and student girl their cousin Ardita, inside the store and all of them were ready to go out while the tourists said to the younger man Zeeshan:

Prince Zeeshan, "God Bless You" and have a very nice trip.

They got out while the younger man Zeeshan said to all younger people and his friends let's take some pictures to this park and so they did, they got picture to one green park that was close with this store.

Also, their cousin student girl Ardita, was taking so many pictures in group with her telephone.

All were happy for this event while Gentius never was releasing the hand of his lovely Prince Zeeshan, but was holding strong the hand of the younger man Zeeshan, looked that he did not want anyone to get his lovely prince. Gentius time by time was watching with his very beautiful eyes that were sparkling bright, the younger man Zeeshan.

His watching was expressing one feeling of huge admiration like he was watching and was holding one Saint person or Saint figure. With his smile looked that he was spreading all around the warm of spring time in this entering of winter season in those two villages "Lunaria" and "Kauntia "of Croatia.

They entered to the minibus and the driver started driving to go to "Lunaria" village. When they were above the bridge, they saw that two villages were greeting each other with their taller trees, while the river water was creating one noise gerr, gerr, gerr, like melody of one whistle, that was coming from one village to other village and were expressing their love for each other.

The beautiful tower light aside the bridges looked they said we are witness of love of those two villages and signals that they are giving time by time by wind, by noise of river's water and by birds in spring summer and autumn time.

All were watching from windows of minibus this beautiful view while the beautiful silver moon was sending its light to all around and to river's water her lights was moving up and down by waves of the water that was coming by mountains and was going somewhere maybe to meet the Adriatic sea's blue water too.

They were talking enthusiast while they saw to the corner the table advertise with village's name "Lunaria". The driver was driving more slowly until arrived in front of the Gentius and Agneza' house aside the road of village.

They stopped over there, all the youngest people gave their hand to the younger man Zeeshan's friends, after that, all the youngest people got out with them and the younger man Zeeshan with his leader of bodyguards too.

The younger man gave his hand to all of them, he wished for success to student girl Ardita, and to Armina, Dalmet, Gentius and Agneza. During this greeting, he said to Agneza I will be in touch with you, I have now your information of communication.

At the time that he gave for the second time hand to Gentius was so much emotional moment because Gentius hugged him so strong and was not leaving, until Agneza and Dalmet, pulled him from the younger man Zeeshan, while they saw his tears to his beautiful eyes.

Gentius made one longer Ooooo his expression while he was covering his eyes with his hand that they not to see the tears in his eyes but all of them laughed, while the younger man Zeeshan, hugged again Gentius and said to him:

I promise to you that I will come to meet you and all of you again.

Gentius said to him: So, you are giving promise to me now, right?

Yes, I am promising you said the younger man Zeeshan.

Gentius said to him: I believe that.

The younger people got walking with all their gift – bags in their hand while were talking loudly with full happiness and time by time were greeting with their hand to the people in minibus and to the younger man Zeeshan and his friend leader of bodyguards Emin, that were staying for some minutes out of the minibus.

Really this separation gave one strong emotion to the younger man Zeeshan, he loved those younger teenagers and more Gentius but he started to have social and lovely feelings for beautiful younger girl Agneza.

He whispered with himself. This feeling inside me is beautiful love for this beautiful younger girl Agneza, she gave me so much emotions today. I feel different person myself now, plus the love that gave to me those innocent sincerely beautiful teenagers.

During those minutes of his whispering in silence, he felt the hand above his shoulder of his loyal and lovely friend the leader of bodyguards Emin, he turned his head to him, while his friend that understood his situation said to him with sweet voice and smile, let's go.

Really at the moment the younger man Zeeshan felt his tears were filling his eyes without his permission, all those feelings created to him so much emotions not only because of Agneza, but about all this huge enthusiasm by those, teenagers and their truly love of them to him. He said to his friend Emin, what a beautiful day today.

His friend Emin, said really it was so beautiful day today, with so many aspects, I never imagined all this variation for today. So many beautiful moments of diversity and humor we spent today. We did very good that we came here to see and meet those lovely teenagers.

They entered in minibus, while they found all their friends that were discussing so much enthusiasts, about this day and about those lovely teenagers, that were so much enthusiast.

All they said to their boss the younger man Zeeshan: We did very good that we came today here and all credits are yours and all laughed. It was so much happy day today. Also, they said to him: You did one beautiful action about buying those gifts to them, you will have so much credit to universe and you will get blessing by all billions stars up to the Galactic.

They started to imitate all actions of the lovely teenager Gentius, when he called every one of them to get their gift bag, while when every one of them said you need my help, he said come on, I do not need your help, but get your gift bag by my lovely Prince Zeeshan and leave us to work quiet here and got out wait us out. All they laughed.

At that time the account lady Adara, was so emotional while said: Those lovely teenagers, made our day today. After she said:

Prince Zeeshan, "May, Allah Bless You" and your family with all his super power.

The younger man Zeeshan, said to her: Thank you very much.

I wish that "Allah" to bless all of you friends of mine that were with me during this trip in those three countries, Slovenia, Croatia and Montenegro of Western Balkan.

At that moment the driver said to all of them:

I will drive carefully and with slow speed because it is night, so will take mor time to go to Ljubljana, Slovenia. They all agreed with driver. The younger man Zeeshan, said to this friends: When we will arrive over there, we will eat dinner to hotel's restaurant.

I know that all of you are tired was longer day with trip and coming all around so we need to take rest to be prepared for tomorrow about visiting some places in Ljubljana od Slovenia. I am sure that our friend account lady Adara has prepared her schedule what to visit tomorrow.

The account lady Adara said: I have everything ready so I think tomorrow we need to visit some institutions of art, university of Ljubljana, also museums because it is Friday, Saturday we will visit Cathedral, center of older city and three bridges and as you said we will be ready at later afternoon or at the evening to fly to our home city and our lovely country too United Arab Emirates, (UAE) so Sunday we will have time to take rest with our family, and Monday to be ready for job.

The younger man Zeeshan said to her:

Excellent schedule. For the moment I forget that is coming weekend so fast.

Was very heavy schedule of this week with so many beautiful stories and very lovely people, that never I expected that warm situation by all for really. I am very happy about our trip. All they said it is true was so beautiful week for all of us.

Ljubljana, Of Slovenia

THURSDAY – EVENING.

THE DRIVER STARTED DRIVING SLOWLY, AT 7:00 P.M., THROUGH ROAD OF the village until got out to modern highway. People inside were talking with each other but the younger Zeeshan, did not speak anymore but he jumped in deep thinking. Time by time Emin, the leader of crew of bodyguards was seeing him carefully, because he understood that he was suffering something.

One time he asked the younger man Zeeshan:

Are you feeling good? Are you Okay?

The younger man Zeeshan, answered with smile: I am good, I am feeling good, but I was thinking for those teenagers and all of those that we saw today and those days make me to think this time to create my memories. I need to write in notebook about everything, also I am thinking and for something else, but I am not ready to discuss for that.

The leader of bodyguards Emin, laughed and said we have time to discuss for something else. During this trip from "Lunaria" to Zagreb the younger man Zeeshan, was not able to see from window different fields and hills, because he was focus to his feelings about that younger girl Agneza.

The tower's light aside highway in period time were giving sparkle through the window to eyes of the younger man Zeeshan while looked that wanted to put him out of his thoughts, so they wanted to distract him, while he interrupted his thinking, and was seeing after the big green table with advertise of different street, or other cross highways.

They did this way around one hour when they entered inside of area of Zagreb, capital of Croatia. They went straight to airport, at 8:00 p.m. while they left the minibus to cars' center, and went to the plane. The pilot started flying 8:30. P.M. to go to Ljubljana of Slovenia.

During this flying they were seeing faraway in distance some place with light but not so much, while when they entered in Ljubljana, they, saw lighter, in distance, while in airport the field was with bright light.

When they arrived in airport was 9:10. P.M. They went to cars' center and rented minibus again while started their driving inside Ljubljana to go to their hotel. During driving they saw so many advertises of different stores or institution, and some residential palaces they saw antic tower light that were creating one diversity with modern light of the city and of course were giving creating one interesting view in city.

When they arrived in hotel the time was 10:00. P.M. really it was later and they were really tired so most of them ordered only chicken's soup without bread while some ordered only cheese, tea and biscuits. They finished the dinner and went right away to their rooms.

The leader of the bodyguard Emin, campaigning the younger man Zeeshan to his suite after he said Good Night to him and was going to his room. The younger man Zeeshan saw so much compassion to eyes of is friend when he left him in his suite. The younger man Zeeshan whispered, I am blessed for my friend and for all others that are with me.

He got out his sweater, shirt and pants and went right away to bathroom to take shower. After he got out of shower, wore pajamas and opened the door of balcony. He was very tired but really, he did not want to sleep.

He was watching the stars up to the sky that looked that moving like wanted to show up, aside the other big brighter stars. The younger man Zeeshan, for the moment was thinking for the younger girl Agneza. He whispered: I do not know what is happing with me, but really, I like this girl, she made me to think so much for her.

I do not know what will be the future of me with her? I think it will take so longer time because she will study university four years while it is so much distance between our two countries, so those will influence not in good term for my thoughts.

He was thinking that first I need to resolve problems with my family and my current wife, after to decide about this girl. I am sure that with my family I will have some obstacles, but I do not want to make sad them, too.

About my wife, she created this situation but I must to be sure that I will break this relationship and to put in end my marriage that is a long time like ice in North Pol. At that moment when he thought for his marriage to end, he felt something pain inside his chest and said loudly Oooo "Allah" what about my two small children I cannot live without them.

At that moment he felt the tears were filling his eyes. He started to sweap his tears and was listening the easy noise of leaves of the trees that were campaigning the big noise of the waves of water river in distance.

In distance was the hill with pine trees and some tallest trees, that creating one beautiful green frame I this part of this beautiful city of Ljubljana of Slovenia.

He was listening in distance one noise by some younger people that were speaking and laughing loudly, while were walking on side walk aside the hotel.

The younger man Zeeshan, saw them, and thought they are happy people here in this city of Ljubljana, as I saw when we came here, looked like they do not have different problems in their life, while those younger people as I see are careless about problems in life but in future, they will face like all of us.

With those thoughts he said to himself I must to sleep, to get awake early in the morning so tomorrow Friday, to follow the schedule that account lady Adara, has prepared so strict and in time everything.

Saturday to finish the visit to others historic objects, Cathedral and older town and other objects too, while afternoon to fly to our home city Dubai and our lovely country United Arab Emirates. (UAE). He said like he was talking with moon: I miss so much my small children.

He closed the door of the balcony and went to the big bed on this suite, to sleep. Strangely his eyes did not have force to close, while the younger man Zeeshan, to enjoy beautiful night in deep beautiful dream. He continued to think for all this trip in Western Balkan, and for all people that he met, that really, they were lovely people too.

After some minutes he thought, I feel myself so bad and sad that I am leaving this girl here. I do not understand myself, I came here to be so happy but I feel that now I am sad more than before to come here.

While when I am thinking in my home that I will find more colder situation so this sadness will be stronger, so I will, suffer these feelings.

This aggravation between my family and my wife's family is bothering me so much, I need to find solution absolutely this time.

Anyway, my situation will change when I will meet my small children that are waiting for me that is it. Tomorrow I will write every notice during visiting this university of Ljubljana of Slovenia, after to put in good writing in notebook to my home, because during this longer trip in Dubrovnik, Montenegro and Zagreb, I did not keep attention to write about all.

Our Earth planet has so many big stories, because all those historic objects and monuments that I saw here are witnesses of those stories, while those people has protected those in very good condition, this is telling me that those people love their countries and are very proud for their big stories to those objects. Most of all they respect and honor their heroes that made possible their existence during all the different centuries.

With those thoughts the younger man Zeeshan, started his journey of the beautiful dream through this night while close his eyes.

FRIDAY. VISITING LJUBLJANA OF SLOVENIA!

Next day early in the morning the younger man got awake by one noise on the glass of the door of balcony, tik, tik, tik, tik.

He got wondering by this noise and stand up to see, while one big white bird looked was saying to him, get awake and Good Morning, while opened its arm with very white feather and flew away through the taller trees.

The younger man whispered one expression: Today is the Peace Day, the sign came this morning by this big beautiful white bird. He prepared himself fast like, got fast short shower, shaved his face, comb his hair, got his perfume, dressed classic suit with one blue open shirt with longer sleeves, and one very thin elegant bold blue color with some very thin white strips tie.

Really, he wanted to take one open lily color or bold purple color but he wanted to be with serious elegant, dresses today not fancy clothes

Also was confuse what kind of socks to wear this day to go in harmony and smooth with his grey suit, so definitively he wore grey socks. Also, he changed his shoes and wore one par bold grey classic leather shoes.

So, at the least, he wore very elegant with easy beautiful grey color suit, socks and shoes also blue open shirt with longer sleeve and very elegant bold blue color with very thin white strips, so he dresses, was so elegant good quality.

He got his black bag design for document also one par sun dark glasses with gray frame too. While he was preparing himself, he heard that his suite's door was opening by his very loyal friend the leader of bodyguards Emin, while gave greeting to his boss the younger man Zeeshan, he said you are ready let's go.

It was 7:30 A.M. when they went to the first floor, of hotel and entered to restaurant while all the others people were waiting over there sitting in two different big tables. The younger man Zeeshan, gave greeting Good Morning to them and got sit. They ordered the breakfast, strangely all ordered biscuits, milk, butter, boil eggs, and cream cheese. They liked the biscuits that were preparing the kitchen of this hotel's restaurant. They were talking with happiness while they did not feel how fast was going the time.

The account lady Adara, said: We must to go now to follow the schedule today and half of the day tomorrow if we want to fly tomorrow afternoon to our home city Dubai of our country United Arab Emirates (UAE) too. They, got out of restaurant and hotel too and got the minibus to go to visit those objects, the cameraman Jassim, established his equipment and supplies of media and the driver started engine of minibus.

During driving the account lady started her explanation about Ljubljana capital of Slovenia. Ljubljana is big city and capital of Slovenia, while is known for its university, population and green spaces including expansive "Trivoli" park.

In two sides of Ljubljana's river, lined outdoor cafes is dividing old town form his commercial place. Ljubljana has so many museums including the "National Museum" of Slovenia displaying historic exhibition. Ljubljana has museum of "Modern Art", home of the 20th century Slovene painting and sculptures.

Ljubljana of Slovenia, located along trade route between Northern Adriatic Sea, and the Danube river's region, North of country, largest marsh inhabited since prehistoric times.

Ljubljana is the city of Slovenia's country' cultural, educational, economical, political and administrative center.

The account lady said to her boss the younger man Zeeshan: I think we to visit first those two museums of Ljubljana and after to go to the university of Ljubljana, if you will approve my suggestion.

I think so because already I gave to all of you information for those museums and city so we can visit in short time those two museum and we have time to go to University of Ljubljana. If we will spend one hour to every museum it is enough time, so we will be able to be to university in 11: A.M., after we can go to see old town with his commercial square and different store. Tomorrow we can see two those famous churches and the triple bridge, this the last we can see in short time and today afternoon anyway.

Her boss the younger man, Zeeshan was seeing her very carefully while was smiling, and was thinking she is very smart, very hard working and very strict in explanation. I think she likes research so much, I must to give promotion to her in near future.

As explained before the account lady Adara, that Ljubljana has so many museums including the "National Museum" of Slovenia displaying historic exhibition. Ljubljana has museum of "Modern Art", home of the 20th century Slovene painting and sculptures.

They went first to "National Museum", while they spend about one hour over there, where they saw so many diversities of Slovenia in different decades of developing, economy and art and after that they went to "Modern Art Museum", that they saw so many interesting painting and sculpture of the 20th century.

They liked so many of them and specific painting with different view. About nature, about people, about abstract painting too about portrait of people too etc. after that they decided to go to university of Ljubljana.

This visit over there was very important for the younger man Zeeshan, because he was thinking to make great reform of education system in his very beautiful and modern home city of Dubai, of his very lovely country United Arab Emirates (UAE). He was very interested to see this university and was happy that they finished visit in two museums and were able in time to see this university.

They got the minibus and driver started driving in direction to the University of Ljubljana. All were discussing about those two churches so enthusiast. They arrived to University of Ljubljana and they saw in front of building one crew of people adult and students.

The account lady Adara, has informed them since in the morning that approximately around 11;00 A.M they will be over there. Really. they were over there at 11.00 A.M.

In front of this building was Rector of university, some professors and some students too. They gave their hand to each other's and entered inside the building, while they saw in the hall so many pictures with wood frame of some professors and some group students in different activities.

So many others student get out of the classes from the second floors and were getting pictures, through the stairs in distance for the younger man Zeeshan and his crew of people. They got up the stairs for the second floor of building and some student to aside the stairs, gave their hand to meet the younger man Zeeshan with so much happiness and smile in their face.

One professor lady very beautiful with very white face with her eyes that color was interfering from grey to blue mixer, while her hair were open brown with highlight color, she was so taller and so much elegant, her dresses were official, while, in her very white hand was holding one grey folder with some papers, so the younger man Zeeshan, was seeing her and he thought with himself:

Looked "Allah" created her beauty, and through to her face, her eyes and her hair some beautiful nature's colors. During walking to the office of Rector of the university the main leader of this university that was one taller, good-looking man, his name was Janko, professor lady introduced herself and said:

My name is Bojana, I am giving Law class in this university. We got news about you by one our student Ardita, that was with you in "Lunaria" and "Kauntia" villages of Croatia, she is studying her for Law. She sent to me and to her friends so, many pictures that you with your people have done over there.

So, students were so much curios and enthusiast too, to see you and they were not silent during the hours of classes because they were seeing from window of different classes when all you were coming. Sorry that you saw so many students through the stairs. The younger man Zeeshan replied:

I am very happy that I saw those students with so much enthusiasm this is big and very good sweet surprise for me really, thank you very much for this warm welcome. During this time, they entered to the office of big leader of this university that the younger man saw his diploma and his title of PHD, doctorate degree and so many paper for different achievement during his career in this institution of high level of education.

The room was bigger with one big, oval, shape, wood table, color normal brown and so many chairs around. Some big high wood shelves with so many books were covering one side of wall of this room, and some pictures of him and his family too, and some pictures with group of students in different activity, while window were bigger too.

One very beautiful but small chandelier hangs above this big table.

One big world map was to the other side front wall. While the marble on the floor were different color like dark red, with some brown color that were creating one very interesting mosaic on the floor. In one corner of this big room were two coaches, cover with luxury silk merchandise and one law circle wood table, brown color with beautiful, design in itself of the wood.

So, the rector of university Janko, with the younger man Zeeshan, his leader of team security Emin, professor Bojana, one secretary of this office, got sitting to this corner and started their conversation.

During this time the journalist Hamad, was writing so fast that got attention of all people around this table while cameraman Jassim, was registering with his video - camera. The conversation was in English language, because the leader of university Janko, and professor Bojana were speaking fluently English language, it is understandable with accent.

The time was going so fast but they did not understand that how was going one hour of really, when they finished their conversation that topic was about education system in Slovenia, and specific in Ljubljana that is capital of Slovenia.

They exchange so many ideas about experience of two countries and they decided that to send to each own country group of professors and students for experience.

During one hour the conversation was so warm so calm with so many smiles, when they finished the rector of university Janko, of Ljubljana gave to the younger boy Zeeshan one very beautiful Art figurine made by white "Alabaster" material, that was building of university of Ljubljana.

One very beautiful leather notebook with name of the university of Ljubljana and one pen blue color with name of university of Ljubljana, also one colorful paper package with one beautiful glass bottle with design in glass itself that was with tradition alcohol produced in Ljubljana alcohol's factory.

While to all the others, to journalist Hamad, cameraman Jassim, account lady Adara, and to secret service team's members and their leader Emin, he gave one beautiful leather notebook with name of university of Ljubljana and one pen blue color with the name of university of Ljubljana too. All said thank you to this lovely leader Janko, of university of Ljubljana.

After that the younger man Zeeshan gave his hand to this leader while said to him that was so happy that he met him and wished to continue this relationship in future. After the younger man Zeeshan all the others gave their hand to Janko, this leader of the university of Ljubljana and got out of his office.

They were walking with professor Bojana to go to her cabinet. During this time in hall, they saw some students that came in front of him and they wanted permission to get picture with him while they were speaking English with him in freely way.

The younger man Zeeshan, liked their confidence and their freely speech in front of their professor Bojana. He got picture with them in crew and he saw their happiness for that action while they left them and were discussing with so much enthusiasm while they were seeing pictures and commenting with each other.

The younger man Zeeshan, saw their action and their enthusiasms and was laughing with happiness, while professor Bojana said to him we have very good and smart students in this university they have high grade in their major for really and they are studying so much foreign language like English, French language etc.

At that time was 12:00 P.M., they entered first to one big room, that professor Bojana introduced them with three people two man and one woman, that were standing up in front of their tables, while they gave their hand with full smile to the younger man Zeeshan.

Those were professors of architecture's major of this university. She told their name, this is Tristan professor of architecture, this is Lian professor of architecture, also this is Alenka professor of architecture too. it was another more small room that were three more people over there two man and one women. Professor Bojana went over there and called them to come in this big room. She introduced them this is Mirko assistant architect, his name means "Peace", the other man is Izidor he is assistant architect too, his name means "Gift of the Isis" and this lady is Katica, assistant architect too, her name means "Pure". All will become professor of architecture in future. All of them laughed with her introduced and explanation.

The room was really bigger with three bigger table and some papers all around, three big computer, one big metallic big shelf, with so many rolling papers that were with different design projects.

It was another metallic table with big frame that serviced like black board that they were opening there those papers with different project to see and to discuss.

They were very happy to see the younger man, while they started to discuss about architecture of the younger man Zeeshan's home-city Dubai, and his country, United Arab Emirates (UAE) too.

They have full information about his beautiful modern city, while they started to speak with technical term and to comment about everything, so the younger man felt happiness that they have so much information about his lovely beautiful home city Dubai, and his country United Arab Emirates (UAE).

They said to him that they will visit his country United Arab Emirates (UAE)and his city Dubai, in future because now they have another reason that they meet him and his friends too. All smiled, while journalist Hamad, was continuing his routine job writing fast everything and taking some pictures so and cameraman Jassim, was registering all the time with his video -camera all conversation in this room with all those - happy people.

The younger man Zeeshan, said to those three architects: You are welcome in our beautiful city Dubai, and our lovely country United Arab Emirates too. After that they went to office of professor Bojana that they found over there three other women so beautiful really dressed with official suits. The younger man Zeeshan when saw them he thought, this university of Ljubljana is choosing people by their knowledge but in harmony and with their appearance with their very good looking.

Professor Bojana introduced those three ladies while she said their name Amalija, this is professor of Law like me, this lady Agata is it my assistant that is becoming professor in future, while this other lady is professor of psychology in this university while she told her name Ilana and her assistant lady her name is Miha that meaning of her name is" Like God" she will become professor lady too in future. Professor Bojana explained for her name too, that meaning of Bojana it is "Fighting Battle" and I am fighting person for progressive way, and all laughed.

At that time the younger man Zeeshan explained the meaning of his name and said: My name Zeeshan is Arabic name, Zee is the "Someone who has" and Shan is splendor, all means someone who has a high resolve, high standard of following, or what one plans to do or a standard high status.

They were smiling while in their very white face with their smiling looks, they were spreading all around spring time in this beginning of the winter time in Ljubljana of Slovenia, while their very beautiful white teeth looked like "Margaritar" stones.

They started right away so much enthusiast to speak fluently English with the younger man Zeeshan. He got shocked with their speech and their confidence. He thought this is unbelievable situation, is big and beautiful surprise for me for really with this excellent, staff in this university of Ljubljana of Slovenia.

He did not want to hidden his strong feelings of happiness and why so many people are saying for him that is shy person and why he is big leader in his city Dubai, and his country United Arab Emirates, so he said to them:

Really, I am very happy that I did this visit in this university of Ljubljana of Slovenia, and I saw so many interesting things, that are giving me some very new great idea for our education system in our country and for our students to have more confidence and to express their idea more freely without any hesitation about any impression.

This is great job that we have done during this trip. While he turned his head to the account lady Adara and journalist Hamad and asked them:

Am I right about this comment? They laughed and said you are very right this is wonderful job that we have done during this week and during this trip in those countries of Western Balkan.

When they finished conversation, they exchanged their telephone numbers e- mails, and they promised that they will see each other again.

After that professor Bojana gave to all of them small package with one cover' s leather notebook and one blue pen with symbol green color of "Dragon" of Slovenia printed like design to those notebooks and pens too.

During this action the younger, man show his sensibility while he felt the tears filled his eyes, really those, action touched his heart. When they finished visit to cabinet of professor Bojana the time was 1:00 P.M. and they prepared to get out of her office too.

They gave their hand to each other while they promised to see them again. They got out while professor Bojana campaigning them until out of building to their minibus. At that time that they were giving "Good Bye" to each other the younger man Zeeshan, holds, strong her beautiful white delicate hand while was seeing her straight to her beautiful eyes, he said we will see each other soon.

He saw that her beautiful, white face got one easy pink color while she said of course we will see each other. After she said: It was very nice to meet you today. She said "Good Bye" and have a save trip to all others and they started driving out of the area of the school.

Strangely the younger man Zeeshan, felt something impression, and one strange feeling during this short time and this separation with this people and this lady Bojana too, but of course he knows that he is so much sensible man.

Anyway, he was thinking for this beautiful elegant professor Bojana of Law class, in this university and said like whispered to himself: Really, I do not know myself what is happening with me in this trip in those countries too, but I liked people in those three countries of Western Ballkan.

The younger man Zeeshan, proposed to all of them to go to eat lunch in center of old town where they are cooking tradition meal, after to continue schedule. At that time the account lady Adara, said, I think you are very right, because after we can go to Philharmonic's center and will continue to see two museums if we will have time today later afternoon.

All they were agreed and the driver got direction to the center of old town. They stopped to the street where were in line so many restaurants. The driver put in parking the minibus and all others entered to restaurant, where were cooking tradition meal.

They ordered different meal that all were tradition of Slovenia meal, while they ordered bottles of water too. So, during this lunch, that started in 1:30 P. M, all were happy for that visit plus they were happy that next day they will go back to their home city Dubai and their country United Arab Emirates too.

The waiter saw them happy and asked them did you like Ljubljana? All said yes, we liked this city, while the younger man Zeeshan said to the waiter really, we did not finish yet, we need to see and some objects today and tomorrow to see center of city and park also and triple bridge too.

The waiter said to him: You are very right; you need to see those parts of our city. They left the restaurant in 2:30 P.M. and driver sent them to Philharmonic's center.

The account lady Adara, started to explain since they were in car that this Slovenia's Philarmonic is the central music institution in Ljubljana of Slovenia. It holds classical music domestic and foreign performers as well-educated youth. It is established since in 1701, as part of Academia "Operosorum Labancensis" and is the among of the oldest such institutions in Europe National opera.

Also, Slovene National Opera and Ballet – Theater, has so much activities domestic and foreign performers. Ljubljana city is famous for different summer festivals too. They entered in building and saw all around while one woman was telling them the history of this Philharmonic - center. They got out in 3:30 P.M.

The account lady Adara, said to the younger man Zeeshan: I am very happy that we will have time to see this artisan and folks (clothes and other items) museum too, that have product of Slovenia since some centuries before so tomorrow we will continue with two churches and center old town and triple bridge.

One hour it is enough to visit this, museum because it is open until 6: 00 P.M. (six a clock) I think until 6;00 P.M. (six a clock) we will finish and we will go to hotel to prepare for tomorrow. The younger man Zeeshan said to her: You are very right.

They went to this artisan and folk's museum too, that they spent over there one hour and half. They got out in 5:30 P.M. (five and thirty minutes), and were driving to hotel while the younger man Zeeshan, said we will eat dinner and to drink coffee in hotel's restaurant too. All were agreed.

They went to hotel straight to their room and the younger man Zeeshan went with his leader of team of security to his suite and said to him in 7:30P.M (seven and thirty minutes), we will be in restaurant to eat dinner. He approved and left him in his suit and got out. The younger man Zeeshan said loudly "Thank You, "Allah" for this very loyal friend Emin, that I have.

At 7:30 P.M. (seven and thirty minutes) the younger man Zeeshan, went to the restaurant with his loyal friend Emin leader of security team. He found his friends over there and after they ordered their preference meal, they started to discuss so much enthusiast with each other.

At that time the younger man Zeeshan understood that they miss their home city Dubai and their families, so they were very happy that will fly and will go back next day in the evening to their families. After dinner all went their room. The young man Zeeshan after left his room the leader of security team Emin, he was thinking so much about all this trip.

After he prepared himself to sleep but the eyes can not find power to close it selves, so he was continuing to think and why he was very tired. He started to create his imagination about this new relationship with this new younger girl Agneza.

He was thinking when she will finish her university for Law, is good she to be specific in her major for International Law so together they will work for big cause of society in future. He was smiling with himself and whispered: If my imagination will find the way to become reality and true story, will be miracle, but who knows what will come in future for both of us, those are mysteries of the life.

Also, he was thinking how will be his life during her studying of four years of university, how he will afford with his feelings and emotions, because really, he is in deep love with her.

After he got something cold inside his chest while he thought but if is happening, Agneza, to know someone over there and to love some one else, because she is so beautiful and probability is so high, that any younger boy to be attracted to her.

At that time the younger man Zeeshan, got out of the bed and went to drink some water, he opened the refrigerator and got one small glass bottle with water, between other glasses bottles with red wine, beer and different soda like sprite, coca cola, lemon, strangely all were small glass bottle.

After some minutes he got calm, while was staying some minutes in front the glass of the balcony and was watching the trees outside. He thought I must to be careful with this relationship and why I feel that I love Agneza, but are so many different conditions that will create obstacles about it. He become more calmer and went to bed to sleep. The night with its magical power made that the younger man Zeeshan to get sleep.

Visiting Center Of Ljubljana, Two Churches And Three Bridges, Old Town Of Ljubljana

SATURDAY.

NEXT DAY IN THE MORNING AFTER THE YOUNGER MAN ZEESHAN, prepared himself to go out while he dressed quality sportive dresses, jeans pants, cotton shirt with square design blue and white color and blue cotton sweater too, than he got out.

He felt himself that morning like younger boy he wanted to walk free that day. Emin his bodyguard came to take him to his room and together went down to the hotel's restaurant.

They found over there their friends. They ordered their meal for breakfast, while all were happy, and all strangely ordered biscuit, milk, butter and strawberry jam, as ordered their younger boss Zeeshan. All looked very happy that morning.

The younger man Zeeshan laughed and said to them: I know why all of you are happy this morning. Some of them asked him with smile: Tell us why we are happy today in this morning? I am telling you now: All of you are happy today this morning, because we will travel tonight to our home city Dubai and our lovely country United Arab Emirates.

After their breakfast they entered to the minibus, and the driver started engine to drive straight to visit two churches first

The lady of account Adara started to explain about history of city of Ljubljana, as they understood that she was so strict about that.

During antiquity a Roman city called "Emona" stood in the area. The city was first mentioned in the first half of the 12th century. It was the historical capital of "Carniola" on one of the Slovene inhabited parts of the Habsburg monarchy.

It was under Habsburg rule from the Middle Ages until the dissolution of the Austro – Hungarian Empire in 1918. After world war the second (WWII), Ljubljana became the capital of the Socialist Republic of Slovenia, part of Socialist Federal Republic of Yugoslavia.

The city retained the status until Slovenia became independent in 1991 and Ljubljana became capital of newly formed state. The city symbol is the Ljubljana's Dragon.

This symbol it is depicted on the top of the tower of Ljubljana's castle, in the Ljubljana coat of arm on the Ljubljana crossing Dragon Bridge (Zmajski Most).

This symbol represent: "Power, Courage, and Greatness". Several explanations describe the origin of the Ljubljana's dragon. According to Slavic myth slaying that dragon releases the water and ensures the fertility of the earth, and it is thought that myth is tied Ljubljana Marsh, the expansive area, that periodically, threaten s Ljubljana with flooding.

It is historically believed that the dragon was adopted from Saint George the patron of Ljubljana Castle Chapel built in the 15th century. In the legend of the of the "Saint George" the Dragon represent the old ancestral paganism overcome by Christianity.

Visit Churches

CATHEDRAL OF SAINT NICHOLAS.

CATHEDRAL OF "SAINT NICHOLAS" IT IS VERY BRILLIANT AND ELEGANT, it is gothic church of 18 (the) century. This cathedral has two twin towers with Green Dome and stands at Cyril and Methodius Square, (Ciril-Metodov) and Town Hall. Religion in Slovenia affiliation Catholic.

FRANCESCAN CHURCH OF THE ANNUNCIATION!

The Franciscan church of the Annunciation> the red or pink color of church is symbolic of the Franciscan monastic order. In 2008 it became cultural monument. This church is built in site where were two or three churches, since 1646 and 1660 while the Bell – Tower, following around 1720 under management of Francesco Oliveri and Francesco Rosina.

The exterior of this church was redesigned in 1858 according to plan by Franz Kurz Zum Thum and Goldenstein. The interior frescoes were added in the middle of the 19th century, by Matevz Langues. The main altar was made by "Baroque" sculptor Francesco Robba. This church is in square named: Francescan Church of the Annunciation!

After that to visit those two churches after we can get to the area where are the triple bridges or Tomstovje explained to them the account lady Adara.

First they went to Cathedral of Saint Nikolas, after they went to Francescan church. They were prepared before about information about those two churches by the account lady Adara.

So, they did not make host to explain everything, while he got shocked by the information of account lady Adara, that was interrupting with delicatesse the host and was doing some questions and was doing some addition of explanation during host's speech.

He asked here: How do you know so many things and so good about our beautiful and very older with great story of Cathedral Saint Nikolas! She answered fast, I was doing research in online before to come here.

He smiled and said to her: Thank you very much for your research and for big interest of our great cathedral of Ljubljana and Slovenia too.

So, and to the other Francescana church they did not spent so much time because of full information by account lady Adara, while at time 10: 50 A.M. they finished visited of two churches while the journalist Hamad, was writing fast notices and was taking pictures of those and his group of people too, and cameraman Yassim, was registering everything with his video camera.

As explained before the account lady Adara, in two sides of Ljubljana 's river, lined outdoor cafes is dividing old town from his commercial place. They put in parking the minibus and started to walk all around. They went to triple bridge or Tromostovje, comprises three bridges spanning the Ljubljana River in the Ljubljana the capital of Slovenia.

It connects the historical medieval town on the on the Southeastern bank with the central "Preseren" on the Northwestern bank dating back square, 13the Century. It stands as the oldest bridge in Ljubljana, in the early 1930 the architect Joze Plecnick, redesigned and expanded it.

In August 2021, the Triple bridge was added to "UNESCO WORLD HERITAGE", list as part of Plecnik enduring legacy.

When they went to "Triple Bridges" they saw so many people and so many tourists that were registered with video- camera and were doing different pictures, so and the younger man Zeeshan with his crew started to make different pictures in crew also cameraman Yassim, was registering with video-camera them and all other people around this area of this triple bridges also and tourists too.

At that time the account lady Adara, started again her explanation, Slovenia is well-known for love about art and culture. Ljubljana is the European capital, of culture, art, festivals, and adventures with its distinctive identity.

Ljubljana is famous for its vibrant cultural scene contemporary creativity, quality of life excellent, cuisine an atmosphere that is hard to forget.

Also, Slovenia has free education free health insurance and medical examination. Transportation is provided, for younger children is secure and if they living with four kilometers of the school building.

The economy of Slovenia is a developed economy and the country enjoys a high level of prosperity and stability as well as above – average GDP per capita by purchasing power parity as 92% of the EU (Europe United) average in 2022.

When the account lady Adara, finished her speech the younger man Zeeshan said to her. You need to teach student in university, in account major, while all others said; That is true she needs to do that and all were talking and were happy with her explanation. She smiled and said it is in online is for free so needed only dedication to make research. The younger man replied: You are very right; it is true what you are saying now.

After they finished walking around "The Triple Bridges" area, they got the minibus to go closer to center of old town where were in line all restaurants and shopping-center.

They arrived over there, and put in park the minibus, while started to walk and to see in line some boutiques with different art figurine and souvenir, they all started to buy something, for their family member to give like gift.

When they finished their shopping, they continued walking and went to one restaurant with Slovenia's tradition's meal. They got two tables close to each other and were sitting close to each other while they started to talk with full happiness.

The waiter was one younger, taller girl, with blond hair with blue eyes, she introduced herself that she was student but was working for weekend in this restaurant, her English language was good.

She asked them where come from? The younger man Zeeshan told her about their home city Dubai, and their country, United Arab Emirates, UAE too. She started to make beautiful comment about their city, looked that she has so much information about that. That situation made so much happy the younger man Zeeshan. They ordered meal as was their preference while they were continuing talking about this day. Really all were happy this Sunday. The Account lady Adara, said to all:

Listen me we have done this visit in those three states of Western Balkan, in record time, we perform everything as was schedule in short time because will take more days. All were agreed. They said really, we did one wonderful job but credit is yours because you gave so much information to us so we did not need to listen host to different object like museum or church.

The younger man Zeeshan, smiled and said it is very true she has so much credit, but now I want to ask you something very seriously but I want truly answer by all of you? The journalist Hamad, asked the younger man Zeeshan: What is your question for all of us?

The younger man Zeeshan, after some seconds silence he said: Are you happy today because we will travel, we will fly today to our beautiful home city and to, and to our country too?

They answered loudly: Yes of course we are very happy that we will fly to our country United Arab Emirates (UAE)and our home city Dubai, too. Again, the younger man Zeeshan asked them while was laughing: So, you miss your family?

Yes, they answered loudly and after that all they laughed.

After they finished lunch they ordered coffee while they were drinking coffee, they got some pictures in restaurant, that has traditional table and chairs dark brown wood, table-clothes were blue and white with small squares design, and the napkin were same textile with color white and blue with small squares design, while glass for water were thick glass, while in window were some short curtains colorful with square design.

They finished the lunch, said one sweet Goodbye to the younger blond girl waiter while the younger man Zeeshan gave to her one fat tips that shocked her and make her so happy, while from her beautiful lips came the words: Thank You very much sir, after they got out got the minibus, the driver started driving straight to hotel.

They went to hotel at 3:00. P. M. they got their luggage while the equipment and supplies of media were in minibus, they gave their hand to the receptionists, younger boy and the younger girl too, and they got out of the hotel and were walking to the minibus. The entered inside the minibus, one man said at last we are ready to go back to our home, all they laughed and said yes: We are ready to go to our home now for really. The driver started driving to airport of Ljubljana. They arrived over there, they sent the minibus to the center of cars and after performed some formalities that got their time, they entered in aircraft. The pilot started flying at 5:00 P.M.

The account lady Adara, spoke were happy: Uauauaua I am very happy, that we are starting flying now in 5:00. P. M. because I have calculated to start flying after 7:30.P.M or 8:00P.M. at evening. So definitely we performed one heavy schedule for really in very optimal time.

After that the leader of the secret service team Emin, said to his boss, the younger man Zeeshan: Thank You very much for this trip in Western Balkan, in those three countries like Slovenia, Croatia and Montenegro, that was one wonderful trip with so many interesting things and Thank You very much for all what you have done for us during this trip too! This was one big pleasure for all of us and one very good experience too. So, I wish that "Allah" to bless you and your family too.

All said with one voice: Thank you very much. Really it was one big pleasure for all of us. "Allah" Bless you and your family too.

Their flight got about six hours it was night anyway the pilot was flying so carefully. Strangely all were anxious about this flying they did not have patience until to arrive in their home city Dubai, of their lovely country United Arab Emirates, (UAE) too.

All the time they were seeing map and time on aircraft and saying ooooh we are going close now to our country. The younger man Zeeshan while was seeing, them was laughing, while was saying: You miss your family and your home - city Dubai.

All were saying loudly: Yes, it is true and were laughing too. At 11:00 P.M. they saw that the aircraft was doing more noise and was flying slowly around airport of their city.

They opened the plastic cover of windows and they saw all full light by electric tower above airport. When the aircraft landed all were happy and applaud while said: Thank You "Allah", also they said to their pilot: Thank You very much, you have done good job and you brought us safely.

All they prepared their luggage and cameraman Yassim, prepared to take the media 's equipment and supplies too. After going through control for passport and their staff they got out the airport while they got taxi as destination of their home they have, while the leader Emin, with his secret service entered to one minibus with their younger boss Zeeshan and went to his palace too.

They campaigned him until to the door, and left him while he was entering to is palace, they continued their trip to go, everyone to his home too. The younger man Zeeshan entered to his beautiful big palace at 12:00 A.M., of this night.

The younger man Zeeshan, did not have patience to see his two children while he left his luggage to the hall and was taking so fast the stairs until he arrived to second floor. He went to their room, kissed them and after entered to his studio.

At that time Aasma the lady of kitchen came fast while said "Welcome" in home and asked him what he wanted to eat. The younger Zeeshan said I do not want to eat only bring me one glass with orange liquid and that is it.

It was one quiet and beautiful night while the fresh wind was coming from ocean too. Their huge city showed its magnificence by different colors of light, that looked like were dancing between different very high building. The younger man Zeeshan and his friends, understood the difference of their huge and modern city with the others city that they saw in Slovenia, Croatia and Montenegro of Western Balkan.

They understood the source of this big difference, that was because of two different systems that have those countries. The countries of Western Balkan, came out from one system, that did not allow to practice different corporations their activity and to create so much rivals while to give so much developing of them.

In their city during this night, they saw big difference was showing in bold way since in airport with huge dimensions with so much domestic people and foreign tourists too.

Also, they saw so huge numbers of big very high buildings that they putting their roof – head inside the clouds of the sky, also so many different colors of lights of so much different big advertise of businesses too.

It was really big difference between their home city and the others cities of the countries of Western Balkan. The younger man Zeeshan, was thinking and remembering, all the conversations, that they have done when they arrived in their home city Dubai. The leader of secret service team, Emin, said to his friends: We must to say to our leaders of our home city and our country too, one big: Thank You, very much, what they have created for our people for our nation.

All the other approved his expression. They said to him: Really, we are blessed that we are living in our country with all these beautiful high buildings, stores, and wonderful environment too, created by hard working people and by leader with big and futurist vision.

During, this night the younger man Zeeshan, was drinking the orange liquid in one luxury cup glass with gold color decoration and was staying in deep thinking. He opened the window of his room – office, while the fresh air that was coming from ocean was touching in gentle way his face.

He was thinking about this trip, about those people really with simple life and strangely about their happiness too. He was thinking about this younger girl Agneza and felt something inside his chest, like difficult breath. He thought: Something interesting is happening with me, one new feeling is growing up inside me about this girl, about her lovely brother Gentius and about all her friends.

He felt that big compassion was growing up for those youngest people in "Lunaria" village of Croatia that were expressing great happiness while were with him. Their honest feelings and their big wondering for the gift that they got by him their great "Thank You" to him, while their eyes were sparkling strong, all of those touched the heart of the younger man Zeeshan.

The lady Aasma, that was servicing in kitchen came and asked him if he wanted something else, while she got answerer by her boss that he did not need anything else. After she asked him: You are very tired why you are not going to sleep. He answered:

Really, I am very tired, but I cannot sleep and some minutes because I need to send some text message to people that I visited, that they were very lovely people and treated us so good, to tell them that I with my friends arrived good in our country United Arab Emirates, (UAE) and our home city Dubai, too.

The lady Aasma, said to him. You are very right, you need to send to them this text message and to give "Thank You" to them for their good treatment and their lovely behavior to all of you. After she said "Good Night and left the younger man Zeeshan alone.

He was in deep thinking and was not understanding that the time was going fast. The younger man Zeeshan, was thinking and for this professor lady Bojana, for her high level, intellect and knowledge and her beauty too. He whispered: She was sweet lady too. This trip to Western Balkan, gave one big impact to the younger man Zeeshan about so many things of social life and education system too.

He was thinking that those three countries Slovenia, Croatia and Montenegro of Western Balkan, did not have our richness situation, but the education of people it was in more high level that in our country too.

The youngest people over there they were speaking most of them so good different languages like English language, French language and Italian language too, that wondered me for really, it was same situation in airport, in hotel in different stores and different restaurants too.

I understood that they have in their public's education system class of foreign language to teach students, that is very good thing. So, I must to think for that matter, in our education system and to make some good reform that will have big and good impact for our country and city's students in their future life too.

During this time, he sent text message to the professor lady Bojana, to the youngest lovely boy Gentius and to beautiful lovely girl Agneza. He felt that time that their eyes got tired, he got up, fixed every item, on the table of his studio while, decided to go to take shower in bath room and to sleep.

The younger man Zeeshan did shower, he did not go to his bed room, but went to another room to sleep, really, he wanted to think again in his lonely night, until his eyes to got tired and not to resists anymore to be open, after to send, him in beautiful world of dreams too. Really, he was very tired in this beautiful night.

When he went to sleep, he was listening noise of leaves of the trees around that were moving from the wind that was coming from ocean. He was thinking with himself that so many interesting things are going in my life, inside my family and outside in social circle also for this trip now.

"Allah: is giving so much diversity now, only to get out my desperation that I have by this conflict of those two families, mine family and my wife's family too.

So, the powerful" Allah" is creating so many others occasions and so many new other people is sending to my life last time. So that is something interesting that those new people that I know were not coming by chance, but by powerful force, to give me another destiny in my life, to open more "diapason" in my life to think for more great things than only for my personal problems.

That situation is telling me that I need to work with myself and to prepare to work hard for more and great case for society and never to be desperate for my family 's situation because every problem has one solution so and for my family's problem will have solution too.

With those thoughts the younger man Zeeshan that tried to close his eyes but appeared to him the face of the younger Albanian girl in Croatia Agneza with her magical smile, while he felt some arrythmia in his heart he whispered what is going on with me, I do not know myself anymore.

Slowly, slowly the kingdom of the night sent the magical stick with ingredient of the stars and silver moon and made possible to close the younger man Zeeshan's very beautiful big black color eyes. Through his eyes he was expressing all feelings that were boiling inside his chest about this younger beautiful girl Agneza.

Definitely during this very longer night the younger man Zeeshan that was very tired got sleep, but strangely the magical night with power of energy of universe did not leave him quite but send him to very interesting dream.

He saw himself that he was walking through one very heavy green forest around one hill, while the sun's rays were entering "interekalary" through the branches of those very taller trees. While he walking through this forest the sun's rays were playing with his eyes and were not leaving him quite to see around.

At that time one grey dark shadow came around his head and was blocking his eyes to see clear.

He started to say what is going on? I cannot see good, to walk through this forest. While some dark figures like grey dark cloud's ingredient appeared in front of his face. Those dark figures have shape like human body but not face not features in it.

Those dark figures started to walk close to him and one voice that came from nowhere entered to his ear with force while said: We are not leaving you to go away. We have a lot to do with you. You have obligated to compensate us for so many things that you have done with us. They said to him: You will come with us! After that they started to make one diffuse noise and one voice said like whisper: We have someone in your home by us that you have created problem

The younger man Zeeshan, started to scream loudly with terrifying feelings: I do not know you, I have nothing to do with you, I have done nothing with you. At that time, he felt dizzy and he has very difficult to breath. I have my big family with my siblings I do not need to work with anyone of you. The dark figure shadows said and we have big family and we will fight you.

After that the younger man Zeeshan, fell on ground above some wet older leaves that, fell by taller trees. He lost himself he was dizzy he did not have power to stand up while felt that all his body become cold and wet.

After that he started his praying: "Allah" help me, and save me from those dark shadows, dark figures, that have shape like human. He was continuing his praying like whisper because he felt that he did not have power to speak loudly, he was thinking that one invisible hand was blocking his normal breath.

Strangely after some seconds appeared in front of him one very white figure with material like cloud. He started to say loudly: What do you want by me, I feel not good I have difficult breath, I cannot breathe.

The white figure got his hand and started to lift up him and to walk like was flying with the younger man Zeeshan, that he did not understand how fast he was going through those taller trees and sometimes, above of top of them, only when he saw himself close to the bottom of the hill.

He saw that behind him was standing up with proud for his beauty the green forest while in front of him appeared one very beautiful green field with so many beautiful colorful flowers.

The field was border by so many different trees taller and most of them subtropical and tropical trees with their heavy circle green crown. So many beautiful wild flowers like "King Protea" flowers, "King Crocosmia" flowers, already red color, "Arlind" flowers, different color "Iris" flowers lily colors.

Some white sheep were on field and one small crew of children were playing in distance with one very white small dog. He thought where I am now?

While the white figure with material like white cloud left his hand and one melodious voice entered to his ear while said:

This is the place where you must to be and those dark shadows, figure never are coming to bother and scare you anymore, whomever they are, your negative acquaintance, your family's enemies, your opposite humans in your job and whatever. This is beautiful and peaceful place to live and to build your new career.

He saw children with that white dog and he thought for his beige or milk color small dog "Zoros" while he felt tears to fill his beautiful eyes. In distance he saw one small very blue lake. The sun was sending, his rays to the lake, that were creating some reflexes with small weaves of the blue water. At that time, he felt one easy touching above his shoulder, he turned his head to see while the white figure like beautiful white cloud with interesting shape started to fly up to the sky.

The younger man started to scream and was calling her: Where are you going? Where I am here in this place? The white figure sent one melodious voice again and said I finished my very good job for you, while you are in very beautiful place where really you must to be. This is beautiful, clear and so much peaceful place for life of people. Really it is magical place but I am alone here he started to scream. At that time, he heard one strong voice:

My dear Zeeshan are you okay? He opened his eyes and he saw the lady Aasma, that was staying in front of him with big wondering and some expressions of scare. This lady was servicing in his home since his childhood, so she was taking care so much for him like he was her son. She continued:

What is going on? She did not stop her asking: Why You are sleeping in this room and not to your bed room?

Why you left this door of this room open?

Why you are screaming and calling someone?

What is going on? Did you have good trip?

Did you meet good people over there?

Did you have any problem over there?

You scared me with your screaming. I heard you dawn to first floor in hall and I came with emergency I though what happened with you?!

The younger man Zeeshan smiled and said to her: My lovely, mother Aasma, he called her like she was his mother, I had a wonderful trip, I met over there the most lovely people, while I have with my friends and those people over there the beautiful time and big pleasure, while yesterday night I was very tired and I slept here, but I saw one dream that created that situation for me.

I need to tell you this dream and you to comment me. While she said:

Okay tell me your dream but not now, you need to take shower to eat good breakfast, and after to go to your office, later afternoon tell, me your dream and I will do comment about it.

When she left, he was thinking for her. She was very lovely for him and his siblings since childhood time, she was like second mother to all of them. At that time one "idea- question" came through his head like very fast light on the sky in sunny day.

How is possible that this lady heard my screaming and my wife to the other room did not hear my screaming and talking loudly too?! After he said loudly to himself: Wife?!

The younger man Zeeshan get out of the bed and went right away to his bath - room to take shower. He finished shower, cleaned his teeth put his favorite perfume, combed his hear, gave another more elegant shape to his beard during shave his face. So, he started big changing about appearance more elegant about everything.

Really this day he wanted to dress sportive beautiful pants and shirt and to show full enthusiasm to his people in his office and to the other offices in his giant floor of job. That day the younger man Zeeshan was very happy that he was in his country United Arab Emirates (UAE) and to his lovely beautiful home city Dubai, he wanted to meet his people and to tell, about everything. He ate fast his breakfast he called his friend Emin, leader of secret service team and was waiting them to come.

He got out of big palace and found all his secret service team in front of his door. He said with happiness Good Morning to them and entered to his car that the leader of secret service team Emin, was campaigning others were behind.

During driving he was commenting about last trip to Western Balkan, while said that he was happy now that was in his very beautiful city. The younger man Zeeshan, said:

That his grandfather, also his father has done a great job for this giant modern city that before 40 years was only desert place like village with direction fishing business. Today we all are working hard to create other space more beautiful and so much green space too.

Our city escaped beyond measures all other big cities in Europe and around the world, for its beauty and high buildings with super modern architecture. Our city created one long line rivals of others countries around the earth planet to follow us with high towers like our high tower "Burja - Kalifa".

This is one unspoken rival, battle in silence that which country to build higher tower above the ground, but difference is that our beautiful city Dubai, not have only one very high tower that is sending its head above the white clouds but has and so many others very high buildings that are claiming to be close to this tower. Definitely our city is power until now for its architecture and beauty of all around the world.

We created that to this city Dubai, that to come now million tourists every year and to come emigrants from all around the world to work here and claim for more better life. But difference between our city and those more small and older cities with great history in Western Ballkan is that they have more high level about social life and more better education's system.

So, I think that needed big reform to our city about education's system. With those words they came in front to their office's building. He left the car out and together with Emin, leader of secret service he entered in building to go to his office. When he entered to his office his secretary came fast and gave greeting to him:

Good morning, and Welcome Prince Zeeshan. We all are happy to see you back. After secretary lady Salma came to his office and some others employees. They gave greeting "Good Morning" to their younger boss Zeeshan, while they said after one big Welcome, also all were curious about their trip and they wanted to listen him.

They were asking so many, questions in same times that make the younger man Zeeshan, to laugh. He said to them: Wait I am telling you so many things about this trip be calm take sit and listen what I am telling to you now. All got silence and were listening the younger man Zeeshan. He started to tell in line about three different states of Western Balkan, like Slovenia, Croatia and Montenegro too.

The younger man Zeeshan said to them: We saw so many historic places so many buildings and churches and mosques built in period time since 15th century until to 19th century and later. They were every interesting and beautiful buildings too, beautiful art was inside of them.

Most important is that people over there were so friendly and lovely, while the younger simple citizens and students were speaking well foreign language like English, French and Italian language of course and their native slavic, language too. We visited one university that leaders and professors of this University gave to all of us one very warm welcome.

The meal in different restaurant to three of those countries was very good quality we ate most of the time native cooking meal really. All trip was wonderful we went and to two beautiful villages too, it was really one very good experience.

People over three were working very hard because they came out from different system, that was monist system and everything was in hand of the government not to people. Now they started different life in different system of democracy, that they faced some difficulties because like individual they came poor from former system but they were doing hard and good job and they have a lot progress in their life and in their economy too.

I will prepare one longer material for that trip and for that education that will be leader of our new program about some changing that we need to do about education system in our city Dubai and after widely in all our country United Arab Emirates (UAE). The younger man Zeeshan, said to them: We finished now, while you, he was speaking with his secretary lady Salma, must to bring to me all materials, that you have scheduled during this week and all, correspondence that were by others to our office too.

The secretary lady Salma, said: Yes, I will do now, while they prepared to leave office when their boss Zeeshan said to them: Wait some minutes I have something else for all of you. He called the leader of the secret service Emin, that was out of office but inside of building, and said to bring the staff that he left to his car.

After some minutes came his friend leader of bodyguards and brought one big bag and left to the table of office. The younger man Zeeshan, said to him Thank You and started to get out one by one some small package and was giving to everyone. They got surprised for this new gesture of their younger boss Zeeshan, while started to open with happiness their package.

All really got so much happy, while they were seeing those gifts like symbol. The secretary Salma, saw in her bag, one leather orange beautiful notebook with design in itself, with one blue open pen with, name of Ljubljana of Slovenia with bold lily color writing and one art figurine like older writing machine. She shocked and smiled while said one big Thank you!

The other man saw in his package, one brown leather beautiful, notebook with design in itself, with one green open pen with name of Dubrovnik of Croatia, bold blue color writing, and one art figurine one beautiful building, because he was architect of this office. He loved that.

The architect got impression and said to his boss Zeeshan: To say

Thank you to you is less, I must to find another powerful word to express my happiness and appreciation. I wish all the best on this Earth planet for you and your family too.

The other man opened his package and saw one bold cherry color leather notebook with design in itself and one pen with bold red color with name of "Ulcinj" black color of Montenegro, while one art figurine one beautiful modern yacht, that made him to give loudly sound uauaua, how beautiful. He was engineering mechanic that was working in that office with different projects for this city. He said to his boss Zeeshan: Thank You very much!

While the other lady opened her package with delicatesse, and saw one mixer color red and white color leather notebook with design in itself, one pen milk color with name Zagreb of Croatia with bold red color writing also one art figurine like book with writing title "Law". The lady that was lawyer to his office expressed loudly her happiness wile said this is wonderful: Thank You very much.

At the end the younger man said to them: I just to tell you that I was thinking for you in this trip. All of them said with one voice: "Allah" Bless you and your family" Prince Zeeshan!

Travel To "Lunaria" And "Kauntia"

TRAVEL TO CROATIA.

TURNING BACK TO LJUBLJANA SLOVENIA.

AFTER SOME DAYS IN HIS HOME CITY, VERY LATER AFTERNOON, HE GOT one strange calling to the number that he gave to Professor Bojana of university of Ljubljana in Slovenia.

She said it is me Professor Bojana from Ljubljana of Slovenia Mr. Zeeshan.

He got shocked and for moment he did not answer but when he heard again, he said to her: I am happy to listen your voice where are you now?

She said I am here in your city Dubai, in this hotel where the owner is one Albanian man from Kosovo, plus he made me one favor he gave me discount for the room. The younger man Zeeshan did not feel enthusiasm, but he said I am coming right away to the hotel to meet you.

After that he felt nostalgia for the younger Albanian girl Agneza, that he went to her country in Croatia to her village "Lunaria: to visit her. He was thinking deeply, about her. He called his secretary woman Salma, and gave some instruction for her while he said to her: I will be out today. I am busy.

After that conversation with his secretary woman Salma, he was driving to this hotel and when he arrived over there all the people that were working over there were scare by his unexpected visit. Employees were coming around to fix something.

He went to cafeteria and he saw the Professor lady Bojana with decolte dress while her white breast looked like wanted to tear this dress to show its sexuality beauty.

When she gave her hand with longer white nails of fingers, decorated with some golden jewelry, while with her sweet smile she showed her white teeth that were under the frame of red lips that gave to her very white face so beauty.

Her open brown hair with some high light, were collected behind. The younger man Zeeshan, gave his hand to her and he felt her soft hand, while he put her hand between two his hands but strangely, he felt so cold inside himself for this meeting and for the moment he was thinking:

What is going with me?! I do not know myself?! I gave so much hope to this professor in her city Ljubljana of Slovenia now I am like frozen ice in North Pol inside me. He got sit and started routine questions.

During their conversation he ordered whisky for both of them while he explained to her this is unusual action of him because he did not drink alcohol but to respect her, he will drink one small glass of whisky.

Professor Bojana said I understood you, but you can order for yourself one soda drink. So, he ordered, on orange drink. When the waiter brought whisky and orange drink, the younger man Zeeshan, was seeing with attention professor Bojana the way how she got the glass with whisky and started to drink.

They started their conversation with smile and Professor Bojana, was drinking whisky in average glass, and the younger man Zeeshan was drinking orange liquid. During their talking the younger man Zeeshan was seeing through the window the silver moon that was shining through the dark night while the bright stars were giving their greetings to silver moon.

The younger man Zeeshan, said to her: We can go to balcony to enjoy this beautiful night. She said yes, while he with delicatesse got her hand to his hand and together walked to balcony. Over there he was watching her in her eyes. She felt impression by his sensitive watching. She was not talking but was whispering confuse, with expression of happiness.

At that time, she was showing with her arm up one beautiful bright star up to the sky while when she put her arm down accidentally, she touched with force him in his arm and said sorry, sorry. The younger man did not speak while he was watching her straight in her eyes.

He got her arm, hold strong while with the other hand he put around her neck while started to play with her hair. At that moment started magic moment. With his passionate kissing he covered her red lips and her mouth, while she felt like drunk lady full with happiness. His kissing was longer while the silver moon was sending its rays 's light like wanted to bother them for fun during their sweet moment of happiness.

His sweet longer kiss gave to her one feeling that tested like strawberry's jam. Professor Bojana was thinking: I am now in beautiful dream.

After some minutes they went back to the hall of cafeteria and after the younger man Zeeshan paid they got out, he gave his hand to her, and said that he will see her next day in the morning.

She was walking to the stairs to go to her room in second floor while time by time she was turning her head and was seeing him with full smile. The younger man Zeeshan, got out his secret service crew were waiting him. While he got the leader of secret service Emin, and was driving to his huge palace. When he arrived to his palace, he said to them:

I see you tomorrow and entered to his beautiful garden.

He entered direct to his studio was seeing to his telephone and saw some messages by Agneza, her brother Gentius and their cousin Armina. He felt happiness inside him but he felt nervous too about what happened that evening with this professor Bojana.

He was confused, what he was doing. he was not secure to control his feelings, or he felt some compassionate about Professor Bojana because she did action that he did not accept so fast. So, she showed to him her full passion to meet and to see him, she did not have patience to wait longer.

Next day he prepared himself to meet this lady Professor Bojana while he did shave perfumed himself with his with his favorite perfume, really he liked the Channel perfume for men but he did not want to use that day because he was using that perfume just to remember his friend from 'Europe that liked that perfume. The younger man Zeeshan, dressed up, and was driving with his secret service people to this hotel.

During this day he saw in front between two windows on the wall outside was created with marble one black Eagle with two heads that is symbol of flag of Albanian people in all countries on Western Balkan and all around the world.

He was seeing with full attention this marble while he was entering inside this hotel. He saw professor lady Bojana that was waiting in big hall with sportive dresses with beautiful smile while gave her hand with sweet smile to the younger man Zeeshan.

He gave is hand to her but he did not leave but was holding strong her hand with his hand and said: I know where we will eat breakfast today while he smiled, at that moment Professor Lady Bojana approved while was moving her head like sing Okay.

The bodyguards were campaigning him. They went to one traditional native restaurant where the owner was friend of the younger man Zeeshan. So, they saw one big welcome by people that were working over there and the younger man Zeeshan with Professor lady Bojana got one table to the corner of this hall.

They ordered white cheese, two eggs, small package with butter, milk and biscuits, not bread. When they started conversation in quiet way he said to Professor Lady Bojana, I have one proposition, to make some changes to your schedule of activity those days that you are here.

We are going to "Zayed" University, after to National Museum later to "Exposo 2020" building next to see the modern area of the beach. Tomorrow we are going to one meeting with women, after to field of horses, later afternoon to "Galleria" modern shopping center also to "Burja Khalifa Tower".

She approved his proposition while she touched his hand like Thank You sign. He was feeling shiver inside him while was staring his eyes to her. It was like one electric ray that was going through between both of them.

He whispered to himself. What is happening with me I do not know myself. After breakfast they went to "Zayed" university building. They met over there students and professors that were enjoying that modern building of the "Zayed" university.

They entered to one big auditor, during this meeting they were doing so, many questions, also were so many answers and reactions.

She forced herself not to react when she saw some many younger students' girl and professors' ladies, with black gown and scarf too. She thought: Unbelievable ins this super modern building in this beautiful luxury environment of this education's center to see this contrast of this black dress of women gown and scarf too. I am understanding, that is conservator religion.

They got so many pictures with professors and students also cameraman Jassim, registered to his video camera. After meeting with a lot good impression by this meeting the professor lady Bojana, was shocking by huge modern building.

She was thinking and with her mind was comparing with building of university in Ljubljana where she was working, while she was feeling that the tears were filling her beautiful eyes.

The younger man Zeeshan saw her and asked: What happened with you? She was speaking short and strict while her voice has some vibration, she did not want to cry in front of him, but she said:

There so many big differences between my country Slovenia and my home city Ljubljana with your country United Arab Emirates (UAE) and your home city Dubai, too. He was watching but he did not speak. After that they went to the car and were driving to National Museum, and after to "Exposo 2020".

She was taking so many pictures and she was writing so fast about everything that she was seeing. She said I do not need lunch when he proposed for lunch. It was heavy schedule that day and professor Bojana felt herself tired.

She wanted to go to take rest in room and to prepare some materials that she wrote short. He sent her to hotel, also he ordered for her food to send to her room in the evening, and she got so much enthusiasm and said to the younger man Zeeshan: Thank you very much.

After he said to her: I will call you later from my home to talk with you. She smiled and said I will be busy with writing. I know but you will find some minutes to talk with me and both laughed. She was seeing him straight to his eyes while her eyes were expressing so much love to the younger man Zeeshan.

When he went in his palace, he did routine action he went to his two children' room kissed them and went to his studio. He saw e-mails and after he saw telephone. He thought to call later night Professor Bojana because she will write longer and later night, but after he changed mind and called her right away.

She answered with laughing. The younger man Zeeshan said to her: I know that you will write so I decided to call now, not to interrupt your thoughts later. Both were talking with happiness. After he said to her: Have a Good Night. He cannot sleep but that night he called one of his bodyguard friends, and said to him: I need to go now with you out. His friend said it is any emergency problem. No said the younger man Zeeshan just I want to go out tonight, I cannot sleep.

His friend replied: Yes, I understood always is problem of this beautiful younger Albanian girl Agneza. The younger man Zeeshan did not speak only said to him I am waiting you. So, he did not sleep but with his friend that came so fast they both went out to the beach while were enjoying the light of silver moon above the ocean's water blue.

The younger man Zeeshan, started conversation, he said to his friend:

When this Professor lady Bojana to go back to her country, we need to travel again to the village "Lunaria" where is living this younger girl Agneza, because I do not know why I am thinking so much for her. His friend approved while he said: Okay we will go over there.

After that they started to discuss for that trip. For moment the younger man Zeeshan, was seeing faraway to the water while he said: Look how far away are going the waves.

His friend body guard said to him, yes, I know together with waves are going faraway and your thoughts to that village where is living your lovely girl. After they started to play and throw faraway some stones to the water, it was like race who of them will send faraway the stones on the water.

They were continuing with this game while they did not understand how fast was going the time, it was already three a clock (3:00 A.M.) in the morning. After that they went to their home.

Next day in the morning the younger man Zeeshan wore his tradition native white longer gown and his scarf like hat above his head and went to hotel, to meet Professor lady Bojana from Ljubljana of Slovenia.

She was waiting to the big hall in front of receptionist place, she shocked when she saw the younger man Zeeshan with his native dresses that day. He gave his hand and said to her we are going to eat breakfast here in the restaurant of this hotel.

They went to restaurant and she ordered "Petulla", honey, milk and two small package butter and white cheese. The younger man laughed and said: I will eat same thing what you ordered for yourself.

After they together with security team 's members got the car and driver started driving to one center where they had meeting with women of different institution and nonprofit organization.

When they arrived to one glass building with modern architecture, they entered to one big room that were with so many big circle tables where were seating 6 (six) to 8 (eight) women in every table. Professor Bojana got shocked when she saw all women adult and younger with black gown and black scarf, while all of them were intellectual women.

Professor Bojana, started to speak fluently English Language, about emancipation of the women, about intellectual women, about economy and politic. When she finished her speech, she said that: It is a big conflict between beautiful faces of the women here that, are like spring time, that are giving inspiration to all of us and those black – dark clothes so something needs to change.

After that last sentence of the speech one strong applause by all women in this hall. At that time professor Bojana asked the younger man Zeeshan about five women in this hall or big room that have wear classical dresses.

Professor Bojana said Okay but who is this beautiful lady with silk colorful dresses? The younger man Zeeshan answered to her that she is her sister Mahriam, she is progressive women and has studied in Western Europe

The younger Zeeshan answered to her that: Two are professors from Western Europe and are teaching student in university, while three the others are counselors for business, they are from Western Europe too, and are working with some Corporations here in Dubai.

Meeting was so much enthusiast while, were so many questions by those women and so many answers by Professor Bojana and the younger man Zeeshan.

Some of them spoke for their experience in daily life -job. They were speaking fluently English language. Professor Bojana thought with herself: They are so much smart women, but they do not have courage to fight for their right, for their dress code to change.

She thought at least those women that really have so much good looking, to wear color dresses, and to continue their religion tradition but open color dresses to wear if with scarf and gown.

When meeting was finished so many women came and surrounded Professor Bojana, they were very happy and started to speak freely and enthusiast, while were taking so many pictures together.

They all were happy that they saw professor Bojana and their leader prince Zeeshan and they did so many beautiful pictures. After meeting, Prince Zeeshan with professor Bojana continued their schedule to go to the fields of Horses and Camels.

When the younger man Zeeshan and professor Bojana wanted to go out, the women said that they very happy the meeting was so wonderful and they never experienced that kind of meeting with years they said that they wish to come more like this meeting in future.

All women were happy and the younger man Zeeshan, was happy too. at that time journalist Hamad was writing and taking pictures with all of them while the cameraman Jassim never stopped his registered, with video camera.

They got out and driver started to drive to horses' field. When they arrived to horses's field Professor Bojana saw big field with white fence and shelter of horses were big buildings so modern and good with red brick wall and roof. While some workers were doing maintains, they meet professor Bojana and the younger man Zeeshan.

After Horses' place they went to Camels' place. Professor Bojana shocked and screamed when she saw that one camel came to the window of the car and put its head inside the window and touched the face of the younger man Zeeshan, while he gave some seeds to it and started to touch the head of Camel with gentle way.

Professor Bojana got picture for that moment of the younger man Zeeshan with Camel. When they got out of the car, Professor Bojana saw one beautiful beige younger Camel was running and came to the younger man Zeeshan and put is head to his face and after to his throat while he was giving seeds to eat Camel.

Professor Bojana got picture of him while said to the leader of bodyguard Emin: Please I want you to get one picture, for me with Prince Zeeshan and this Camel. The leader of security team got picture of three of them Prince Zeeshan, Professor Bojana and Camel too.

Professor Bojana was very happy and sent that picture right away to her Friend of University in Ljubljana of Slovenia. When the driver got out of the area of those fields of Horses and Camels, he entered in highway, at that time Prince Zeeshan heard Professor Bojana that said to him:

How it is possible those animals love you? Prince Zeeshan said to her: all animals and people love me! ..and was smiling. They were continuing their way and when they arrived to Galleria and the driver Stopped the Car while all others security members were to the other car, Professor Bojana said to Prince Zeeshan:

I want to be member of those "All" that love you. Prince Zeeshan saw her in her eyes and did not say anything but was watching her with longer watching.

Over there Professor Bojana was seeing this giant and modern Galleria with full attention again to her eyes came tears down to her face, while the younger man Zeeshan saw her and he understood. She was comparing her country Slovenia with this country too and this city of Dubai.

They entered to one cancelier's store and over there, Professor Bojana saw some notebooks with colorful leather cover and some colorful paper with beautiful with beautiful graphic design on the top or to the bottom of the page.

She wondered for their price and made one uauaua how expensive they are I wanted to take for myself and my friends but No I can't buy those. The younger man Zeeshan laughed loudly and said how many notebooks you want?

She got red to her beautiful white face and said one for leader of university and two for my office friends, professors. She wanted more but she was shy person. The younger man understood her while bought for her six colorful notebooks with leather cover and six packages with colorful paper with graphic design to the top or to the bottom of the page and eh advised her:

You can give to your office friends notebooks and to leader of university, while to architects you can give those beautiful, colorful, paper. She said:

Thank You, very much and gave compliment to him while said:

Brilliant mind. Both laughed with happiness.

The younger man Zeeshan entered to one perfume's store and she followed him but she was waiting him what was doing he bought one bottle of perfume "Dior" for her.

She got wondering when he said enjoy it. She got red in her very white and beautiful face but he said it is for you. She said Thank You, very much she saw that was expensive. After that, they entered to one store with leather bags and he asked her:

What kind of bag and what color you want. She said, Thank You no, I do not need, it is enough the perfume. The younger man Zeeshan said to her with smile: I did not ask you if you need or not bag, I asked what kind of bag and what color you like, she smiled after she said:

Okay, and she choose one classic black leather bag, while said thank you to him. They got out from the store and were seeing around; they saw one store with winter suit for women. The younger man entered inside she was staying outside he called her come inside: She entered inside the store and the younger man showed to her one very elegant blue suit with some very thin white stripe, sweater and skirt. She said it is so elegant and so beautiful. He said to her find your size.

She opened her eyes, but he said short find your size. We need to pay and to go out we have a lot to do today and he was laughing. She chose her size while the sales person put in a very beautiful big bag this elegant winter suit for woman.

She said to him a big Thank You and was smiling while was seeing him straight to his eyes. After they saw one store with leather shoes and boosts. He said to her good for you to get one par shoes or boost for your self for winter.

She said that it is enough but he said to completed everything, for winter and laughed. She wanted shoes like half boost black color too, he paid for that and sales person put the box, of shoes to one beautiful bag too.

To one store of books the younger man bought for her one thick book with brown leather cover with history of the United Arab Emirates (UAE). The book was in English language and has history of his country, and his city Dubai and his family too. After he bought for her one beautiful watch without asking her.

He entered to one gold jewelry store with her and he choose and bought without asking her one very beautiful gold necklace and said to her to have present by me and to remember me and laughed she got shocked it was so expensive.

She did not have breath to say Thank You to him both laughed. She said after God Bless you and your family too. He said Thank You and "Amen". They entered to one small restaurant that was doing product like Doner and Fast food, meal, she said let's eat short lunch and to go to see Burja Khalifa, tower.

It was coming evening and the electric light started all around. They got out to Galleria and went to see "Burja Khalifa" from outside that was one wonderful view with all its light advertise.

Professor Bojana whispered with herself: This is magical night with all its miracle. She was thinking for all those gifts by the younger man Zeeshan. She understood him, he wanted to respect her. During walking around to square close to "Bruja Khalifa"- tower, the younger man Zeeshan said to her: I want to honor you that you came right away alone to see and meet me, and Thank You, very much by you.

After they went all together with his friends of security team and professor Bojana to restaurant of hotel to eat dinner. They went to restaurant and ordered their preferred meal as they wanted.

They were eating and they were discussing with happiness with Professor Bojana. During this time professor Bojana wanted to make ritual to go to the balcony to see stars with the younger man Zeeshan.

They left their friends over there and went to balcony. She said to him: This night I never can forget in my life Thank You very much what you have done for me. He got her hand and was holding to his hand while he saw tears to her beautiful eyes.

He promised to her and said: We will see each other again and again. I want our friendship to have very longer term. After they entered to the restaurant, when they got seat, to their table came the owner of the hotel Kosovar man his name was Adriatic.

He smiled, met all of them and said to the prince Zeeshan:

Thank you very much for your coming to my hotel and my restaurant, it is honor for me and my family too. I got new by my receptionist for your coming and this lady, Professor Bojana, that is coming from our region of Western Balkan, I tried to help as I can and to respect her.

My name is Adriatic because my father loved Adriatic see and his beach and he was smiling. As you know Adriatic see with his blue water is giving fresh air to Slovenia, Croatia, Montenegro and Albania too. While I am Albanian from Kosovo.

After he said this package with this Whisky bottle is for our guest in Dubai Professor Bojana, and this whisky bottle is for you Prince Zeeshan, while all dinner is gift by me for all of you.

Thank You, for your coming to our hotel and restaurant all of you. All of them said thank you to him. After he left and said Good Night to them. They left restaurant while the younger man said to his leader of security team Emin: Tomorrow in the morning you will send professor Bojana to airport early in the morning. In big hall of Hotel, he gave the hand to professor Bojana and told her that his security team's members will send her to airport early in the morning. She hugged him, and prince Zeeshan saw tears in her eyes. He said to her you must to call me the moment that you will arrive to your home.

He saw her that all the time that she was going to stairs or the second floor was turning her head all the time to see Prince Zeeshan.

During the time that driver was driving to prince Zeeshan's palace, he was thinking about Professor Bojana and felt empty inside himself. He felt his compassion for her. He thought it was beautiful time, those days with professor Bojana anyway. I wish for her the best. She will be my good friend in Western Balkan.

During that night prince Zeeshan went to balcony, while was drinking one coffee in big cup and was watching the starts up to the sky. He started to pray for his wish to come true about this "Suddenly White Dream", while he saw that one bright star looked that moved and the younger man Zeeshan thought is coming true my white dream is becoming reality.

Suddenly one beautiful idea came through his brain. He thought to go for ski in one center of Austria and over there to meet Gentius and Agneza and professor Bojana with her friends from Ljubljana

While was drinking and was praying to stars, looked that starts were saying to him what is your request that you need our help. At the moment suddenly he got calling by Agneza from "Lunaria", he shocked and he whispered with himself the stars gave answer and was smiling, after he shouted "Allah" Thank You very much for this good night, while he moved from his chair, he thrown to his pants the few coffee that was left in his big cup.

At that moment he decided to call his leader of secret service. He answered right away what is going on?

Prince Zeeshan said to him: I want to talk with you tomorrow.

His friend bodyguard Emin, said to him do you need me to come now to your palace. No answered Prince Zeeshan tomorrow I need to talk with you. Through telephone he heard his friend voice is about your new people in West Balkan?

Yes, said Prince Zeeshan. He was thinking with himself I do not know myself anymore. What is happening with me? But I am sure that I am very happy now. I do not know what kind of feeling is this about this younger Albanian girl Agneza.

Now that I was thinking for new way of my life is happening something strange with me, because my wife is changing now. But whatever to happen big problem for me is about my children I can live without my children.

141

Also, I will have problem with my wife 's family and my father too, that he designed that marriage for me out, of my wish. Really, I do not want to think about those anymore I want to think only about beautiful things and time that I will spend for ski in Austria while I will invite and the younger boy Gentius with his sister Agneza and his friend Dalmet with his sister Armina.

Next day Princ Zeeshan went to his office with his secret service people while, in his office he was doing conversation in private way only with his leader of this secret service crew Emin.

We are going two days in Croatia and to "Lunaria village I need to see this girl. The leader of secret service team Emin, said I am understanding you are under pressure of this new feelings, so I will support you to go over there, this is to help you, to know yourself where you are standing with your feelings about this girl.

You need to be ensured, for yourself about this girl and these new feelings, that not to regret later. Really, I do not want to see you in bad situation later. I do not want to happen again your situation like some times before. I want to see you happy and to be concentrated in your job too. How many people will take in this trip? Asked the leader of secret service. The younger man Zeeshan said:

Only you with my secret service team. We are going the beginning of next week only two days. We are going first day and will sleep one night over there the second day we will travel during night to come back to our home city Dubai. So they decided to take another trip.

During this day the younger man was Zeeshan, doing his ritual job and strangely he was very happy that his loyal friend was supporting him for this trip in Croatia and specific to "Lunaria" village where the younger Albanian girl Agneza was living with her brother Gentius and her parents too.

When he went at later afternoon to his palace after he saw and spent some times with his two small children he went to his studio and opened computer, and saw so many e-mails by those people that he has meet in west Balkan.

He saw e- mail by student of Podgorica of Montenegro, he saw e-mail by the youngest people of "Lunaria" of Croatia and e-mails by professors of university of Ljubljana of Slovenia.

He replied to all of them with one greeting and send one – e-mail to Agneza just was asking her how she was doing, but he never wrote to her for this trip he wanted to make surprise to her.

At that time, he heard one short easy noise of his phone, he opened the telephone and he saw text message form Agneza. He was very happy and did not have patience to see the text message.

He saw one short cold sentence that make his heart from hot feeling to cold immediately. He was reading the text message by Agneza from "Lunaria" of Croatia. "I, am sure that you are very happy because I saw this happiness in your face and professor Bojana's face in local newspaper, so I understood".

The younger man started to whisper with himself while he said: I must to go to meet this younger girl Agneza. He was thinking with himself: What kind of Telepathy is this today I was talking about her with my friend and she was thinking for me too. She starts to doubt to me!

I think that I started to love deeply this younger girl Agneza. Really, she is so beautiful, and her eyes are spreading all around light with their sparkle. Her eyes mixer color green to blue are showing great and strong rivals with blue color sky, and green color of leaves of the trees and green grass too.

When she is smiling that looked, she is bringing spring time and when she is watching with her eyes, is giving full glad to my heart and I feel lost in her watching at that moment.

I am very happy that I met this younger beautiful Albanian girl Agneza.

He was thinking that when she was walking with crew of people in "Lunaria" village and "Kauntia" village when she was seeing up to the sky looked that the white clouds up to blue sky were moving fast and opening their place while were creating big space for her sparkling light of her beautiful eyes.

The green trees were moving their branches down to whispers with each other with jealousy while their leaves were doing easy noise to disturb the multicolor flowers all around, that those not to give attention to this younger beautiful Albanian girl Agneza, while they were opening their petals and spreading all around their scent fragrance.

The younger man Zeeshan said with low voice: I think that all elements of nature were jealous for this beautiful younger girl Agneza, and why the Universe with its positive energy created her beautiful appearance. Her beautiful heavy hair brown, color looked that were rivaling the trees on the forest during while the wind weather, that was taking care for hair while were moving around with force like branches of forest's trees.

Days were going fast with routine job. The younger man Zeeshan was continuing with happiness inside his chest and his hear his daily job. During this time, he started to see some changing, in behavior of his wife Laylae, that she was acting more sweet, softer was not using irony during her speech.

She was not acting like wild, capricious and criticize person, but during her speech and behave the younger man Zeeshan, was seeing to her watching and to her face more compassion, and more love.

Those phenomenon like behave, watching and talking in this soft way and with love, that were missing for a long time inside this beautiful and luxury huge palace, between those two people, husband and wife. It was a long time that the younger man Zeeshan was feeling cold when he was coming in his palace, looked that the walls were spreading cold rays, while he tried so much to prevent conflict and contact with his wife, not to speak so much that all the time will end with strong argument.

Time by time he was justifying his distance with his wife that he has something to do intellectual job, while he was losing in his studio – room and was leaving behind in air her expression:

You did not have time in your office to finish your job?! It was not enough time for you over there to do this job where are working so many people for you?!

So, during this time he saw drastic change of his wife's behavior, while he was preparing divorce 's document and that time that he was thinking for the younger beautiful Albanian girl, Agneza for new beginning for new faze, in his life.

He was thinking so much serious for this matter and was so much enthusiast. He thought that his wife Laylae, something she understood by his cold behave and now has changed mind but anyway he did not care so much because now he was swimming in water of happiness for this younger girl Agneza.

Suddenly, he was thinking that one hot strong feeling of love was growing inside his heart too while he started to forget all problems in his life between him and his wife, also between his family and family of is wife too, that really those problems were driving him crazy and distracted him.

Now in front of him appeared one orange to gold sunrise in fresh morning after one ugly heavy dark – grey color storm and one pink to orange sunset that was closing the beautiful day.

Those beautiful and happy days he was feeling since he got out of the door of his palace, that all the multicolor flowers were opening their petals with happiness and were spreading their scent fragrance that was smelling so good and made him and all his friends to feel dizzy with pleasure.

Also, the branches of the trees, were spreading their whispers rumor by their leaves outside to the others multicolor flowers and trees and specific Palmas trees aside the highway and different road that all of them were giving pleasure to the younger man Zeeshan and his friends with their moving and their fragrance.

At that time the younger man Zeeshan whispered to himself when his friend was driving his car to go to his office:

I think that nature changed and it is very happy for me too.

Came the day when the younger man Zeeshan will travel with his team of secret service only for two days in Croatia, to see this younger girl Agneza in "Lunaria", village. They started their flying early in the morning at 7:00 A.M. but when, they arrived in Western Balkan the weather was so grey, so the pilot was flying very carefully.

Strangely from the plane the view looked clearer because was not strong sun's light and the most of the trees were without their green leaves, so the younger man Zeeshan, and his friends were seeing the fields, hills and mountains with their grey and brown color. To the top of some mountains, they saw the white snow that was covering like hat above the mountains.

They arrived in Zagreb of Croatia around 1:00 P.M. in middle day. They got the minibus to airport and started their driving to Zagreb of Croatia. They arrived to hotel at 1:40 P.M. They, went to receptionist got the key of their room and went to leave their small luggage and bags. They decided to eat lunch to any restaurant during the driving in highway and to go straight to "Lunaria" village. The day was short of this winter season so they did not like to be later.

During their trip they saw one tradition restaurant to one exit of highway, that to his advertise has one white lady with folks' dresses. They understood that to this restaurant were cooking traditional Croatian meal.

They put their minibus to the parking and entered to this restaurant that was with longer hall with two longer lines of tables with four chairs each of them, while the windows were with short textile cotton curtains, with strip design blue and red color.

145

The tables clothes were with white shining color quality cotton and four big napkins with same material like short curtains of the window. So, the napkins were bigger with strips blue and red color cotton. There were with thick glass cup for water. So, the design and supplies of this restaurant was classical tradition native Croatian. They saw some people that left their big truck in parking and came inside to this restaurant looked that their, were so familiar with the owner lady of restaurant because they started to make so many jokes with her.

They ordered lunch and they started to drink since the beginning alcohol with those thick glass cup. The younger man Zeeshan saw them and thought: They are working hard with their big truck also is winter cold weather they are learn to drink alcohol. His friends were seeing these people and they said strange, we know that these people on Balkan and Western Balkan, they are drinking so much alcohol since in the morning.

After that the younger man Zeeshan with his friends ordered lunch, some ordered rice with meat, some soup with chickens and some eggs with cheese and water. Also, they ordered salat with boil white cabbage with olive fruit, also with olive oil and vinegar, that was tested so good.

The lunch was so good in that cold day of the winter time in Croatia. After lunch they started driving to "Lunaria" village. They arrive to "Lunaria" village later afternoon, they started driving straight to school to ask, but the man to the door said that these younger people had class in the morning not afternoon.

The younger man called the younger girl Agneza, but she did not got answer he left message, but he did not got answer too. He wrote text message:

Dear Agneza I am here with my friends and I am waiting you here to come in front of your school with your brother. She sent one sign like shocked for his coming and short answer I am in home. They waited some times and after they went to the road that was close her home. It was grey weather and the dark night was coming more early so some light to the street of village were open early.

They stopped on the corner of the street close to her home, and the younger man Zeeshan, and the leader of secret service Emin, got out of the car and were going close to the home. They saw one big white paper to window. The house was bigger but one floor. The younger man Zeeshan went to read this letter, he understood that Agneza as smart girl she was has created that scenario.

He started to read every sentence that were pointing with numbers.

1. I saw your pictures in online, with professor Bojana of university of Ljubljana of Croatia, both of you looked so much happy. She looks beautiful. She came so fast to you to your home city and your country too.
2. I will study university in Ljubljana of Slovenia, that is taking four years and more maybe.
3. I spoke in general way about you, with my mother and father too, but they blamed in bold way, because they cannot accept that I to marry with one man that has other, wife. It is not our tradition, does not matter what is your situation now in your family, you still married.
4. Your beautiful and rich country and your home city is so far away from my country too.
5. I cannot stay far away from my family.
6. I cannot lose my new profession that I will study university, because I do not know your native language and will take me so longer time to learn it and to practice my profession.
7. We have so many differences about our two families about tradition and so many other things.
8. I love you but I see so many obstacles for both of us for our relationship.
9. Distance in time and distance in geographic line is impacting so much maybe in negative and will make weak our relationship.
10. Needed so much effort that our relationship to have success, while I think for myself. I am very young and I am fragile now for those strong efforts. I am not ready for that. I hope you will understand me!

With love,
Agneza.

The younger man felt his tears in his eyes and whispered slowly, I am understanding you but I am in love with you. So, he decided to call he brother Gentius. He got so much enthusiasm and started to speak fast, with loudly voice.

He said to the younger man Zeeshan, Agneza cannot come now but I am coming out now to meet you. Gentius did not have time to answer to the question of his mother, about what is going on, but got out, all of this conversation, the younger man Zeeshan was listening by phone and laughed.

So Gentius got out and met his lovely Prince Zeeshan while was kissing with full love and was doing oooooo, after he met the leader of secret service Emin. They discussed some minutes, and the younger man Zeeshan said: Tomorrow I need to meet Agneza. I am not coming here but after school I will send my friend to take you and Agneza and to bring to Zagreb, and after we will bring again here in "Lunaria".

Gentius said: Ooo, very good because tomorrow all the pupils of this school has only three hours because they will send us to one botanic garden, so I and my sister Agneza will not go over there we were so many times over there. So, the class of teaching are 45 minutes we have three hours, so in 11:00 A.M. We are ready to travel because we are finishing the class in 10: 45.A. M.

Prince Zeeshan said Okay and left Gentius to go to his home and they started their driving to Zagreb. The driver was driving slowly so they arrive to Zagreb after one hour. They were to their hotel in 6:50 P.M. they entered to the hotel's restaurant and ate their dinner. His friends understood that their younger boss Zeeshan was not so much happy but with deep thoughts.

After dinner they stayed more longer in restaurant and were discussing with each other they did not want to go out to walk, it was a little cold weather outside. Later they went to their room while the leader Emin, was campaigning his younger boss Zeeshan until to his room.

After the leader of security team said good night to his boss Zeeshan and left him in his room. The younger man Zeeshan got out his sweater and laid dressed in his bed and was thinking so much he was desperate.

He whispered to himself: What is going with me? How will be my life?

I understood that I am in love with this beautiful younger girl Agneza.

He felt that his tears were going down to his cheeks without his permission.

He felt very weak himself that evening and he never understood how the sleep got him in dark night kingdom. Suddenly he opened his eyes later and he saw himself dressed laid to the bed, he did not understand where he was, and why he was laid on the bed with his classic dresses. He saw his very expensive watch and got shocked that was 12: 00.A.M. in the middle night, also he was desperate that was not the morning and said who is staying all this night here.

He got out of the bed changed his dress opened for some minutes the window and went to get shower while he was thinking that shower will make fresh his mind. After he got his luxury pajamas and was seeing television while was laid to the bed until the sleep came quietly and close his eye with gentle.

In the morning the strong knock of the door awaked him and he understood that was the morning of new day in Croatia. Strangely he was very happy that was not longer, night. He said to his friend good morning and went to change his dresses and to get prepare for that new day. While his friend was preparing coffee for both of them to the machine that was to the other corner of the room.

They started to discuss while the younger man Zeeshan said to his friend you are going with one man to get Agneza and Gentius to "Lunaria", in 11:00 A.M. you must to be over there, you need to drive around the 10:00 A.M.

It is about 40 minutes driving to "Lunaria" but because off traffic let's thing about one hour, so I think after 12:00 P.M. you will be with them here. They will stay with us for lunch until 3:00 P.M.

After you have another hard job to do to send them in "Lunaria" village and to come back so after 7:00 P.M. in the evening we will start flying to our country tonight. This trip was not so good for me said his younger boss Zeeshan. His friend said to him: Do not say that, wait until you to see this, younger girl Agneza.

The younger man Zeeshan, continued his speech I will stay with the other men to see something around the center of this city Zagreb until you to come so now let's go to eat breakfast to hotel's restaurant.

They went to restaurant that their friends were waiting them. They ate breakfast, eggs, white cheese, butter and milk some have and peach or strawberry jam too.

In 10:00 A.M. the leader of secret service team Emin, started driving with his two friend s to "Lunaria" village, while his boss Zeeshan went out with three the other his friends of secret service to walk around to the center of Zagreb. They rented one hotel's car. So, he said to his leader of security team we are waiting you in 12:00 P.M. here. In 12:15 P.M. the younger man saw the younger girl Agneza with her lovely brother Gentius dropped the car and run to him. Gentius did not leave space to his sister but was kissing and hugging prince Zeeshan, while he hugged both of them Gentius and Agneza, with his arm and he kissed both of them with full love.

This day looked that was not Agneza, that she wrote the letter last evening last night. She was very lovely. The younger man Zeeshan was seeing her was smiling and was thinking: She became wild jealous because of visit of professor Bojana to my home city Dubai, and pictures that I have done with her.

He was holding their hand both of them and said to his friends let's go to eat lunch to any restaurant in center of Zagreb. He was very happy and all his friends strangely were happy too, for that situation. Really, they love their younger boss Zeeshan.

They went to one traditional restuarant with Croatian meal, while they found so many people over there. They got two tables. The younger man Zeeshan stayed in table with Agneza and Gentius and his friend Emin the leader of the security team the other got another table.

They ordered so many different meals for lunch, they wanted to test so many meals in small quantity from Croatia. Lunch was so good, and they conversation was so lovely and very interesting. The younger man never discussed anymore her letter to Agneza because she was seeing him with so much love straight to his eyes.

She said to him this was the lovely, surprise for me, because I thought when will be the time to see you again? The younger man Zeeshan said to her: Agneza you will see me again and again. At that time Gentius said to his sister:

Yes, you will see again and again because this time he came, only for me, spoke with longer voice and with full smile. All they laughed, but Gentius was giving so much diversity and humor conversation and never was stopping his questions as much curious he was for everything.

After lunch they started to walk around this center of restaurant and small shopping, but Agneza did not allow the younger man Zeeshan to enter in stores, he understood and laughed. All they were very happy. Was coming 3:00 P.M. and was time that those two younger people to go to their "Lunaria" village. The younger man Zeeshan started to feel something anxious. When they went minibus, he said now is time you to go to your village because we need to travel tonight to our country I came only for you this time.

So, all of them with minibus got riding to go to "Lunaria "Village". The driver was driving slowly but carefully so after 4:00 P.M. They were in front of the home of Agneza and Gentius too, they parents were waiting for them, because they know that they were going to meet their lovely prince in Zagreb.

During this time Gentius called his mother but she was in store in center of "Lunaria" village, and prince Zeeshan heard that she said ooo thanks God that you came in good way. Said hello to your lovely Prince Zeeshan.

While Gentius said to his mother I will say I will do it I will do it.

Came the time to give greeting to each other at that moment prince Zeeshan felt tears to his eyes and he saw tears to beautiful eyes of Agneza and Gentius too. He hugged and kissed both of them. He was full emotion and can speak any word.

Gentius and Agneza said to him we will write to you. When they left Prince Zeeshan with his friend got to the minibus and driver started driving straight to Zagreb. He was driving slowly, so they arrived to their hotel in 5:30 P.M. because were so much traffic.

They got their luggage and got riding to airport, during driving the younger man Zeeshan said it is good to drink coffee to any cafeteria before to go to airport.

So, they stopped to one cafeteria before to enter to highway. The leader of secret service Emin, said this trip came with happy end all smiled and their younger boss Zeeshan too. They went to airport, they sent the car to the center of rent, also they passed control of passport, and went to their private jet of their boss Zeeshan.

At 7:00 P. M. their pilot started flying. Really all of them were happy that will go back to their lovely country United Arab Emirates, (UAE)and their very beautiful modern home city Dubai. It was very quiet night and pilot was doing very carefully flight.

They were thinking how much difference is between their country and those countries of Western Balkan too.

All of them were discussing about lovely Gentius for his humor and his curiosity for everything and they got wondering how much he loved Prince Zeeshan. He was speaking with so much love and with his deep of soul.

The day were going so fast, with routine job. During this time the younger man Zeeshan was enjoying his time with his friends of secret service while was going to so many corporations to discuss about this new project of new town close to desert area.

All different specialists and Chief Executive Officer of different corporations were enthusiast for his idea and were ready to help him. More enthusiasts were group of architects and they started right away their job to create beautiful architecture for this new town but that will not be with very high buildings.

So, day were going very well, and the younger man Zeeshan was doing his routine daily job plus new activity about this new project of new town. He was enjoying more time with his two children this time, also he was seeing every day the big changing of behave of his wife Laylae, and everything was going smooth in their relationship.

He was asking his wife time by time like accidentally when he was coming early afternoon in his palace, about her idea of new project. One afternoon he spoke straight to her while asked her: Oooo, I did not ask you about new project? How is going your preparing for your project with your group of women architects, and business-women too? By the way if you need, any help tell me for everything you need.

His wife saw, his pride that with his speech he wanted to show to her that he was not interested for her new project but wanted to help her because he had a lot experience about business and new projects and buildings too.

Strangely he got one strict answer with irony by his wife Laylae, that he got shocked: She said to him: Thank you very much my dear husband for your asking and taking care for my project, but do you know something because I know you are so much busy as you were all the time with your daily life's job so I do not want to bother you. By the way I have one perfect high-level group of intellectual women architects, business-women, account and lawyers too, so I think this time I do not need your helping.

Really, I am very busy this time about preparing this project and she was smiling. The younger Zeeshan, said to her: Really you are very busy now also you do not need help by me?

His wife Laylae, replied to him: Yes, it is, true really, I am busy this time and I do not need now your helping, but more later, of course all of us need you help because you are leader in this beautiful modern big city Dubai, now I am going to take children to send out to the garden they to play.

The younger man Zeeshan said to her: Okay go while I am here in studio to work in computer some material. When he went to his studio and got sitting to his chair in front of his computer he was thinking for his wife and her reply that afternoon.

He said to himself: She loves me. I see her feeling to her eyes when she is speaking with me. She changed so fast in good way. Love is changing people for good. She wants to challenge me with this project now.

Maybe she is scare, and is feeling something inside her for my last two trips in short time in Western Balkan, she does not want to lose me. She is not giving priority to situation that is created to our two families by us, she wants to protect our family with our children she wants to protect her marriage too.

So, the younger man Zeeshan, got calm and before to start his material in computer he saw e-mails and his telephone in quiet way. He received some e-mails by professors of Ljubljana in Slovenia, also he saw text message by Agneza and his new lovely teenager friend Gentius. First, he was reading e-mails of professors of university of Ljubljana of Slovenia.

When he finished reading of the e-mails and wrote to them in short way with expression "Thank You" to them, for their writing, he was reading Agneza's text message, he was happy for her very lovely text message, he felt that all his body got fast warm like by electricity. He whispered: I am in love with this beautiful Albanian younger girl Agneza that is living in "Lunaria" village of Croatia.

He started to pray: "Allah", give good direction to my situation now, I am experiencing new love but I did not believe changing so fast behave of my wife and turning back with her warm feelings to me. She loves me too. Another reason is that I cannot live without my two children I love them so much.

Anyway, the younger man Zeeshan was very happy this time whatever to come situation in near future. He said to himself: Thank you "Allah" that turned in calm situation in my palace and peace to my wife, so we do not need to argue in wild way.

After he was reading the text message of Gentius and he was laughing loudly with humor written by teenager boy. At that time came his wife with two children and the lady that was servicing to their palace. His wife said to him: I did not see you a long time to laugh with happiness is any good news?

He answered to his wife while was laughing: Yes, it is, a great news because is writing me one teenager boy from Western Balkan, from one village of Croatia that I met over there and has so much humor plus he is so much curious for everything.

His wife Leylae, when she saw that he was quiet, happy and told to her about this teenager boy, and he was explaining to her and was writing to him in same time, she left his studio and went with two children to their room.

Really his wife Leylae, did not bother him anymore because she saw that he started to change, he was coming more early in home not like before that he was so much anxious and during this time, he was spending more time with two children.

Their life was going quiet smooth without big conflict and their small children were giving so much happiness to both of them

The younger man Zeeshan, started to work with his material in computer. He was thinking that time was going fast. He was serious about this new project. He needs to deal with so many banks and companies about this project but he was remembering one older saying that:

"Money is going and is coming again, but the time is going and never is coming back anymore." So, the younger man Zeeshan, thought that he did not need to waste time but to start as soon as possible about this new project close to Desert's area.

After he called Emin, the leader of secret service team and told him that he needs to discuss with him about one important matter. So, in the morning before we to go to my office we will go to any cafeteria to drink coffee and to discuss together about this matter.

He heard his loyal friend answer: Very good let's do that tomorrow in the morning. I think is for Western Balkan, said his friend. The younger man Zeeshan said to him: You are right it is related this matter with people of Western Balkan but the place will be in center of Europe.

Okay said his loyal friends let's discuss tomorrow in the morning when we will go to Cafeteria. Also, he said to his younger boss your voice is sounds good.

His boss Zeeshan replied: Yes, I am very good for this my voice sounds good. The leader of the secret service Emin said to him:

Have a Good Night!

His younger boss Zeeshan said to him too: Have A Good Night to you!

Next morning his secret service team came to his palace and he said to his driver we are going to cafeteria of one my friend.

They went over there and the owner was very happy that saw the younger man Zeeshan while said to him: Thank You "Allah" that I see you this morning to my cafeteria. What happened that you did not come for a long time. I miss you, also, my wife and my children asked me: Why is not coming Prince Zeeshan to our cafeteria? I said to them, that you are so much busy.

Prince Zeeshan said to him: I traveled two times in Western Ballkan during last time for that reason I did not have time to come here. The owner started to ask him about Western Ballkan while he called his wife and told her that their lovely prince Zeeshan was in cafeteria with his friends too.

After some minutes came his wife, she was very happy when she saw the younger man Zeeshan came and hugged him and said welcome, we missed you. After some minutes of conversation, the wife of owner left them to talk.

At that time some people came in cafeteria and the owner left prince Zeeshan with his leader of secret service, on their table while said to them:

Coffee today it is by me for all of you! The younger man Zeeshan started conversation with his loyal friend leader of team of secret service.

He told him that they will travel to Austria they will go to one center for ski. Prince Zeeshan said to him I think that we will go December 25 until December 30 so for holiday of New Year we will be in our home to celebrate New Year evening, or we can go after holidays, January 5 until to January 10. So, what do you think about this schedule.

His friend bodyguard Emin, said to Prince Zeeshan: I think is better for us to go December 25 until December 30, because will be big and beautiful surprise. I know that in Europe students and pupils are starting their winter vacation in December 28 until to January 10 or 15. His friend said to him call these people that we are going over there.

After their conversation Emin, the leader of secret service left the office of his younger boss Zeeshan and get out.

Prince Zeeshan did not have patience to wait but he called the younger boy Gentius, while his through telephone he heard Gentius voice that was cheering and was speaking fast with full happiness.

Prince Zeeshan told to him that he will go to Austria in December 25, until to December 30, and he is thinking to invite him, his sister Agneza and his friend Dalmet and his sister Armina but they need to get two days off from school and permission by their parents.

So after that Prince Zeeshan told him that he will pay tickets of plane to come four of them in Austria, to this center of ski also he will pay and two rooms for them. Prince Zeeshan told to Gentius that he will meet and some other people from Ljubljana of Slovenia.

Gentius said to him: I know professor of university of Ljubljana and her friends that made advertise for you, your country and your city too. Very good, meet them, Prince Zeeshan said Yes, I will do and all of us will have very good time I think.

Suddenly he heard the scream with happiness by Gentius and after he heard him that said: Really you Prince Zeeshan will invite us and will pay for us tickets and rooms to this center of Austria to make ski.

Really answered serious Prince Zeeshan. Gentius said: We will take two days off by school and by director woman also we will take permission by our parents four of us, I promise to you Prince Zeeshan, after he was doing, Ooooo, what beautiful and big surprise for us for this winter vacation.

After some seconds silence by both sides because prince Zeeshan was laughing with Gentius and his happiness, he heard Gentius to said:

Prince Zeeshan, I love you so much and I miss you.

While prince Zeeshan with laughing said to him I see you over there. After that conversation, Prince Zeeshan called professor Bojana in Ljubljana of Slovenia.

She answered right away while she was showing her wondering for this calling that day and her happiness too. Prince Zeeshan told her that he will be in center of ski in Austria December 25 until December 30.

He continued his speech: So, if it is possible, you with your friends to come over there two days and to meet each other will be very good for both of us and all of us. She was glad and answered fast Yes, I will come and I will tell to my friends if they want to come with me over there. They ended their conversation with their expression. "I see you over there" and one sweet Good Bye!

So, Prince Zeeshan decided to go with his secret service people and his journalist Hamad, cameraman Jassim, and his account lady Adara, to Austria in December 25 and to stay until December 30. He was taking all the crew that he had in first trip of Croatia and Slovenia.

The younger man Zeeshan started to make arrangement that center of area of alps of Austria for hotel's room for himself for his crew of secret service and for Gentius his sister Agneza and his friend Dalmet with his sister Armina.

When he finished arrangement with that center of ski in Austria, he went out to different stores to buy something new clothes and boots for ski 's center in Austria.

Really Prince Zeeshan was regular for ski to different area of alps of Austria, Switzerland, France, it was done like ritual now for him.

He was very happy, and his people that were working with him in his business and in his office were seeing big changing to him those last months but the never know the reason the source of this happiness.

Before he was in deep thoughts and so much serious looked like the universe has thrown to his face all the grey clouds of the sky, while now he was more open and was doing jokes time by time.

Since he met all those people in Western Balkan, he understood that in our earth planet has so many good people that can change bad mood of any person in good mood. Prince Zeeshan understood that so many people have problems in their life some have big problem and some have small problems but all they are finding way to resolve or erase those problems and why some of them are not rich people.

Days were going fast, with their heavy routine job, so came so fast the day that that Prince Zeeshan will travel with his crew. He will take in this trip his secret service crew's people, cameraman Jassim, journalist Hamad, and account lady Adara and his pilot. So, he got all crew that he has in first trip.

They started flight very early in the morning at December 25, but their flight was more slowly when they entered in space of Europe, because the weather was not good and sky was with heavy grey clouds. They arrived in Vienna of Austria later after middle day. In airport of Vienna, they got one minibus and were driven to this ski- center.

When they arrived over there, they found people that gave them one big sweet of welcome and started to help them to hold their staff like media supplies and equipment too.

To registration's table Prince Zeeshan was talking with the younger lady that she was speaking English language fluently. She said to him Sir, everything is Okay about rooms for you, and your people that came today, all their windows are in front, of the hills with pines trees and others trees that are covered with white snow, it is really one magnificence view while you will enjoy this view too.

With all respect that I have for you, maybe I ask you about four others younger people, that you did arrangement for room it is standing this schedule that they will come tomorrow or is changed for them? Prince Zeeshan said:

Thank you for your asking but the schedule is same, they will come tomorrow before middle day. After that he with his people went to their room to establish themselves, really their room were big while from window they will see that beautiful view.

Prince Zeeshan has suite, bigger while they were two windows one small to part of living room and the other window of bedroom was bigger. Really it was one wonderful view outside.

All the pines trees and others were covered with white snow and their branches cannot afford their snow's weight in their body but they stayed down and they did not care for their pride to show their beauty like in spring and summer time with their leaves.

He got sitting to the big bed and called Gentius. Gentius answered fast with glad while was speaking loudly and fast, we are coming at that same time, Agneza was speaking with happiness Yes, we are coming.

Prince Zeeshan felt, warm inside him and his happiness was spreading all around the room. Gentius was continuing: My father will send me, Agneza, Dalmet and Armina in airport of Zagreb.

At that time Prince Zeeshan heard the voice of Gentius's father that was speaking Albanian language and said with accent "Hello". Gentius translated in English language: Prince Zeeshan my father said hello to you.

Prince Zeeshan said Thank You, and felt that all his room was happy like him, and all white snow looked more brighter to him now, while the branches of the trees that started to move slowly because of their snow's weight looked very happy and were greeting him. Prince Zeeshan promised to Gentius that he will come with his bodyguard to take them in airport of Zagreb.

Next day Prince Zeeshan went in the time that was coming the plane from Zagreb to Vienna. They have schedule of their plane to start flight from

Zagreb in 8:00 A.M. and to arrive in Vienna at 9:00.A.M really the flight was only 55 minutes by plane.

Anyway, Prince Zeeshan went over there with his crew of secret service and were waiting those younger people. When Gentius, Agneza, Dalmet and Armina arrived at airport and enter to hall of airport, after they got through control, they were happy when they saw Prince Zeeshan with his people, Gentius called loudly:

Ooooo dear Prince Zeeshan we came and he started to run while left behind his sister Agneza, and his friends Dalmet and Armina. He went to Prince Zeeshan and hugged him strongly and was leaving all the others were laughing some others people were seeing with attention Prince Zeeshan because they heard younger boy when called him.

So, many people came around Prince Zeeshan while he was meeting Agneza, Dalmet and Armina. They were waiting him to meet these younger people, after some of them said hello to him and started to ask him for his visit to Viena after them came so many others people and created one big crew. All of them were taking picture of Prince Zeeshan and his people with those younger boys and girls too.

They were happy when Prince Zeeshan told them that this visit was only for fun in the ski's center and that he liked Austria, and his capital Vienna beautiful city very cleaning and very quiet too.

Also, he liked that ski- center, he loved the building and rooms were so beautiful with windows in front of hill and he was enjoying one very beautiful white view with so many trees full covered with snow. At that time one younger couple pleased him and said:

Can we take one picture with you Prince Zeeshan? He said of course. They got picture after wanted and the others, but the leader of secret service told to people that Prince Zeeshan was so busy he has not time for all, but better let's do on picture like group with all of you, so they were happy they said Okay, and got one picture with Prince Zeeshan and his people too.

After that they all said to him: Prince Zeeshan, we wish for you a good vacation in Austria, thank you very much that you are visiting our country:

God Bless you Prince Zeeshan and your family too. Prince Zeeshan said: Thank You to all of them and gave them greeting with his hand after that they started their driving to ski center.

After that they got the big car "Vene" and the driver was driving to hotel in center of ski. All around the white snow has covered the field and the hills aside the street. When they arrived over there all the youngest people got shocked that they saw so many people in front of the hotel that were talking so much enthusiast.

They entered inside the hotel to make registration and after they went to their room, really Gentius wanted to stay with Dalmet, in room so Armina went to stay with Agneza to the other room. Room were bigger with window with two glasses, also were very warm inside, while the two bed were single but bigger. They have television and refrigerator too, one dark wood classic closet also one small table with two chairs.

The bath room was bigger with big mirror and every kind of shampoo with small bottle and small soap were over there and so two big white quality towels two more smaller for face and two other smaller for hand

Agneza and Armina prepared their staff in closet while they were seeing from the window the beautiful view that pines tree has their branches down by the weight of the white snow.

They said in same time how beautiful view. They heard the voice of Gentius that were calling them while knock to the door and entered inside with full happiness. Gentius started to speak enthusiast for their beautiful big room and all furniture and television too, also he said that the bath room was bigger with big mirror and so many white towels and shampoo and soap too. After he asked Agneza.

My dear sister tell me, why are small those bottles of shampoo and soaps are small too, cover with beautiful paper on bath room. Agneza laughed and Armina too, after Agneza explained to her lovely brother that was curious for everything:

They are putting small bottle shampoo for two people and small soap for two people because they are bringing every day shampoo and soaps too. They are changing every day all the white towels, while are cleaning room every day, bringing everyday small package of coffee and sugar and cream milk and are living to the table where is coffee machine. When people are staying longer, they are changing sheets and velvet, so everything is very cleaning.

During summer time they were in hotel on beach to the country United Arab Emirates (UAE)to the beautiful city Dubai, of the younger man Zeeshan, but over there they have suite like small apartment and Gentius did not get attention because their mother has brought and some soap and shampoo and sun cream from Croatia. So, he got attention here about those items.

After Agneza's explanation, her lovely younger brother Gentius said: Ooooo now I understood, this is very good. He asked again his sister: Did you hear that my lovely Prince Zeeshan said that he will send us to see Vienna one day. Both those beautiful, younger girls laughed loudly when they heard Gentius that said my lovely Prince Zeeshan. Agneza said: Yes, I heard, all of us heard him is sure that he will send us to see Vienna, I am sure for that because what he said he is doing.

So, they got out to hall to meet the younger man Zeeshan that was waiting over there with his secret service team. He smiled with them and said let's go to cafeteria or to restaurant you to eat something.

Agneza and Gentius said to the younger man, we have eaten because our mother prepared some sweet like biscuits and we have and some others, we will give you to test, because we promised to our mother that we will give to you. We gave and to Dalmet and Armina too.

The younger man hugged Gentius and said: Okay, I will test biscuits that your mother has cooked but now all of us are going to eat breakfast to restaurant after, we are going to cafeteria to drink hot chocolate.

They went all of them over there and they got three average tables, and ordered breakfast. The younger people wanted boil eggs with cheese and milk, and biscuits, so ordered and the younger man Zeeshan, the others people they ordered, tea, butter, white cheese, and small biscuits.

They all started to do conversation happy and freely because there were no people in restaurant only them because the others tourists, ate very early breakfast and went to make ski.

At that time Gentius, asked freely the younger man Zeeshan while was handing his hand with his two hands with full love. Prince Zeeshan, are you sending us to see Vienna? The younger man Zeeshan, said strongly: Yes of course I will send all, of you to see Vienna.

We are going all together to visit Vienna of this beautiful country Austria. Today and tomorrow, we will do ski, here after two days we will go to see Vienna. The last day that is the fourth day for you, all you youngest will travel in your "Lunaria" village of Croatia, while me with my friends will travel to our home city Dubai in our country United Arab Emirates, because for us is going five days' time, here we came yesterday and I am so much busy in my country with my job every day. Gentius said: Ooo very good I understand you are busy, you have a lot job to do.

Thank You very much dear Prince Zeeshan, that you came again to see us and got us here to see Austria this center of ski and Vienna too.

They finished breakfast and after they went to cafeteria that was full with people inside, they got sitting to the chairs, to one big table in corner of this huge cafeteria and ordered all of them big cup with hot chocolate.

After that they got out to make ski. The younger man Zeeshan got Gentius to help to make ski. They started together and all people were listening screaming with happiness of Gentius while was saying, Oooooo, while his smile was mixer with some feelings of fear, while the younger man Zeeshan, was laughing with him and said do not be scare I am with you.

Dalmeti, was going together with another member of secret service and Armina was going with Emin, leader of secret service team of the younger man Zeeshan. Agneza was scare, she said I will stay here to see you, so she stayed on the top of the hill.

The younger man Zeeshan turned to the top of the hill from the other side and saw Agneza was alone was staying over there. He felt warm inside his chest and went over there with Gentius and said to her: Why you are here? Agneza answered: I am scare to do that. Your friend said to me that he will help but I was scare to go.

Gentius spoke enthusiast, I was scare too but my dear Prince Zeeshan helped, me and I did very good ski in small distance, so go and try now, because prince Zeeshan knows very well and he will help you. Agneza said: No, No, No I will see here I am good while her face got pink color.

The younger man Zeeshan got her hand and said to her come with me I will teach you, we will do ski not so longer distance. Gentius was saying enthusiast, go Agneza, go try to make ski. So lovely voice and warm smile of the younger man Zeeshan and his persistence while was holding her hand and enthusiasm of her lovely brother convinced her mind to do ski.

They started together while Gentius was doing applauded with his small hand cover with wool, colorful gloves. After some meters Agneza got confuse and screamed, while the younger man withdraws her close to himself to help Agneza not to fell, but suddenly both of them fell on the white snow. The younger man Zeeshan try to hold and to protect her not to get wound, so at that time, they enrolled on white snow while he kept his hand behind Agneza neck to protect her. When they stopped, he loughed and asked her if she got hurt.

Agneza got pink color in her face and said with sweet voice: No, I am okay, at that time he touched, with one hand her head her hair out of the hat and at that delicious moment he kissed her in her beautiful natural red lips, while said to her, I came for you in this country to meet and to see you and to make this small vacation together.

Agneza said with low voice: Thank You while her face got more red color. After that he helped her to stand up and all together got away to turn back to hotel. They were talking together with full happiness, when they arrived in front of hotel, they found Gentius that was running to meet them.

Gentius came with full love and said to his sister Agneza: You see, he knows very well ski, you see, you see and was hugging with full happiness the younger man Zeeshan. The younger man Zeeshan thought about Gentius and thought: This very lovely good-looking teenager boy, stole my heart for really. After they went close to hotel to wait his friends and Armina with Dalmet, that they did not arrived yet.

In distance they saw the crew with friends of the younger man Zeeshan and Armina and Dalmet that were talking and laughing loudly, who knows maybe some of them fell over the white snow, down to the hill.

Afternoon the younger man Zeeshan, proposed to his friends and to four younger and teenager boys and girls to go to one village close to one small town to see one very important Library that is inside one older antique castle, also over there to this village is one bigger aquarium with only river fishes that are unusual about shape and color of their body.

All they were agreed. After he told them that to this village it is one very good restaurant with native Austrian meal and international meal too. All they were happy so they decided to go to drive to this village at 4-00 P.M, afternoon.

After they went to their room to take their bags and to dress different, so at 4:00 P.M. all were in front of the minibus. The driver started driving through one good road that was coming around the one hill covered with white snow. When they finished the driving to this road at the bottom of this hill, they saw one huge field covered with snow all around.

They were seeing and enjoying one very beautiful view on right side of this white field covered by snow, while on the left side they saw one long line of hills with pines trees on those hills that their branches were going down to kiss the ground by the weight of the white snow above it.

After 30 (thirty) minutes driving they saw the roofs of the houses covered with snow, so they understood that they were close with village that the younger man Zeeshan told them. They entered in village that has so many solid red brick houses and some houses were older built by solid stones.

All houses were in two sides of the road of this village, while in front of them, after 10 (ten) minutes driving inside the village 's area they saw at the bottom of one hill and around this hill some flat one floor buildings, they understood that over there was center of this village and shopping center too.

Really was like that, when they arrived over there, they saw some luxury cars in front of those buildings. They put in parking their minibus and started to walk together in front of those buildings. They entered to one store and asked for Library. The lady that was owner of the store got out of the store together with them and told to them in distance one small building like castle that was in distance to the bottom of the hills.

They started to walk while they saw one beautiful classic cafeteria, after that they saw one restaurant, that looked so beautiful through the window full with people inside it. After they saw one club that was servicing for classic dancing with his circle stage too, inside his big hall.

During their walking they saw one small chancelleries' store with so many colorful supplies for pupils and students of school, also for different offices too.

The younger man Zeeshan, thought with himself. It is very interesting this village to have so many facilities, all of those for really. When they arrived to castle, they saw one big building in circle shape with two floors on the field.

They asked one man: What is that building on that field with that big garden in front and around that was surrounded with one elegant iron fence?

The man answered to them: This big two floor circle shape building, it is complex, for medical service for village, for day care for children of village also it is laboratory, and center of nutrition and fitness too.

Also, it is another small building close to that circle building that is servicing like maternity for mother and new babies born, while building of school two floors it is in area when you entered in village, from highway.

All those buildings, the circle complex, two floors building, the maternity building and the two floors school building are brand new in this village that commune has built, for people. The younger man Zeeshan, thought with himself: I have read about this village but never I imagined that this village will be so much organize like small town, plus another small town is close with this village too.

They together entered in castle where library was inside it. They saw so many people inside it too. The castle looked small outside but inside it was two floors, and was adopted one small electric elevator that was servicing for tourists.

When they saw around, they shocked that really were so many sections with different books, while looked small outside for really. All the time the younger man Zeeshan had his eyes to Agneza, he felt so much happiness that was close to her in this trip.

When they were walking and they were crossing their watching with each other Agneza, was taking one easy pink color, to her face while the younger Zeeshan was feeling heat inside his chest and arrythmia in his heart.

So many time, he was touching her like accidentally in her arm or shoulder since one time in front of others he spoke loudly, Agneza do not move fast that are so many people here, do not be far away from us, od not loss, at that time her brother Gentius, said with laughing: So said all the time, our mother to her when we are going to the town close to our village "Lunaria" for shopping because she is losing between people.

At that time the younger man Zeeshan laughed and he got benefit by his Gentius speech and said: Okay Agneza come stay close with me and he got her hand and was holding to his hand, because you are losing and I invited you in this trip, I do not want problems with your family.

All laughed, so the younger man Zeeshan made factice, his action to hold her hand to his hand and to walk together hand by hand with Agneza, while he said you do not see your cousins and friend Armina with her brother Dalmet that are staying everywhere together close. Agneza spoke with low and melodious voice:

Look my brother Gentius is moving so fast all around for that I walk alone. Okay said the younger man Zeeshan he is younger, so you need to take care for him, at that time he said to Emin, his leader of secret service to hold by his hand Gentius and not to leave alone in this big crew of people in different sections.

So, his friend, Emin, leader of secret service got the hand of Gentius and was holding him everywhere, they were walking and laughing together. He was enjoying good time with lovely Gentius.

At that evening started the full happiness of the younger man Zeeshan, while he was holding the hand of Agneza and time by time where they were seeing different section with different books, he was full emotion he cannot believe that he was hand by hand with her, while time by time was touching more stronger her hand too.

When Agneza was lifting her head to see him in his eyes to make him to understand that was holding strong her hand he was smiling and was releasing a little bit. When they entered to one section, they got shocked they saw, that were some classic books with brown color with thick cover with leather and some were with orange color thick leather cover while aside the pages were with silver shining color.

At that time Agneza gave one sign like uauauau, how beautiful, no one was in that section for that moment. She lifted other arm and with hand tried to get the book in high shelves.

The younger man Zeeshan, helped her to take that book. At that moment he saw around no one person- tourist, was in that section, only his friend Emin, leader of the secret service was behind them, and he kissed her in her face in gentle way, while lifted her hair above her forehead. His friend Emin only smiled.

She got easy pink to red color on her face and smiled, while the younger man was seeing her and thought the spring time is showing in her face now, he was the happiest man at that moment. This is my beautiful lovely evening he whispered and said: Thank you "Allah".

After he got that book with thick leather orange cover that was going in harmony with silver color of outside of pages, and said so beautiful design for really. It was one classic book. They saw that this Library was so rich about different books and more interesting so many were with very beautiful design.

To the other section he saw so many tourists, that were seeing those books with very beautiful design with thick leather cover and different colors but majority of books, were with brown color and some dark green color, or black color. Some books, were with easy orange color but some of the books they have design some figure printed in itself of leather cover.

The younger man Zeeshan said to Agneza, I see here so many high qualities books about material and their expensive and beautiful cover plus what is material inside. This is big surprise for me for this village, this is great experience for me.

When they got out of this section and got to the hall that was with this red wide, rogue and wanted to get the electric elevator for second floor, some students were coming down and they saw the younger man Zeeshan while they shouted loudly: Uauaua this is Prince Zeeshan, of Dubai of United Arab Amirates, (UAE) all people- tourists around turned their head to him.

The students came in front of him they did not open the way to go to elevator but said to him in English Hello: May we take one picture with you. The younger man Zeeshan laughed while he did not release the hand of Agneza and said to them: Of course, we can take picture together now.

They got picture like crew with the younger man Zeeshan and his younger lovely friend Agneza too, that he never released her hand, while students were seeing her with the corner of their eyes so she got attention of them but anyway they were very happy that were getting picture with prince Zeeshan too.

At that time so many tourists that were in different sections came to this hall and they wanted permission by him to take picture with prince Zeeshan so he decided with all of them like crew to make picture together. It was one wonderful evening for really.

So, some of them after got picture started to ask him about his country United Arab Emirates, (UAE) and his country home city Dubai too, also they asked about his opinion for this country Austria too and center of ski.

So was one suddenly one not planned but beautiful interview, one of tourists was journalist while he said that he will right three colons to French newspaper, "Mondial" for this beautiful evening and unexpected meeting with this great younger leader of the Dubai of the United Arab Emirates (UAE). All tourists were speaking fluently English language but with accent of course.

Really this evening was beautiful for everyone that was participating in this unusual meeting in this castle center of culture. The younger man Zeeshan said to Agneza we need now to go to the second floor to see what is interesting over there.

So, they said greetings to the other tourists and got the elevator, while some of them said loudly: "God Bless", you Prince Zeeshan, and we wish for you a very good vacation with ski in Vienna of Austria while all of them were taking picture with their camera of prince Zeeshan in open elevator when was going in second floor.

The younger man Zeeshan saw so much enthusiasm and happiness to European tourists about his presence in this center. He felt so much happiness and inspiration about that, but happier, he was because he was very close in open way in front of others with Agneza while he was holding strong her hand all the time and his leader with his team of secret service Emin, was all the time around him.

The leader of secret service Emin, was seeing this younger boss Zeeshan happy and was smiling all the time with him. While one moment in second floor he said to the younger man Zeeshan, I am very glad for you, to see like that because it is a longer time that I did not see you so much happy.

It is a longer time while he said with longer voice all the expression and after said: "Thank You "Allah" for my lovely boss friend Zeeshan, that you gave happiness to him. The younger man Zeeshan smiled while said yes, I am very happy while he saw that tears were filling eyes of his friend Emin, leader of. the secret service.

The younger man Zeeshan, loved his friend this leader of secret service team and he filled that his eyes were full with tears too. The younger man Zeeshan, was very happy for Agneza and was very happy for this good friendship and his loyal friend too, while he said with normal voice: "Thank You Allah", and saw that Agneza was seeing him very carefully with full attention.

They started to see in different aisles of the second floors for all books that were in line in different shelves in this floor were and section for children and kids 's books.

They liked that atmosphere, while the younger man Zeeshan liked some book for kids with colorful figure with soft animals and he bought four books for his two children. Two for his son and two for his daughter, while Agneza saw him so much dedicated to choose the most beautiful books for his kids and laughed, the text was in English language.

The cover of one book was with figure of deer, the other was with figure of dolphin, while two others books, their cover were one with white rabbits with their carrots in their mouth, and the other was with colorful, "Mandarin" ducks so beautiful.

He was laughing wile was seeing those books and said they will love those books with those beautiful figures with soft animals. When they were walking to the other aisle the younger man saw one book with beautiful cover color blue open while in front was one very beautiful dog with beige to milk color, while he said with laughing, this is like my "Zoros" small dog, that I have in my home, I am buying and this book.

After that they went to cashier to pay, when the cashier heard his English language with accent, she said do you want one very beautiful dictionary book with leather cover in two language, Croatian language and English language too. He said to her with smile I want to see. She brought two dictionary books with leather cover one was with green color the other was with blue color, while the title of the book was with golden color, the books look so beautiful outside, plus importance of the two languages inside.

He loved those and said I will buy two of them. Agneza was seeing him with attention, while she thought that he will buy those for his two small children to have for future to learn Croatian language for culture, but really it was not like that, because he said to her put in two different packages, that the packages were with shining letter so much elegant with some small easy figures design figure in itself.

He got the package with green dictionary book and gave to Agneza and said to her: Enjoy it and start to study for university. Really, he bought dictionary book for her and before close to her area where she was living. But those books were so beautiful with their cover too.

When he finished the payment, he saw that face of cashier younger girl was shining with big smile, while she said: Thank You very much! The younger girl gave to both of them two small chocolates.

They said to her Thank You and got the elevator to go to the first floor. The younger man Zeeshan said to Agneza we can take cup of hot chocolate, I want medium size what do you want, maybe you want large size cup? Agneza said: Really, I want small size cup, but the younger man Zeeshan laughed and said no, no, no, you will get like me medium size to be equal together and they both laughed.

They did not see around to this section of cafeteria their friends or Gentius and with Dalmet and Armina while the younger man Zeeshan said to Agneza, that they have lost to different sections anyway they are with my secret service people, so Agneza smiled and they got one small table to drink their hot chocolate with medium size both of them, as he said to be equal.

The younger man Zeeshan said to Agneza this is good spot because we will see them when are coming to go out, so we will stay here in this table to wait them. Agneza was agreed. After the younger man Zeeshan said to Agneza:

We need to go to visit and this big aquarium with river fishes, that in guide of tourists the text was describing very interesting. Agneza said: Yes, I like keto see it, while she got one easy red color in her face while she faced the strong, straight and sweet watching with good intention by the younger man Zeeshan.

She was seeing around and again saw the younger man Zeeshan but he was continuing his full attention watching, like so she felt herself like was swimming in very cold water and made one gesture like shiver was going to her body.

The younger man understood her gesture and smiled, he though she is so beautiful, I think really, I am in love with her. Thank You "Allah ", for this beautiful gift in my hard and difficult time of my life about feelings and relationship too.

At that time, he got courage and said to Agneza: I think you to come to my home city Dubai, to my country United Arab Emirates, (UAE) to continue your university. She shocked from his speech that time and rise her eyebrow. She spoke with half of her voice: but my parents… but he did not allow to continue her phrase while he said to her: One day you will leave your parent anyway.

Agneza said: They like to study in Croatia and they did not like to go to Ljubljana of Slovenia, they think is far away, but to say to them that I will go more faraway maybe they will get heart attack while she smiled. The younger man Zeeshan said to Agneza in serious way. Prepare them since now that not to get heart attack because you will leave them in future and you will be in big distance anyway. At that time, he was watching her straight to her eyes to see her reaction.

Agneza started to whisper with herself, she was not giving strong reaction because she was scare to destroy this beautiful day and his very good feelings for her, she was continuing to whisper and to move all around with her very white elegant and delicate hands the empty cup of hot chocolate.

The younger man Zeeshan, understood her position but he did not want to make easy that situation while he said to her: Listen me Agneza, I am feeling that I started to love you, also I am very busy with my job and our distance will create problems, so I cannot, see you often plus university is four years a longer time, so all those factors, maybe will influence not in good way for our relationship.

Definitely I want you to think seriously about this matter in near future what you will decide. I want to do action and to be close with you in my home city.

I want you in my life. She saw him, she smiled, while through her face was spreading with speed wings of happiness that were giving shining to her eyes, while her very beautiful natural red color lips were showing her beautiful white teeth like "margaritar".

At that moment the younger man Zeeshan, thought all the world is of him, and he got her hands to his hands was holding strong while he said with low voice: "I love so much, you Agneza"! I hope you understood my feelings too.

Also, I want to say to you: You are so beautiful I am saying "Thank you very much" to "Allah" for the gift that gave me that day that I saw you on the beach to my country and my home city too.

At that time that they were seeing each other in their eyes with full happiness and they did not care for people around they heard one strong noise of the Gentius that made: Ooooo, while he saw them with their cross hand to each other. All of them laughed while the younger man Zeeshan hugged Gentius and Gentius hugged him in strong way with full love as lovely teenager he was.

He was enthusiast about what he saw around this library because he liked so much books to read, while he said for Emin, the leader man of the secret service, that really, he is very lovely man, and he had very patience with me explained Gentius to the younger man Zeeshan.

The younger man Zeeshan made with sign to the lady to prepare another hot chocolate while he said to Gentius to go to take his medium size cup with hot chocolate. He said to him you will drink same size like us hot chocolate and all laughed. Gentius went over there got the cup and came to their table while started to explain with full enthusiasm about what he saw in this library and store of the boos too for selling.

After some minutes came all others people in this section and they said to the younger man Zeeshan, we need to go to visit this aquarium with river's fishes, because the time is going fast. So, the younger man went to pay for the hot chocolate and all of them got out of this beautiful and very interesting library that for surprise was full with foreign tourists.

They got the minibus to the parking and the driver started driving to go to the big aquarium with river's fishes. The road was in two sides with very taller trees that strangely were green but cover with snow, those were trees that were resisting the winter and were doing challenges to winter too with their bold dark green color of their very unusual interesting leaves.

They arrived to one building with circle shape that has one wide corridor with big glass window in front of one beautiful small park with colorful flowers around. While when they entered inside, they saw the corridor was going like labyrinth in different section.

They shocked that inside of this building were so many diversities of river's fishes with different shape and different colors. There were different aquariums with blue glass inside with water and fishes that were swimming with full pleasure and happiness and quite way.

Some other aquariums were horizontal like shape of merchandise refrigerators. Kingdom fishes the most beautiful fishes blue open color, green color, red open color, blue color, bold pink color, and mixer color looked that the universe in their small body has thrown all the colors of rainbow, so beautiful small fishes that were doing so beautiful inside blue water environment, through the green algas inside the water.

The most beautiful were the kingdom bigger fishes, that their body was quite bold blue, their heads were green pink and blue, while short arms were pink color with decoration to the top bold blue color so were and their tale colorful small pink color small green and most of the others were blue very beautiful fishes,

"Phylum" fishes copper color, with some rings in itself through body. "Class" fishes, were small grey color a little bigger than sardines, small fishes. "Order" fishes were, small grey color there were and some in this group named pet fishes multicolor so beautiful.

"Family" fishes were so beautiful one group was bold green color and one was open green colors body while the others were colorful but strangely all those three different groups of fishes, were swimming in group together while were creating three different colors groups of fishes in aquarium looked so beautiful.

While Gentius and his friends never stopped to do uauau oooo and so they were expressing their pleasure. Gentius fishes were small or average size with grey color and some with pink color or open grey color. "Species" fishes were with different measures and different very beautiful colors plus one specific kind of specie was "Siamese" fighting fishes, were with pink to orange color average body and their tale was white transparent like crown behind so beautiful fishes for really.

Fishes can feel pain, they have a good sense of test sight and touch, many fishes test without opening their mouth. Fishes are cold blooded and they cannot control their body temperature. Fishes like "Trigger" fishes can swim backwards. While "Gold" fishes were kept in a dark room it will lose its color.

"Agnatha" jawless fish were elegant taller like linguine, while "Cedar" river fishes or "Salmon" that were white with unusual form with white tale like peacock form but more small so beautiful fishes, "Otoliths" white fish small looked like mendusa like flat octopod transparent body.

Some of those, "Otolith" fishes have one red color outside around the white transparent body. Some other small fresh water fishes were with red tale. "Bothriolepis" fishes, were longer elegant with grey horizontal stripe throw white body. "Tiktaalik" fishes that were longer very elegant with longer tale silver color.

Agneza was expressing so much enthusiasm and time by time accidentally was touching the arm of the younger man Zeeshan to tell him while was pointing the most beautiful fishes in aquarium.

He was happy with her gesture while was seeing her in her beautiful eyes and he got her harm in his hand and never released until they got out of Aquarium, that was the most beautiful evening for the younger man Zeeshan that was together hand by hand with Agneza.

After they all got out of this aquarium to go to parking where was their minibus. They entered inside the minibus and all were discussing so much enthusiast about this library and this aquarium with river's fishes.

The younger man Zeeshan was seeing with full attention Agneza, through the mirror in front of the minibus, while he was talking with the leader of the team of secret service. Time by time he was involved in conversation of the younger people so he wanted to see straighter Agneza.

She understood all his intentions during this evening and she was very happy that he was watching all the time her and was carrying so much for her. The trip to go back the hotel of the ski got more longer time.

The driver was driving so slowly, he did not want to make any wrong doing or any accident, because some small cars were driving so fast through this road and why was so much snow around and on the road too. Anyway, the trip was going so well, until they arrived to the hotel of the ski center.

They entered direct to the restaurant but some of them did not want to eat dinner, only to take hot tea or hot chocolate, while for the younger people the younger man gave with smile order, you need to eat something for dinner.

They ordered eggs with cheese and one cup of milk, while all of them Agneza, Gentius, Armina, and Dalmet, were eating and were discussing with full happiness about what they saw in that village.

Gentius started to speak loudly for different colorful fishes, while his very white, nice face and his cheeks were red from cold weather and his nose too, he was doing some happy gestures while was describing the shape and color of fishes, and was telling to them some pictures that he got with his camera.

At that time all the others that were listening Gentius were laughing loudly, with his enthusiasm while he was said to them: Why you did not like those very beautiful fishes. They answered with one voice. Yes, we liked so much them.

So, this enthusiasm was spreading all around the big hall of this restaurant that were only few people inside for really because others have eaten their dinner and they went to their rooms.

When they finished and the younger man Zeeshan paid for all, they got out of the restaurant while said to each other Good Night and went to their room. Gentius was talking with the younger man Zeeshan while he was holding his hand, they stood some minutes to hall and he said like order go to sleep now because tomorrow we will have another busy day with ski.

Gentius kissed him in his face and said I am going to sleep now. When Dalmet and Armina said to him Good Night while Agneza was seeing him, he said straight to Agneza do you want to stay some minutes here and to see the beautiful silver moon and the stars from this big window or you are going to sleep?

She answered quickly, I want to stay and to enjoy this view. Dalmet and Armina, smiled while Gentius that was walking up to the stairs to go to the second floor to his room said to Agneza, my dear sister stay and campaign my dear Prince Zeeshan, all they laughed loudly.

When they left the leader of secret service Emin, the loyal friend of the younger man Zeeshan said to his boss I am going some minutes to my room but I am leaving here with you two my people. So, he called again with telephone his friends and they came down to the first floor while got sitting to another sofa in corner of this hall.

The younger man Zeeshan and Agneza got sitting to one sofa close to this big window while in front of them was one small circle table. At that time came the receptionist one very handsome younger man and asked the younger man Zeeshan if he with his girl needs something to drink, but both of them said no we do not need anything now.

The receptionist smiled and left them while was going to his place to take care for one couple that need him to ask for something. The younger man and Agneza open in full way the white lace curtain with beautiful floral design in itself, so they created more clear vision to see during this dark night the beautiful silver moon and the stars that were decorating the sky around the moon. Looked that all of them were in race who will give more bright light.

The younger man said to Agneza maybe we will see tonight the fallen stars so prepare yourself for any good wish in your life. Agneza answered very fast:

I am prepared I have ready while her very white and beautiful face sparkle from happiness. Tell me said the younger man Zeeshan while he smiled. Agneza said: I wish to go to the university of Ljubljana in Slovenia, and this time to go fast.

The younger man Zeeshan laughed loudly and said I thought maybe you have another beautiful wish. Agneza said this is the most beautiful wish for me for my life. Okay I understood he said I know that is very important for you this education as for everyone in this world while he was seeing in direction of the stars through the window. Agneza was seeing him with wondering but he did not turn his head to her while he was seeing her with his corner of his eyes.

She got red in her very white face and got confuse because she thought maybe she answered wrong and gave hurt to him, so he was not seeing him but was seeing serious in direction of the stars to the sky.

Agneza toughed him with delicatesse to his arm and asked with soft voice:

Can you tell me, what is your wish? He turned his head to her and asked her while was seeing her straight to her beautiful eyes. Really you want to know the best secret wish now under the bright star. Agneza smiled and said: Yes, I want to know because I am curious and is so much important for me.

The younger man Zeeshan asked her: Why is so much important for you my best secret wish?

Agneza started to whisper because she found herself unprepared for this question or counter-question. At that time the younger man Zeeshan smiled and said, to her: Okay I am telling you now my best secret wish under the bright star.

While the younger man Zeeshan, got serious and started his recite:

My dear very beautiful silver moon and all of you brighter stars help, me with my best, secret wish that I will tell you now, while I am pleasing you with full of my heart that this secret wish to become reality under your bright and positive energy.

I want that one very beautiful girl that suddenly I saw her, It was only one coincidence, but now I started to love her with full of my heart to be with me all my life. Make me calm, give peace to my heart because when I am not with her, I cannot sleep all the night, the arrythmia of my heart is giving signal to my brain, while is creating some diffusion of my thoughts up.

So, during this kind of night that really are so much in line, my thoughts are getting hot, while are creating to my imagination some lovely vibrant wild. At that time, I am flying in the beautiful imagination world while I am doing with this girl love, such everything around me, looked brilliant.

While when I am focusing in my mind, I see nothing is around, only some silver moon's rays are coming through window and playing with me hard.

While when I am with this girl, very close with me aside, I feel confuse to speak and my words are playing inside my mouth but never are coming in right way out, so I am not able to express my great love, because of my shy character and at this moment my heart is very hot.

When I tried to say to her I love you, I mixer with another confuse question, what is the reason that people like you? So, my dear bright stars, give to me your positive energy and bright up and make calm my heart. Also, your positive energy to melt my love to her heart.

I want from all of you to make hear heart to love me too. I promise to all of you stars in universe, when you full fill my best wish secret, I will love this girl in eternity, while she will grow older together with me.

I will treat her like one beautiful white rose in delicate glass bottle while nutrition for her grow up will be my full love, while from retina of my eyes I will send to her beautiful eyes so much bright and sight, that in her life together with me never to have dark.

From my heart I will send so much vibrant of my feeling of love, so in her face I will see always peace and smile. Her happiness will fill our home all around with, beautiful scent of love, while I want to be dizzy by her love's fragrance.

So definitely I am waiting, by all of you bright elements of universe, that during the day with silence you are living the place to golden sun's rays, while during the night you are doing sparkle with your light make my love to have so much sparkle too, because I love so much this girl as I love all of you, also make my, best, secret wish to become true.

At that time, he felt to is harm, the hand of Agneza and he turned his head to her while saw to her tears in her eyes, while she said to him: So beautiful, all the stars will help to full fill your secret best wish.

At that time the younger man Zeeshan, touched her beautiful hair and kissed her with delicatesse in her cheeks but looked that his eyes' tears wanted to show up in front of eyes' tears of Agneza so to show their presence too.

He kissed again Agneza fast in soft way to her very beautiful natural red lips, while only his two friends, receptionist, younger boy, and the stars were witness that were enjoying this beautiful love's show with smile, while the light of the stars came fast from the big window in this beautiful night.

They stayed over there another one hour while they were talking and laughing and after they decided to go to their room also and his two friends were going with them in second floor to their room.

It was one very beautiful evening for the younger man Zeeshan and his younger lovely girl Agneza, that was planting in his heart and growing up one new beautiful delicate love.

They said to each other have a Good Night, and every one of them entered to their room. Agneza went to her room and found Armina that was reading in computer. Armina asked her:

It was beautiful evening for you? Did you enjoy this evening with younger, Prince Zeeshan. Agneza felt her red to her very white and beautiful face and said short and strict. It was a wonderful evening and outside it was one miracle image by the silver moon and all bright stars in this dark night while they all were giving one light to the white snow around. From the big window I was enjoying one panorama so beautiful like in movie.

Armina was laughing and said I love your artistic speech about this miracle image outside in this dark night that was light by bright stars. Both of them laughed while Agneza change her dresses and wore her pajamas and went to her bed, while Armina said close the light.

Really this night Agneza cannot get sleep quite her thought was coming in her mind about everything that she was enjoying in this trip. She whispered with herself and said: Something is happening to me; some feelings are growing in my heart that never I had before.

She said to herself like whisper: I think, that this is love, I will name it love, and really, I am scare for this love now I have another direction to follow next September about studying in university of Ljubljana of Slovenia or maybe in Zagreb, of Croatia so what is that that is happening with me now. With those thoughts her eyes started to close and send her in this night in beautiful dreams.

The younger man Zeeshan did not go in bed because he was sure he cannot sleep by his thoughts about this girl that he started to love in deep way, now but he decided to get busy and went to the table to write something, but really his hand was not able to take order by his brain to write.

He was thinking for Agneza he smiled with himself and went to change his dresses got his pajamas and went to the bed, that he was sure that will take longer time until his eyes to get closed during this night.

He started to think so many things and most of all for this younger Girl Agneza how will go their love story in future. He whispered with himself, a lot problems are coming in future about this beautiful my new love story but I will escape all of them, I love this girl.

He got sleep very later, and the moon was witness about his thoughts. He did not want to stay until in the morning with those thoughts, so he decided to close with force his eyes and to enjoy beautiful dream of this longer winter night in Austria.

In the morning in 8:00 A.M. all were waiting the younger man Zeeshan, in big hall of first floor. His leader of secret service Emin, went to his room and told him that all are waiting in hall to fir floor.

The younger man Zeeshan smiled already he was prepared, while he has washed his face shaved his beard and left small but elegant, get his perfume, dressed thick sportive - suit for ski and got out with his friend. Over there he found, his people and younger people too, and all together went to restaurant to eat breakfast.

They ate breakfast with their favorite meal and got out of restaurant it was around the 9:00 A.M., in the morning but when they went out, they heard one big noise.

They got wondering but two big busses were in front of the hotel and some people were dropping the bus without luggage but with sportive dresses for ski.

One lady came from inside hotel and went straight to the younger man Zeeshan. She said: Sir we have one problem now suddenly we were not prepared for that problem that is related with you. The younger man Zeeshan got wondering and asked: What is this suddenly problem that you were not prepared and related with me, please tell me?!

She continued you see those two busses that are over there to big gate of the hotel. Yes, answered the younger Zeeshan. I see those two buses. What is about that?

Okay I am telling you now, one bus is from Wienna with professor and some excellent students of university of Wienna, they got news they you are here and came to spend this day with you and with ski and will go back again in city of Vienna.

The other bus is with professors and students from university of Ljubljana of Slovenia, and some of them are your friends so they called their colleagues in university of Vienna and decide to make one pleasant, surprise for you.

So now they are here today for you and those students and professors of University of Ljubljana will spend this day with you and will go to their hotel in Vienna while tomorrow will fly to their country Slovenia and their lovely city Ljubljana.

Really the younger man Zeeshan, got shocked it was really big surprise for him this suddenly, event he did not have time to answer or to discuss because in distance he saw professor Bojana, that was doing with her hand in distance sign to him and was smiling with full happiness.

At that time, he turned his head to see Agneza that she was seeing him with wondering what was about this lady of hotel, what she was saying to him what was any problem about hotel or room maybe, but she did not see that professor Bojana, was coming straight to the younger man Zeeshan.

The younger man Zeeshan, said thank you very much to the lady of hotel and was seeing at that time, Agneza and Bojana. Bojana came fast and gave her hand and hugged him while gave his hand to her with full smile and said welcome and was doing with sing to Agneza, like I am wondering, I was not prepared for that.

He said to professor Bojana this is really the most beautiful surprise for me, while she told him that her friend and leader of university of Ljubljana of Slovenia, was here for him. Bojana was speaking so much enthusiast and with full smile.

The younger man Zeeshan with love and smile said to her: Very good so I need to change my schedule with my people and some my visitors I need to tell them.

Professor Bojana said Okay to him, we are coming all here to meet you, while during this time, you can make arrangement about schedule with your people too. She left the younger man Zeeshan to go to his people and went to the bus where were her colleagues and students too.

He went right away to Agneza that was waiting in distance and said to her: Really this is big surprise for me. I never know about this small event really, I told to Professor Bojana, that I will be here, and if possible she to come with her friends that I have met before in University of Ljubljana of Slovenia, but never I knew that will be here her other colleagues and friends of university of Vienna of Austria, but anyway we will spend our day with them, to honor them because are two groups of two different universities one from Vienna of Austria and one of Ljubljana of Slovenia.

Anyway, we will handle that situation together this unusual day, plus you will have opportunity to know some professors and students from university of Ljubljana of Slovenia. Agneza saw him with full love because she understood that he was so much dedicated to her but he wanted to respect and those people that came to meet him and to talk with him.

So, this day was one good occasion for both sides, to discuss so many things about education also to enjoy this beautiful cold but sunny day with ski with professors and students of those two countries.

The younger man Zeeshan, was happy that Agneza understood him and supported him in that unusual day. He was very happy that was with her and put his arm above her shoulder, while started to whisper to her ear some beautiful love's words.

He whispered to her in soft way, in this beautiful cold but sunny day, I see your beautiful white face that is not different by this very white snow, while snow is sparkling by the golden sun's rays, your eyes are sparkling by my love and my presence to you, while your very white beautiful face is shining with happiness, because of my full carries to you.

He said to her: Agneza I am blind now by your beauty, also I am dizzy by my love of you. So, help me to escape this difficult situation because of my love. Agneza was laughing with full happiness while saw that the younger man Zeeshan was seeing her straight to her eyes and kissed in easy way with delicatesse to her cheeks. For both of them this was the most beautiful moment.

After 30 (thirty) minutes all the people, of two buses came in front of this hotel and they entered to one big hall of meeting. It was one unexpected meeting for the younger man Zeeshan, but he handled in very good way with his team of secret service and his inspiration and motivation by his younger girl Agneza that was supporting him in this meeting too, together with Armina.

Professors of university of Ljubljana of Slovenia, were very happy to meet again with prince Zeeshan, while the professors of the university of Vienna of Austria, were very happy to introduce with him by their colleagues like professor Bojana. Also, some students of university of Ljubljana of Slovenia, were very happy to see again Prince Zeeshan, while the others students of university of Vienna of Austria were happy to see and introduce to him too.

So started one very interesting meeting this cold but beautiful morning of Wednesday, in this center of ski. Always professor Bojana was aside the Prince Zeeshan to one big table in front of people and leader of University of Ljubljana of Slovenia and leader of university of Vienna of Austria were in center of this big table too.

Agneza with Gentius and Armina with Dalmet, were in first line of chairs that were reorganized in this way for this meeting. Aside them were some students from both two countries of Austria and Slovenia and behind them were all others professors and students too.

Suddenly one silence like serenity was created in this big hall when professor Bojana made introduced in English language the Prince Zeeshan in this auditor. After her Prince Zeeshan started his speech in English language.

Prince Zeeshan started to explain so many things about education system in his home city Dubai and his lovely country United Arab Emirates, (UAE), also he spoke so much about developing of his country about economy and most of all about business in his country and his beautiful lovely city too.

There were so many questions by professors and students also so many answers and replies by Prince Zeeshan. The meeting got to get hot when one younger girl student from Vienna of Austria asked him about black clothes, like black gown and black scarf that were using in his country the women and specific the younger girls and students too.

She asked direct without fear and without tension: When the Local government of your city Dubai, that you are leader and central government of your country United Arab Emirates, (UAE) will give freedom to younger girls and specific students not to use anymore those heavy black jihad clothes black clothes?

Also, I understood about the religion of this country, really your country too, and about adult or older women that are continuing to respect this religion with their black dresses, but I think to give some new breath and freedom to the younger girls to release from those heavy black clothes gown and scarf it is very important and big request or demand of modern time.

So definitely when the government of your country United Arab Emirates, (UAE) and specific your home city DUBAI, will work to help the younger girls and the younger women in your country to be free from those heavy black clothes that is taking from them the younger fresh looking from their beautiful face?

At that time one strong applauded was spread all around the big hall by all students and professors of two countries of Austria and Slovenia. While all students and professors started to say in one voice: When, when, when. This calling, was spreading like waves on ocean that were pushing each other to the shore, around the hall while was coming stronger.

At that time the younger man Zeeshan got shiver to his body, but when he saw that Agneza was laughing with full happiness, and Armina too, while Agneza was lifting her two hands up like was praying for good, he smiled he felt that all this weight got out of his chest.

He cannot stop to see Agneza that his watching got attention to professor Bojana that she got something one very easy red color to her face when she understood his very lovely watching to this very beautiful and younger girl from Croatia and she felt that for him she did not exist in that hall.

Really this action instinctively of the prince Zeeshan created one strong shake, situation inside the chest and heart of Professor Bojana, that after that moment she never get out her eyes by this younger very beautiful girl Agneza. Professor Bojana at this moment she understood that she has fallen in love with the younger man Zeshan, really with prince Zeshan.

While during this time of the screaming really with happiness by all professors and students of those two countries in this big hall of this hotel of ski, Emin, the leader of secret service of prince Zeeshan got alert and spoke with radio with his people to be alert.

Some of them, member of secret service came around the big table where were, Prince Zeeshan, professor Bojana and others leader of university of Vienna of Austria and university of Ljubljana of Slovenia.

Really the younger man Zeeshan did not think for any rise of tension in this hall because as longer and very good leader in his big and very modern beautiful city, he understood that this calling and screaming with happiness was like one friendly protest to support the women and younger women and younger girls of his country United Arab Emirates, (UAE) and his home city Dubai.

Really, he was in tension for the answer that he will give to this very good and intellectual people too, but he was very happy that Agneza was so much happy too. That day morning presence of Agneza gave to him one hug inspiration and he understood that he was in deep love with this younger girl and he forget for one moment that beautiful professor Bojana that went the first to his city Dubai, to meet him, while now was present in this meeting and to his table too.

The younger man Zeeshan started his speech with delicatesse he was choosing his words, very carefully because he understood that he was speaking in big crew of the very smart people with different major of the university.

He thought that in future they will remind his speech what he said to them and will write to different newspaper in Europe and Western Ballkan because some of them were excellent students in major of journalism too.

The younger man Zeeshan, started his speech for so many reforms and progresses were done to his country about social life and about the integrate of women in science in education in medical field and every branch of economy. All were listening in silence, and looked like nobody was inside of this hall, so the younger man Zeeshan understood very well how important was for them his answer for that matter of women's jihad.

He said that we are working and we are in progress with this process but you must to understand that my country has strong feelings for its religion, while we need to deal with so many conservator people that are so much fanatic and loyal to ritual and dresses of this religion of Muslim.

Now I am promising to all of you that I will work hard with my team with all others nonprofit organization with women's organization with youth's organization to forward in this process maybe will take some times but we will do big changing for good of new and future generation of women and girls too.

Really, I am for progress and for big changing in my very beautiful home city Dubai, and in my lovely country United Arab Emirates (UAE)too. I will work very hard for this matter I want to be proud for our women and girls in our country to dress like all the other women and girls in developed world.

I want to leave this legacy and for my wife, my sisters, my daughter, my aunts, and my nieces in future. I want to make easy this process and for all my brothers, my cousins my friends about their spouses, their sisters their daughters, their aunts and nieces in future.

When the younger man Zeeshan, finished his sentence all the people, in hall applauded and said with high voice we hope and we trust you that you will do that. After that professor Bojana that all the time is excellent for her job and creative job too, stand up from her chair and went in front of students where she has put one white board.

Professor Bojana, started to put monitor and to show to them, all pictures that she has done in the very beautiful and modern home city of Dubai of prince Zeeshan, the pictures were coming in line everywhere.

The most interesting were the pictures of the meeting with professors and students in "Zayed" University of Dubai, that was one magnificence and huge building with super modern architecture but in contrast they saw in one huge modern hall so many women and girls with black gown and black scarf in their head.

Also, they saw another pictures with meeting with women from different branches of economy and nonprofit organization's leaders but all of them were with black gown and black scarf on their head.

The people in hall got silence they saw those really beautiful women covered with black gown and black scarf and looked they felt bad for that and one full silence was spreading in hall.

One younger student girl in middle of the hall said this is humiliation of the beautiful, girls and women in your home city Dubai, and your country United Arab Emirates, (UAE), and another younger student boy close to her started to speak loudly: This is to persecute women and girls for their right in their life.

The younger man Zeeshan understood their point also he thought maybe they are in major of journalism and he got inspiration by their courage of their expression. He saw Agneza that made sign with her hands like they are right, so he got full smile in his face.

Professor Bojana was continuing after with the most beautiful area of this modern city of Dubai. All gave one huauhauhuaa, that they liked so much all those objects and modern areas of that city. One younger student said loudly: This is big contract between this unusual beauty of this city, to exist this black clothes situation all around.

When professor Bojana finished her very intellectual job, for Prince Zeeshan really it was one wonderful job and big surprise for him he said thank you to her. During this time, he was in deep love with Agneza and he did not give attention of big love of professor Bojana that was preparing this quality job for him.

Prince Zeeshan was between two deep love situation one love for Agneza that he was deeply participated and another great love of professor Bojana that she was participated totally why he was standing static but with respect to her.

Professor Bojana when finished her explanation and got so much applauded by people she said: Now it is time together to enjoy ski with our lovely friend Prince Zeeshan, his crew and his youngest guests too from Croatia.

All said with one voice yes, let's go for ski. Professor Bojana with very carefully action got close to Agneza while asked her about her name and where she was living in Croatia.

Agneza was very happy to see her and explained to her about "Lunaria her beautiful village close to Zagreb of Croatia, also she told her that she was hopping that next year at September to come student in university of Ljubljana of Slovenia for lawyer or maybe other major was in option yet. Professor Bojana tried to hidden her jealousy and said to her that she will help her for everything while prince Zeeshan came to them and was listening.

Professor Bojana was watching Agneza that was reacting, with love feelings and smile to her face, she thought with herself she is so beautiful for really, while was seeing with her corner of her eyes Prince Zeeshan, that was staying serious without expression in his face, but inside her chest and heart professor Bojana felt that she is her strong rival to Prince Zeeshan.

After meeting all were happy to go to make ski, they said they did not have so much time because later afternoon they will travel all of them to Vienna. When they go to take supplies for ski professor Bojana was talking with Prince Zeeshan while close to him were four younger people Agneza, Gentius, Armina and Dalmet.

They were very happy, while professor Bojana saw that teenager Gentius that was so much energies was listening carefully their conversation and time by time was asking the younger man Zeeshan, I do not know very well English and I did not understand some words that she said while all were laughing.

Professor Bojana started to explain to him in Croatian language that was Slavic language, was close with Slovene language while Gentius was so much happy while said to professor Bojana: He is my very lovely Prince Zeeshan.

Professor Bojana said to him: Really, he is very lovely Prince Zeeshan.

Gentius said with full smile in his very nice face, yes, he is very lovely prince, I know that, and all others were laughing with his enthusiasm and innocent reply and behave.

The younger man Zeeshan was watching very carefully Agneza and time by time was giving sign like: Be quiet! So, they go for ski. Agneza said I am waiting here you can go. She was calm and was seeing with happiness and love straight to the eyes, of the younger man Zeeshan. The younger man Zeeshan said to professor Bojana we can go together while Gentius is going with my friend Emin, leader of my security team, while Armina and Dalmet they are together and they know to make ski, while Agneza she is not prepared for that is first time for her so let's stay here.

He decided that one men of his secret service to stay with Agneza and to wait them when they will return.

So, they started ski while were going down to the hill and the sun's rays were hitting their eyes. All were happy from distance they were listening the scream, with happiness of Gentius.

Big crew of students and professors were going down with ski to this beautiful hill covered with white heavy snow. All around were coming noise of laughing and some scream of some people that were falling on the white snow. It was one very beautiful view on this hill that day and so much enthusiasm.

When they arrived to the bottom of the hill professor Bojana came very close to the younger man Zeeshan while with provocative watching and gesture with her hands like to hold to him, but he did not react to her behave, he stood correct with respect but serious and cold with one longer quite smile, like she to understand that we are now only good friends

She started to ask him with some questions in line, while she did not gave time him to answer until she finished.

Why you prince Zeeshan are so much different from the last time that I met you in your home town Dubai to your country United Arab Emirates, *(UAE)?

Really what is the motive of your visit this time here simple for ski or something else?

Has something to do your visit this time with this younger beautiful girl Agneza, that you have invited her with her brother and her your cousins too?

Why you did not call me and to tell me that you will come here with her?

Really, I got news by another cousin Ardita, of this younger girl, that she is student of law major in our university.

Prince Zeeshan got her hands to his hands hold strong those and said to professor Bojana.

Please, better not do discuss this topic this matter today, let's enjoy this beautiful day with happiness both of us and all the others, because I have nothing to say to you now, about those questions. We never know what surprises will bring our life in future, about me about you about her etc.

Really, I came for ski this time with my friends because I was tired with my heavy job and my last time that was so much heavy about schedule that we visited so many cities and towns and villages.

We visited those three countries like Slovenia your beautiful country and your home city Ljubljana, Croatia, with Zagreb and Dubrovnik, and "Lunaria" and Kauntia villages also Montenegro with Podgorica, Ulqinj, and so many other.

So, I decided only to come for ski to spend with peace this small vacation, to visit and Vienna of Austria, and to go back to my country.

Professor Bojana understood that was not time and place to say anything anymore while she changed the way of conversation with delicatesse, while she covered with her smile the hurt that she got by his diplomatic reply.

She understood that Prince Zeeshan has changed about her, she did not see any silver line, about her suddenly love for him, also that will continue with him because he was not in same page of love with her, but she thought to save their friendship at least and last. She continued her speech with smile while put her arms around his shoulder and said: Okay you are very right. I got your point.

Also she continued to explain to him about preparing her material for last visit in his beautiful modern home city Dubai of the country United Arab Emirates,(UAE)

About material I have prepared a long time ago and I wanted to send to you with video to give your opinion, but when I got this news that you will be here, I was very happy to show to you this material.

I organized with my friends, others professors that all were happy to do that, and some professors of Vienna that we are cooperating about education and about some seminars of science.

So, both sides of two universities we did one very good job, while we chose some excellent students to come with us.

Prince Zeeshan said to her with smile and love in his face: Really you did one wonderful job, it was for me one very beautiful surprise and this meeting was going so well. I am really very happy how beautiful and interesting day was for me and all others people in this meeting and this activity for ski.

I hope that we will see each other in future more and more. Professor Bojana was very happy, her beautiful eyes were sparkling when she heard his words, that they will see each other more and more in future.

She was very happy for his statement and she did not want to analyze about what they will see each other about education system of two countries or business or whatever simple, she was very happy and why she did not want to ignore her intellect, but she really was happy. She said to herself this happiness of myself, I will put only one name "Love".

This is love for this man. I am really in love with Prince Zeeshan while she was seeing him in his eyes. Strangely Prince Zeeshan was seeing her in her straight to her eyes with smile and he did not want to hidden, his pleasure of her presence.

Who knows?!, Those are mysteries of universe about man in relationship with woman. His action was with so many meanings while he gave one strict statement about friendship.

So, his statement did not allow any space for any alternative for love during his conversation. Anyway, this conversation was going so well both of them were happy that their happiness was showing with their lovely watching to each other.

They decided to go back to the center of ski's hotel with other people and to eat lunch wile to prepare for trip later afternoon. When they arrived in front of hotel, they saw that Agneza was over there with friend and member of secret service of Prince Zeeshan.

They were sitting to one concrete bench when they saw Prince Zeeshan they stand up with happiness and Agneza did not control herself but run with speed and hugged Prince Zeeshan, while he was holding stronger with his arms and he felt that in his eyes were coming tears without his permission and drooping to his cheeks. It was so much touching feelings of him, about her action to run with speed and to huge him.

Professor Bojana saw very carefully this scene, she saw his tear on his cheeks and his lovely hugging of her, while she whispered to herself. This is great love. At the moment prince Zeeshan saw professor Bojana that her face got strong red color and changed her very white beautiful face, but she said with calmness: Let's go to eat lunch all of us, because we need to travel later afternoon.

After that professor Bojana put her arm and hand to shoulder of Agneza and were walking together to restaurant with Prince Zeeshan and his friend of secret service. Really Prince Zeeshan loved her gesture and said to professor Bojana in her ear in friendly way:

Thank You very much by you. She replied: We will be very best friends in longer run-in longer term. Yes, approved Prince Zeeshan we will be the best friends in long run. They entered in restaurant and found over there, big crew of professors and students together around to different big circle tables and some square tables.

Some of them called Prince Zeeshan to go to their table but he said to them I have my team you see. They approved and said you are right. After lunch came to the table of Prince Zeeshan with his small crew two leaders of two universities of Vienna of Austria and of Ljubljana of Slovenia.

After some minutes came and two architects of university of Vienna of Austria and friends' architect of professor Bojana of university of Ljubljana of Slovenia that prince Zeeshan met him in first visit in Western Ballkan.

They started to discuss for some futurist projects of architecture of Austria and Slovenia and they expressed their wish to visit his country United Arab Emirates, (UAE) and his very modern and so beautiful home city (....).

Prince Zeeshan said to them: You are very welcome to my beautiful country United Arab Emirates, (UAE) and to my lovely home city Dubai. I promise to you that I will be the leader of this guide and you will see so many beautiful things.

Really prince Zeeshan while was speaking he was seeing time by time Agneza to secure her that he has all attention to her and was taking care for her. His watching with attention to Agneza, was not going without attention of professor Bojana and other leaders and professors of architecture of two universities of Vienna of Austria and Ljubljana of Slovenia.

They were seeing this beautiful younger girl with their corner of their eyes but they never gave reaction to Prince Zeeshan. After all were going out to enter to their bus, while prince Zeeshan and his younger crew with his secret service team went to their two buses, to shake their hands with them and to say Good Bye, for meeting next time.

Before to enter to two buses they did so many different pictures with professors and students in crew. Really it was one lovely day. They entered in buses and their driver started driving.

They were greeting with their hands from window. When the buses were going up to the hill people started to sing songs that their melody was coming through some open windows that they were continuing to give greeting with their hands, while they blocked the road because some other small cars and one bus with tourists was coming to hotel.

The younger man Zeeshan with Agneza, Gentius, Armina, Dalmet and his secret service crew were staying in front of hotel until they saw that two buses were going down to the hill and lost through the pines - trees full with white snow, to the road that was going down around the hill.

After that all of them entered to hall of hotel while were discussing with enthusiasm. They decided to go to their room and to see each other at the evening because this day was unusual day, with one unexpected schedule but really it was surprised very interesting and beautiful day, with full enthusiasm by those people.

At that time that so many other tourists came inside the big hall with their luggage and some of them with their sportive bag on their shoulder, behind. All were talking loudly while they created one longer line to receptionist to make registration and to go to their room that they have done arrangement before to come here.

At that time Prince Zeeshan said to Agneza better of for you and all of us to be out of this big noise, he did not want to show to her, that he was uncomfortable that some people that came were seeing her with attention.

His caring about noise, was to erase his suddenly jealousy. Agneza said to him while was giving, to him one longer lovely watching:

You are very right we need to go to take rest to our room and we will see you at the evening.

Agneza, went to her room while was talking with her friend cousins Armina and were watching television too. Later at the evening they went down to the first floor to see other people crew of the younger man Zeeshan, and to eat dinner. They found all of them in hall that were waiting them, and their brother Gentius and Dalmet were over there.

The younger man Zeeshan, smiled and showed so much happiness when he saw Agneza with her cousin Armina were coming to them. He put his arm with smile to the shoulder of Agneza and said to all let's go to eat dinner while Gentius was talking with so much enthusiasm with the leader of security team Emin they became friends now.

They ordered their preference meal for dinner and all were talking with each other while they were sitting in two tables that they make together.

The younger man was sitting between Agneza and his office account lady Adara, while Armina was sitting aside Adara too and all the others were sitting in line close to each other, while Gentius and Dalmet where in two sides of Emin the leader of security team.

After dinner the younger man Zeeshan said to all of them: I like to see stars outside some minutes what do you think? The account lady Adara said to him: Really it is cold but I like to see some minutes how looked in this night the stars up to the sky. All the others said loudly let's go to see the stars outside. So, they got out to see the stars outside in this beautiful night. Really it was one magical view outside. The silver light by moon and stars was reflecting to the white snow while the pines trees in distance looked darker with their originally bold green color, so all the environment looked white and black only the electric light was more open yellow color.

All were watching the stars while the loudly voice of Gentius that was telling with his hand some stars to Emin the leader of security team was not leaving quiet the crew of people and they were laughing. Gentius happiness were giving inspiration to other people around to love environment around.

At that time the younger man Zeeshan whispered to Agneza: Do one important wish for yourself while was telling one very bright star, and please make my name part of you wish do not forget it, and started to laugh while was touching her hair with gentle.

Agneza smiled and said to him one strong yes. I will do that very important wish for myself and for both of us and smiled. Really for both of them it was magical evening while the love was spreading itself to their face and their chest and heart also this evening was so beautiful for teenagers and friends of the younger man Zeeshan.

They stayed outside about 20 minutes (twenty) with their enthusiasm they afforded the cold weather of this night and after they entered inside the hotel to go to their rooms.

The younger man Zeeshan, hugged Gentius that was saying: It was beautiful evening my dear Prince Zeeshan, while Prince Zeeshan said to Agneza with love and smile: I see you tomorrow. All said to each other have a good night and went to their rooms to sleep. Next day they will have another schedule to go to visit, beautiful and historic Vienna city capital of Austria.

Agneza when entered with Armina to their room, they started to discuss about this beautiful evening and about stars, while Armina said to her: Prince Zeeshan is very good and lovely person with big heart, while he is respecting all of us. I think he has special feelings and good intentions to you Agneza. I love how much he is taking care for you. Really, I love that situation. Agneza saw her friend - cousin Armina, she got red color to her face and said: Yes, he is very good person.

Austria

VIENNA.

ONE DAY BEFORE TO VISIT VIENNA WITH THOSE TEENAGER AND HIS secret service crew, and his journalist Hamad and his cameraman Jassim, the younger man Zeeshan called one center of information for tourists and he made request for one host to campaign them in tour in Vienna and to tell them about this city.

The day that they were going to visit Vienna they ate breakfast, and started driving after 9:00 A.M. (nine a clock). The host one younger man that was speaking fluently English came one day before to meet them and stayed in that hotel so they were all together in this beautiful trip.

They were enjoying all relieve cover with snow mountain and hills in one road that was going all around to the bottom of the mountain and after some hills. After they entered in highway to go straight to Vienna.

They saw big green table with information about direction in highway to Vienna. At that time the host said: I am giving some information now, the others I will explain when we will be in center of city of Vienna.

Vienna is Austria the most populous city and its primate city with about 2,000,000,00 (two million) inhabitants while with metropolitans, 2,900,000,00. (two million and nine hundred thousand) inhabitants. This city has population nearly, of one - third of population of all country of Austria.

Vienna is center cultural economic and political of Austria. It is the fifth largest, city by population in the European Union and the largest city in Danub river by population. Vienna is the capital and largest city also it is one of nine federal, states of Austria.

The city Vienna bordered on eastern edge of "Wiennerwald" that is Vienna woods, in northeast is bordered by most foothill of the alps that is separating Vienne with western part of Austria at that transition to the "Pannonian" Basin. Vienna it is on Danube - river, also is traversed by highly regulated" Wiennfluss" (Vienna River). Vienna is surrounded completely by low Austria, and lies 50 (fifty) km 31 (thirty-one) miles west of Slovakia and its capital Bratislava. Vienna is lies in northwest 60 (sixty) km 37 km (thirty-seven) miles of Hungary and 60 km (sixty) 37 (thirty - seven) miles of south Moravia of Czech Republic.

The existence of Vienna, back in time is since habitants Celts settled since 500 BC. on side of Danube - river. Vienna in English name is homonymous Italian name. the German name Wien comes from the name of the river Wien. Modern name Wien came from "Uueniam" in 1881.

The one Celtic settlement of "Vedunia" was converted by the Romans, that in 15 BC fortified the frontier city and called it "Vindobona", a province of Pannonia in the first century and was elevated with roman city rights in 212. They fortified "Vindobona" to guard the Empire against Germanic tribes to the north.

Vindobona supposed to mean white village. Celtic roots "Vindo" means white, while in Welsh is Gwyn or Gwen, while "Bona" means settlement village same like in Older Irish and Welsh. This followed by a time in the sphere of influence of Lombards and the later the "Pannonia Avars" when the slavs reated majority of region population.

From the 8th century the region was settled by the Bavarii, (Baiuvarii). In 976 the Babenbergs established the Margraviate of Austria. In 1221 Vienna was granted city of rights by Leopoldi VI. The reign of "Habsburg", started in 1278.

In 1440 Vienna became the resident of "Habsburg" dynasty. In 1437 Vienna became cultural center for art and science music and fine cuisine. Hungary occupied city of Vienna between 1485- 1490. Vienna in 1558 became capital of "Holy Roman Empire" (800 - 1806). Also, Vienna was the capital of the Austrian Empire from 1804 – 1867 and of the Cislethanian part of Austro – Hungary from 1867- 1918

During Napoleon Bonaparti's wars Vienna became the capital of newly formed "Austria Empire" during this time Vienna play one big role in politic of Europe including the Congress of Vienna in period time 1814- 1815.

During period time 1867 – 1918 Vienna became the capital of Austria until the beginning of the 20th Century. Vienna was the largest German speaking city in the world and before splitting of the Austro – Hungarian Empire in the World War the First (WWI). The city has 2,000,000,00 (two million) inhabitants. Today is the second largest German speaking city after Berlin.

Later of 19[th]century until to 1938 the city of Vienna remined center of high culture and modernism. Vienna at that time was world capital of music.

Strangely during period time of 1919 until to 1934 Vienna became the center of socialist politics, while this period sometimes named and referred like "**Red Vienna**".

During Austrian civil war of 1934 Chancellor Engelbert Dollfuss sent the "Austrian Armed Forces" to shell civilian housing such Karl Marx – Hof, occupied by the "Republikanischer Schutzbund" that was socialist militia.

During the November's the program specific at 8 November 1938, 92 Synagogues, in Vienna were destroyed. Really only the city temple in the1 (first) district was spare. Adolf Eichman held office in the expropriated in Palais Rothschild and organized expropriation and persecution of the Jews of the almost 200,000, 00 jews people in Vienna around 120, 000,00 were driven to emigrate and around 65,000,00 were killed.

After the end of the World War the Second (WWII) the Jewish population was only about 5,000,00 people. On April 2, 1945 Soviet Red Army launched Vienna offensive against Germans that were holding the city and besieged it.

Vienna was also center of one very important resistance group around "Heinrich Mair" which provided help to allies with plans for V1 – V2 rockets.

After the World War the second (WWII) Vienna was part of Soviet occupied Eastern Austria until September 1945. As in Berlin and Vienna was divided in sectors, by four powers like the U.S.A., The United Kingdom (U.K.), France and the Soviet Union while was supervised by an "Allien Commission".

The four – power's control of Vienna finished or lasted until the "Austrian State Treaty" that was signed in May 1955. They decided to be Austria neutrality, after of withdrawn of four allies' troops, really power states at that time. This law of neutrality of Austria, passed in late of October 1955.

This law ensured that Austria would align with NATO, or neither with Soviet block, and this important fact is considered one of the reasons that Austria in 1995 delayed to enter in European Union.

Today, Vienna is host to many major international organizations including United Nation (U.N.) OPEC (The Organization of the Petroleum Exporting Countries) and the OSCE (Organization for Security and Cooperation in Europe). In 2001 city center was designated a UNESCO (United Nations Educational Scientific and Cultural Organization) world heritage site. In July 2017 it was moved to the list of the "World Heritage" in danger.

Vienna has been called the "City of Music" due to its musical legacy as many famous classical musicians such as Bethoven, Brams, Haydin, Mahler, Mozarti, Schoenebrg, Schuberts, and Johan Strauss, Called Vienna Home.

Vienna, it is well known for having played a pivotal role as a leading European music center of the age of "Viennese Classicism" through the early part of the 20th century. Vienna Is also said to be the "City of Dream" because it was home to the first psychoanalyst, "Sigmund Freud".

The historic center of Vienna is rich in architectural ensembles including "Baroque" Palace and gardens and the late 19th century lined buildings monuments, and parks.

During his explanation the younger man Zeeshan whispered with himself very interesting story and Information for this city of Vienna.

SCHONBRUNN PALACE, SCHONBRUN 1130. VIENNA.

It is imperial palace the Habsburg summer residence in the Muesum Quarter district historic and contemporary building display works by Egon SchieleGustav Klint and other artists.

Schonbrunn Palace

SCHÖNBRUNN PALACE (GERMAN: SCHLOSS SCHÖNBRUNN ['ʃLɔs ʃøːnˈbʀʊn] ①; Central Bavarian: Schloss Scheenbrunn) was the main summer residence of the Habsburg rulers, located in Hietzing, Vienna. The name Schönbrunn (meaning "beautiful spring") has its roots in an artesian well from which water was consumed by the court.

The Baroque palace is one the most important architectural, cultural and historic monument of the Vienna of Austria. This Schonbrunn palace has 1441 rooms while his history and his garden has is more than 300 years. This palace with his garden are reflecting the changing tastes, interests, and aspiration of very successive Habsburg Monarchs.

ThiS Schonbrunn palace has great history It has been a major tourist attraction since the middle 1950.

In 1569, Holy Roman Emperor Maximilian II purchased a large floodplain of the Wien River beneath a hill, that was between Meidling and Hietzing. The former owner, in 1548, had erected a mansion called Katterburg.

The emperor ordered the area to be fenced and put game there such as pheasants, ducks, deer and boar, in order for it to serve as the court's recreational hunting ground. He also ordered that in a small separate part of the area, were settle "exotic" birds such as turkeys and peafowl. Fishponds were also built.

During the next century, the area was used as a hunting and recreation ground.

When died the Ferdinand II his wife Eleonora Gonzaga, used that like residence and spent so much time over there plus she loved haunting too.

During the period time of 1638 to 1643 Eleonora Gonzaga added a palace to this mansion Katterburg. In 1642 the name Schonbrunn, came in invoice of this palace so the Schonbrunn orangery seem to go back to Eleonor Gonzages as well she has credit for that.

During the period time 1740- 1750, the Schonbrunn palace was build and was remodeled, with the from that has today, this happened during the reign of Empress Maria Theresa, who received the estates as a "**Wedding's gift**".

Franz I commissioned the redecoration of the palace exterior in the neoclassical style as it appears today.

Franz Joseph, the longest-reigning emperor of Austria, was born at Schönbrunn and spent a great deal of his life there. He died there, at the age of 86, on November 21, 1916. Following the downfall of the Habsburg monarchy in November 1918, the palace became the property of the newly founded Austrian Republic and was preserved as a museum.

After World War II and during 1945- 1955 that named time of the Allied Occupation of Austria, Schönbrunn Palace was requisitioned to provide office space for both the British Delegation to the Allied Commission for Austria, and for the headquarters for the small British Military Garrison present in Vienna.

In 1955 when Austria, reestablished itself like Republic, the Schonbrunn palace once again became a museum. It was used sometimes for important events such as the meeting between United States of America (U.S.A.). president John F. Kennedy and Soviet premier Nikita Khrushchev in 1961.

Since 1992, the palace and gardens have been owned and administered by the Schloss Schönbrunn Kultur-und Betriebsges.M.B.H., a limited-liability company wholly owned by the Republic of Austria.

The company conducts preservation and restoration of all palace properties without state subsidies.[3] UNESCO catalogued Schönbrunn Palace on the World Heritage List in 1996, together with its gardens, as a remarkable Baroque ensemble and example of synthesis of the arts (Gesamtkunstwerk).

SAINT STEPHEN 'S CATHEDRAL

St. Stephen's Cathedral (German: Stephansdom [$\widehat{\int}$ tɛfans͵doːm]) is the mother church of the Roman Catholic Archdiocese of Vienna and the seat of the Archbishop of Vienna, Christoph Cardinal Schönborn, OP.

The current Romanesque and Gothic form of the cathedral, seen today in the Stephansplatz, was largely initiated by Duke Rudolf IV (1339–1365) and stands on the ruins of two earlier churches, the first a parish church consecrated in 1147. The most important religious building in Vienna, St. Stephen's Cathedral has witness of so many important events during the time of the Habsburg and Austria's history too. this Cathedral has its multicolor tiles roof and is more recognizable symbol of city of Vienna {1}.

HISTORY.

By the middle of the 12th century, Vienna had become an important center of German civilization, and had four churches including one Parish church that was not in used anymore because did not meet the town religious at that time.

In 1137, Bishop of Passau Reginmar and Margrave Leopold IV signed the Treaty of Mautern, which referred to Vienna as a civitas for the first time and transferred St. Peter's Church to the Diocese of Passau.

Under this treaty, Margrave Leopold IV also received from the bishop extended of land beyond the city walls, with the notable exception of the territory allocated for the new parish church, which will become St. Stephen's Cathedral.

It is believed that new parish church Saint Rupert church, was built outside of city walls on an ancient cemetery dating back intime of ancient roman times. During the year 2000, archeologist discovered graves 2, 5 meters (8, 2 feet) below the surface that supposed to be of the back time of 4th century. This is telling that that history of this place is older that Saint Rupert church that is considerate the oldest church in Vienna a of Austria.

In 1137 while following the Treaty of Mautern, was done constructed partially of Romansque church that was solemnly dedicated in 1147 to Saint Stephen in presence of Conrad III of Germany, bishop Otto, of Freising and other German nobles who were about to embark on the second Crusade {2}.

At that time the first structure was completed in 1160{3} while major reconstruction of this church finished in 1511, while repair and restoration are continuing and the present day. During period time 1230 until to 1245 Romanesque structure was extended to west ward, while the present day the west wall and Romanesque Towers date back from this period.

Although the first structure was completed in 1160,[3] major reconstruction and expansion lasted until 1511, and repair and restoration projects continue to the present day. From 1230 to 1245, the initial

Romanesque structure was extended westward; the present-day west wall and Romanesque towers date from this period.

In 1258 a great fire destroyed much of the original building of this Romanesque church. Romanesque church and reusing two towers was constructed over the place of ruin the old church and consecrated on April, 23, 1263.

The anniversary of this second consecration is commemorated each year by a rare ringing of the Pummerin bell for three minutes in the evening. This church has so many reconstructions, during 1304 the time of King Albert I and his son Duke Albert II, the work of Albertine choir finished 1340 of 77 anniversary of the pervious consecration.

So some part of this church like middle nave largely, is dedicated to Saint Stephen and all saints, while north and south nave are dedicated to Saint Mary and the apostles. During that time until in 1365 just six years after beginning the Gothic extension of the Albertine choir Rudolf IV disregarded Saint Stephen's status as a mere parish church but at that time started first step to of chapter be fitting the large Cathedral

This move was only the first step in fulfilling Vienna's long-held desire to obtain its own diocese;

In 1469, Emperor Frederick III prevailed upon Pope Paul II to grant Vienna its own bishop, to be appointed by the emperor. At that time the Bishops of Passau who did not want to lose control of that area the diocese of Vienna was established on January 18, 1469 with Saint Stephen's Cathedral as its mother church.

In 1722 during the reign of Karl VI, Pope Innocent XIII elevated the see to an archbishopric.[3]

The most interesting fact is that during World War II, (WWII) the Cathedral was saved from intentional destruction at the hands of retreating German forces when Wehrmacht Captain Gerhard Klinkicht disregarded orders from the city commandant, "Sepp" Dietrich, to "fire a hundred shells and reduce it to rubble".[4] On April 12, 1945, civilian looters lit fires in nearby shops as Soviet Army troops entered the city.

Because was wind the fire was spreading so fast to the Cathedral, while damaged the roof, that caused it to collapse.

Fortunately, protective brick shells built around the pulpit, Frederick III's tomb, and other treasures, minimized damage to the most valuable artworks.

However, the Rollinger choir stalls, carved in 1487, could not be saved. Reconstruction began immediately after the war, with a limited reopening December 12, 1948 and a full reopening on April 23, 1952.

EXTERIOR.

The church was dedicated to St. Stephen, also the patron of the bishop's cathedral in Passau, and so was oriented toward the sunrise on his feast day of December 26, as the position stood in the year that construction began.

The Saint Stephen's Cathedral is built of limestone, the cathedral is 107 meters (351 feet) long, 40 meters (130 feet) wide, and 136 meters (446 feet) tall at its highest point. Over the centuries, soot and other forms of air pollution accumulating on the church have given it a black color, but recent restoration projects have again returned some portions of the building to their original white.

TOWER.

The Saint Cathedral is standing at 136 meters (446 feet) tall and affectionaly, referred to by the city's inhabitants as "Steffl" (a diminutive form of "Stephen"), Saint. Stephen's Cathedral's massive south tower is its highest point and a dominant feature of the Vienna skyline.

Its construction lasted 65 years, from 1368 to 1433. During the Siege of Vienna in 1529 and again during the Battle of Vienna in 1683, it served as the main observation and command post for the defense of the walled city, and it even contains an apartment for the watchmen who, until 1955, manned the tower at night and rang the bells if a fire was spotted in the city.

The double – eagle imperial emblem with Habsburg – Lorraine, coat of arms on its chest surmounted by a double- armed apostolic cross, which referred Apostolic Majesty, the imperial style of kings of Hungary was replaced earlier crescent and six -pointed star emblem. Really the original emblem as well as a couple of later one, in present time can be seen by tourists in Vienna City Museum.

The north tower was originally intended to mirror the south tower, but its design was so much ambitious at that time, because the architecture of Gothic of Cathedral, at that time was coming to the end so construction was halted in 1511.

After that in 1578 the tower – stump of Cathedral was made in greater size and value with Renaissance Cap for that reason they put nickname the" Water -Tower -Top" top by Viennese people. In present time the tower, stands at 68 meters, (223 feet) tall, so it is the half height of the south tower.

The main entrance to the church is named the Giant's Door, or Riesentor,

Possible referring to the thighbone of a mammoth, that hung over it with decades, after fell in 1443, while they were digging the foundation for the north tower or were working to give funnel shape of the door to risen for water (middle German risen is sink or fell of the water.).

The tympanum above the Giant's Door depicts Christ Pantocrator flanked by two winged angels, while on the left and right are the two Roman Towers, or Heidentürme, that each stand at approximately 65 meters, (213 feet) tall.

The name for the towers derives from the fact that they were constructed from the rubble of old structures built by the Romans (German Heiden meaning heathens or pagans) during their occupation of the area.

The originally bells of south tower were lost during the World War II (WWII) while square at the base and octagonal above the roofline, the Heidenturme originally housed bells.

The north tower remains an operation bell tower.

From all of those the oldest parts of the church are the Giant's door and the Roman Tower, that is telling to the world for "Giant, great and very quality job has done at that time by people that were working with soul and their heart in their hand".

Their good job made to resist this very beautiful unusual Cathedral of Vienna with centuries, from damaged by the weather or earthquake or by different terrible war so it is showing its magnificence view in present time.

This cathedral is showing with proud her beautiful art and pride too, and why is so much older in age in centuries, also is showing to people the pride and beauty of art and architect people at that time.

Roof

THE GLORI OF THIS SAINT STEPHEN 's CATHEDRAL STAND UP TO ITS roof very rich colored loner 111 meters (one-hundred-eleven) (364 feet) (three -hundred -sixty four) while is covered by 230,000, 00 glazed tiles (two- hundred -thirty thousand).

On the south side of the building, above the choir, the tiles have form of mosaic of double headed eagle that is symbol of the empire ruled Vienna by the Habsburg dynasty.

The coats of arms of the City of Vienna and of the Republic of Austria are painting on South of building.

During the World War II (WWII) in 1945, the building of Cathedral got damaged by fire in height until up to the North tower also was destroyed the wooden framework of the roof too.

The roof is 38 meter (thirty eight) above the floor, but to renovate this roof like original before have been cost approximately so over more 600 (six hundred) meters-tons of steel bracing that were used. The roof is so steep that is cleaned by the rain and not often is covered by snow.

Bells

Saint Stephen, Cathedral, of Vienna has 22 (twenty) bells. One curiosity is about composer Ludwig Van Beethoven that discovered the totality of his deafness when he saw the birds were flying out of the bell tower as a result of the bells' tolling but could not hear the bells.

The largest bell that it called "Pummerin" (Boomer) and hand in North tower. This bell has weight at 20, 130 (twenty thousand and one hundred and thirty) kilogram (44, 380 LB) (forty-four thousand- three hundred and eighty).

This bell is the largest in Austria, and the second – largest swinging bell in Europe, after the 23, 500 (twenty-three thousand and five hundred) kilogram (51, 800 LB) ((fifty - one-thousand and eighty hundred) Peter in cologne Cathedral.

The bell founder by Johann Achammer that was captured by Muslim invader in 1711, was replaced partially from its original metal in 1951 after crashing onto the floor when its wooden were burned by fire in 1945.

The new bell that was gift by upper Austria has a diameter of 3.14 (three meters, and fourteen centimeters) meters (10.3 ft) (ten feet and three inches. It sounds on only a few special occasions each year, including the arrival of the new year.

Also in this tower are two older bells really formerly they were three, but no longer are used. One is "Small bell" named Kleine Glocke that weight 62 (sixty two)kilograms or (137 LB)(one hundred and thirty seven) cast around 1280.

The other is "Dinner Bell" Speisglocke, (240 (two hundred and forty) kilograms (530 lb) (five hundred and thirty) cast in 1746; and "Procession Bell" Zügenglocke ("processions bell") 65 kilograms (sixty five) (143 lb) (one hundred and forty three) cast in 1830.

However, the Kleine Glocke was restored at the "Grass Mayr" foundry in Innsbruck in 2017 and rehung in the North Roman Tower. To those bells the loud ringing of eleven electrically operated bells build (cast) in 1960 that hangs in south tower.

The others ancient bells that are replacement because are damaged or lost by fire in 1945 of World War II (WWII), are used during Masses at the Cathedral while four are used for an ordinary Mass. The quantity of bells increased to close, to ten bells for a major holiday Mass, of Vienna of Austria.

The eleventh bells and largest or more is added when the Cardinal Archbishop of Vienna himself is present in Mass. So, the Cardinal Archbishop of Vienna is giving "Glory of Glory" to himself like religious figure and leader also and to Saint Stephen Cathedral, with loudly ringing of the more then eleventh bells, so all around the Vienna.

I think that day all white angels are opening their arm up to blue sky while birds and all other items that are doing noise have not space that day under the space of blue sky above all of roofs of buildings and houses of Vienna.

The loudly ring of those so much bells, of this famous Saint Stephen Cathedral of Vienna, of Austria, will never allow other sounds to be heard in Vienna that day. Only smile and happiness of people that are listening that loudly ring while are praying wherever they are in Cathedral or around while they are giving thank you to this Cathedral with their praying.

With that loudly ring of her powerful bells eleventh or twenty-two this Saint Stephen Cathedral is spreading all around the "Faith" and "Peace" to people of Vienna of Austria and to people all around the world.

This Cathedral is spreading its grandiose story for so many centuries, is spreading its resistance to so many factors social and climate too, it is spreading feeling of courage to people that never to give up for every hard and difficult situation.

Its loudly ring is attracting mind of people never to forget the longer journey in so many centuries of this Saint Stephen, Cathedral and her people that contributed and built with so many difficulties and protected its until now. This Saint Stephen Cathedral is giving loudly ringing for people with meaning that will "Faith", persistence, courage, patience and hard working everything can achieve everyone.

This "Saint Stephen" Cathedrale's loudly ringing by so many bells is giving inspiration to people of art and architects too, to work with full passion and to create beautiful things for people and for new generation, in long run, and if is taking longer to achieve their goal.

The "Saint Stephen", Cathedral's loudly rings is giving so much hope to people in their life, for "Peace - Faith and Love" and for interacting with each other.

From the largest to the smallest, they are named the St. Stephen (5,700 kilograms (12,600 lb)); St. Leopold (2,300 kilograms (5,100 lb)); St. Christopher (1,350 kilograms (2,980 lb)); St. Leonhard (950 kilograms (2,090 lb)); St. Josef (700 kilograms (1,500 lb)); St. Peter Canisius (400 kilograms (880 lb)); St. Pius X (280 kg); All Saints (200 kilograms (440 lb)); St. Clement Maria Hofbauer (120 kilograms (260 lb)); St. Michael (60 kilograms (130 lb)); and St. Tarsicius (35 kilograms (77 lb)).

Also in this tallest tower are the Primglocke (recast in 1772), which rings on the quarter hour, and the Uhrschälle (cast in 1449), which rings on the hour.

The north Roman Tower contains six bells, four of which were cast in 1772, that ring for evening prayers and toll for funerals. They are working bells of the cathedral and their names usually recall their original uses: Feuerin ("fire alarm" but now used as a call to evening prayers) cast in 1879; Kantnerin (calling the cantors (musicians) to Mass); Feringerin (used for High Mass on Sundays); Bieringerin ("beer ringer" for last call at taverns); Poor Souls (the funeral bell); Churpötsch (donated by the local curia in honour of the Maria Pötsch icon in the cathedral), and Kleine Glocke (cast in 1280 and is the oldest bell in the cathedral).[

Fixtures on outside on walls. During the Middle Ages, major cities had their own set of measures and the public availability of these standards allowed visiting merchants to comply with local regulations.

The official Viennese ell length standards for verifying the measure of different types of cloth sold are embedded in the cathedral wall, to the left of the main entrance.

The linen ell, also called Viennese yard, (89.6 centimetres (35.3 in)) and the drapery ell (77.6 centimetres (30.6 in)) length standards consist of two iron bars. According to Franz Twaroch, the ratio between the linen ell and the drapery ell is exactly$\{\displaystyle {\sqrt {3}}/2\}$.[8][9]

The Viennese ells are mentioned for the first time in 1685 by the Canon Testarello della Massa in his book Beschreibung der ansehnlichen und berühmten St. Stephans-Domkirchen.[10]

A memorial tablet (near location SJC on the Plan below) gives a detailed account of Wolfgang Amadeus Mozart's relationship with the cathedral, including the fact that he had been appointed an adjunct music director here shortly before his death. This was his parish church when he lived at the "Figaro House" and he was married here, two of his children were baptised here, and his funeral was held in the Chapel of the Cross (at location PES) inside.[11]

Adjacent to the catacomb entrance is the Capistran Chancel, the pulpit (now outdoors at location SJC) from which St. John Capistrano and Hungarian general John Hunyadi preached a crusade in 1456 to repel Muslim invasions of Christian Europe. (See: Siege of Belgrade).[12] The 18th century Baroque statue shows the Franciscan friar under an extravagant sunburst, trampling on a beaten Turk. This was the original cathedral's main pulpit inside until it was replaced by Niclaes Gerhaert van Leyden's pulpit in 1515.[citation needed]

Interior

ALTAR.

THIS CHURCH IN MAIN PART OF IT CONTAINS 18 (EIGHTY) ALTARS, WITH more various chapels. Two famous altars are the Hugh Altar (HA) and the Wiener Neustadt altar (German: Wiener Neustadter Altar.

The High Altar that is attracting the watching of visitor in distance is built for seven years from 1641 to 1647 as the part of the first refurbishment of the cathedral in the Baroque style.

The high Altar was built with marble from Poland, Syria and Tyrol. This High altar was built by Tobias Pock by the direction of Vienna's Bishop Phillipp Friedrich Graf Breuner. The High Altar represent the church's patron Saint Stephen. This altar is framed by figures of patron Saint Stephen and surrounding areas with Saints Leopold, Florian, Sebastian and Rochus also it is statue of Saint Mary which her eyes are to heaven where Christ waits for Stephen (the first Martyr) to ascend from below.

The Wiener Neustadter altar was ordered in 1447 by Emperor Frederick III whose tomb is located in the opposite direction. This altar is in north of building.

Frederick ordered it for the Cistercian Viktring Abbey (near Klagenfurt) where it remained until the abbey was closed in 1786 as part of Emperor Joseph II's anti-clerical reforms. It was then sent to the Cistercian monastery of St. Bernard of Clairvaux (founded by Emperor Frederick III) in the city of Wiener Neustadt, and finally sold in 1885 to St. Stephen's Cathedral when the Wiener Neustadt monastery was closed after merging with Heiligenkreuz Abbey.

The Wiener Neustädter Altar is composed of two triptychs, the upper being four times taller than the lower one. When the lower panels are opened, the Gothic grate of the former reliquary depot above the altar is revealed.

During the week days, the four panels are closed and display painting of scene of 72 (Seventy - two) saints. During Sunday the panels are open and are showing the wood figure of different events in the life of Virgin Mary.

On weekdays, the four panels are closed and display a drab painted scene involving 72 saints. On Sundays, the panels are opened showing gilded wooden figures depicting events in the life of the Virgin Mary.

Restoration began in its 100 (one hundred) anniversary, in 1985 and this restoration got 20 (Twenty) years, were restored 10 art, got 40, 000 man hours, and this primary restoration cost 1, 3 million euro, because its large surface area of 100 (one hundred) square meters or (1,100 square /feet) (one thousand and one hundred)

MARIAPOCS ICON,

The Maria Potsch, icon (MP) is a Byzantine style icon of Saint Mary with the child Jesus. The icon got its name from the Hungarian Byzantine Catholic shrine of Mariapocs (pronounced Poach) form where was transferred to Vienna. It is very interesting about this picture that shows the Virgin Mary pointing one child (the meaning is that:" He is the way.") and the child a three- stemmed rose that symbolizing the holy Trinity and wearing a prescient cross from his neck.

This icon with measure 50 x70 centimeter was commissioned in 1676 from by painter Istvan Papp, by Laszlo Csigri for his release as a prisoner of war during the time that Turks (Turkish) were invading Hungary at that time. Csigri was unable to pay 6 (Six) forint fee the icon was bought by Lorinc Hurta who donated it to the church of Pocs.

One unusual story happened in 1696, that they were claiming that two miraculous incidents happened with the mother in the picture allegedly shedding real tears, so after this incident the Emperor Leopold I ordered that picture of mother to send, to Saint Stephen's Cathedral, where it would be saved from Muslim Armies that at that time still controlled Hungary.

Upon its arrival after a triumphal five-month journey in 1697, Empress Eleonora Magdalena commissioned the splendid Rosa Mystica oklad and framework (now one of several) for it, and the emperor, personally ordered the icon placed near the High Altar in the front of the church, where it stood prominently from 1697 until 1945. (248 years period time).

In 1697 when empress Eleonora Magdalena arrived after a triumphal five months journey, she commissioned the splendid rosa Mystica oklad and frame work one of several.

Emperor personally ordered the icon to be placed near to High Altar in front of church, where it stood prominently from 1697 until 1945.

Since then, it has been in a different framework, above an altar under a medieval stone baldachin near the southwest corner of the nave – where the many burning candles indicate the extent of its veneration, especially by Hungarians.

Since that time was in different framework above High Altar, under medieval stone, close southwest corner of nave where were burning candles by Hungarians. Since that time the picture has not been seeing weeping again but happened some others miracles, and answered to different prayers by so many people too, that attributed to this picture- icon.

One occasion was the victory of Prince Eugene of Savoy over the Turks (Turkish) at Zenta after weeks that the icon – picture's installation in the Stephansdom.

Another very interesting story about this icon is that when the people of Pocs wanted to return to them, this holy miracle- working painting, but the emperor, sent to them only copy of this painting instead the original.

It is said that since than the copy has been reported to weep real tears and work miracles, since that time the village's people change the name of village from Pocs to "Mariapocs". Since that time this village became one very important pilgrimage for people all around area and all tourists from all around the world.

PULPIT.

The stone pulpit is master work of Gothic Sculputure that it is attributed to Anton Pilgram, but today Niclaes Gerhaert Van Leyden is thought or supposed more likely to be the carver.

So, the local language sermon of priest sermon could be better heard by the worshipers in the days before to be used microphones and loudspeakers. The position of pulpit stands against a pillar out in the nave instead of in the chancel at the front of the church.

The sides of pulpit erupt or have like stylized like petals from the stem supporting it. On those Gothic petals are relief portraits of the four original doctors of the church that are: Saint Augustine of Hippo, Saint Ambrose,

Saint Gregory the Great and Saint Jerome that each of them are in one of four different Temperaments and in one of four different stages.

The handrail of the stairway curving its way around the pillar from ground to the pulpit that has one the most fantastic decoration with some interesting figures like toads and lizards that biting each other that is symbolizing the fight of good against evil. At the top of the stairs, it is a stone puppy that protects the preacher from intruders.

Beneath the stars is one of the most beloved symbols of the cathedral: it is one stone self portrait of the unknown sculptor gawking out of the window and this famously known as the Fenstergucker.

The chisel in the subject's hand and the stone mason's signature mark or the shield above the window led to the speculation that it making to think, it could be a self – portrait of the sculptor.

CHAPELS.

There are several formal chapels in St. Stephen's Cathedral:

St. Catherine's Chapel, it is in the base of the South tower, it is the baptismal chapel. The 14-sided baptismal font of this Saint Catherine Chapel was completed in 1481, and its cover was formerly the soundboard above the famed pulpit in the main church. Its marble base shows the four Evangelists, while the niches of the basin feature the twelve apostles, Christ and Saint. Stephan.

St. Barbara's Chapel, in the base of the North tower, is used for meditation and prayer.

Saint. Eligius's Chapel, in the Southeast corner, is open for prayer. The altar is dedicated to Saint. Valentine whose body (one of three, held by various churches) also it is in another chapel, upstairs.

Saint. Bartholomew's Chapel, it is above St. Eligius' Chapel, has recently been restored.

The Chapel of the Cross (PES), it is in the Northeast corner, that holds the burial place of Prince Eugene of Savoy in the vault containing 3 coffins and a heart urn, under a massive stone slab with iron rings.

The funeral of Mozart occurred here on December 6, 1791. The most interesting is that the beard on the crucified Christ above the altar is of <u>real hair</u>. The chapel is not open to the public.

Saint. Valentine's Chapel, it is above the Chapel of the Cross, in current time has the hundreds of relics that belonging to the "Stephansdom", including a piece of the tablecloth from the Last Supper.

A large chest holds the bones of Saint. Valentine, that were moved here in that place about a century ago, that now is the Chapter House to the south of the High Altar.

TOMBS, CATACOMBS, AND CRYPTS

Since its earliest days, the cathedral has been surrounded by cemeteries dating back to Roman times, and has sheltered the bodies of nobles and commoners. It was honor for some people to be buried inside the church close to physical presence of the saints that relics of them are preserved over there. Very interesting it is that some people that are more less honor were buried outside but near of the church.

Inside this cathedral are tombs of the prince Eugene of savoy (PES) that was commander of the imperial forces during the War of the Spanish Succession the Chapel of the Cross (Northwest corner of the cathedral) also the tombs of the Frederic III, that was Holy Roman Emperor (FR3) under whose reign the Diocese of Vienna canonically erected (built) on January 18, 1469 in the Apostles' Choir (in southeast corner of the cathedral.

The construction of Emperor Frederic's Tomb spanned over 45 years that really started 25 (twenty-five) years before his death. The body of the tomb has 240 (two hundred forty, statues and is a glory of medieval sculptural art.

In 1735 when happened the outbreak of bubonic plague to the eight cemeteries and to charnel house the church closed the wall and while the bones were moved to the catacombs below the church. Burials directly to catacombs continues until in 1783 when the new law refused most burials within the city. Really there are over 11.000. persons in catacombs, that they said maybe will be toured.

The basement of the cathedral also hosts the bishop, Provost and ducal crypts (room grave underground). In 1952 completed construction the Bishop crypt under south choir of cathedral where they put the 98 year- old Cardinal Franz Konig in 2004. The Other members of cathedral are buried in special section named the Zentralfriedhof.

The ducal Crypt located under chancel and holds 78 (seventy-eight) bronze containers with bodies, hearts or viscera of 72 (seventy-two) members of Habsburg dynasty.

Those are some of so many others curiosities of this cathedral how they had honor, their people their saints or their members that were working and contributing in this cathedral with great older history for really.

ORGANS.

The Saint Stephen cathedral has organ that supposed to have built in 1334. (13; 15) After the fire of 1945 Michael Kaufman built one great pipe organ, 166

The Kauffmann organ at the west end was only used for about 35 years before falling into disuse. In 1991 the Austrian firm of Rieger rebuilt the choir organ. It is a mechanical organ with 56 voices and 4 manuals.

The Austrian firm of Rieger rebuilt in 2017-2020 the west end (Riesenorgel) organ that use 160 façade and some old pipework that this resulted in organ of 5 manuals with 130 stops. (17).

The choir organ has its own console, but is another separate console that is built in 2017-2020 that has 5 manuals with 185 stops, that is making possible that Riesenorgel and choir organ to play at the same times (18), also the Cathedrale has and 3 smaller instruments too(19)

CONSERVATION AND RESTORATION

The renovation, preservation of the fabric of the medieval cathedral has been one longer process at Saint Stephen Cathedral since started its construction in 1147 and is continuing too in current time in different parts of this cathedral for really.

During the times the porous limestone were subject of the weather, so when they were coating with a sealer of silicone that can create trap moisture inside the stone and that caused the crack of the stone when was water freezes.

After this phenomenon, the permanent "Dombauhütte" (Construction Department) uses the latest scientific techniques (including laser cleaning of delicate features on stonework), while was doing investigation time by time the process while were soaking with substance or putting something in stone that can create a place to make infiltration of water.

The multi – year renovation of the tall South tower is the most current visible repair for that reason the scaffolding has been installed and is preventing advertises that were costing. This repair of majority of South tower finished in December 2008, while the most of scaffolding were been removed.

In this cathedral of Saint Stephen, the cleaning of interior walls and outdoors is doing systematically and is doing gradual processing, while and outdoor relief of the Christ in Gethsemane is being restored.

It is after a long time that a major project has been recently completed for which visitors and worshippers in Saint. Stephen's Cathedral, had been waiting since 1147:

Now the cathedral has better heating during the winter. Previous systems, including fireplaces, just deposited in consideration amount of soot and grease on the artwork, but the new system uses apparatus in many different locations so that there is little moving airflow to carry damaging particles. The Cathedral is now heated to around 10 °C (50 °F).

Now in cathedral is used laser measurement because some architectural drawing that date from Middle Ages, are on paper 15 feet, and are to fragile to hand, so definitely now the digital 3 – dimensional virtual model of the cathedral exist in computer, while the modern plans can be output at will.

When the weather is causing something to stonework and needed to replace or to repair, the computerized system can create life sized model the nine full – time stonemasons on the staff on the site of workshops against the North wall of cathedral.

One 37-year-old man vandalized the interior of the cathedral on March 29, 2014, by pushing the statue of Saint. Jude Thaddeus from its marble base.[20]

Some art historians discovered in January 2020, a mural under layers of dirt on the wall that is now the cathedral's gift shop. Art historians believed that this mural to be the work of the Renaissance artist Albrecht Dürer.[21]

HOFBURG,

German: [ho:f.buʁk]) is the former principal imperial palace of the Habsburg dynasty in Austria. Hofburg is located in the center of Vienna, it was built in the 13th century and expanded several times afterwards. Hofburg palace served as the imperial winter residence, as Schönbrunn Palace was the summer residence. Since 1946, it is the official residence and workplace of the president of Austria.

Since 1279, The Hofburg area has been the documented seat of government since 1279.[1] The Hofburg has been expanded over the centuries to include various residences like "Amalinburg" and the "Albertina". Also has residence of the imperial chapel "Hofkapelle or Burgkapelle". The other building is the imperial library "Hofbibliothek", the treasury "Schatzakammer", the Burgtheater, the Spanish Riding aschool," Hofreitschule" and "imperial news," Stallburg" and "Hofstallungen"

During the reign of Emperor Franz Joseph, this palace faces the Heldenplatz ("The Heroes Square") that was to be planned to become the Kaiserforum (de) but it never completed.

Numerous architects have worked at the Hofburg palace during its expanded, with diversity architecture like Italian architecture, some engineer like the Italian architect-engineer Filiberto Luchese, Lodovico Burnacini, Martino and Domenico Carlone.

During this expanded of this Hofburg palace worked and some otherS architect with the Baroque architecture like architects Lukas von Hildebrandt, Joseph Emanuel Fischer von Erlach, Johann Fischer von Erlach, and the architects of the Neue Burg built between 1881 and 1913.

HISTORY.

The "Castle of the Court", which constructed during the Middle Ages. Initially planned in the 13th century as the seat of the Dukes of Austria, the palace expanded over the centuries, as they became increasingly powerful.

This Hofburg palace it was the seat of the Habsburg kings and emperors of the Holy Roman Empire, from 1483 to 1583 and again was continuing its role again from 1612 to 1806 and thereafter until 1918 the seat of the Emperors of Austria. Since that time, the Hofburg palace has continued in its role in years to come as the seat of the head of state and is today used by the Austrian Federal President.

The "Hofburg" Palace, it is also the permanent home of the Organization for Security and Co-operation in Europe (OSCE).

The whole palace complex is under the administration of the governor (Burghauptmann), that is part of the Burghauptmannschaft, an office which has been in existence since the Middle Ages under the auspices of the Burgrave. At present the Burghauptmannschaft is under the jurisdiction of the Federal Ministry of the Economy.

In September 1958, parts of the Hofburg palace turned like convention center and were opened to the public. In the first ten years, the "Burghauptmannschaft" operated the convention center for public;

One private company named Hofburg Vienna – wiener Kongresszentrum, Hofburg Betriebsgesellschaft has done management of this place for international congress and for different event center.

Every year the convention center hosts about 300 – 350 different events with around 300,000 – 320,000 guests. So, with those events, meetings and conventions this center is servicing as well for banquets, trade fairs, concerts and balls too

STRAUSS AND MOZART CONCERT

In Vienna of Austria people can enjoy the true essence of Vienna with classical concert dedicated to Strauss and Mozart that is brought to people by the world- class interpreters of classical music, the Salonorchester Alt – Wien.

People and tourists can explore the very place in the heart of Vienna where the Waltz King, Johan Strauss II used to charm and to give full pleasure to crowds of people with his outstanding composition.

JOHANN STRAUSS.

Johann Strauss II was an Austrian composer and conductor of the 19th century and became famous all over Europe as the "**Waltz King**" with his popular waltz composition, such as "On the Beautiful Blue Danube", "Vienna Blood" or the "Emperoro Waltz".

His unique "oeuvre" (work of art) includes more than 500 waltzes,16(sixteen) operettas, polkas, quadrilles, one ballet and one opera.

WOLFGANG AMADEUS MOZART.

Wolfgang Amadeus Mozart, was an Austrian composer and renowned as a piano- and violin virtuous. Today, many people regard him as the "**most significant artist in the history of classical music**".

Despite his early death, he created an extensive collection of compositions which enjoy great popularity among classical music lovers around the world.

DANUBE CRUISE.

So many luxury cruises ships are giving gorgeous, itineraries, in different destination through Europe and to legendary Danube river that is passing in beautiful city of Vienna of Austria, while tourists really enjoying one beautiful view.

BELVEDERE SCHLOSSGARTEN.PALACE, WIEDNER GURTEL 1. 1040 VIENNA

The Belvedere is a historic building complex in Vienna, Austria, that has two building with Baroque architecture (the Upper and Lower Belvedere) the Orangery and Palace Stables. The buildings are set in the Baroque-park landscape that is in the third district of the city, on the south- eastern edge of its center.

It houses the Belvedere Museum. On the ground are so many decorative tiered and fountains and cascades, so many Baroques sculptures and majestic wrought iron gates. The Baroque palace complex was built as a summer residence for Prince Eugene of Savoy.

The Belvedere complex palaces were built during the time when Vienna was Imperial capital and home to the ruling of Habsburg dynasty, also during this time has so much extensive construction on it. This period of time was full prosperity while during this time the commander in chief Prince Eugene of Savoy's successful got victory to so many series of wars against the Ottoman Empire.

LOW BELVEDERE.

On November 30, 1697 one year after construction of the Stadtpalais, Prince Eugene purchased a sizeable plot of land south of the Rennweg, the main road of the Hungary, at that time was created immediately plan for Belvedere Garden complex.

The prince Eugene of Savoy, chose Johann Lukas von Hildebrandt as the chief architect for this project rather than Johann Bernhard Fischer von Erlach, the creator of his Stadtpalais.

The General had met Hildebrandt during the time of military campaign in Piedmont, that he had already built Rackeve Palace for him in 1702 on Csepel and island in the Danube of south of Budapest, of Hungary. Later he had built so many others facilities in his service.

The architect Johann Lukas von Hidelbrandt, had studied civil engineering in Rome under Carlo Fontana and went into imperial service in 1695–1696 in order to learn how to build fortifications. From 1696 records show that he was employed as a court architect in Vienna.

Johann Lukas von Hildebrandt architect had so many achievement during this times, like Belvedere complex palaces, also the Schlossh of Palace, which also commissioned by Prince Eugene, the other is the Schwarzenberg Palace that was knowing as the Mansfeld – Fondi Palace, that was before former name, The Kinsky Palace too, and the entire Gottweig Monastery estate in the Wachau Valley.

At the time that the prince was planning to buy the land on the outskirts of Vienna for his Belvedere project, the area was completely undeveloped, so was the good time to do that purchase of land by him, for the garden in future and the summer palace too. –

One month before that prince Eugene of Savoy to buy that land the Imperial Marshall count Heinrich Franz Von Mansfeld, Prince of Fondi purchased that land and put the architect Hildebrandt to build a garden palace in this land

Prince Eugene was forced to take loan against his Stadtpalais that was in process of construction to buy that part of land. he bought this land in 1708, again in 1716 and again he bought in 1717 – 1718 so he can expand the garden in stages.

So was not easy and that time about the law or about buying land in easy way and to build big building too, but the artist soul can give inspiration to great people to create something very beautiful

Record showed that the construction of the Lower Belvedere had started by 1712 when prince Eugene submitted the request for building inspection on July 5, 1713.

Work proceeded quickly (with speed) while, Marcantonio Chiarini from Bologna started painting the quadrature in the central hall in 1715. The ambassador from the Spanish Flanders visited the Lower Belvedere, as well as the Stadtpalais, in April 1716.

Extensive work was doing out on the grounds at the same time as construction was progressing on the Lustschloss, as the Lower Belvedere was described on an early cityscape.

During that time, Dominique Girard changed the plans for the garden significantly between January and May 1717, so that it will be completed by the following summer.

Dominique Girard, who was employed as Fontainer du Roi, or the king's water engineer, in Versailles from 1707 to 1715, he also had started working as a garden inspector for the Bavarian elector Maximilian Emanuel from 1715 and forward.

Latter with recommendation he worked for Prince Eugene. The permission for the balustrade is the best-known work of Giovanni Stanetti too.

GARDENS.

The Belvedere Gardens were designed in the formal French manner with graphic, graveled walks or path walks and jeux d'eau ("Fountain Playing Water"), by Dominique Girard. Domenique Girard was trained as pupil of Andre Le Notre. Also, throughout the gardens were so many mythological figure allude to the rise of Prince Eugene with different sculptural program that were linking him to god Apollo!

A great water basin in the upper parterre also stairs and cascades that were full with different nymphs and goddesses that were in upper and lower parterres survive, and some patterned bedding that has long been grassed over were restored most of them.

UPPER BELVEDERE.

The construction of the Upper Belvedere began as early as 1717, as testified by two letters that Prince Eugene sent at the time from Belgrade of Serbia, to his servant Benedetti in summer 1718, that he was describing the progress of the work on palace. The construction of the palace was so much advanced by October 2, 1719, that make prince Eugene to be able to take the Turkish ambassador Ibrahim Pasha over there.

In 1718 started the decoration of the interior, while in 1719, Prince Eugene commissioned the Italian painter Francesco Solimena to do the altar piece for the Palace Chapel and the ceiling fresco in the Golden Room.

Really, in the same year Gaetano Fanti was commissioned to do illusionistic quadrature painting in the Marble Hall, while in 1720 Carlo Carlone got task to do of painting the Ceiling Fresco in the Marble Hall, that was done from 1721 until to 1723.

The building was completed with construction in 1723. During this time the Sala Terrena was at risk to collapse because of structural problems so in winter of 1723 until to 1733 Hildebrandt, was forced to install a vaulted ceiling that supported by four Atlas pillars that gave the room the current appearance

Salomon Kleiner, an engineer from the Mainz elector's court, produced a ten-part publication between 1731 and 1740 containing a total of ninety plates, entitled Wunder würdiges Kriegs- und Siegs-Lager deß Unvergleichlichen Heldens Unserer Zeiten Eugenii Francisci Hertzogen zu Savoyen und Piemont ("Wondrous war and victory encampment of the supreme hero of our age Eugene Francis Duke of Savoy and Piedmont"), which documented in precise detail the state of the Belvedere complex.

AFTER THE DEATH OF PRINCE EUGEN.

When Prince Eugene died in his City Palace in Vienna on April 12, 1736, he did not leave a legally binding will. A commission set up by the Holy Roman Emperor Charles VI, so they named the prince's niece Victoria as his heir.

She was the daughter of his eldest brother Thomas and the only surviving member of the house of Savoy-Soissons. Princess Victoria moved into the Belvedere, known at that point as the Gartenpalais, on July 6, 1736, but immediately she made clear that she was not interested in her inheritance and wanted, to put in auction off the palace complex as soon as possible.

On April 15, 1738, Princess Victoria married with Prince Joseph of Saxe-Hildburghausen (1702–1787), who was several years her junior. Princess Victoria, married in the presence of the royal family in the Schlosshof in the Marchfeld region, Lower Austria. Victoria's choice of her younger husband proved an unfortunate one, so was short time marriage, however, and the poorly-matched couple divorced in 1744, (so only 6 {six} years together).

After Princess Victoria finally decided to leave Vienna and returned to her home city of Turin, Italy, eight years later that Maria Theresa, the daughter of Charles VI, was able and decide to purchase the estate.

The imperial couple never moved into the Gartenpalais, which was first described as the Belvedere in their sales contract of November 1752.

The Belvedere buildings' complex, was somewhat eclipsed by the other imperial palaces, and as result of this, at first the buildings were left unused during that time.

Later Maria Theresa decided and created an ancestors' gallery of Habsburg dynasty in the Lower Belvedere as was tradition to all other palaces that were belonging to the imperial family.

In April 17, 1770 when masked ball was staged in palace for occasion of honoring marriage of the Imperial Princess Maria Antonia (Antoinette) with the French Dauphin, who became later Louis XVI. The Lord Chamberlain, at that time the palace got awakened from its slumber

In this ball that will participate 16,000 guests that were invited, while two people were charged to take care for all extensive preparation, those were Prince Johann Joseph Khevenhuller – Metsch and court architect Nicolaus Pacassi.

Maria Theresa and her son Emperor Joseph II decided to transfer in 1776 the "Gemaldegalerie" {"Imperial Pictures Gallery"} from the Imperial Stables that was part of the city 's Hofburg Imperial Palace to the Upper Belvedere.

Maria Theresa and her son Joseph II were inspired by the idea of enlightened absolutism, their intention was to make the Imperial collection accessible to the general public. Really this gallery was opened five years later and made it most successful the one of the first public museum in the world. (*online)

So that is telling in this modern time that people when they have passion they can create miracles and if they are going through difficult time, so they can create their legacy and they will leave their legacy for art or science or whatever to future generation to come.

Many painters served as director in charge of the Imperial collection of pictures in Upper Belvedere building until 1891 when it was transferred to the newly built "Kunsthistorisches" Museum, ("Mueseum of Fine ART" on Vienna's Ringstrasse.

So during this time while the Upper Belvedere building was transformed into a gallery of very beautiful pictures at the end of eighteenth century, while the Lower Belvedere building, served mostly to royal family members fleeing from the French Revolution. (French Revolution May 5, 1789- November 9, 1799.).

The younger man Zeeshan was listening with full attention the host explanation while whispered with himself: Very strange and so important history in this world everything can happen.

Between others royal members, one was Marie Therese Charlotte, that was the sole surviving child of Marie Antoinette and Louis XVI, also Archduke Ferdinand. Marie Theresa Charlotte resided in the palace until her marriage with prince Louis Antoine, Duke of Angouleme in 1799.

Archduke Ferdinand that was former Governor of the Duchy of Milan until 1796, went to live there after the treaty of Campo Formia in 1797

After the Habsburg Monarchy was forced give up Tyrol to Bavaria in the treaty of Presburgs (now Bratislava Slovakia after Napoleon's victory) in December 26, 1805, so it was one agreement that Austria signed to end participation on the war, and to handed territory to France that has decisive victory and its allies, so one new home must to be found for the Imperial collection's pictures from Ambras Castle near Innsbruck.

Again, the younger man Zeeshan whispered with himself very interesting history, the world is changing in every century, older system replaced by new systems of society, and is changing and social life of people all around the world.

All the time we must to accept big changing without big conflict. Also, in current time new modern technology is changing the world and social life of people and their concept for life.

As the beginning the collection was taken to Petrovaradin (now is Novi Sad, Vojvodia of Serbia) to protect it, not stealing or looting got by French troops. The emperor Francis II ordered in 1811, that this collection to be installed in Low Belvedere, that really was small for that collection of pictures.

This part of Belvedere named Low Belvedere that took in that time function of Museum had started to draw so many visitors during the time of Congress of Vienna. (1814 -1815)

The Prefect of the Imperial Library, Moritz, count of Dietrichstein-Proskau – Leslie, that he was director, got management of Collection of Egyptian Antiquities and the Antiquites room and added those to the Ambras Collection in the Lower Belvedere collection from 1833 and in progress too. The Roman milestones which have been stored before in the catacombs of the Theseus Temple up to the point, were relocated in 1844 to an open – air in the Privy Garden.

Anyway, the Watercolor by Carl Goebel the Younger that was participating in Lower Belvedere beginning as a Museum, as was description by Joseph Bergman for collection since existed dates 1846. This situation of collection of the pictures did not change until those moved to the newly building Kunsthistorisches, Muesum in the Ringstrasse in 1888- 1889.

BELVEDERE AND FRANZ FERDINAND

After relocation of the Imperial collections, both of Low and Upper Belvedere were opened to be public museum for a while at least. After Emperor Franz Joseph I decided in 1896, that the Upper Belvedere building to serve like residence for the heir to the throne that was his nephew Franz Ferdinand.

The palace remodeled under supervision of the Architect Emil von Forster, that he was also imperial Undersecretary, so this palace served in future like Franz Ferdinand's residence. The Modern Galleria, was opened a few later on May 2, 1903.

This museum was the first collection of the state of Austria that was dedicated to modern art of Austria, and came like result of demanding or request of Austrian Artists that was known as the Vienna secession.

This museum was place of gathering or to juxtapose Austrian art with International, modernism from starting with works by Vincent Van Gogh, Claude Monet, and Geovanni Segantini, that were bought by this Modern Galleria.

The museum was renamed later like Staatsgalerie ("Imperial and Royal Gallery" in 1911, later it was decided that this Galleria to expand the focus beyond modern art and to include to itself and works by more early eras.

During the time one tragic event happened assassination of the heir apparent Archduke Franz Ferdinand of Austria, and his wife Sophie duchess of Hohenberg in Sunday - June 28, 1914, in Sarajevo, capital of province of Bosnia – Herzegovina, that formally was annexed by Austro – Hungary Empire, in 1908.

Really their assassination made to collapse the Habsburg Monarchy in 1918 that created the beginning of new era for the Belvedere.

They were assassinated by one Bosnian – Serb student, Gavrilo Princip, during their driving in Sarajevo. Gavrilo Princip was "Merchant" major -student, also he was member of "Young Bosnia" organization or more

exact one secret association, that had goal to free Bosnia from Austro –
Hungary Empire, and to Achieve Unification of South Slavs.

Gavrilo Princip was arrested with all 24 (twenty-four) other students
all Bosnian that were subject of Austro - Hungary. He was younger age 19
(nineteen) years old; he was spared the death penalty but he got 20 (twenty)
years in prison. At his trial Gavrilo Princip said:

**"I am a Yugoslav Nationalist, aiming for unification of
all Yugoslavs and I do not care what form of state, but it
must to be free from Austria"**

**Brave, younger student, Bosnian Gavrilo Princip for
really, to stand up in front of one powerful Empire of
Austro – Hungary at that time.**

He was imprisoned at the Terezin Small Fortress the Czech Republic,
this Small Fortress was center of military in 18th century and served like
prison in 19th Century where was prisoner and student Gavrilo Princip.

The assassination of Archduke Franz Ferdinand, was the key of outbreak
of the World War I. Gavrilo Princip died on April 28, 1918 in this prison of
Terezin aside the "Ohre", river, on Small Fortress, of Czech Republic in very
young age of his life 23, (twenty-three) years old from tuberculosis, that
cause was poor prison conditions.

Really the Serbian's Government did not inspire that action of
assassination of archduke Frantz Ferdinand but the Austrian Foreign office
and Army used the murder as a reason for preventive war that used that led
directly to the War World I. (WWI).

BELVEDERE IN THE FIRST AND
SECOND REPUBLIC

After the end of the war in November 1918, the art historian Franz
Haberditzl submitted a request to the Ministry of Education, that the palaces
to be left to the Staatsgalerie. This application was granted the very next year.

The nationalization of the Belvedere palace complex was also another
possibility that to create the draft document to reorganize the former
imperial collections drawn up by Hans Tietze in 1920– 1921.

In addition to the museums that still exist today, it was created plans to set up an Österreichische Galerie (Austrian Gallery) and a Moderne Galerie. During the 1921–1923 was done reorganization the Baroque Museum in the Lower Belvedere that was added to the existing museum ensemble while the Moderne Galerie was opened in the Orangery in 1929.

During the World War II this palace got so much damage with parts of the Marble Hall in the Upper Belvedere and the Hall of Grotesques in the Lower Belvedere that really were destroyed by bombs.

The Postwar restoration of museum extended from 1945 to 1953. On February 4, of that year the Österreichische Galerie reopened, followed by the Baroque Museum. The Museum "Mittelalterlicher österreichischer Kunst ("Museum of Medieval Austrian Art") opened in the Orangery on December 5,1953.[3]

The World Monuments Fund (WMF) released one report in 1996 that was explained, was citing that all this postwar restoration had left the "Sala Terrena" and Grand Staircase without much of "Their Original Character". {4}. Also the same year the World Monuments fund added in list about the Belvedere Garden to be "highlight"," The state of disrepair of the much – loved Viennese landmark.{4}

During the year 1990 there were done multiple restoration about physical and aesthetic issues under a Federal plan to modernize the nation's museums. {3}. This program returned the garden to their original Baroque character also renovated in significant way "The Sala Terrena and grand Staircase".{4}.

The Lower Belvedere and the Orangery have been specially adapted to stage special exhibitions. The architect Susanne Zotti, turned the Orangery into a modern exhibition, after winning an invitation-only competition, also hall whilst still preserving the building's original Baroque fabric.

This {**venue**}??opened in March 2007 with the exhibition Gartenlust: Der Garten in der Kunst (Garden Pleasures: The Garden in Art). A few months later the Lower Belvedere reopened with the show Vienna – Paris.

The redesign of the building was done by the Berlin's architect Wilfried Kuehn, that he moved the entrance back to its place in the cour d'honneur, also he created free line vision form the Main gate of the Lower Belvedere via the marble hall until to the Garden façade of the Upper Belvedere too.

The different sections of the original Orangeries that annexed to the

Marble Hall were returned to their original condition while provide space in current time for the new exhibition rooms.

Some section like the magnificent Baroque state rooms – the Marble Gallery, the Golden Room, and the Hall of Grotesques – never changed and are open to the public.

VIENNA STATE OPERA.

Vienna state opera considerate done of the most important house in the world. It is the house with the largest repertoire, that has been under the direction of the Domenique Meyer. In this house are playing and is performance of such famous opera like Aida. Toscana, La traviata etc. Vienna has three opera houses. Tourists from all around the world and musicians' people are enjoying this Vienna opera house.

"ALBERTINA" MUSEUM OF VIENNA.
ALBERTINA PLATZ 1010. VIENNA.

The Albertina is a museum in the Innere Stadt (First District) of Vienna, Austria. It has, one of the largest and most important print rooms in the world. This museum has approximately 65,000 drawings and approximately 1 million old master prints, as well as more modern graphic works, photographs and architectural drawings.

"The Albertina Museum" bought with permanent loan, apart from the graphics collection, two significant collections of "Impressionist and Art" early in 20th century, some of them will be permanent display. "The Albertina Museum" serviced and for temporary exhibitions.

The museum Albertina, had 360,073 visitors in 2020 it was down 64 % from 2019 because of pandemic covid -19 but this museum is ranked 55th in the list of the most visited "Art Museum" in the world{1}

HISTORY.

The Albertina was built on one of the last remaining sections of the fortifications of Vienna, the Augustinian Bastion. Also, the originally, the Hofbauamt (Court Construction Office), which had been built in the second half of the 17th century, stood in that location.

In 1744 it was renovated by the director of the Hofbauamt, Emanuel

Teles Count Silva-Tarouca, to become his palace; it was known as Palais Taroucca. The building was later taken and used like residence by Duke Albert of Saxen-Teschen.

Albert later brought his graphics collection there from Brussels, where he had acted as the governor of the Habsburg Netherlands. He extended the building by Louis Montoyer, so since then, the palace has immediately bordered the Hofburg.

The collection was expanded by Albert's successors. When his grandson Archduke Albrecht, Duke of Teschen lived there until his death in 1895 it was called the Palais Erzherzog Albrecht. {By Online}

The collection was created by Duke Albert with the Genoese count Giacomo Durazzo, the Austrian ambassador in Venice. In 1776 the count presented nearly 1,000 pieces of art to the duke and his wife Maria Christina (Maria Theresa's daughter). {By Online}

Count Durazzo, who was the brother of Marcello Durazzo, the Doge of Genoa – "wanted to create a collection for posterity that served higher purposes than all others: education and the power of morality should distinguish his collection...." {By online}

In the 1820s Archduke Charles, Duke Albert and Maria Christina's foster son, later did the modifications of the building by Joseph Kornhäusel, which affected mostly its interior decoration.

After Archduke Charles, his son Archduke Albert then Albrecht's nephew the popular Archduke Friedrich, Duke of Teschen lived in the building. {By online}.

In early 1919, the new socialist government of Austria confiscated, without compensation, both the building and the collection belonging to the Archduke Friedrich and evicted him. In 1920 the collection of prints and drawings was united with the collection of the former Imperial court library. In 1921 the building was renamed The Albertina.{By Online}

In March 1945, the Albertina Museum was so much damaged during the World War II, by United States Army Air Forces, {USAAF} bomb attacks. The building was rebuilt in the years after the war and was completely renovated and modernized from 1998 to 2003.

Different modifications were done of the exterior entrance sequence, including a distinctive roof by Hans Hollein were completed in 2008, when the graphics collection finally reopened.

In 2018, the Albertina bought the Essl Collection of 1,323 contemporary artworks, including pieces by Alex Katz, Cindy Sherman, Georg Baselitz, Hermann Nitsch, and Maria Lassnig.[2]

On May 27, 2020, "Albertina modern" opened as a new museum for modern art. The collection of Albertina modern encompasses over 60,000 works by 5,000 artists.[3]

HILTON VIENNA PLAZA.

Hotel in Vienna are built between lake and hills and mountains. Between others hotel there some luxury Hilton hotels in Vienna, like "Hilton – Waterfront", hotel, "Hilton Vienna Plaza", hotel, "Hilton Vienna Park", hotel, "Double Tree by Hilton Vienna", hotel, etc, that are creating luxury and comfortable environment for tourists from all around the world.

All the time the younger man Zeeshan said to the host: It is very interesting story of Vienna of Austria.

That afternoon they were very tired when they came back from Vienna, he stayed with his lovely girl Agneza to the hall after dinner and next day all they got their luggage and went to airport early because he sent the youngest people in airport with his security team members, while later in middle day they got flying to their country United Arab Emirates (UAE) to their home city Dubai.

Next day after the younger man Zeeshan turned back with his team of secret service to his country United Arab Emirates (UAE) and his home city Dubai he, went to office saw some documents signed some of them and said to his leader of secret service team Emin, prepare your crew because now wea are going to desert land.

The leader of secret service Emin, told them and everything was ready so all of them were going to desert land. The younger Man Zeeshan told to driver to get another highway with speed so they can go fast to desert land. When they arrived over there the younger man Zeeshan told them that he will build one small modern new town in that place step by step, segment by segment.

The younger man Zeeshan started to explain with full passion in some details about this new project, while he was speaking his friend leader of secret service team Emin, was seeing him and he thought: My younger boss Zeeshan is in deep love and he has full passion and for job and for this project now.

He was thinking that this is one good point about his enthusiasm and this new love because he is very happy to work and is not desperate or in deep thoughts anymore, but other negative point is that his story with his wife never is ending so what will be for him in future. Let's "Allah" to decide for him, now we all to enjoy his enthusiasm for job.

At that time the younger man Zeeshan said: It will be three sections of this new modern town.

First Section: It will be residential area with condominium with modern architecture. To enter in this section will be one mermer (shine, special marble) gate with green color with some white lines in itself like design through this mermer of gate.

To the top of this gate will be the name of my father with golden metallic letters. Between condominiums will be one wide road, while aside the road in two sides will have wide sidewalk, with green trees and to the bottom of the trees we will plant multicolor flowers also modern with beautiful shape of electric tower.

Second Section: it will be only administrative section, with official building, with medical center – building, public library, cultural center – building, computer center building, also human resource center building for people.

It will be one cinema here also one research science center. We will build in this administration section one huge building with four floors elementary school, another one four floors building of high school, also one huge with two floors building for professional college and one modern shape four floors building of university of this new town too.

Will be some statues on this second section like in front of the school, in front of university, in front of medical center and in front of cultural center too.

Between second section and third section will be one empty space land for to build in it one field for football game and two other field one for volleyball game and another for basketball game so this space will be sportive section.

All around those administrative buildings we will plant trees and multicolor flowers. The wide road will build from first section and will go through in middle of second section, also to third section and will extend until to lose in desert land where will be another medical curative center over there for healing people for different illness.

Over there will be the last word of science because science people are working to use the elements of sands of desert for healing different illness. I think my father will build and take care for that medical center with my brothers too.

The mermer gate of this section will be with blue open color with some white color lines design in itself of mermer this color will put clarity to mind of people. To the top of this mermer gate will be with silver color metallic letters the name of my mother, while two branches of olive tree will be to the top of the name of my mother too, that are symbol of peace for people

Third Section: It will be modern villas' section. Villas will build with different shape of architecture some will be modern some classic architecture. Villas will be flat one floor or two floors. The wide road that will extend from first section to second section will continue in middle of the third section between villas.

Willas will be separated in two sides of this wide road and some of them will build up on hills in line of this section.

Trees and multicolor flowers will plant all around this third section and around villas too, while one line of the bus will have in those three sections. The color of the mermer gate of this third section will be bold silver color with some lines with open egg color. This silver color with those open egg color lines of this mermer gate will give serenity to people.

So, guests when will come to visit their family or relatives or friends will understand that this section of villas it is saint section will good people with full peace of living. The third section of villas will have exit to beginning of desert area. The name of this gate with golden color metallic letters will be: "Peace – Nature".

All his friends the member of his security service – team, were listening their younger boss Zeeshan with full attention while they pointed his enthusiasms that they did not see to him and to his face for a long time.

They saw his gesture with his hands and arms that was doing visual around the area also they saw his eyes were sparkling bright looked like he has in front of him one big paper of design project for that his imaginary idea about this new town with three sections. They understood that he was very happy and so much energize and full optimism too for this project. Really, they were happy for their younger boss Zeeshan while the leader of secret service – team was listening and all other people saw in his eyes' tears.

He felt something different strong feelings inside him for his boss while he whispered with himself, he is better now, he is not desperate anymore, he is so much optimist and so much enthusiast.

Definitely he escaped his difficult emotional situation. The leader of secret service Emin, of the younger man Zeeshan loved, his younger boss. Really that moment the leader of secret service team was very happy for his younger boss Zeeshan.

The younger man Zeeshan was continuing his explanation, that this new town needs so much job but when we will start absolutely, we will find way to finish it in optimal time.

First, we will start with infrastructure with road in middle of three sections with channel with big concrete tube for water to go underground, and with side walk. Aside the sidewalk we will plant different kind of trees with different shape so to create diversity in town. After we will start with buildings.

We will cooperate with different giant domestic construction corporations of our country United Arab Emirates (UAE) and foreign construction corporation too. I am calculating with my mind but we will discuss with our architects, so I think that this new town at least to finish in five years.

While my father will work for medical center in desert that will be modern building with super modern technology and luxury room for people. In this medical center they will use the dessert's sand for healing of different illness of people.

I think that this road of those three sections that will be so beautiful will connect with new modern highway that will go through the desert to this new modern medical center with very beautiful building. After maybe will be open way for different centers to build in dessert by different corporations because the science and technology is forwarding.

All said with one voice: This will be the most modern project to use the dessert of our country that has so much space. At that time that the younger man Zeeshan, was happy for his good friends that approved his creative idea, because he needed their support. He loved his friends he was all the time with them they were like his family, he said to them:

Let's go now to eat one good lunch to the restaurant that is close to the field of horses and other animals too. All were happy for that lunch with their boss. During the driving all were involved in conversation about this new town. They said: If is coming so beautiful and will be quiet, we hope so, we must to think to move in this new town and all were happy about this idea.

The younger man Zeeshan laughed and said maybe is going to happen that you to be here but I need to find another crew of secret service, after because it is some distance by my current palace and all laughed. They said: We want to work with you but we will find solution.

With this glad conversation they arrived to the restaurant that they were enjoying so many times. They got Coca-Cola and the leader Emin, lifted the glass with coca cola and said let's drink that glass with cocoa cola for this new town for new beginning and to have success. All they lifted their glass with coca cola and said: we wish good luck for this new project of our boss Zeeshan.

During eating lunch, they were discussing so much enthusiast and everyone was giving one new idea. So, this lunch was really like meeting for business with different ideas and with different imagination while in their face of members of secret service - team, showed smile and happiness too.

They finished lunch and started driving to go to the city to their home. They left behind this very quiet place while entered in noise and super modern highway that was full with different cars.

They were seeing and enjoying their beautiful modern city with very high building that looks were rivals who will kiss the first the blue sky. While the fresh air of blue water of ocean was splashing the glass of those very beautiful glass buildings that were standing pride for their height and were skeptical to the people and cars that looked in miniature from their top level of their roof.

The leader of secret service said loudly: Really our modern city Dubai, is so beautiful and this is credit of family of our boss Zeeshan. They all said: That is very true. We must to say one big, "Thank You" to his family! This is the most beautiful and so much value gift that they gave to our people of this lovely city.

When they arrived to the palace of the younger man Zeeshan, they left him inside his garden of his palace and continued their way to go to their home. The younger man Zeeshan entered inside his palace and was seeing all around the luxury situation of the hall while got stars to go to the second floor.

In front of his studio came in same time his wife Leyale and the lady

Aasma that was servicing to the kitchen. They said both of them with full smile, welcome in home and what do you want to eat?

He got wondered by full smile of his wife Leyale, after a long time of cold situation, while the other lady Aasma, was all the time with smile and love to him.

He said to both of them: Thank you very much but I have eaten with my friends, lunch and I got coffee too to this restaurant close to field of the horses and camels too.

He asked both of them with politesse: How was yours, day today.

They answered in same time: Our day was very good. The younger man Zeeshan did his respect for both of them because he did not want to keep attention about was the day to his wife Leylae.

After he said I am going to see two children and I will work to my studio until to evening. I have one material to prepare for meeting tomorrow. So, he was going to the room of their two children and his wife was going behind him.

They enjoyed some minutes with their children while were laughing with them. His wife Leylae, was telling with smile, about what children have done during their day with their toys. He kissed his children and went to his studio. He left his wife Leylae, with children in their room.

He started to work with computer, while was thinking what is going with me now? I do not understand the behave of my wife now? She changed in drastic way since I came from this trip? She gave me warm today, she created situation that I am in good family with her and our children too.

I am feeling dizzy now, because before some moments I felt like nothing has happened to us. I felt like the first time of our very happy marriage and why I did not want to show to her my good feelings for that situation to the room of our children.

Why my wife changed this time, while we are prepared for divorce?! What is her goal now with me? I do not know myself anymore. I liked those moments of my family but I am thinking so much for the younger girl beautiful Agneza.

She is so calm so beautiful so innocent also she was so happy with me during this trip. Also, her teenager brother Gentius, was so much happy and he gave so much love to me during this trip, he wanted to show to everyone that he possesses me, he was my favorite person in that crew. He is very younger boy very dreaming boy too. At that time the younger man Zeeshan started pray loudly:

"Allah" help me for this strange situation that I am now and give peaceful and good direction for everyone that is involved in my romantic story too, and my family's story too. Really now I wish to realize my "Suddenly White Dream", because I feel I am in love with this younger beautiful girl Agneza.

Suddenly came his wife Leylae, with big wondering and asked him:

What have you done today to this field of horses and camels with your friends?!

The younger man Zeeshan wondered for her question and said nothing we have done over there. What is problem that you are asking me?

One friend of mine called me and gave news and television gave one short strict flash news for your new idea for new town close to dessert and the name that you have decided to give to those three sections?

She continued with smile but with potence: Why you did not want to put and my name over there to this project to any section?!

The younger man Zeeshan replied to her: Why I need to put your name to those sections while is not your creative idea and you did not do anything for this idea, plus I am not putting my name why I must to put your name?

I decided to put the name of my father and my mother also and the name of third section, "Peace – Nature" because over there to this section will live good and peaceful people. He continued his speech but something with irony: If you want to put your name create one vision project and I will put your name in it.

She said serious and proudly: Of course, I will do one vision project you will see, and of course will be my name over there!

The younger man Zeeshan, started to laugh in easy way and said to his wife:

Forward do it! After you will enjoy your name in that project. His wife said to him. I will do for myself and for our children they to be proud for me too. The younger man Zeeshan, said loudly with smile good luck with your project, start its design with your creative idea I will support for your project.

With this conversation they created one strange but warm situation in their palace. While his wife Leylae, went again to see the children while he was continued to work in computer. Next day in the morning the secret service was waiting the younger man in front of his palace.

The driver started driving straight to office of the younger man Zeeshan, that he will do meeting with his specialists of local government for this new idea of this new town close to dessert area.

The leader of secret service Emin, was with him until to his office after he went out. The younger man called his secretary Salma, and said to her to call all specialists to come to his big office. He explained to them about what was this meeting and started to give in details about his new creative idea for this new town close to dessert area.

They started to discuss with so much interest. After one hour of meeting while all were in their room with so many questions and answers with so many replies, while one longer ring got attention of the younger man Zeeshan, and all the others people in his big room – office.

He got permission by them to leave some minutes this room and went to another room to answer to this longer ring of his cellular. When he answered he heard the voice of his leader of the secret service Emin, and asked what is problem?!

I got news that your wife Leylae, is to one business's building, but we did not have news that she will go out today so she is alone not anyone of our security team's members is with her.

He said to Emin, his leader of secret service team wait one minute I will call her. He called his wife and she answered immediately. The younger man Zeeshan, asked her: Where are you now?

She answered I am to one office with one group architects, women. What you want with this office of architects asked the younger man Zeeshan?!

I told you I will start my new creative idea for new project where I and you, both of us we will decide to put my name to this project. The younger man Zeeshan started to laugh in easy way without noise, and asked her again:

Why you did not tell me for that schedule today? So, I will put my secret service team to campaign you? She answered in telephone: I thought to make surprise to you. Also, I will go with this lady leader of architects to another office in this building that is for business to ask about so many things and about budget too, how will cost this design project.

The younger man Zeeshan said humor: So, you are serious for this your new creative project?!

Yes, of occurs I am serious she said for that I came here in this office to discuss in this office, I to give my creative idea they to create architecture of project. After the younger man Zeeshan asked her:

Where you think to do this project to which area? She answered right away: I will do this project aside the river. First, we will start to plant trees aside the river because there are a few trees and the land looked empty and dry, after we will build, infrastructure after to start buildings and everything.

The younger man Zeeshan made only one sigh, hm, hm, hm, after he said to his wife: Okay I am sending to you to this building my security team to campaign you in home when you are finishing job over there, for your creative idea we will talk in our home. Now I am going because I interrupted my meeting with my specialists.

His wife was continuing enthusiast her speech: Those architects' women and their boss woman were very happy when they saw me and when I explained to them my creative idea. They promised to me that they will work with me and they will do the best project for my creative idea.

Their boss woman advised me to go with her to another office to this big high modern glass building to discuss with some other specialists of business and about, cost of project. So, I am doing and this conversation with this architect and her friends, women of business and after I will go to home.

What about children? Asked the younger man Zeeshan. She answered right away: Children are with their lovely nanny as always. Our children will not miss me for some hours they are learn to stay with her as always, because she is very, lovely for them.

Okay I am going to continue my meeting and you finish your job that you have started. I will see you in home. Have a nice day and good luck said with longer voice the younger man Zeeshan while was smiling with himself. He went to meeting discussed so many problems with his people and when meeting finished he went to his office.

The younger man Zeeshan got wondering and was thinking for this big changing of his wife Leylae, for this suddenly courage that she showed for starting active life and specific about new project. Really, I do not understand that big changing of her, maybe those three trips made her to think deeply about our situation.

So now she understood about importance of our family than hurt feeling between two our families because of our disagreement. He was thinking anyway I have not time to think for that I have so many jobs, to do and this project of the new town to follow.

While about this younger girl Agneza I am happy that I know her and I will have a lot time to think for that because she is going to study in university for four years in Ljubljana of Slovenia, while I will continue to work here.

Anyway, I never know what will be my destiny, "Allah" will give good direction of my life, so during this time is big potential about emotions and feelings between two different situation the current cloudy situation with my family and my wife and the other situation, that for now is very happy situation with this younger girl Agneza.

At that time, he was seeing in his telephone and his computer too, he got enthusiasm when he saw e- mail by Professor Bojana and her other friends, professor of law and other professor of architecture, also he was happy when she sent to him some picture that they have done in ski 's center. She was writing to him that she will take care next September for his new friend the younger girl Agneza. He saw and some e-mails by professors of University of Vienna of Austria that he met in ski's center of Austria.

At that time the younger man Zeeshan felt warm in his chest also he felt that tears were filling his beautiful eyes. He whispered to himself: Professor Bojana, is very good person with very good feelings, she is hiding her hurt feelings but she wants to keep strong our friendship.

Professor Bojana, understood my deep feelings for this younger girl Agneza, she accepted that, because she has high level admiration for me or more specific beautiful feelings that named love, but she is very smart woman too.

Really, Professor Bojana is very beautiful and high level, intellectual woman. I am very happy that I meet those people in my trip to Western Balkan, like in Ljubljana of Slovenia, in Zagreb of Croatia, in Dubrovnik, in Lunaria and Kauntia of Croatia, also in Ulqin of Montenegro and in Wienna of Austria, too.

I am very happy for my new and good friends too. Thank you, "Allah" for those good trips in Western Balkan and for those good people that you gave gift to me, was whispering the younger man while was seeing all e-mails.

But when he opened his cellular, telephone he made one big uauaua, with pleasure when he saw text message by Gentius, by Agneza and by the student that he met in big park close to Podgorica of Montenegro.

He started to read the text by Gentius and started to laugh at that time came his secretary Salma, she got wondering when she saw her boss so happy and was laughing while was reading. It was a long time that the secretary lady Salma did not see with happiness and smile her younger boss Zeeshan, but all the time in deep thoughts.

She asked him with smile: You have good news?!Yes said her boss Zeeshan. I have a very good news I have one beautiful, text by one very lovely teenager boy that is with Albanian ethnicity but they are living in Croatia.

He said to his secretary come here and see those pictures in my computer. She saw his e-mails by his foreign friends that have written in English language and so many beautiful pictures that they have done in ski 's center. Her younger boss Zeeshan told to her Gentius in picture and said I laughed with text of this younger boy? She saw him and said he looked so lovely so younger and with very good looking.

The younger man Zeeshan said yes, he is like that very lovely teenager with very good looking also he gave to me and my friends, so much humor and happiness about his questions for everything he was so much curious.

His name is Gentius and he was saying to all others this is my lovely Prince Zeeshan and my lovely friend and he came for me in Croatia and invited me in this ski center of Slovenia too with my sister and my cousins' brother and sister too.

The Secretary lady Salma, was glad that was seeing her boss Zeeshan, very happy with humor too. When she left his office after she explained to him so many things about job's problem and so many appointments that he needs to do in near future, she was whispering with herself:

Thank you, "Allah" that brought good time and happiness to my boss. Really the younger man Zeeshan, was very good with his employees, but all the time he was serious and with deep thought for his personal problem.

So, his staff were not feeling good and comfortable with his situation and were speaking with restriction to him because they did not want to bother him and to make him more desperate.

After those three trips to Western Balkan all people in his building's office saw so much difference and big change to him and to his behave and they loved that situation too. Meeting those new people to Western Balkan, gave to the younger man Zeeshan so much enthusiasm, also this new and very beautiful feelings for this younger girl Agneza made him to feel himself younger.

He was seeing his environment around and the world with bold colorful view not gray color like before. Definitely this time the younger man Zeeshan was very happy. He decided to put some very important appointments, within the week not to extend time, because he wanted to start right away the new project of this town close to desert area.

He was thinking, that he did very good job with those trips to Western Balkan.

The younger girl Agneza, was the reason of those trips and she had credits for all those people that he met over there while he was seeing the world in different angle too. He worked all the day while later afternoon close to the evening he said to leader of secret service Emin, I like to go this evening to the restaurant that is close to the beach where we went with professor Bojana of university of Ljubljana of Slovenia.

The leader of secret service agreed and prepared his team to go over there with their younger boss Zeeshan. They went over there and got coffee, while the hall of cafeteria in second floor was full with people. The younger man Zeeshan said to his leader I want to be some moments alone in silence to balcony.

The leader Emin, agreed but he did not leave alone him, because he loved his friend and younger boss Zeeshan, but got sitting in one chair to the corner of balcony, he knew older situation and new situation of his boss he understood his request while the younger man Zeeshan was sitting to one chair in middle of balcony.

The silver moon was sending its bright light to the face of the younger man Zeeshan, while the stars were dancing around above his head and were giving so much light to the water of ocean during this dark night.

The stars looked like were respecting the bright light of the beautiful silver moon that was full that night while was putting like flux light to one specific place of ocean while her rays were covering and face of the younger man Zeeshan.

The stars were sending their bright light around the light of the silver moon like decoration and were creating to water of ocean one magical view. The white calmer waves during this night were getting reflex by those light of silver moon and stars and were changing their color like in frequency from grey to white.

The waves of water ocean in cooperation with their noise and the noise, crau, crau, crau, of some flamingos that were flying above water of ocean to the sand, were creating one easy beautiful symphonia during this dark night.

The younger man Zeeshan was seeing and said to his friend to the corner of the balcony this is one magical night. He approved with one strong yes and was continuing in silence to see in distance of water of ocean.

The younger man Zeeshan started to remember meeting with professor Bojana here their beautiful moment also he thought I gave to her one different idea about our communication and our relationship but thanks to "Allah" gave path to got good direction and to understand my situation.

Professor Bojana, is very good lady, and she is very smart lady, to understand that never to create hope for something that was not going to happen. I really did not want to give to her disappointing.

After he was thinking for the beautiful younger Albanian girl Agneza that was living in Lunaria village of Croatia. I do not know who will get direction my life now, but I feel so good for this girl, I think I am in love with her.

What is going with me?! I do not know myself anymore. It is going to be so longer without her, four years of university and those six months to finish high school with summer too, they are going five years totally, far away a long time and a long distance, plus her parents are not approving some of our tradition and principles of life and marriage.

Also, I cannot live without my children and my wife cannot live without her children so those are some bigger and very important issues, so both of us cannot live without our lovely beautiful children. Another reason is for me the big change the behave of my wife too.

Really, I love this younger innocent girl Agneza and I wish with full of my heart that this "Suddenly White Dream ", to happen and to became reality, but I will pray to "The Great Allah". He said to himself: This is the most beautiful quite night and is bringing to me only beautiful memories for really. Thank You Allah!

During this time the younger man Zeeshan, saw in distance on sidewalk close to the beach some different younger couples that were walking while one of those couples, were hugging each other and were laughing. When they were close to one, subtropical green trees, that its crown was bigger in circle shape, they went close to tree 's body where light of electric tower was not interfering and the boy kissed his girl while the other couples were walking forward in distance.

It was this couple under this beautiful tree, silver moon up to the sky, that was doing investigation for them with her light, while the stars were happy for this couple and gave diffuse light to make confuse their silver moon with its light, while the waves of water ocean were doing some noise like one romantic melody.

So. the universe with its power sent all those elements of nature to congratulate the love of this younger happy couple in this dark night.

The younger man felt so much warm inside himself and felt his eyes were full with tears, maybe he was reminding his love story with his wife Leylae, that after marriage have some problems as so many others couples on this earth planet.

... Or maybe he had tears in his eyes for this beautiful younger girl Agneza, that for that relationship, was foreseeing so many obstacles, like family's obstacles, emotional' s obstacles and social's obstacles too, in his life. Those are mysteries of universe about what and, why? at that time the younger man Zeeshan had tears in his eyes.

The leader of secret service Emin, saw him that he was covering with his hand his eyes, he understood that his younger boss Zeeshan was so much emotional and asked him: Are you okay?

The younger Man Zeeshan answered right away I am very okay but this night is so beautiful. The leader Emin, saw that he can speak clear was full emotional and came close to him while he saw tears in his eye. The leader friend of the younger man Zeeshan did not speak, while his boss Zeeshan said direct, that is life for this you see tears in my eyes.

The younger man Zeeshan said to him we can go now, after they left their balcony, went to their crew inside cafeteria and got out of this luxury building and got car to the parking and started driving for to go to the home of their boss and after everyone to go to their home too. it was one beautiful and quiet evening to this luxury cafeteria aside the ocean.

During their driving the younger man Zeeshan said to his friends. Today and specific tonight I understood how good job we have done for our people and specific for the younger people with this center and this sidewalk aside the ocean.

We have created one beautiful environment to give pleasure to people so they can spend some happy time during off day or holiday or during evening and specific during summer time in this beautiful environment while they will enjoy fresh air of the water of ocean.

All agreed with his speech and they said really this is beautiful environment.

So many people are coming here for weekend with family and their children too, and are enjoying walking on side walk while children are enjoying all sweets and popcorn that are buying in those ambulant stores.

The younger man started to walk through his beautiful garden with a lot different green color flowers that were resistance of this season creating one beautiful green carpet with their design by specialist of silviculture. The trees around were moving their branches with delicatesse under influence of the wind that was coming from the water of ocean during this night. The light of the beautiful of silver moon was giving light shining, to the path that he was walking.

Suddenly he stopped in front of the door of his beautiful palace and saw up to the sky for moment, he lifted his arms up and said loudly: Universe with all your beautiful stars and beautiful silver moon give to my life so much light, also and so much warm by your golden sun too.

While he entered inside of his palace and his lovely Zoros, dog was coming down to the stairs with speed and came to his feet while was moving all around his short and beautiful tale. The younger man laughed loudly when he saw his lovely dog Zoros that came with full love to him and got him to his arm, while, Zoros, dog was touching his chest with his head and was opening his eyes and was seeing all around.

The younger man with his lovely Zoros dog, entered to his studio at that time Aasma, the lady that was servicing to his kitchen came fast and asked what he will eat. He said: I want nothing really only one ice tea in one big cup glass and I am drinking to balcony. The younger man loved this evening and wanted to continue his thinking to balcony.

The lady brought the one big glass cup with ice tea and left to one small table to balcony in front of the younger man Zeeshan. He left his dog Zoros to the floor while he was coming around and he started to drink the ice tea.

He was thinking for life of the people in those country of the Western Balkan, and said most of them had very simple life but they were so much happy and so much friendly with each other.

He whispered with himself: I have everything but those walls of my palace are so cold and are sending to my body some frozen rays that making my heart frozen and my mind with deep confuse thoughts. Definitely I need to spend more time with my family with my children and to spend some happy time with my friends freely by job's problem.

I really need to apply some elements of life to the country of Western Balkan. Also, I will organize some picnics with my family, with my friends and their families and their children too. So, we will create some diversities in our life that is full with job's problem. My city is so beautiful and has so many cultural centers that, really, I need to visit with my small children.

Another problem is my story with this lovely younger girl Agneza. Really, I think, I love this girl but I do not want to put her in my family's problem, because I do not want to hurt her. She must to prepare herself with full enthusiasm to study the university next September because I never know how will go my situation with my wife Leylae, and why she started to change and to become warmer.

Definitely I do not want to distract Agneza from her objective, from her new direction of education, I think she started to love me too. I will support her and will make her time during university so much easy, so she never to think for anything in need but only to study.

She is very good student and very good girl too. She has her face so beautiful and looked so innocent in her thoughts, also she is very carefully about spending money too. At that moment with those thoughts the younger man Zeeshan started instinctively to write text message to Agneza. He wrote to her with some questions: How are you? How is going everything and your school too.

How you are taking care for Gentius? How you can give answer to all his questions about everything and the end he put one smile sign. He was very happy that he wrote to her. He felt that all the doubts thoughts that were so heavy to his head got out and he did not feel anymore, big weight to his head and to his chest.

After some minutes he heard one click to his cellular telephone and he open it right away. He saw replied text message from Agneza. The younger man Zeeshan started to read very fast. Agneza was writing simple English language, but in strict way she was writing answer for his questions.

The younger man Zeeshan felt like one invisible hand was touching his forehead and he felt so much calmer inside him and so much peaceful. He thought: What is happening with me? I do not know myself anymore. I think that I am in love with this younger girl Agneza.

He closed his eyes and started his imagination under the light of silver moon during this beautiful dark night decorated with all those stars up to the sky. For the moment he saw like flash light one white light in form of feather of big bird that was flying around his head.

He heard inside his head one noise like easy whisper: I know what are you thinking! It is one very longer way with so many obstacles. You must to prepare yourself to be strong for this new situation. There are two ways in front of your cross, one has table "Adventure" and another has name "Love".

If you have "Adventure" better not to start, because will be failure and for your family too, and will leave one bold sign like wound in your current and future relationship. This wound will not leave quite you and your current wife Leylae, too.

If you have "Love" really love you need to take so much efforts while now you are not prepared for that, needed so much hard job to create solid foundation for this new love. With those efforts you will win of course and will be really big change of your life too, because you have one experience now.

At that time, he saw that this white feather of big bird started her slowly flying up to the sky during this dark night, while the younger man Zeeshan started to speak loudly: What will happen with my two small children I cannot live without them?!

The white father continued its flying to the sky at the dark night, so the younger man Zeeshan, did not get answer, but he felt touching by one hand to his shoulder and heard those words: My dear Zeeshan what is happening with you? What you are talking loudly?

The younger man opened his eyes and he understood that he was speaking with himself, while saw Aasma, the lady that was like his mother, she raised him that was asking him. He smiled and said to her looks I was suddenly in one dream I saw one white feather of one big bird that was flying and I heard its voice or noise that was speaking with me and asked for my children, but I did not got answer.

She smiled and kissed him to forehead while said you my very dear son Zeeshan, are very tired and you have some fascinating figures about your problems, but anyway the white feather is faith sign or more exact every feather whatever color to be is faith sign, that is older 's saying in ancient.

Really it is very good that you saw one white feather, so definitely this is sign that you must to have faith for your children, because you asked with loudly voice, with full emotion, this white feather for your children. I heard you. So, your mind is working hard nonstop for your children whatever to happen in your life.

The younger man Zeeshan smiled and said: It is very true I love my children and never I can leave them alone in my life. The lady said to him. I know and I am sure that you love your children so much and never you will leave them alone. I see every day how much you are taking care for them, but now you need to go to sleep, because you are tired, is later night, and tomorrow you will go to work again to your office.

The younger man replied with smile and love: You are very right I am very tired and tomorrow I have so much to do to my office, I need to go to sleep now. At the moment that he stands up from his chair and started to walk to balcony he asked Aasma, the lady that was cooking and taking care for him and his family.

Please tell me from your experience how was your marriage with your husband and what is secret of your longer-term marriage, plus that you have some children too. She saw him with deep thoughts and said: I am telling you know.

Our families married us me and my husband. We were not rich families, but me and my husband after wedding we started to work right away. I was very lucky that your parents hired me in their home. I was working very hard because I wanted to establish myself in long term and so I did.

After that I established myself to your parents that I love them so much, so I secured my family and my four children two boys and two girls, that came more later in our life, with my job so if my husband will lose his job, I was secure here plus your parents were taking care so much for my family for their well-being.

My husband worked hard all his life and he never he lost his job too. So, our life was Okay about normal financial situation, and we secured four our children good life and their good education too, that was big sacrifice for us, but we worked and saved so much to give them education and you know them too.

Now we are happy that they have good job too. Now my four children all they are married while me and my husband are living close to your area, because of my job here.

While about all other problems as every couple we had some problems and specific with my husband's family because they were in poor situation and all the time, they needed help plus other problems but the key of my success of this longer-term marriage is one word: "Tolerance".

I applied tolerance with my husband and when happened that he was so much nervous, I was going to the other room until I calculated that his nervous situation was going down and was going again to living room and I said to him calmly:

We can drink one small cup of coffee now?.. or to take one small cup of ice cream? He was seeing very serious and with wondering after was smiling and said to me: Okay let's drink coffee, or let's take one cup of ice cream. So, his nerves were down and we were normal in communication.

So, Tolerance between couple is success of longer-term marriage.

I wan tot make bold and another point my dear son Zeeshan do not forget me and my husband we are old fashion so we were seeing the word divorce like one ashamed sign in front of our families, our relatives and our family's friends too. Another reason was and financial situation for our children so we never saw like alternative divorce for every conflict that maybe we had in our life.

The younger man Zeeshan, said to this lady: I understood the key of your success of your longer-term marriage. This is great experience for really, because family is very important. Since in family is starting rules and law of social life.

After he asked during the hall of his palace the lady: What is about your children's marriage – life? She answered while was laughing, Oooo they never are like me and my husband. They have so many disagreements, with each other, and they do not have so much patience. Really, I am working and advising them all the time, but they are saying to me: Mother is not your time now things are different.

I am saying to them things changing but family' rules about respect of each other about tolerance, and patience never are changing. With her last sentence they said to each other: Have a Good Night! So, the younger man Zeeshan, went to sleep in his bed room.

During this night he never can sleep but was thinking the words of the lady that took care for him all his life until now in adult age. The younger man Zeeshan, was thinking with himself:

These people were not rich but they started their life from ground zero and built with hard job until they achieved their good standard life, good condition for their children and good education for them. They have done so much sacrifice but all the time they were happy like couple.

While me I have everything that has created my grandfather and my father, I am living in very good and very rich environment since I have born but I have not happiness, that I was dreaming and I am not rich in love.

Now that I am feeling something really great love inside my heart, is coming this duplicate life for me between two women in my life. My current wife Leylae, that we were in some times in very difficult situation about our marriage that was going to the end and this very younger beautiful Albanian girl Agneza, that she is so much innocent and I understood that she started to love me now.

"Allah" with your super power give clarity to my mind and to my situation, but if you want to know that true for me now if you are asking me with all your "Angels" or "Meleqe" around you what is my situation?, I am telling you right now I am in very deep love with this girl Agneza.

With those thought he was coming around his bed but he cannot force himself to sleep. Strangely he got out of the bed and went to balcony, while was seeing the stars up to the dark sky.

He started to pray with his hands up. After he whispered to himself. I do not feel good myself, I do not get normal breath. He really was in big dilemma for his new situation. He felt anxious and he got walking to his kitchen to drink very cold water, after he got very cold water with ice too, he felt himself better.

He went again to balcony and was thinking: What to say now to Agneza for my new situation with my wife Leylae. I told her that I love her and I wanted to get her here not to go to study in Zayed University, and now this current situation came suddenly to me, but really I love this younger beautiful girl Agneza, I love her.

Anyway, I need to sleep because tomorrow I have meeting with so many people about this new project of new town close to desert's are. After meeting I will discuss with my secretary Salma, she to follow some of my duty and I need absolutely to make some day of from my job and to be quiet to see after where I am standing with my new situation in my family.

Nex morning he went with his secret service team to his office and did meeting with people that he invited for this new project. After he discussed with his secretary Salma, and told her that he really did not feel good himself, he explained to her, that he was not sick but something happened to him during those three trips in Western Balkan and he feels himself very tired for really.

He said to her that he will go with his family some days to one quiet village close to this city Dubai, that has beach but to be far away from noise of big city. He said to her, if you need me for any emergency call me or text me or e - mail to me.

The secretary Salma said to him everything will be oaky and I will put some appointment for next middle week. He approved her. With her words she wished to her younger boss Zeeshan a very good short vacation. He left her and got out while he told to Emin, his leader of secret service team that he will go with his family to the beach of the small village and they will be with him over there. He agreed and all of them agreed with him, they were happy to go for short vacation to this beach of this small village, that was not so much far away from their beautiful big modern city Dubai.

When he went in his palace, he told to his wife Leylae, that next day, they will go with their children for short vacation some days to the beach to the small village. He explained to her that he felt himself so much tired by those three trips in Western Balkan in short time, for business so he needs some days off now.

She shocked, she opened her eyes, she was not prepared for that vacation after what they have gone through in their relationship. She smiled her eyes started to fill with tears and she said I like that idea, let's go over there, and is very quiet place over there, while our children will be happy over there. We will have time to enjoy our vacation and to stay together with our children, days and night.

She said with full happiness I am going now to prepare clothes for our children and my clothes too since now afternoon. During this conversation he heard sign of his cellular that was telling to him that he has one message. The younger man Zeeshan said to his wife Leylae.

Okay, just do it! I am going to my studio to see some materials in my computer and who is sending me any e- mails also after we both are going to balcony, of the other room to drink hot chocolate and to enjoy this evening and to discuss for this short vacation.

His wife Leylae, did not believe to her ears what she was listening, she saw one big changing to his behavior she felt herself so much happy and said to her husband Zeeshan Okay, we will drink together hot chocolate to balcony.

She left him in hall in front of his studio – room and get to the children 's room. The younger man Zeeshan went to his studio and opened his cellular telephone and saw message by Agneza.

He felt glad for her message and was reading so fast and replied so fast to her. After he whispered to himself: I do not know myself anymore what I am doing for really. But really, I love my family and absolutely I want to be the very good father for my children too. So, this is very delicate situation for me for really.

Now I need to do this vacation that is it. With these thoughts and he did not understand how fast he was writing to this younger girl Agneza with some beautiful, expression of love while sent his message.

Very fast Agneza replied, she was writing that she was very happy for his very lovely text that he replied to her. She was continuing to write: Really, I am thinking so much for you those days, because you gave to me, to my brother Gentius, and to my cousins Armina and Dalmet some very beautiful days with great memories for our life.

You created for me in my youngest time one very beautiful necklace with so many value stones and pearls, "margaritares", diamonds, that will be hang to my brain for all my life. I am very happy that I know you. Now I want to tell something that maybe will be big and very beautiful surprise for you.

Now I changed my mind for this university and I am taking in consideration this option that you said to me to come to live with you over there when I am finishing this high school and in future I will study over there, university in your home city Dubai. I am feeling now that I miss you so much and I want to be with you all the time all my life.

She was continuing her writing with those words: You bought so much clothes for me so I do not need anymore, to buy anything over there but I will be with you over there. She was so much innocent and naïve too.

The younger man Zeeshan when was reading that he did not control himself but he screamed ooo my "Allah" help me while was continuing:

Ooooo, Agneza do not say that not now! Oooo, my "Allah" help me for this unexpected situation that I have created by myself. He started to write while his hands started to get shake, he was not controlling his hands but he wrote:

My dear Agneza I miss so much you too, about this problem of university we have time to discuss and about my idea that I told you. You are very right, but give me some times to finish this new project for new town that will be close to desert's area.

You must to know that needed so much job to do with so many people, so many specialists, like architects, accounts, businessmen, engineers pedologists, engineer of topographies, engineer of electric, construction companies and so many different corporations.

She wrote again: I understood you are right it is very big job and we have time to discuss for that because now is winter time I need and six months to finish this high school, but I wanted to tell you that I am agreed now with your idea that you told me to live with you in your country United Arab Amirates (UAE)and your home city Dubai.

The younger man Zeeshan was in deep thinking. This time came for the younger man Zeeshan, with so many new situations, some known and some unknown while some unexpected for their new direction that were following. Really life has so many surprises for anyone so no exception and for the younger man Zeeshan.

But this time the line of graphic for going for him from low level to high level and from high level to the line was going straight after was going down to low level and suddenly to high level again. So many big changing about reaction by current wife Leylae, during this time, and his new younger girlfriend Agneza too.

Another point of this graphic was fever of those, low and high waves of feelings cold and hot fever too. The younger man Zeeshan thought with himself:

Really is difficult to understand the nature of women, but now I need to focus, to this new project of the new town while to adopt with new situation that is creating by my wife Leylae, and this younger girl, very lovely Agneza. It is good for me for my health and for my state of my mind to see in distance the feelings of those two women in my life and to see where I am staying with them while to put balance in my life.

Really my love for Agneza, came in unexpected way. It was like one ray light in one dark situation. Thank You, "Allah" that you sent to me this lovely, younger, beautiful girl Agneza, in my life and brought so much optimism to me, also so much love to my heart and to my chest.

This new situation of this new love serviced like one big generator that gave so much energy in every vein of my body, to see brighter, my life and to have big hope for future that was one strong foundation of feelings about starting this new project.

This strong energy gave power and happiness to fly to Western Ballkan, and to see different levels of life of people in those different Balkan's countries also to know so many wonderful new people. I am very happy now. Thank you very much, "Allah" for this new situation and this strong and new love that you brought to my life like one precious gift.

My life with this new strong love it is like one jewelry with beautiful stones that their color is like the hour when the golden sun is going down below to the horizon, while the sky glows the warm and radiant the hues.

At that time is created the magical view, while in the sky is created one specter colorful started at the bottom with bold to easy purple color, while it is interfered, to easier, blue open after to green color, the other lay to red color, and other lay is bold pink color, in wide lay that is going to enter in intercalary way to yellow color.

This beautiful conglomerate of colors during Sunset is giving so much pleasure, to people, so and for me this new love is giving so much pleasure to my heart. I did not believe that during my cloudy, turbulent time "The Great Allah" will bring in my life this beautiful gift that turned right away the desperation situation to full happiness and new vision and clarity in my mind.

This is one of some others mysteries of Universe that showed in my life. During this situation the Universe with its powerful force that is full with positive energy by billions stars up to the sky, is giving to me, the hard creative job of this project about building new town close to desert's area, that I never to be depressed or down but to be more active in my job like leader of public service and this project too.

The younger man Zeeshan whispered with himself: I wish for everyone that is going through difficult situation like me to get that positive energy by Universe and to be happy. I want that the soft hand of "The Great Allah" to sweep from forehead of everyone the desperation and negative thoughts while to print peace with its hand and feelings of happiness, also to give free breath because the life is continuing anyway.

At same time the younger Zeeshan was thinking for Agneza about his love for her. He said to himself while was doing monologue. I know that Agneza now is struggling to believe that I truly love her. While instinctively he started to write message to her:

I want you always to trust to my divine love for you. Agneza you are so precious to me, more than you will ever know. I hope that you will understand me and will trust me that this unexpected love for you gave so much flood of light to my darkness situation and illuminated my mind, while gave so much enthusiasm and so much confident hope for my life now.

This my new love for you that came from an unexpected way that day that I saw you on the beach with your brother Gentius, and your friends, it was like one "ortek", that collected all my open and hidden feelings of love and together with those feelings made me to fly to Western Balkan and to meet you again, and again.

My friends did not wait any second to explain to them about those trips in Western Balkan and Center of Europe, in Vienna of Austria, but they said it is because of this younger beautiful girl Agneza. I think my love for you never will fail, but I hope our love will be bright.

This is strong love for me, now I am understanding, "That no one knows and understand love until to receive love", so I will wait you because I love you. After he sent this text message to his younger girl Agneza.

The younger man Zeeshan was thinking in deep way and said "How came my life in this way? How my life got this stranger direction?, really now I am in cross-road with my family and my new lover. With my new love story, I feel myself so much happy and so much younger.

Anyway, I have time for solution until Agneza is going to study for four years in university of Ljubljana of Slovenia. Now I need to concentrate all my knowledge to this new project and I must to be focused about preparing and starting this new project of new town close to desert's area.

This love for Agneza gave me so much inspiration for my future life.

The younger man Zeeshan said to himself my situation is coming so much complicated. There are times in relationship when is big conflict and is coming time to prepare for deep separation while is born new love so without expressing with voice but inside the chest I think one of women must to leave, but really no one of those is leaving while I am now in deep love with this younger girl Agneza.

Now there are two women in my life that they want full love and two children they absolutely they want unconditional love above every conflict or bad situation in couple. In my heart is now one very beautiful new feelings of great love that is growing up with speed but potential of my wife that is claiming to posses' place in my heart because of her power of our children is giving shadow to these new feelings.

This feeling is like the fresh green grain plant that is coming above the ground on field and one wild plant is blocking it while is coming around the green leaves of grain and is not allowing to grow to get sun's rays and to create photosynthesis.

So needed to get out the wild plant on the field, so to allow green grain plant to grow up and to give fruit. Really in my situation I am not sure for really whom I must to select.

Changing behave of my wife Leylae, is giving me some dizzy situation, but is giving and some happiness for her coming back with feelings to me, while for the younger girl Agneza now it is really love but are so many, obstacles in long run in our journey that is giving some doubts and shake to the foundation of this new love.

Also, her parents and she, do not practice our tradition about marriage with more than one spouse or wife, if they will accept that condition, will be so much easy for me, without any problems by me. Really, I am in cross road now and I do not know myself anymore.

Let's hope what is coming in future, maybe the sun with its hot's rays will make to change situation about wild plant, while will dry and will release the fresh green grain plant to grow up.

So, and for my situation the universe with its positive energy will give way in peaceful, to open space for one of them, one of those two women. For moment I am enjoying in unexpected way, for really the quiet situation of my family and I am dreaming so much for this "Suddenly White Dream ", with this beautiful younger Albanian girl Agneza to become reality.

Really, I do not have courage like one strong with full experience farmer to get out the wild plant that is attachment to culture plant. To make selection about feelings of people, to one two or more persons, it is not easy for really. I am sensible about this point.

I love this calm situation in my family now, but I cannot sleep quite while thoughts are dancing to my head all the night with one strong melody about this younger girl Agneza.

During this time of this small vacation, I need to concentrate to my project of this new town, while I will spend so much time with my small children while I will give them pleasure with my full presence during those days.

With those thoughts the younger man Zeeshan, close that day while left his studio and went to sleep. Next day they started all family, their trip with car and his full team of secret service to go to this quiet place of beach.

When they arrived over there, the beach was to one corner that all around was surrounding with some soft beautiful hills with some rare trees for really. They arrived to one flat building that some people were waiting them in front of this building.

They came to say to the younger man Zeeshan, to his wife Leylae, and his children and all others men one sweet "Welcome". They got their luggage, some plastic supplies, of children for to play in water of ocean, and some small boxes with different items inside.

The younger man Zeeshan, whispered with himself: "Ooohhh Allah" help me something I felt inside my chest, I cannot breath. This beautiful place is like the section of the beach that I saw for the first time the younger girl Agneza. The leader of secret service Emin, came close to him while he saw that the younger man Zeeshan was putting his hand to his forehead and asked him: What happened you have pain? Do you have headache? At that time, he ordered one lady that were servicing in this flat building: Go and bring fast one glass water with ice.

They were in front of the building, while his children were asking their mother for so many things about this beach and who knows what they were pointing with their finger straight to ocean. At that time his wife Leylae, heard the leader that order for water and saw the younger man Zeeshan, her husband that got one easy yellow color in his face.

She got scared, and asked fast what happened while left her children to take care another younger lady and came to her husband Zeeshan. She asked him: What happened with you. He did not answer only was seeing her straight to her eyes and said to her:

All the time you must to take care for our children whatever to be and whatever to happen with me. But now I am better. Maybe was this situation because I did not eat breakfast, only I got and was drinking one cup of coffee.

When the lady came with one glass with water and another silver tank with so many ice's cubes, she gave to the younger man Zeeshan, at this moment the younger, man Zeeshan, said to his friend Emin, leader of secret service team.

This place is like the place of the beach that we saw those Albanian people with their children that really are living to Croatia, and reminded me the moment that I saw this very younger, beautiful, girl Agneza.

Really, I do not feel good myself now. I do not know but I cannot get out her face from my mind. His friends Emin, saw his younger boss Zeeshan, that was weak and some tears were filling his beautiful black color big eyes. His friend said to the younger man Zeeshan, drink this water and do not be sick get calm because "Allah" with his power will give good way for both of you for you and your lover younger girl Agneza.

He wanted to make calm his younger boss Zeeshan, because he loved so much his boss and he did not want to happened something bad to him. He knows that his boss Zeeshan, was in deep love with this girl Agneza and that he was so much sensitive too. The leader of secret service Emin, said to the younger man, Zeeshan:

We all came here for fun not to be desperate so please focus now in this situation and later, you must to call, Agneza in telephone and you will feel quieter yourself. The younger man Zeeshan, started to explain to his friend:

I feel that I left her over there so far away, like she is alone but she has her family. I saw myself with my wife Leylae, and my children here in this beautiful place and all of you and I thought about Agneza, I felt weak myself and something came up to my stomach like acute pain.

I was very close with her last trip that we were for ski, in Vienna, Austria, that was the most beautiful, vacation in my life, really was cold winter but I found full hot love to this girl Agneza for me, I was very happy over there. Also, I was very happy for all people from universities, that came from Ljubljana of Slovenia and Vienna of Austria, to meet all of us. It was one wonderful, vacation for really.

The leader of secret service team Emin, replied: While was laughing. Really it was the most beautiful vacation for all of us, Thank You, very much by you for this opportunity that you gave to all of us, because we are really your friends and we love you so much plus, our duty for you to protect you and your family and people that you love.

More beautiful was curiosity of Gentius and strong love that he was showing for you in front of all, looked that he did not want anyone to touch or to take you. Also, I have fixed the calm and beautiful face of your lover girl Agneza and her very lovely watching to you all the time, she was so calm, so soft, really so lovely and beautiful.

We all were happy for your happiness with this girl Agneza, but what to say now, this is life with so many mysteries and surprises. You have your family now that situation took turn U so fast. Definitely this situation it is up to you now, what direction you will give to your life.

Of course, we all never will forget your desperation time, but now situation changed, and you have changed for better, now you are stronger. This girl Agneza gave to you so much inspiration for life and to be more active.

Also, those three trips in Western Ballkan were so beautiful, so much interesting with very lovely people and were decisive and gave big impact to you, to your life and to your big changing. I am happy for you for this big changing.

I am proud of you for your strength and optimism in life and job and so many others in your office and your department are commenting for good your situation and your big changing but really, they do not know the secret. "This is the power of love".

The power of love it is making people to get healing, it is making people to climb high mountain, it is making people to escape the most difficult situation in life, definitely the power of love is giving to people so much hope.

The power of love is making the life of people like one very beautiful melody, that everyone wants, to listen all the time, again and again.

At that time the younger man Zeeshan, smiled and said yes, it is true, "The power of love is making, people to escape mountains, seas and oceans, like me that I went three times in Western Ballkan with all of you my best and lovely friends.

The power of love is like very beautiful dancing like Waltz of Strauss in big concert of Vienna of Austria, that most of the time is ritual for every new year, and when one couple is dancing so happy and beautiful, all are happy to see them and to campaign them in waltz, so it is, the power of love for one couple that is getting support by all the best friends.

When the love of one couple is getting support by all their best friends and does not have intrigues to separate them for so many unreasonable reasons this is the most beautiful situation, it is like one correlation of two beautiful rare flowers on green grass of the field with so many other multicolor flowers that making addition of their beauty in nature.

Really, I love my family as always, I loved it, but what happened it was not in my hand so this difficult situation was escalating by so many sides of our two families and other acquaintance that were doing intervention in different ways with different opinion and were creating distract and diffuse but not with bad purpose.

Suddenly in this very turbulent time, came this new situation, that you know very well because I was with all of you my friends to that beach, last August, when I saw this girl Agneza. Maybe "Allah" that is the Great sent that beautiful gift this girl Agneza, and her very lovely brother Gentius, for me to make drastic change plus all those teenagers that gave to all of us so much enthusiasm with their innocence and their full optimism. Above of all I am very happy that I have with my side all the time all of you my best friends. Now let's enjoy all of us with my family too, this small and short vacation in this beautiful small beach.

When the younger man Zeeshan, entered inside this summer - house and he saw that his wife Leylae, that was preparing children for the beach was changing their dresses. He took seat to one chair and was seeing his children that were so happy and were doing noise that they wanted to go out so fast to the beach. The younger man Zeeshan, started to laugh.

At that moment his wife Leylae, said to one lady to take care for children and their dresses and went close to her husband Zeeshan. What happened with you today? She was showing her wondering but strangely he did not see to her face and to her eyes to her watching, pain. While she started to speak with some irony but not in bold way. Maybe you got some sick in Western Balkan or maybe any other matter that is not leaving you quiet.

The younger man Zeeshan, was thinking at that moment: She is not changing, or more exact she is playing role now, but I do not know that she knows something or maybe somebody told her who knows!

The younger man Zeeshan, replied to her while was laughing: Okay can you tell me what is this matter that is not leaving me quiet? There are so many matters about you no to leave quiet his wife Leylae, said to him, but was not seeing him in his eyes but was enrollment her beautiful eyes all around the room.

The younger man Zeeshan, was continuing this conversation, he wanted to discover, if she has any information about that younger girl Agneza in Western Balkan.

Tell me with your very bright mind and you do not want to move your eyes all around the room, but make more specific what is this important matter that is not leaving me quiet, maybe you know more better than me.

His wife Leylae, was doing with her finger all around the room and said: This room is so beautiful, with design and furniture too, for this I am moving my eyes all around. Really, she wanted to win time with that kind of reply to her husband Zeeshan, and to think what matter she will tell to him. The younger man Zeeshan, said to his wife Leylae, this room is very beautiful and you are so beautiful, but when I am speaking with you, it is not affecting me this beauty of this room but I am seeing straight to your beautiful eyes and beautiful face too.

So please tell me and help me what is this matter that is not leaving me quiet? His wife replied: Okay I think is something serious this matter for you that you travel three times in short period of time in Wester Balkan.

Plus, this matter maybe is putting some new clouds to our last hard relationship that has related and with our difficult situation that was between us about communication and about of our two families. The younger man Zeeshan, said: It is true that we were going through one difficult situation in our relationship, last times, but this does not mean that we cannot find solution and to change better our situation.

His wife Leylae, said to him: Yes, it can happen but is depend to you how you will turn this situation for better. The younger man Zeeshan, said to her: I think this is depend more to you than to me to come better situation.

For the moment the younger man Zeeshan, felt inside him one cold feeling that touched all his body and was moving from head to toes of the feet. He thought she is not changing but maybe her parents want to have some profit by her from my family.

I feel that I love that girl Agneza, she looked so much innocent and so much clarity, I saw in her face and during her speech. I love her, I will take care for her, really, I do not want to lose her. Definitely I will wait her and time by time I will go to visit her in university of Ljubljana of Slovenia.

While for my current wife Leylae, I will see what will happen in our communication and our relationship and most of all I will see her family what plan has now after our difficult situation. If is going more worse situation, I will see them what they want like compensation in the name of their daughter that is now my wife and mother of my two children.

If is coming bad situation I need to stay close with my father by his side and to help him to manage this situation calmer. Really, I am very happy that I am in strong and deep love with that younger beautiful Albanian girl Agneza in Lunaria of Croatia of Western Balkan. After the younger man Zeeshan said:

Thank You "Allah" for that great love that is gift by you this time.

The younger man Zeeshan, did not continue this conversation anymore but said in strict way, I am changing my dress and I am taking children to go to the beach, you can finish what you have started and come over there, we are waiting you over there.

His wife Leylae, said to him: You are right I must to establish all those clothes in shelves and I am coming over there. After some minutes while her husband Zeeshan, got out with two children that were doing noise with happiness with some plastic toys in their hand that they will play in the water, she was establishing the clothes and was putting in two separates wood 's shelves.

She was thinking about her situation with her husband, while was whispering with herself, so many big changing by him. I am scare that I will see our marriage to the end, while I cannot stop my jealousy about everything, really, I created this conflict and my family escalated in high level.

Really, I love so much my husband and I cannot imagine my life without him, but I cannot stop myself with, those doubts. I see that last time he is not sad like before that I was thinking that he is suffering and I will be priority for him.

I feel that he is so happy maybe by someone new lady, that gave to him inspiration for job and those trips in Western Balkan. I see that during my conversation with him, he does not show pain to his eyes when I give some hard words, but he is quiet and his mind is somewhere that is giving peace to him.

The other phenomenon that I see now to him is that I do not see that his eyes to fill with tears when I am blaming or giving any provocation to him, really this situation is giving deep pain inside of me. I am very scared to think that I am losing my very lovely husband Zeeshan.

For the first time I think that it was in need for me to listen my parents for this situation, and to make more worse situation with my husband and his family. Excuse me "Allah" that I am thinking in this way for my parents that they tried everything good for me, but I love so much my husband Zeeshan, and I do not want to lose him and to destroy my very beautiful life that so many people are dreaming it, on this Earth planet. I was not controlling myself by jealousy and I sent in dead point of sadness my husband Zeeshan, that was trying so much to shut down that conflict during that time.

Now I see big difference to him because he is not saying like before, I like this dress or get and wear the other dress to go out, also he never is saying to me I like that way of model of your hair today, or I like this kind of color of lipstick or change this lipstick today with those clothes. He is not seeing me with feeling of admire like before about my appearance, he is not like before.

Most of all he was not jealous when he got news, that I got out alone to this department of architects' women and center of business. He only asked me with laughing what was the reason that I went over there and after he said he will send his security team for protection of me when I will go back to our palace and that is it.

Really it hurts me because I thought he will be mad for my action. I cannot accept that he is becoming more tolerant because I know him, he was overdue jealous for me before, since he cannot concentrate himself if in front of others with his wild, watching. Really is not him that I know before is big changing and this kind of changing is not sounding good for me and our situation.

Now he wants to stay more time alone and is justifying himself when is coming from his job that he has something to do in his studio. Only one thing is true that he never changed with our two children that he loves them so much.

He is trying to keep silence and quiet situation in home but his passion is gone it is not like before, this is hurting me for really. I want him to come back to me with his full passion. Ooo Great "Allah" help me for this situation, please help me and turn back the great love of my husband Zeeshan.

At that time, she felt her tears were dropping to her face in heavy way and she cannot, stop her suddenly crying, while she did not hear the other lady came to ask her something and saw her crying. The younger lady asked her if is any big problem, but Leylae the wife of the younger man Zeeshan, replied:

No, it is not any big problem but I was with my children some days to my parents to visit them, and all the time separation with people is giving me pain and nostalgia and I miss so much my mother too.

The younger lady said, yes, it is true, and I miss my mother when she is going to see her family and stayed over there some days, while I with my siblings, brother and sisters, we are staying with our father and our grandparents by father side to our home.

After she said to her: Do not get sad you will spend the wonderful time here and we are here to service to you. We are very happy that you came here with your husband and your two children too, really all people that are working here are happy, we got glad since the day that we got news that Prince Zeeshan with you with your children, all family will come here.

After that Leylae, the wife of the younger man Zeeshan, wore the colorful dresses for beach and her beautiful bath suit, put one big hat white color with one blue open silk ribbon, for protection by sun and got out of the room and building to go to her husband Zeeshan and her two children to the sand close to ocean.

She was walking to the sand while was seeing her husband Zeeshan with theirr two children were playing on the sand with one small beautiful turtle with mixer color that dominated green color and some, interference of yellow color.

They were trying to push the turtle to the ocean but turtle was walking so slowly and noise of children while laughing and screaming with happiness, with turtle were giving enthusiasm to this empty beach. She said: Thank you "Allah" I have the most beautiful and happy family.

She went over there, and they were together, during this beautiful day while the sun was giving his golden rays to blue water of ocean, while was coming one easy wind and temperature was around 24 Grade Celsius, so was not cold but was not very hot but beautiful weather to enjoy the beach.

Her husband Zeeshan, said to his wife Leylae, welcome, and he kept himself busy with his children, so full preoccupation were his children in this beautiful day on the beach. She was seeing him and said to herself he changed so much with me, but I will pray and hope that he has not fell in love with someone for a while all the others we will fix together. "Allah" help me for my problem and for my husband too, and I will try to prevent my jealousy that really it is something difficult and I will prevent my other provocative behave in future too.

She went close to them and her children came to her with full happiness, while she hugged and kissed them took sit on the sand while said to her husband, that weather is so beautiful today, while got out of the big colorful bag of the beach two small bottle with orange liquid and gave to two children. But they did not want orange liquid they started to say that wanted strawberry liquid.

She got out two the other two small bottle with strawberry juice (liquid), and gave to them, she knows preference of their children she was preparing for that, while she gave to her husband one more big bottle with orange juice.

Two children were very happy and started to drink that strawberry juice, while the younger man Zeeshan, started to prepare their plastic small boats and to go with them in water of ocean to play with them.

He did not have attention for another thing but was focused to prepare those two plastic small boats for children and he did not hear the ring, or more exact he heard the ring but he did not give attention to that to his telephone, he was full occupied to his children this day, he really wanted to give them one beautiful and joy day on the beach. He decided those days to be able only for his children not others people.

Strangely, and suddenly pop up one unforeseen problem, because after ringing was one sound that is specific of text message in cellular telephone. So, the wife of the younger man Zeeshan, opened with delicatesse but not in hidden way the telephone and was controlling the text message.

She thought whatever to be I will say to him that I thought maybe was coming from your job's office this text message and I wanted to tell you. When she opened the telephone and was reading the text message by Agneza, that has some expressing of love but not in bold way but everybody that will read that text message will understands feelings of love.

She felt one high level fever was rising inside her chest and her breath was taking, difficult, she felt herself in bad situation one big jealousy exploded from her chest and her heart while her tears suddenly were coming down with speed through, her beautiful face.

This unexpected problem came like one fast light during sunny day, that no one foreseeing. Really those are the mysteries of universe with its magical power to make clear to couple or people about one shadow situation so the universe is bringing in surface the truth, and after that people or couple must to deal with this true situation and what solution they will give to the truth not to lie or to cover up situation.

She got the telephone and went to her husband, Zeeshan, she did not want to yell and scream like before because she saw he was working hard for his children was a little difficult to prepare those plastic boats, also two children were so happy around their father while was seeing him to work and were waiting those plastic boats to go to the blue water of ocean.

She said to him while was showing his, telephone, one lady Agneza, is writing to you one text message because you did not answer to her calling, but during this text message I understood some romantic points.

She felt that her body was going to fell to the sand and her hands were taking shake. She was waiting his replied while was commenting to him, I opened because I thought are your people from office, but I saw different situation that is lucky for you and strong sad pain for me.

At that time the younger man Zeeshan, understood situation while he did not want to escalate the big conflict and said to her:

First it is very good that came this text message and you feel some romantic point, this is very good that is telling me that people love me and do not forget I am "PRINCE" right, he repeated again right. She said right you are "PRINCE", she spoke something with irony in bold way.

The younger man Zeeshan, continued and you loved me for this reason that I am Prince, right? Right?, he spoke again. She said: Between others reasons it was and this reason, I loved that you are "PRINCE".

Okay let's love me people what is difference?! You never can stop people to love me for others reasons and for this reason of my monarchy' status that I have and I am enjoying. Good for you to be this way, you to make me to love you so much. Your strategy is to hold our beautiful family and to have long term our marriage, and tactic is you to make me to love you.

If you are continuing with this way of fighting all the time you will become sick, our marriage will get one hard and deep crack and will get break up until to the end to divorce. While I will see in front of me one huge like water blue of ocean with so many people, ladies, (and their parents that want to give their daughters or their sisters or their cousins in my life to marry with me), that like fishes inside water to swim straight to me and to claim to love and to marry with me, that is it.

So, you will lose me, your lovely and hard- working, husband that is doing everything, for his wife and his two children, so you will lose me with your jealousy. The younger man Zeeshan, was speaking and was working with those plastic boats for his children, he did not yell and never spoke with jealousy.

He did not want to scare his very lovely children but he thought better that she saw, if it is coming to the end our relationship and our marriage, she will know who will be in line. Really, he was happy that Agneza was taking care for him and was calling and writing text message, he felt so much happiness, so he did not get mad with his wife, he understood her situation, but he wanted to make her calm.

To finish his conversation about this topic he explained to her: Listen me very carefully, during those three trips on Western Balkan I met so many wonderful people between them and students and professor ladies. All of them are in touch with me all the time during this period time.

One of them came to visit me in our city Dubai, right away after first trip, and we have created so much activities about life here we had meeting with women- organization, with leaders and student of "Zayed" 's University and so many visits to our city, Dubai, so during that time that you with your families were preparing strong war and scenario, against me and my family too, I was busy with activity.

I respected her and she never can forget but all the time is honoring me while all newspapers in her beautiful city Ljubljana of country Slovenia, wrote for this activity by her notice – writing's memories, while the others ladies are from Croatia, Montenegro, Austria and students too, and others professors.

So just you to know was business trip and experience we to learn by them and they to learn by us in our city Dubai and our Country United Arab Emirates (UAE), so this lady is one from those students and that is it nothing more, they have different culture from us and are very lovely people.

Now I am advising you my dear wife Leylae, do not destroy this beautiful short vacation those days with our children because I need to relax from problems. Those three trips in Western Ballkan's countries were in short time very heavy with schedule I was with full my staff- people of my office, so I was tired but you will see when I will write my book, about those three interesting trips and about those countries.

So, and for problems in my office those days I was and got tired and I decided to do this short vacation and to be happy with my family with you and with my very lovely children.

I thought this vacation we will improve and consolidate our relationship and our marriage, so I am doing everything to achieve my goal, but if not happening the universe will give way to our marriage. So, I am praying to "Allah" to give good direction what is the best for both of us and our two children.

Really, I want to enjoy this vacation and not to think for any bad and negative thing. It is very interesting what "Allah" is giving so many problems to the richer people on this Earth planet.

We have everything in our family that others people are dreaming and for all their life they cannot achieve that situation and this high financial situation, but we do not have happiness all the time fighting.

I saw in Western Balkan in those three countries, Croatia, Slovenia, and Montenegro, that people younger and older, were not rich were working very hard in different job with different way to create something good for their families, some of them were surviving but they were so much happy with their families and with their friends too.

This I pointed during my visit over there, strong and happy families also strong and happy friendship all around in store, in hotel, in restaurants, in cafeteria, in universities, in school if and on the street and boulevard people were together with smile. They were full with glad feelings and very well - educated people too.

After that conversation, the younger man Zeeshan, finished his job about preparing the plastic boats and got his two children and went to the blue water of ocean entered inside it.

He put every one of his children in each plastic boat, while was holding with his hands those two plastic boats and was coming around slowly, slowly, through the blue water of ocean. His wife Leylae, was laid on the yellow sand, while was seeing her husband with their two children, and whispered with herself:

I love my husband but I can't stop my wild jealousy. I am scared that with my very impulse behave I will destroy my marriage. "Allah" excuse me but it the first time that I am blaming myself about cooperating with my parents in this wild war, for my husband and his family and parents too.

I felt that I was seeing myself like very co-depended to my parents if this situation was going to the end. I was very selfish and I did not think about my children that are and his children too. Really at that time with my jealousy and my capriccio, I was thinking only for myself, also it was risk I to lose and custody of my children depended to my financial situation.

Definitely I need to see any Doctor Psychology, I must to start psycho-therapy, with psychology. I need to help myself anyway and to save my marriage.

Also is happening one good thing and I need to prepare myself for this project for one new section of this new town that I will put my name in it. So, I will keep busy myself and I will not have vacantly time to think for negative things.

During this time that she jumped in her deep thoughts, she saw in distance one crew of white Flamingo, (Pelikans) birds, some of them were big white Flamingo birds, and some of them were white small Flamingo birds, that were flying above the blue water of ocean. When they were flying close to the small plastic boats, two small white Flamingo (Pelikans) birds, came down while stayed each of them to each small plastic boats where were staying two children.

At that time two children started to cheer with full happiness, each of one white Flamingo, (Pelikans) birds, were seeing with wondering each of one of children with their cheers and were not moving.

The younger man Zeeshan, whispered with himself: Thank You "Allah" that you brought those two white Flamingo to my children, so my children will have peace in their life in future. After he turned his head in direction where was his wife, to see her while said to her with loudly voice, that she will be able to hear in that small distance over there laid on the yellow sand:

Look our two children will have peace in their life. Look carefully each of those white Flamingo birds, stopped their flying and came down while each of them is staying to each small plastic boat in front of our children.

His wife Leylae, laughed while was seeing others white Flamingo (Pelikans) birds, that were flying up to the sky and were doing crau, crau, crau, crau.

The younger man Zeeshan, spent all the day on the beach with his family, with his wife but most of the time with his two children with their small plastic boats on the blue water of ocean.

After this quiet beautiful day that really the younger man Zeeshan, erased the conflict that was creating suddenly. They went to building to eat lunch. Later afternoon they were walking on the beach aside the ocean together with friends of the younger man Zeeshan.

The evening was opening the path for the dark night to come with all her beautiful stars. Looked that the golden sun was capricious to leave his place to beautiful silver moon and why both of them are best friends of universe and together are cooperating for the weather of Earth planet.

The golden sun was playing with blue water of ocean while was sending to it the orange to pink color its rays during process of sunset and was happy to see itself in mirror on the blue water of ocean, but the white waves were more capricious and were moving to cover or to destroy its view or beautiful image or golden sun.

The sun started to withdraw and to collect all its orange to pink rays of process of sunset and was putting his rays inside his gas body, while was going with elegance and slowly was moving behind one white cloud up to the sky.

That time so many white waves came with their power and pride for their white color close to the yellow sand, whole the golden sun thought:

Who is spending time with those lazy white waves of blue water of ocean, better, to leave those on the light hand of my best friend the silver moon and her allies the universe's military of billion stars up to the sky.

During the night silver moon and the bright stars are giving fresh air and serenity down to Earth planet so the white waves will not dance like crazy under water. This beautiful evening that was saying welcome to the dark night decorated with beautiful stars, the younger man Zeeshan, was enjoying with his family and his friends too.

After dinner the younger man Zeeshan, was very tired and said to his wife Leylae,: Reall I am very tired and I need to sleep right away. She approved and she went to prepare her two children to sleep. During the night the younger man Zeeshan, was living un-conscience one very interesting dream.

He was swimming on blue water of ocean, suddenly the golden sun was covered by one heavy grey cloud and some big white wild waves were moving his body inside the water and on surface. He was terrified when in front of him appeared one white angel that opened its big white arms. At that time, he heard one female 's voice that was calling:

Prince Zeeshan, looks here it is me Agneza. She was to one white small boat and land one white longer plastic stick to him, to help him to hold himself to that stick and to come to the white boat. He got the stick was holding it and arrived to the white small boat.

Agneza with one adult man dropped one plastic staircase that was attached to the white boat. To one side of the boat, he (the younger man Zeeshan) saw one part in parallelogram shape painted with blue open color while was one title wrote with bold white color:

"SUDDENLY WHITE DREAM"!

THE YOUNGER MAN ZEESHAN, WAS WATCHING THIS TITLE, THIS PHRASE for moment he was confuse while was thinking where and when I have read this phrase, after he climbed the white plastic stairs and entered in the board of the white boat.

At that time came Agneza and hugged him strong while her tears were going down to her beautiful face. She started to kiss him with full of love while said to him: If will happen something to you my life will be full pain and dark because "I love you so much".

The younger man Zeeshan, hugged this lovely beautiful Albanian girl Agneza, while he started to kiss her with full passion and said:

"I love so much you Agneza!", also I cannot live without you!

His wife Leylae, heard that her husband Zeeshan, was talking during sleeping but really, she did not listen, in details, after she moved him in gentle, that her husband Zeeshan, to get awake. He opened his eyes and asked: Where I am now?!

His wife did not tell to him where he was but said to him while was watching him with full attention straight to his eyes in investigation way. You were talking so much during your sleeping. He did not speak but he thought:

Oooo, "Allah", it was only dream and Agneza came and save me she saved my life during this difficult weather like hurricane through wild and big white waves of the blue water of ocean. It was dream, that I saw the title of the white small boat, that is wrote to one part of the side of small boat painted with blue open color, with capital letters, with white color:

"SUDDENLY WHITE DREAM"!

So, my dream maybe will turn reality. I am happy that I saw Agneza. Really, I love so much this calmer, beautiful Albanian girl. I fell in deep love with her.

Thank You "Allah" and please help me in longer journey. I am in difficult situation but really 100% that I am in deep love with this girl Agneza. This beautiful love came from nowhere in the time that never I was waiting and never I was feeling and thought about it. Now I am very happy that I love this girl Agneza. We have so many differences about the life and so many different traditions, and different culture of living, but maybe "Allah" brought this beautiful gift to my life and I need to enjoy it with full of my heart.

The younger man Zeeshan, did not think what said his wife Leylae, but whispered: I love Agneza with full of my heart. When I see her is like the fresh air of the spring time is entering to my chest to my lungs and is giving to me freely breath.

She changed my very deeply desperation situation in full happiness. Agneza gave to me hope for my life in future, plus she gave me oxygen and inspiration to create new vision project. Agneza, her younger brother Gentius and her two cousins Armira and Dalmet, gave me full love and never they counted or thought for my money or my social status.

Ooo "Allah" help me for this difficult situation with my family but the true is that now I am in love with the beautiful younger Albanian girl Agneza.

"Allah" help me now, I am in your secure hand. I am waiting your direction, whatever you to decide I will follow your way, your decision, but I am repeating:

I am really in deep love with Agneza. Without her the day will be not shinning by the rays of golden sun. The park and the field will not have their colorful beauty by flowers in front of my eyes.

When is happening than the golden sun to shine above and around our beautiful modern city Dubai, the rain will not shower the ground will happiness in front of me.

The flowers will not open their colorful petals, while the trees will not open their green leaves to enjoy the rain with its melodious sound but all colorful petals and green leaves will get shrink, while the rain will touch tangent them and will go nervous in the ground for this skeptical environment while will create erosion of ground in capricious way.

During this time the powerful angel Ramuel, that is the closest angel to the God, and is guiding the good souls in heaven will see my good soul to suffer, so will send its thunder and nothing will be in harmony.

While the dark night will not show its magical beauty with its silver moon and beautiful stars that will not doing sparkling while the moon will be painting with dark, grey prints that will bring full bad luck.

I will not enjoy aside the water of ocean the light of beautiful silver moon and all small and big stars above white color waves of water of ocean. So, I will see only dark night and desperate sounds of waves. The white Flamingo birds will not fly with happiness with their noise crau, crau crau crau.

Nothing will be in harmony of nature on daily and night life in front of me. During my suffering for this love maybe the Raguel Angel that is angel of justice and harmony will give justice and harmony for my great love.

The great "Allah", that will be witness of my situation of life's suffering without Agneza,... with those whispers the younger man Zeeshan, got out of the bed while said to his wife Leylae, that she was standing up in front of him:

I need to drink coffee, really, I was tired yesterday. It was very early in the morning when he was going to prepare and to drink coffee. Through window he saw that was starting the sunrise.

He thought: I wanted so much this short vacation, but started not good. I think that is so much quiet here. I am learning with energize city and people that are moving around with energize too, also I saw so much energize people that were moving around in those three countries in Western Balkan.

I do not know why I do not feel happy myself in this place. Only happiness for me here are our two children. Really, I am lucky that I have my friends with me here, also I love my loyal friend Emin, the leader of my security team, he understands me very well.

I am wondering how much I changed with presence of my wife here, before during the time of our conflict, my tears were coming down to my face without my permission and so much pain to my chest, I had. Now no more pain and no more tears. It is strange how is evolution of feelings to people.

The younger man Zeeshan, prepared by himself coffee and was drinking alone in kitchen. He was thinking that he was not in good mood to stay longer to this beach, if for those some days, he was thinking to turn to city as soon as possible. He thought that he will relax somedays in quiet place but strangely he did not like this time, he was under pressure of one big flux of so many thoughts.

He was thinking that for his situation and his transition of feelings during this period time will be good therapy for him to be in city with full activity and with meeting with so many people and energize life because this quiet place was doing more sick him.

He was thinking all the time for his situation, that was creating one battle of different thoughts inside his brain. He thought that will be better for him to be busy and so he will not have so much time for thinking and most of all for some dark thoughts. He loved his family he wanted to go smooth this strange situation, that he was showing up that he was happy but really, he was not happy at all.

The younger man Zeeshan, was thinking with nostalgia all the time in this quiet place, for his younger girl Agneza. He understood that he was not controlling his thoughts about this girl and where he was talking with his friends.

His loyal friend Emin, understood him and time by time he said to his younger boss Zeeshan, you are not here, with your thoughts and was smiling. He was right because the younger man Zeeshan, was thinking for Agneza.

He decided to find one reason and to tell to his wife and friends that they will leave this place very soon they will not stay all the week because he has job to do. Strangely when he was thinking about that matter, he heard early in the morning one longer ring to his telephone cellular. He did not get the telephone and did not open it but really the ring was continuing with loudly sound so he got the telephone.

He heard the voice of his secretary Salma, that started to speak fast:

Sorry for calling today very early, but I thought to call you before I to go to the office, because one group of people from our country's President's office is coming to our office and they want to meet with you. They said that after two days they will be here. Really the younger man Zeeshan, was very happy for this news and he gave big shocking to his secretary Salma, that said with full happiness and laughing that he will come tomorrow in office. She asked him: Really you are coming tomorrow in office and you will interrupt your small vacation? The younger man Zeeshan, laughed and said: Really, I will come tomorrow because I know all of you are missing me. Both of them laughed.

His secretary Salma, explained to him: I thought you will give me any instruction to wait with other people them but is good that you will come by yourself. After she asked him: Are you leaving your family, your wife with your children over there and you will go back again?

The younger man Zeeshan said to his secretary: No, I am taking all of them in home, they will continue to go on the beach to our city it is not problem. I wanted to be in this quiet place but duty is calling so I am coming back with my family too.

After he heard her that say: Okay Thank You, very much and welcome to office. He wished to her a very nice day and closed the telephone. When he heard his wife's voice behind him that said: What happened? I heard that was about your office.

I came to drink coffee with you, but as I see you have finished drinking it. The younger man Zeeshan, spoke with smile and full with happiness that wondered his wife. Yes, it was my secretary Salma, she was calling from her home, she has one news that she named emergency and wanted to tell me before she to go to the office.

In my office is coming one high level delegation from capital of our country from office of our president. She wanted some advice but I said to her that I will be over there tomorrow, so we will leave this place today later afternoon after we to enjoy our day on the beach with our children.

I must to be over there, you understand how much important is for me and for my job plus I do not want to leave you here with two children alone in this very quiet place, that this situation has positive and negative points plus not are not people around so everything can happen.

She saw him happy but she never can imagine why he was happy, she thought it is about this delegation from president, she never can imagine that he was happy to go out of his pressure of dark thoughts in this very quiet place he wanted noise and energize movement around him. He wanted to be busy with people and to escape this situation of so many doubt thoughts.

Really, he was very happy and he shocked his wife when he said: Listen me we get awake early today, so I think to keep busy myself and to service to you my dear wife today for breakfast. I am preparing one omelet with eggs and one glass cup with milk and whatever you want extra. She laughed and she said Okay, if you are happy and with full wish to do that, I will like to eat breakfast by you today.

His wife continued her conversation, while she was seeing her husband Zeeshan, with wondering. During this time that you my dear husband will prepare this breakfast I am going to folder and prepare our luggage and bags with our clothes and children's clothes too, so when we are coming from the beach everything to be ready, and we to go.

The younger man Zeeshan, said to her: This is very good idea to prepare our staff for to go back home. She went to the other room and he started to prepare and cook omelet while he was whistling one beautiful melody, looked that really he was very happy that he was going back to his home and his beautiful and modern city Dubai too.

During this morning he was listening chirping of some beautiful birds that were in crew to the trees that were in front of the kitchen 's window while one breeze was bringing fresh air to the open window of the kitchen while in distance was coming one easy sound of the white waves of the blue ocean.

The younger man Zeeshan, loved this morning while time by time while he was cooking on oven, he was seeing from window of the kitchen and was enjoying this beautiful nature. He whispered with himself: Thank you "Allah" for this beautiful nature that we are enjoying every day in our life. Thank You "Allah" for this big harmony of the different colors of our nature.

He called his wife: Leylae…I The breakfast is ready, are you coming ?.. or I am eating alone. She came right away and both of them were eating and laughing when came one of those ladies that were servicing to this building. She got shocking and said: Ooo sorry I am later.

The younger man Zeeshan, smiled and said you are not later but we got awake very early and so I was happy to prepare by myself this omelet and we are eating now with my wife. The servant lady said to them: Really, I did not want to make noise very early in this kitchen that is close with those rooms.

Really this building was small flat with some rooms and one big living and dining room too, and big kitchen that is it. The younger man Zeeshan, said to her do not worry, you are very Okay, we got awake early because we need to leave this place today later afternoon because one news came suddenly from my office and I must to be over there tomorrow.

The servant lady said: Oooo "Allah" we loved you with all your family to be here, we all are happy with your presence, so you got very short vacation. This is very beautiful place. Really here is very quiet and you are coming from the big city, but vacation will be so beautiful here.

The younger man Zeeshan, explained to her that is coming delegation by president of our country to my office, that is very important for me. The lady said really, this is very beautiful. I am happy that they are coming from his office, good for you prince Zeeshan, and good for this beautiful big city too.

Really our president is great man from powerful and important "Zyed" family too, because they are founder of our beautiful country United Arab Emirates (UAE).

Yes, it is true replied the younger man Zeeshan, they united seven emirates of our country that were separated before and we are today good and strong country too, with economy, culture, military and education too.

You know so many people from around the world are coming to work to our country and to live too, plus, so many tourists are coming from all around the world to enjoy our beautiful country United Arab Emirates, (UAE) and specific our famous city Dubai too. Now you understand how important it is for me to be over there and to wait with honor this delegation.

The lady said to him: You are very right you are leader of this city so you needed to be over there and to honor them. It is not only about me because there are and the other leaders in our city but I need to make beautiful organize and to prepare, one wonderful welcome for those people with the others leaders of our city friends of mine, so we will give one very good name to our city and our people too.

I need to prepare and to put so many flags to different center like galleria, museum, to office of local government and in main street. I will tell to my staff to put some beautiful flowers in bottle attachment with different electric tower around my building so all the city and all around my building to have festive environment. His wife Leylae, was seeing his husband Zeeshan, with so much inspiration and happiness while he was speaking so much enthusiast in front of his wife and this servant lady, that both were smiling.

Really his wife Leylae, was thinking with herself about him: She thought that this time her husband Zeeshan is with full inspiration about his job, he has done drastic change. Inside her was coming in surface one doubt feeling of jealousy. She was thinking what is source of this big drastic change of him and what is source of this big inspiration that never I saw before and never I saw during our conflict's period time.

He looks so much happy and talkative, I do not know anymore him he is different person now, and this big changing it is in positive side. I with my family did not win with him, so who is the source of his happy situation and high inspiration now?

She was seeing him and felt something cold inside herself and whispered:

I wish that I to be source of his happiness and big inspiration now for him. Really, I am doubting for that fact because I gave to him hard time, really, I want to know who is this source of his enthusiasm, but it is mystery and maybe will be mystery for so long or forever.

She felt inside herself from her stomach through to her chest and heart was growing up one new feelings of jealousy that was growing more stronger and why she decided to prevent her jealousy but she was feeling that.

She was understanding that her feeling of jealousy was creating one erosion to her body and to her relationship with her husband Zeeshan, while she repeated with very low voice: I need to start therapy with Doctor of psychology about my feelings and about my relationship with my husband.

When I am going back to home to our city I will put appointment with one Doctor of psychology and to start right away this therapy. I need to help myself and to protect my marriage and my family too. I never will allow others people to involve in solution of problems of my family too, because some are doing to me but some are distracting me with different advices that are not working out when is conflict situation in family. I will start this therapy and I will read books about this matter too.

In the morning when the younger man Zeeshan met his security team's members he told to them that they will leave that place later afternoon because tomorrow he must to be in office to prepare everything before to come delegation by Abu Dhabi, president 's office.

So needed a big job to do and so many preparations. All were agreed and they said: Let's use and this day all the day on the beach and afternoon let's go in city Dubai. The younger man spent all his day with children and time by time he was doing conversation with his wife Leylae, but all the time his attention and his eyes were to two children so he was justifying himself with their two children for not giving so much attention to his wife during this day.

The day was going so soft with so many laughing by both of them, with their two children that were doing so many noises, in their small plastic boats on the water blue of ocean. His wife was thinking with herself and was whispering:

I wish to be so many days in future of my life, for both of us like this day today, with harmony laughing and happiness. Later afternoon after they ate lunch, they started driving for to their beautiful modern big city Dubai. Strangely during this time, the younger man Zeeshan, was talking so much enthusiast with his friend leader of security team Emin.

His joy conversation got attention of driver, of his wife and of course his loyal friend Emin, leader of security team knows the secret really, of this enthusiasm. When they arrived in city and entered to highway, he said to them with happiness let's go to drink one coffee or to get ice cream for all of us and for my children too.

All were agreed, they stopped to one small ice cream 's store and they told to the other car of the security team's members we will go all of us for ice cream they laughed and they were agreed of course. It was one very beautiful evening with its characteristic beautiful sunset for that big beautiful modern city.

In the store the two children were so much happy while they were seeing different advertise for different color of ice cream, they ordered mixer color ice cream and all were laughing. The two children were happier, when the owner of the store gave to them small toys with ice cream that were same in figure of advertise, so their happiness and their scream for those toys, it was without limit and made all the people to laugh in this small but beautiful really luxury store, with its tables and chairs colorful.

The younger man Zeeshan, was very happy for his two children and so was on union of himself happiness and children happiness. He was combinating all his action that day in cooperation with his attention to his children but really, he was very glad for good feeling for his younger girl Agneza and for that reason that she called him and left message. He was thinking, she started to love me, she is thinking for me, she called me and got courage that left message to me. Now I am sure that she loves me.

After they got ice cream, they started again driving to go to their huge and beautiful palace. The evening was coming with its fresh air and the younger man said loudly: This is the most beautiful evening. All in car agreed. The younger man Zeeshan said: I never can imagine for so short time I will miss my home so much. Really at that time two children were laughing and said to their father we miss our home too. All people in car laughed.

They arrived in their palace when they entered in the garden in front of their palace that looked like one very beautiful multicolor carpet by multicolor flowers, was running so fast their beautiful beige color Zoros dog in front of them and it goes straight to the younger man Zeeshan, while the two children were touching Zoros dog all around, they wanted to play with him.

The younger man Zeeshan, did not get the Zoros dog because he left to his servant lady to follow some medication service as advised the veterinary. After dog came from inside the palace the servant lady to help them with their luggage and bags. Returning to is home gave some peaceful feelings to the younger man Zeeshan.

They entered to their palace and the younger man went right away to his studio. He did not have patience to see all the e – mails, also to see all calling and text message to his telephone cellular. He wrote back e- mail to some people, when one e-mail got his attention was coming from one professor of University of Vienna of Austria. He was reading very carefully with full attention. He was explaining to his e – mail that they have created one small group with architects

From two universities of Vienna of Austria and from University of Ljubljana of Slovenia, also between them will be and professor of law Bojana. Really, he was very happy this time he was not anxious like before about visit of professor Bojana, and other people of this group, because he has consolidated his position with this younger girl Agneza.

He said to himself, I will have busy time all this month and this is very good for me because I wanted to keep myself busy but look universe with its mystery is organize all to keep me busy. First it is coming presidential delegation after this architects' group from two main Universities from Center of Europe and Northwest of Ballkan, so definitely I am happy that I will be busy.

After he wrote one longer a- mail, with so many romantic beautiful phrases to express his love and his attention to her. Really his writing was so much enthusiast with all colors of love by hot golden sun, by very good ascent of petals of multicolor flowers, and full love feelings that were coming like crystal river water from his hot heart.

One phrase to this writing that" Life without you will be for me blue" were expressing the impact that this girl Agneza has to his life and she must to be careful because he was so much sensitive and every good or bad of her action will influence in his life.

While the last phrase of this writing that: "Your melodious voice when is coming through my telephone to my ear is like the beautiful chirping of birds to my garden, early in the morning after raining has stopped and all around is beauty and fresh air, and good smells by flowers." While this morning it is one miracle.

So, the writing by the younger man Zeeshan, was one deep conglomerate and melting of beautiful feelings of love and beauty of nature too. His writing was full inspiration, he was feeling that has now in his chest and his heart one beautiful great love and he was feeling himself like younger boy.

He whispered to himself: I do not know myself anymore but I feel that I am happy. I feel that I am full confidence and fearless for my life. I feel more stronger myself now. I do not feel weak myself and desperate like some time before during big conflict in my family and between our two families, mine's family and my wife's family too.

I see my life full color and my children are giving me happiness without limit. Definitely I feel myself now one strong man with full experience for good or bad situation in life, plus I feel myself man in deep beautiful magical love and I feel great and lovely father for my two children too, and very good leader for my people, for my community and my city too.

Later night when he wanted to sleep the younger man Zeeshan, was very tired while he was moving around the bed, he was not feeling quiet himself and his brain was working nonstop about so many things in same time.

His brain was full with different questions that wanted so many answers, while some answers were coming fast and some answers were not coming because so many obstacles by so many unforeseen problems in line so later, he jumped in deep sleep, in dark night.

During night he saw dream again he was seeing in distance faraway one green field but in front of him was one desert space. He did not want to walk in desert, he was not preparing for that situation but he was curious and wanted to see this bold color green field in distance. He was waiting and waiting but when he did not see any solution how to go over there, he decided to go back and not to see that bold green field.

At that moment one strong wind came around to the place that he was staying and lifted up the sand of desert while created one open wide road that was continued until to the bold green field. The younger man Zeeshan, started to run to this road and arrived so fats to the bold green field.

This field was surrounding all around with taller trees that were servicing like border or fence with the other place of the ground. The younger man Zeeshan, saw in distance one younger beautiful girl that was doing sign with her hand like come here. The younger man Zeeshan, started to walk in her direction but how much he was walking, so much faraway was going this younger girl.

During his fast walking one white heavy cloud came in front of him and was moving slowly, slowly to the sky at that time the younger man Zeeshan, heard one distance voice looked was coming from inside of this white heavy cloud. You have a long way to go to meet this younger girl you are walking fast you are running but you cannot arrive her, you have a long way to go to meet her, was repeating this voice in his ear.

The younger man felt so much tired by his running and fast walking too, so he stopped and was thinking I did not arrive this younger girl maybe is fiction by me this figure but how I will go back to my place I am in middle place of nowhere, and he felt anxious and fear.

At that time, he opened his eyes and he understood that he was in dream. He thought it is "White Suddenly Dream. It is my conscience, also are my feelings inside of me for the younger girl Agneza, is only dream by it is one foresee, it is one sign that, "Allah" is sending me sign that I have a long way to be with her and I do not like that fact, I am in love with her. I want her to be here close with me. After that moment he never slept quite until to the morning.

Next morning, he prepared himself to go to his office. He got out and found all his security team's members in garden in front of his huge and very beautiful palace. That morning was fresh with some grey cloud up to the sky.

They were driving through the main highway while his leader of security team Emin, said to his younger boss Zeeshan, we have a busy time this week with those two groups of people, so we need to use three cars and I need to make organize of my security team and to make addition maybe and two or three more people. The younger man Zeeshan, said to him you are right so do it.

When the younger man Zeeshan arrived to his office all were waiting him and all entered to his office for this small short meeting. He started to explain to them for program that they will follow during those days that delegation from the presidential 's office will come.

While when are coming group of architects from Vienna of Austria and from Ljubljana of Slovenia, he said: Some of you will not be in office those days but all the time will campaign this crew together with me.

All were agreed. He decided two women to prepare the big room of conference for those two groups that were coming and to put one flag of country inside of this conference room and some flowers on big table while outside to put some more small flags all around area of building.

The younger man Zeeshan, ordered one man of his office to make in his power and knowledge of management of outside area, on highway that to put some big flags of the country in different segments of highway until to their building also to one big building to order electronic advertise of the portrait of president of their country of the United Arab Emirates, (UAE).

All got their assignment for those days of those two delegations. So came the day that the younger man with some other people of his local government went to airport to wait this delegation from presidential 's office. The group of people from presidential 's office came they all were friendly and happy to see the younger man, Zeeshan. They were campaigned by police cars in front and behind that was organized by younger man Zeeshan, for security.

They were shocked and same times they showed their happiness for this festive environment through the highway, they made one big uauaua for big portrait of president from great family's "Zayed" of the country United Arab Emirates (UAE) in electronic advertise to one high building.

Also, they really shocked for the beautiful design and environment by flowers and small flags all around the building where were offices of local government and of the younger man Zeeshan too. Really those two women of the office of local government have done very beautiful job of course women all the time has talent for beautiful design.

They entered in conference room that was so beautiful environment too, with high quality of big table by walnut wood open honey color with some design in itself and one big crystal bowl with some original orchid white and pink color.

Chairs were with walnut wood with design in itself with one very beautiful, silk, merchandise cover with stripe white and bold green color, of course, green color it is hope so all this conference's room was full with hope for good meeting and good arrangement by local government and federal government or central government too.

The meeting was very important they came to see some institution, some universities some hospitals and some factories. Another very important matter of this meeting was analyses of current situation and plans for budget in future by federal government for this city Dubai. Definitely first impression was so good by this delegation about festive environment and sweet welcome.

They noticed that specialists that were working with the younger man Zeeshan, in local government of this huge super modern and very beautiful city Dubai, were high level like intellectual and they have so much knowledge of their profession.

The first day was going so well, they did that meeting, after they eat lunch in this building the food was coming from one local restaurant that the younger man Zeeshan, ordered for all. Lunch was going so good talking and making some jokes. After they went to visit some universities and at evening, they went to sleep in hotel that they have arrangement from their capital city Abu Dhabi of the United Arab Emirates (UAE).

All the time the younger man Zeeshan, with one man and one woman from his office was campaign this delegation everywhere. When he left them in hotel, he wanted to go to office to take something before he to go to his palace later night.

When he entered to office, he found one small package FedEx, while he got shocked, he turned package from the other side to see who sent that he laughed loudly when he saw the name of Gentius brother of Agneza. He opened so fast this package that gave to him after this very tired day one big happiness.

He found inside one beautiful picture that he has done with Gentius, the picture was inside of one silver color plastic frame. He understood that Gentius did not want to put heavy items because it was expensive transport of package by weight.

He found one beautiful leather notebook open green color cover with poems, inside those poems was written by the younger girl Agneza sister of Gentius, also was and one post card writing greetings by Gentius.

He smiled and was writing right away so fast text message to Gentius he calculated difference of time between his country United Arab Emirates, (UAE) and Croatia country of Gentius. He was sure that Gentius will read right away. He was right after some minutes he heard the sound of telephone, that was telling, to him that has text message.

He opened the message link and he saw the replied of Gentius that were happy, words between others I miss you so much my lovely prince Zeeshan, and I love you too, and one longer ooooo. At that time the younger man Zeeshan, felt that all the world belongs to him. He was so much happy while said loudly:

Thank You, "Allah" for those younger lovely people that you brought present to my life. After he got out of the office and was going to his palace with his secret service crew, he got the notebook with poems by Agneza with himself. He did not have patience to read those poems he decided to read in his studio in his palace.

When he arrived, in home, he said to his servant lady Aasma, that he needs only ice tea to bring to his office and he so much busy, to work in his studio room so time by time come to see me if I need something. Same thing he told to his wife Leylae, that was waiting him with big smile and sweet welcome.

He explained to her short strict what was his day, also he told to his wife that delegation got shocked and liked so much festive environment that he has created with his people have create.

He told to his wife that they visited two universities and tomorrow they will visit two hospitals, and two factories while the third day they will do meeting for budget that federal government will approve for our city Dubai, that is very important for all of us and for our environment for business and social life of people.

I think they were very happy we gave lunch to them in our building the food was ordered to local restaurant everything was going excellent, and all the time I campaigned them outside in those visited with one man lawyer that he is using two names, but we are calling him with his Nassar, name, and Adara one woman of account, that are working with me in local government.

I am happy that everything was going smooth and so good and I did very good job that I came and did preparation of everything and my people too. Really his wife approved him and she said I see that you are so glad for this day and I am happy for you. After that her husband Zeeshan, said to her: I am busy now to prepare one material for tomorrow so I am going to my studio to work. She said: Okay with smile. At that time one longer ring sounded in bold way to his phone.

The younger man Zeeshan, hesitated to open his telephone he thought maybe is coming by Agneza but his wife was seeing with full attention and noticed his hesitation while said with force to him: Open telephone why you are not opening why you are not answering?

The younger man Zeeshan, said "Allah" he thought that he did not want conflict now with his wife for really but he said to her:

I am very busy now I have not time to talk with people.

It is longer ring without interruption maybe is very important said his wife. Definitely he opened the telephone and was thinking whatever to be I am saying they are my new younger friend.

Really it was one his friend that said to him open your telephone and read to local news in online because one journalist that was campaigning the delegation, by presidential 's office has written so much for you, but, he did not explain, what was writing, but said read it now and have a good night.

For moment the younger man Zeeshan, stay some second without saying anything he was wondered what was writing about, because his friend spoke short, he thought maybe it is any problem. His wife asked him what is why you changed you face? One friend told me that their journalist has written fast in local news in online.

His wife said: Okay why you are not opening that link and read material.

My friend spoke so short and I think that I do not want to know if is not good writing because I had beautiful day and I do not want to destroy the happiness by day that is gone and my good evening now. Whatever to be you will know, now or tomorrow it will be same if it is bad, you will feel bad. So open now to know what is and to prepare yourself for tomorrow.

He opened the link and he saw one longer writing. Strangely the writing it was so beautiful about everything, about electronic advertise of portrait of president of the country, about flowers and national flags all around and to local government building, about design of environment about meeting and his very high qualify staff and visited to two universities.

All writing was with details and was using so much artistic figures so many metaphors, and so many beautiful describe and comparing with so many others beauty of city around the world. Also, the journalist was writing for the younger man Zeeshan, it was very friendly.

He was treating his staff of office so good, more important he was loved by his people and was leader with vision of future for his city Dubai

So, he was capacity for this country of the United Arab Emirates (UAE) and for his city Dubai too, that so many must to learn by him and his experience. He explained to us that he is preparing for new modern project for new town close to desert area too, that will be one great thing for this city will be extended of this city in that area and so many other jobs, to be open for people and immigrants too.

He was reading with voice to hear and his wife Leylae, and his eyes started to sparkle from happiness. His wife said to him: I told you maybe it is important so this is very good news for really for you. She said to her husband Zeeshan, congratulation.

Now she understood that her husband Zeeshan, was truly when he said about returning to home and in city because of this delegation and he wanted to prepare that everything to be good. Really everything came success for really. This express, writing by journalist that evening it is evidence for this success.

After that conversation the younger man said to his wife: I see you later I am going to studio. First, he entered to room of two children kissed them play some minutes with them and after he entered to his studio.

He opened the computer while was seeing e- mails that people have sent to him but he did not reply because he wanted to be quiet and to read that note book with poems by Agneza, he was sure that they will be love poems too.

He opened the green open color note book that has one red heart symbol in up right corner of cover, all poems were hand writing. He started to read poems. He saw that poems were separated with chapter; each chapter has ten poems.

First chapter was with poems about describe of nature's, that some were writing with nostalgia about colors of nature and memory. The second chapter was with poems, about people, different friends and relatives younger and adult, some were with humor and some about their portraits those were happy poems, third chapter was with poems of love.

The younger man Zeeshan, was reading first one poem about nature the second he was reading one portrait of one her relative and laughed loudly for really was humoristic poems looked that Agneza loved her relative and has so many points of humor, about his appearance and his funny character.

After he started to read in line poems of love. After he read some of them, he understood that poems of love were about him and their meeting and her thoughts for future and about missing her new lover. Those poems made the younger man Zeeshan, to jump in deep thinking while his eyes were full with tears. He whispered: She loves me! Also, I am in deep love with this younger girl Agneza.

Next day in the morning the younger man awaked early prepared himself to meet with presidential delegation. After he ate short breakfast got out and meet his security team 's members and their leader his loyal friend, while the driver started engine of car and started driving to go to his office.

When he arrived to his office the secretary gave information about schedule of that day. After thirty (30) minutes the ring of telephone interrupted his conversation with his secretary. He heard the voice of the leader of presidential delegation that told to him, that after they will eat breakfast, they will be in his office in 10: A.M. and they will continue to go to visit two hospitals and two factories.

The younger man Zeeshan, was very happy that everything was going so much good with this presidential delegation, he understood from his speech and his voice of the leader of delegation that he was so happy about this visit to this beautiful modern big city.

At 10: A.M. members of this delegation arrived to the office of the younger man Zeeshan. They discussed for 10, (ten) minutes and they got out with the younger man Zeeshan, with his lawyer and account lady too.

First, they decided to go to visit two big main hospitals in this city. They went to first hospital and they saw very cleaning environment of the hospital all around inside and outside, while to so many rooms they saw some the modern electronic medical equipment.

Hospital was huge, with ten floors, with beautiful shape of architecture.

After they visited the children's hospital that was huge too, with seven floors with so many beautiful geometric figures, with different colors outside on surface of wall, painted with color like green open color, blue open color, orange color and easy egg open color. They visited so many big rooms that were with toys for children, they saw one modern big room of physiotherapy with different colors on the wall.

They visited modern hall of surgery with modern equipment and they visited some children that were really sick and they saw how was service, to those children. They faced pleasant situation. Their journalist was keeping writing all the time in every room or hall that they were entering.

After they finished their visit to some access of hospital, they did one short meeting with director in his big office and some doctors of this modern children's hospital. The member of presidential delegation gave their opinion for this children's hospital and after they asked the director and doctors what they have any request to Federal Government, so they will explain to president and to health department too.

The director and doctors of this children's hospital made so many requests, and most of all was about modern medical equipment. They gave one **new idea**, that to make addition one facility aside and attachment to hospital with rooms for sleeping, so those room to be used by parents that were living faraway from tis big city like in rural area, and must to stand close with their children.

In this way they will have some times to take rest and to sleep quiet some hours days or night. All members of presidential delegation were agreed with this proposition of this new idea.

Also, they requested for one small park with different toys in garden outside, so children that were getting recovery and were standing longer in hospital must to go and to enjoy this small park in front of this children 's hospital.

All delegation's members were agreed and with this proposition about this idea of small park in front of the hospital. When they finished the meeting, the director said to them: Now we all together are going to another meeting to the big conference room.

They shocked they got confused but they did not blame the director of the children of hospital. The younger man Zeeshan, got wondering and was thinking what he will discuss more to this big conference room maybe are some other people or parent of patients (children) over there.

They all went over there while were discussing with joy with each other. When they went over there, they saw one strange situation really it was not what the younger man Zeeshan, thought.

They found two big table close together and so many chairs around, while on table cover with very white beautiful cotton, table clothes with design in itself and so many beautiful white dishes with some easy pinks color design geometric figure and some thick glass for water.

In four big dishes were so much food meat, salat, rice with meat, sweet and coca cola and orange small glass bottles. Of course, to every, dishes were spoon, fork and knife. All got shocked for those huge tables with so much food and design, of setting dishes for everyone and those four dishes was so beautiful.

Some white cotton napkins were folder in beautiful way, while four women were standing up to service to those people. All loved this beautiful environment while the smell of cooking was giving provocation to them to get sitting fast and to start eating. Really it was one big surprise for all of them no exception and for the younger man Zeeshan, and his lawyer man and his account lady of his office.

All started to discuss with happiness while were trying this delicious food. The younger man Zeeshan, was so much happy for this welcome of the director of the children hospital. He thought this director got so much serious this problem so he honored all of us and he honored our very beautiful city Dubai.

The journalist did some pictures of this group with leader the younger man Zeeshan. After that they gave their hand with so many Thank You, to the director of the children hospital and got out.

They said to the younger man Zeeshan, we can go right away to two factories now to visit. They went to one factory of conservation of food fruits and so vegetables, meat etc. They faced one modern factory about equipment and quality of plastic and glasses where they were putting food that were conservating.

After this factory they went to another precise metallic products. This factory or plant was super modern with so much precise cutting machine and other electronic equipment. Workers were working in cleaning environment with full security, with uniform dresses with big glasses in their eyes for protection and with big plastic gloves in their hand for protection too.

Everything was modern and excellent. When they finished their visit while their journalist was taking pictures and was writing all the time, they got out of this modern factory and proposed to the younger man Zeeshan, to go aside the beach to any cafeteria and to talk over there that afternoon.

So, they went all together to this modern glass cafeteria aside the beach they ordered coffee and some ordered hot chocolate. It was one very beautiful afternoon that was leaving the place to sweet evening.

They talked with so much enthusiasm while said tomorrow is the last day, so we will do meeting in the morning with your staff about budget for your city and later afternoon we are traveling to our city Abu Dhabi, capital of the country United Arab Emirates (UAE).

After one hour they went to hotel while the younger man Zeeshan, and his two employees' lawyer and account lady were campaigning them after they left to go to their home it was later evening.

The younger man Zeeshan, with his security team was going to his palace strangely he was not talking so much that evening. The leader of secret service, Emin, thought it was heavy and tired day maybe he I got tired and was under pressure. But after some minutes he heard the younger man Zeeshan, that broke the silence in the car and said:

I saw those very sick children yellow in face in danger for their life and I thought about my two children and I got terrified. So definitely our local government must to put more budget for the adult - people's hospital and specific for children's hospital too.

Also, we must to cooperate with nonprofit organization around our country United Arab Emirates, (UAE) to give more donation for those two hospitals and more for children hospital. Those sick children today in this hospital touched my heart they were seeing to us and they were waiting their healing by us.

They were seeing with their open eyes and wanted hope by us. I hugged so much of them I saw their innocent smile to their Angelo - faces.

The younger man Zeeshan, did not have voice to speak more and leader of secret service understood that he was so much impressed by those children. They arrived to his palace and left him in front of his huge very beautiful palace.

He was walking so fast he was not counting the stairs of the big hall and went right away to his children's room he found his wife with children. His wife asked him: How was your day today with this presidential delegation.

He answered very good we visited two hospitals while the director of children hospital has prepared one wonderful lunch with delicious food, we ate in one big conference hall. Everything was with good design setting in table luxury and very good test of food.

His wife asked him: Are so many sick children over there? He saw her, he did not have power to answer but he got his two children in front of him he hugged them and his eyes started to fill with tears. His wife saw his tears in his eyes and she did not ask and did not speak anymore, she understood that he saw so many very sick children over there and was so much sentimental.

After some minutes he said: I cannot imagine what I will do if our children will be sick like some of them over there. I will be terrified and my life will be not the same anymore. Thank You, "Allah" for good health of my children and all my family members too. His wife Leylae, said: Amen!

After the younger man Zeeshan, said with force to his beautiful wife: Listen me very carefully this is my statement first to you: I will do the impossible to turn in possible to help the children's hospital with my power and I will cooperate with so many institutions and nonprofit organization that to give priority donation to children's hospital. Definitely the children's hospital will be my priority in job and in my life.

After they both went to his studio and were seeing in computer for listing of different organization that were giving donation to different business and hospitals too. The younger man Zeeshan, said to his wife Leylae: I need to make research for all institutions and nonprofit organization all around our country United Arab Emirates,(UAE) and to different country that are bordering us.

At that time his wife said to him: I can help you too, with research about this problem, I like to do research so I will spend time with research when when I will be quiet not busy.

The younger man Zeeshan, saw her and said in short way it will be helpful if you will do that job for me. After she left her husband Zeeshan, alone to work quiet in his studio and went to see again two children to their room. He continued to see in his computer but his thoughts were not leaving him quiet. His thoughts were flying with speed faraway to Western Balkan, to the younger beautiful Albanian girl Agnezia in Croatia.

It was really very happy moment when he was thinking for this younger girl Agneza, he was forgetting at this moment all problem that he has in his life in his family or in his job. He was watching through half open window outside, the silver moon up to the sky and all bright stars.

He whispered with himself, all of those stars and silver moon knows my situation, they know that I am in deep love with this beautiful girl Agneza and they are trying to discover more about this romantic story, for this reason they are sending their silver light rays through this window to my studio.

He started to smile and was whispering with himself I think and my beautiful beige color lovely "Zoros" dog, knows my love story because he is opening his eyes, and is watching me very carefully when I am giving to him water to drink.

I felt some days before when I was in field of horses and camels when I was feeding one Camel that was seeing with doubts, maybe Camel knows about my love story with Agneza or has got some rumor by Giraffa with longer throat that they are getting news so fast up to the air.

Maybe for this reason Camel has started those days to put through window inside the car its head and is touching my head, because wants my attention now since got news for my new and beautiful love story.

Also, my lovely horse knows about my love story because now he is coming more closer to me and is putting his head close to my head and he wants my attention maybe my Horse like Camel started to be jealous for me that I love so much this younger girl Agneza. Really, I am very happy that all my lovely animals "Zoros" dog, Camel, Girafa and Horse are close with me in this difficult moment of my life and they are enjoying my happiness about this beautiful new love, does not matter they want more attention by me now.

When is coming Agneza to live with me we will decide to put new name to my lovely animals. She asked me what names I have put for those animals but I told to her that only "Zoros" dog, I put name, so she gave me new vision for my soft lovely animals to put beautiful name to them.

Also, she said to me to put beautiful label by leather with their name to their body or like necklace. I will do that. With those thoughts the younger man Zeeshan, started to dream about Agneza and how will be developed his love story with her.

So, he left to make research about those nonprofit organizations or different institution for donation for children's hospital while he thought that he has time for that job to do in future.

The younger man Zeeshan, was continuing to see the silver moon to the dark night through the window and made one wish to the Procyon star, to make bright his "Suddenly White Dream" but he did not see the shooting star this night.

Anyway, he was very happy what he was dreaming after that he went to get sleep so to be fresh for next day that will be the last day of presidential delegation and more important is that the next day they will decide the new budget for his city, that will be manage by his local government.

Next day he got awake early and was preparing himself to be good in front of his delegation. This day he did not dress his native uniform white longer gown and his white longer scarf, but he dressed elegant classic suit grey open color and one very good quality very gray open color shirt, and one bold dark blue very elegant and thin tie.

His shoes were bold dark color and his socks were open grey with some elegant decoration bold blue geometric figure. So, when he was walking the socks showed up a little bit, between his pants and shoes and when he tried to get seat the socks showed more with their beautiful design so his dresses that day were luxury and very elegant "Shik" dresses. He used his special and very expensive perfume so he was ready for this great meeting. He got his dark leather bag with document while he was preparing to go, his wife Leylae, came to see him and she got shocked for his test that day, that was so much elegant and beautiful. She made one sigh like ouououu, while her husband Zeeshan, smiled and said:

It is very important day today for me, for my local government, for our beautiful city Dubai, and for our people in our city too. Today they will decide for "Project – Budget" after they will decide in federal government in capital city in Abu Dhabi of our country United Arab Emirates, (UAE).

She said: You are very right. Have a good luck in this meeting. I wish to be one big amount of budget too for our beautiful modern city Dubai.

He said to his wife Leylae: Have a nice day. I see you later in the evening. He got out and met his people of secret service that were waiting him in front of his palace. They started driving to got to his office.

When he left, his wife felt cold inside herself. She started to think in deep way and she whispered: He has changed so much. He does not need anymore, my test for his dressing. He was dressing so beautiful and luxury today. I am scared about that, because I think that he is in love with someone new.

Oooo "Allah" help me to see clarity and prove me to be wrong with my thoughts. I love my husband Zeeshan, and my two children too. I love my family but he has changed so much. I see some details that I doubts in his behave and why he is trying to be good with me this time, but I do not see his feelings and sparkle to his eyes that were telling me before big love for me.

He was not anxious today about his meeting and all those days about this visit by presidential delegation. He was so much anxious before and was discussing with me that he needed to concentrate for meeting or different event but not this time. He was happy from the beginning. He showed himself so much confident for this visit by Federal Government offcials. I think he is more strong and happier now.

I wish now to have the past time with my husband, why I created that distance with my capriccio and my family too?! Really, I want to return the pas time about our relationship, what I have done for myself. "Allah ", help me.

She felt that her tears were going down to her nice face, while she heard the voice of her children to other their room so she went over there to see them what they were doing. At that morning the younger Zeeshan, man arrived early in his office and he found his secretary Salma, too that she was working overtime those days, also he found over there his lawyer Nassar, and his account lady Adara. They were preparing every paper in conference room and were waiting presidential delegation to come in 10 A: M.

The member of presidential delegation came in time in 10: A. M. they were in his office. Started meeting in conference room. There were so many discussions about budget some approved and all were agreed about some were some issues by Government's delegation.

One proposition by one official man of presidential delegation, was about creating new modern industry of fishes, of conservation of fishes, and creating one institute of science research for medical staff by ingredient of different fishes that were in their marine in their ocean. All were agreed for that. Definitely need more money of budget of this city.

Came one issue to discuss about very important matter that never anymore to build town like "Palms" town on blue ocean. They were agreed in absolute way, never anymore to put concrete in blue water of ocean for every reason. We need to protect environment and specific our blue water of ocean.

We do not need to disappear or to erase space of water. Most of all we need to protect marina and fauna of ocean. Population is growing up to our country so we need to use everything for food what is produced by agriculture, or about fauna in our environment.

So, finished his speech one man from presidential delegation from capital, Abu Dhabi of country United Arab Emirates (UAE). Most of them were agreed while the younger man Zeeshan, did abstenim. He did not blame, but he did not approve, maybe he got that phrase indirect like critic for spending so much money in not necessary of creating new environment, and why is so beautiful.

Maybe the younger man Zeeshan, understood that official man of presidential delegation was so much right about environment and super huge amount of money of expenses. At that moment came one bright idea of the younger man Zeeshan.

He thought will be more right to build one small town hanged to ocean with steel like we are building bridge inside blue water and in two side of bridge to be some houses for those that will afford, so in future we will replace this steel and to take out if is necessary if it has erosion. But what to do with those thousand- and thousand-ton concrete and big stones, inside the blue water of ocean, that with their cold power ignored the blue water and pushed away with force, while the blue water was with thousand years over there in that position.

This is the power of the strong objects to the soft and sweet fresh blue water of ocean. Maybe one day the blue water of ocean will claim for its place again and will get revenge with any strong flood around, who knows?,.. everything happen int this life of Earth planet.

Maybe he thought right the younger man Zeeshan, but he did not say about his bright idea to them at that time. His pride maybe will not allow to accept that error or mistake about environment and so much expenses while so many empty land around.

Another proposition was to use or plant wild plant or trees, that their, roots were going inside deep of the ground and trees to resist to high fever of environment to expand green space. All were agreed. So needed more money for that too.

The account lady Adara, got courage without asking her younger boss Zeeshan, and her office's lawyer Nassar, but she gave another new idea another proposition while she started to explain in details in strict way but in bold way.

She said: We have a lot Government 's land that is empty. So, I think it is in deep need to build in those land that possess by Government some buildings that will be for immigrants whatever they are legal or illegal.

We cannot leave people to sleep outside. So many of them are coming from poor countries, they do not have money and they are working hard in construction so we need to make easier, their life until them to collect some money and to live later in their own.

When they are leaving those public buildings, they will be free for others that, will come, so our beautiful modern big city Dubai, will not have problem anymore to establish immigrants.

To create this complex of buildings in some hills or close to the river that is land of government so we do not need to deal with private owner to buy their land so much expensive. As we know that immigration of people for reasons, that we know and for unknown reasons, will continue in future as all around the world, but our city Dubai is hope for job with his modern construction so we will have immigrants all the time.

Also, we do not know that tourists that are coming from all around the world to see bad situation in our city Dubai, or to get news by people around for bad condition of immigrants, anyway they are humans being.

They were listening her very careful with full attention in silence when she finished, they said very good idea, excellent we will put this point to rise budget specific for this new proposition that really it is necessary.

Lawyer Nassar, got his time to speak and he said I have another proposition for Federal Government, to help us for budget so our city to build new futurist rail way and futurist station train and this rail way to connect our beautiful city Dubai with capital city, Abu Dhabi, with special electric train.

We can build half of distance and other half of distance to build by local Government of the capital city of our country United Arab Emirates, (UAE) in this way we will rise numbers of travelers to come to our city and to go to capital and profit will be great for both beautiful cities. While in future this futurist railway to connect with Saudi Arabia's land beyond our border.

The leader of presidential delegation said to him. Really this is very great idea futurist rail way with electric train we will win in time and we will win so many tourists in our region plus tickets will be not so much expensive for people. So definitely people will love to travel and to see those beautify cities in vacation time or their off day by job or doing holiday. This situation will help so much local business of those two cities.

Absolutely I will make bold this proposition to Federal Government and I think we will have positive answer because our president is very close and friendly with your leader, here in your city.

At that time lawyer of office Nassar, of the younger man Zeeshan, showed pride appearance and was seeing the account lady, Adara, she smiled she understood his jealousy, for good answer by presidential delegation so he wanted to escape her to rival her and why they were so best friends for really. When the younger man Zeeshan, saw him, he started to laugh, while one member of delegation said to him: Really you prince Zeeshan, have in your local government very smart people with full knowledge and with great vision for future.

The younger man Zeeshan, replied to him: It is true I have every good and smart people with full knowledge and with great futurist vision plus they are working hard every day with innovation. I am very proud of them.

The younger man Zeeshan, explained to them for another project that he will start for new town close to desert area and in future his family has different project in desert area for medical staff to use ingredient by sand and for some research they will do in desert area to use in future for people like environment.

The leader of presidential delegation said to leader Zeeshan: Absolutely we will help you with budget for this new town close to desert area and for all science research and job to desert area.

This is big project and of our Federal Government, so it will be priority to help you will budget for them, because this is science's study for the future of our country United Arab Emirates, (UAE) too.

So, the meeting finished with success. The leader of the presidential delegation said to all: This budget will be for this year, and why there are so many matters, to discuss but let's do one project in time step by step.

Definitely, we agreed all of us about those points:

As conclusion of this report that we will send to our Federal Government in capital city United Arab Emirates, (UAE) will be:

1. About futurist industry of conservation of fishes and science research's institution for ingredient by fishes too.
2. About building complex with buildings for immigrant workers.
3. About building futurist new railway with electric train between two our beautiful cities, half distance build by every city in their own, and after to expand international futurist railway with Saudi Arabia land outside of our border.
4. About building new town close to desert area.
5. About building center of medical with ingredient of sand and to make research in desert land for new environment in future, that really this project is taking time for really. But we need to start.
6. And our opinion not to abuse with environment of marine, with blue water of ocean and never ever, to put concrete anymore inside the water for town only port sea.

All were agreed.

For all the others domestic problems will be in own of local government of your city Dubai, for this year. Are you agree for this report. All were agreed and happy too.

After the meeting they all were to one small luxury restaurant that was located close to building where office of the younger man was and they ate delicious food. Of course, for this food will pay the younger man Zeeshan, because they were his guests in that last day, plus this budget made happy the younger man Zeeshan.

After lunch the younger man Armir, with his friends, lawyer man and account lady campaigned the members of presidential delegation to airport.

The members of presidential delegation before to leave said to the younger man Zeeshan, one big Thank You, very much and that they will be in touch also they were very happy for those three days that they spend with him and his people.

After they got the presidential jet aircraft and started their flying while they said, that they will be in touch with them. When the presidential jet started flying the younger man Zeeshan, proposed to his two friends, employees to go to drink coffee to one cafeteria in airport.

It was so much movement by people in airport also people looked so much enthusiast and so much noise by them too around. The younger man Zeeshan, said to them: We had a heavy time those three days but I think it was success for our and for our city Dubai.

Really this meeting it was big event about this budget for our city and our projects too. Now we need to work for those projects. Now you must to work together with architects about those projects. You need to give priority project of industry or factory of conservation fishes, and architecture of this science — research's institution, about complex of buildings for immigrant and for this futurist railway with electric train too.

I am proud for both of you and for your new ideas, for really you honored our local government and me too. Thank You, very much by you. You did my day today.

Days were going fast and next week was coming the group of Architects, some excellent student s of architecture and Professors, from university of Ljubljana of Slovenia and from University of Vienna of Austria.

So, the next Monday the younger man Zeeshan, went with his crew of secret service to airport to wait this group of people. Really, they got two cars, to one was driver leader of secret service and the younger man Zeeshan, while to the other car were driver and others members of secret service team.

The group arrived early in the morning in airport of the city of Dubai, of the younger man Zeeshan, because their flight was started in midnight in Europe. When they meet each other, they told to the younger man Zeeshan, that they will stay only three days, and the third day they will travel again later in the evening to go back to their countries in Western Balkan in Ljubljana of Slovenia and in center of Europe, in Vienna of Austria.

They brought so much enthusiasms. Really the younger man Zeeshan, was so much happy to see them. He decided to spend all those days with those people. The younger man left those days his office while was campaigning this group of Architects and Professors.

The first day that they arrived after they got their rooms and ate breakfast in restaurant of hotel, they started their visit as was schedule, of the younger man Zeeshan. First, they went to the big center of architects it was one modern building of this Institution of Architecture, in this big city.

They did one meeting professional over there. After they went to the University with major of Architecture. They did another meeting over there. They saw so many interesting things in those two centers. They saw so much modern supplies and equipment of Architecture in those two centers, also they saw so many modern projects in the Institution of Architecture and in the university with major of Architecture too. They got shocked by those modern and bigger projects.

At the evening they all went together to modern cafeteria aside the ocean, while the younger man Zeeshan, left this group on the table and went with professor Bojana to balcony to see the beautiful dark night decorated with beautiful bright stars and silver moon. The eyes of professor Bojana were sparkling while were watching with full attention straight to the younger man Zeeshan.

But this evening it was not like last evening that they were together. Aaaahhhh, this evening it was not the same with the last evening that professor Bojana showed full love, while the younger man Zeeshan, was confused, he was showing love but his was not bold, because his heart it was confuse between two beautiful ladies. His love it was between Professor Bojana and the younger girl Agneza.

While this time he was more oriented to Agneza, he was doing jokes, but his watching did not show romantic love, but more friendly love. Professor Bojana did not feel comfortable with his big changing but as smart woman she understood him, that he was in deep love with that younger girl Agneza.

She was investigating him while she was watching him with corner of her eyes and with smile. The younger man Zeeshan, was seeing her very carefully, while he thought she is very beautiful lady and smart. After they went inside the hall of the cafeteria where the group of people, their friends were talking loudly with happiness too. It was one beautiful evening.

They got seat to the chair to the big table and started to discuss with them for problems of projects of the country, United Arab Emirates, (UAE) of the younger man Zeeshan. The were so much enthusiast when they saw this very modern and beautiful city of Dubai. They said to the younger man Zeeshan, that they saw in documentary and in different magazines and advertises but to see in reality this city it is one miracle. Its architecture it is one outstanding architecture super modern and very beautiful.

They said that they did the best action that they came to see this city. While the younger students they were speech less. Really, they got shocked by the beauty of this big and modern city. They said with one voice this is not only modern and beautiful city this is one fantasy.

After that they went to hotel that the younger man Zeeshan, with his team security campaigned them after he went to his beautiful huge palace. When he arrived in his home, he went first to see his two children and after he went to his studio. Really that night he did not feel that he wanted to sleep.

He was thinking for Agneza but his thought was not living quiet and for Bojana. He was justifying himself while he thought that really, she is so beautiful and high-level intellectual woman, but he saw first Agneza that with her charm she grabbed his heart.

Agneza gave to his heart one strong light of love and changed his life that was in turbulent situation at that time. Agneza gave to the younger man Zeeshan, at that time so much arrythmia in his heart that were created by one new suddenly strong love, that he never imagined at that time to happen.

He was so much furious during that period of time he was desperate while he was fighting with himself for all strange situation that was created.

Suddenly the universe with his stars and silver moon that was seeing him during different night so much desperate, in deep thinking and during the day the golden sun was seeing him that smile, never found place to his lips and mouth with his employees, and why he was acting correctly to them but not with humor and love, so those universe's elements started to move for action.

So those powerful elements of universe that are so close with life of human - beings on Earth planet with their positive divine energy sent like value gift this new beautiful hot love to the younger man Zeeshan, through Agneza that was acting like messenger of universe to act like catalysator to give speed this process in life of this younger lovely man Zeeshan.

The younger man Zeeshan, was thinking about that situation that he was before and how changed in drastic and very beautiful way, he felt at that time one hot wave of love inside of his chest and he decide to write to Agneza right away.

He was starting to write in computer in official way, sometimes universe is giving sign of protection so he has intuition that somebody will control or seeing him and really his intuition did not lie because behind his shoulder was staying his wife Leylae, and was seeing what he was writing. She came without noise. When she saw his writing like official report, she interrupted him and said you have to write tonight this report.

The younger man Zeeshan, smiled and replied to his wife Leylae: I did not hear you when you came, and I did not want to bother you until to finish this writing. When I came, I went to see our two children and I thought you are in bed- room sleeping, or reading so I came here to write short this material what we did today and I was coming to tell you.

His wife Leylae, asked him: Tell me short how was your day today. He answered with full smile it was one wonderful day with so many activities to center of architects and to university with architecture major between two visits we ate lunch while in the evening, we went to cafeteria aside the ocean.

Really, they got shocked by beauty of our city Dubai, while some students that came with their professors said this city it is one fantasy, this environment it is magnificence. His wife Leylae, asked him with wondering:

Why came and students with those professors from those universities?

Her husband Zeeshan answered to her: Yes came and students they were excellent student so the universities paid for their trip to see and to get experience in our country United Arab Emirates, (UAE) and our city (Dubai) too. His wife Leylae, commented really this is very good job and good idea and for students in our country United Arab Emirates, (UAE) and our city Dubai too. After that she said to him: I am very happy for your beautiful day and left him in his studio.

The younger man Zeeshan, whispered to himself while said: Thank you "Allah" that protected me this time and created my idea to write in official way, plus he did not write the name of Agneza yet. So he continued his writing so fast, he was writing, to her for all activity that they have that day and in the end he expressed his deep love to her and wrote that:

I do not have patience until to come soon to meet you over there to your country Croatia to your village Lunaria. After he was seeing around that nobody was behind him or moving around to the hall, while to the top of the letter he wrote: "To My Suddenly White Dream! So, he was happy that wrote to Agneza and he was not desperate that his wife Leylae, was controlling him because this new love gave confidence to him, after all that he was going through, with fear and anxious about everything, about his position his family and their two families, of him and his wife too.

Now he was so much glad because he knows that Agneza loves him, and he did not want think for negative thing anymore. He was thinking I will do the best as I can for my family but this love is making hot my heart and nature all around looks so beautiful and I love my job and my people in my office too.

He was continuing with his thinking: Now only, "Allah" know what direction to give to me, I want to follow my happiness now let's go with flow in future I never know what is coming for me. Really, I am in love now with this younger beautiful Albanian girl Agneza, and I am not guilty.

I never accepted that my wife Leylae, with change for good now, so I am justifying myself, I was Okay, I was waiting so longer but now it is another new love and so many things will be changed in my life. I am taking care for everything for my two children and my family but now I am taking care and for my happiness for really.

He was thinking to buy some presents for Agneza and her brother Gentius, and something for Dalmet, and Armina their cousins, while to give to Bojana so she can give to Ardita) and she will send to "Lunaria" village to her cousins too.

He was thinking that I need to find time tomorrow so I will send this group of people, to huge mall of our city Dubai, and I have time to buy something over there. They are and two days here but the last day they will travel to the evening so I need to finish that job tomorrow about those small gifts.

I am sure the account lady Adara, with lawyer man Nassar, has prepared schedule for tomorrow when to send this group of people. I will be very happy now if Agneza will be here with this group of people to visit my city Dubai and to spent time with me.

With those thought he closed computer and was see from window the silver moon and the stars through this dark night while he whispered one pray and made one wish: Bring to me Agneza that I love so much, make this reality for me!

Next day in the morning the younger man Zeeshan, prepared himself to go to the office and to spend all the day with his guests from Western Balkan and center of Europe. He went to the office and was waiting his guests.

They came in 10.A.M.(ten a clock) to his office but before the younger man Zeeshan, decided to tell them the schedule of this day where they will go while his account lady Adara, was standing up in front of them the leader of this group strangely did one request.

We need to see around this city where are empty land so we can create one idea and maybe we will give you our idea for developing of this area with our specific architecture so this beautiful and modern city to have diversity about architecture.

Really request of leader of the group of professors and students, made to get wonder the younger man Zeeshan, but he liked this idea because he was curious about their other new idea what kind of architecture, they will propose for this empty land that has so much hectares (ha) around the city of Dubai.

The younger man Zeeshan, showed to them so much enthusiasm and said Okay I am agreed with that request let's go since now over there I am telling to you some of empty are that are surrounding our city of Dubai.

They got out of the office and got car and minibus like one day before and started driving to see empty land outside of the city of Dubai. When they arrived over there, they saw huge square of empty land with few trees around while the river was in distance with that place.

The ground was open brown color to easy open like color of sand, so it was not black color ground, it was not argil land. They started to discuss with professional terms. They said that is not in need in this place to build high building because foundation is not secure and is not in need to spend so much money to put foundation in very deep way.

They thought that here, maybe is good to create one beautiful project with flat, buildings, like shopping center, cultural center, with some buildings flat but modern for museum, library, theater, while only some buildings in line in distance to be maybe not more than ten floors.

They made addition, also to create one section for villas and one big green park with benches and some small stores for coffee or soda or whatever for people that like to come to spend time in park with their family and children too. Also needed highway in this section too, to connect with main center of this big city. But we think this will be preferred section of this city so many people will love to come to live here.

Another engineer architect gave another idea: We need to think for one beautiful modern bridge to the river so this side to be connected with other side of river in short way so in future will be created another project for the other side of the river, to build like this section while let's name twins section in both two sides of river with same architecture.

To the other section to have more medical center and different school like high school, college or university, while in this section to have elementary school middle school and high school.

So, this modern bridge will connect those two twins' section also will be created one luxury environment and quiet area too because will be more residential area and school or university will be for resident here, but maybe are coming and from the other part s of city of Dubia, students if they will like it.

Another architect gave another beautiful idea: I think we must to create in one or two sides of the river some stores and restaurants in line or cafeteria with easy material or skelet iron and glass or wood that in future to be replaced if is happening something with weather like flood or hurricane or whatever or tornado or if is coming another project for river area too.

I think that will create one beautiful area specific in the evening by light of the restaurant or cafeteria or small stores boutique, so those lights will reflex to the water of river too, and people will have big pleasure for this view.

While sport field about football and basketball and volleyball will have in two sections except in school but those will be for the children and youth people that will be resident here in those two sections. Needed hotels in two sides too, to be modern but no higher that building ten floors, so we will create one harmony with all buildings and other commercial buildings or cultural center buildings around.

All agreed also the younger man Zeeshan, and his friend lawyer Nassar, and account lady Adara, said: If you think that is coming beautiful this area is going to happen, we will build it with our investitures.

The leader of the group of architects said to them: It is coming very beautiful area very modern and most of all it is coming very peaceful area, so people that will live in this area in future will be privileged people, I am sure for that. In future time so many people will claim to live here in river-twins' area too.

The younger man Zeeshan, was happy for those ideas and this new version of those two twins' section in river's area in empty land of his city of Dubai. He got so much enthusiasm when they said: We will work hard to prepare this project in optimal time and to send to you for those two twins' area.

Really, all were happy for their contribute that they will give in extending of beautiful environment of this city of Dubai, while their leader of group said to them: We did very good job that we came here to see empty land of outside of this modern city of Dubai, so it is one good experience for us and is giving us, so much inspiration and energy to work hard and to create this beautiful project.

After that conversation the younger man Zeeshan, proposed them to go to drink one coffee to one store that was aside highway before to enter inside the city of Dubai. He Explained to them that after drinking coffee to cafeteria we will go to see huge super modern mall of our city of Dubai. All were agreed and they showed their big happiness.

When they arrive to cafeteria, they shocked for the store that was so modern, and beautiful with glass all around not with brick - wall and inside was so luxury environment. They expressed their pleasure while said to the younger man Zeeshan: Thank you very much that you brought here us in this beautiful cafeteria and luxury inside this is another experience in your beautiful city Dubai.

After that the younger man Zeeshan, said to professor Bojana: You will be more campaign during tour to mall because I need to buy something for those teenagers, and I need your advice also I will give to you to give to Ardita she will send those present to those people in "Lunaria" in Croatia.

Professor Bojana, smiled while was seeing him straight to his eyes, and said absolutely I will help you with my advice and I will send those presents for those younger people straight to their hand for sure.

And both of them understood each other and laughed. At that moment was beginning of creating one deep and strong foundation of friendship between the younger man Zeeshan, and Professor Bojana of university of Ljubljana of Slovenia.

After luxury glass cafeteria they went to luxury huge mall that was the magnificence, shopping center in this city. When they entered inside it, professor Bojana asked the younger man Zeeshan: What do you want to buy for your new friends, younger people?

The younger man Zeeshan, answered while was giving the hand to the top of his head with gesture that he was not sure, anyway he answered it is good to buy for them for four of them one electronic tablet.

What do you think? Professor Bojana said to him: This is wonderful idea. While I am helping you what to buy any dress for your new friend younger girl Agneza because she will be student to my university next September so I hope.

So, they entered first to one store with luxury cotton sweater with very beautiful advertises. So, Professor Bojana said to the younger man Zeeshan,: I think is good you to buy for Agneza these two cottons, sweater with longer sleeve, while she chooses one blue open color, cotton sweater with advertise of the City of Dubai, and another pink open color, sweater with two white birds symbol of peace that were staying in one green branch of the tree.

The younger man liked those two sweaters. Professor Bojana said to him it is better to buy for her brother Gentius, this blue bold color cotton sweater with one white ball with design black figure geometric.

That is enough about sweater, two for Agneza because she will be student faraway, from her family and one sweater of her brother Gentius, that he will be in family too. The sales person put those sweaters, in very beautiful colorful bag and gave to them while the younger man Zeeshan, paid for them to cashier.

After that store they went to another electronic store where they bought five electronic tablets, for Agneza, Gentius and their cousins, Armina, Dalmet and Ardita. They got those four packages of tablets, and after paid they went out to meet their crew that were walking slowly in longer hall and were waiting the younger man Zeeshan, and professor Bojana they did not want to lose each other in this super huge Galleria.

Definitely professor Bojana put aside her jealousy and helped about this idea the younger man Zeeshan. During their walking the younger man stopped in front of one store with luxury small bags for ladies. He entered inside and after, him entered Professor Bojana she thought, maybe he will ask her for anything for his younger girl Agneza, but when she was close to him, he asked her what color you like, one of those small luxury bags.

She wondered and said: Thank You, very much but I do not need. He said to her I asked which color you like I did not ask if you need or not it, and was smiling.

She chooses one grey color leather small elegant bag that has design in itself. She was very happy and said with full of her heart: I never can forget that. Thank You, very much, but anyway you bought for me presents last fall when I came here.

He was smiling and said to her: Enjoy it. He paid for this small leather bag while the sales person created one very beautiful package for that bag and they went out of this store. They were walking together with other people of this crew while in front of them showed up with very beautiful advertise one liquor store.

The younger man Zeeshan, entered inside this store and behind him entered professor Bojana that was acting like his loyal campaigning person in this tour around the Galleria.

While his security team were together with other people in front of the door of the store. The younger man Zeeshan, ordered for two directors and two architects professors three big glass bottles with Whisky, while for three students and one architect professor lady ordered four small glass bottles of whisky to give present to them.

He asked professor Bojana, I am okay now with those, tell me if you need one glass bottle Whisky. Professor Bojana answered to him fast I am not drinking alcohol at all, so I am single woman, and one girl in my family and I have only my mother in home she is not drinking alcohol too, my father passed away a long time ago, so I do not need it.

The younger man Zeeshan, saw her and really felt pain for her, that she has only her mother in her life. Professor Bojana got out of the store and called her friend architect lady and three students to come to take those glass bottles with Whisky and to give to them.

The younger man Zeeshan, paid for those bottles with Whisky that the sales person of the store, gave beautiful package for everyone bottle with Whisky.

When they got out of the store professor Bojana gave instruction to students that four big bottles were for two directors of university of Vienna of Austria and university of Ljubljana of Slovenia and for two professors of architecture major.

She continued with her instruction, while four others glass small bottles, are one for the lady professor of architecture and three others are for them younger students. All were very happy because bottle with whisky was expensive in this store to this huge modern famous galleria of this super modern city of Dubai.

They were continued this tour through the Galleria while were discussing for so many different matters and topic. All looked so much enthusiast. When they got out of this Galleria the younger man Zeeshan, said to them to go to eat to one restaurant close to this area that has traditional cook of this city.

One of those directors said to him: Better for us will be to go to another area because here is luxury environment and maybe is expensive restaurant too.

The younger man Zeeshan laughed loudly and said to him: Do not worry let's be expensive I want you to try traditional meal, they are doing so good service.

The director understood the expression of the younger man Zeeshan, and did not speak anymore but stayed silent and smiled. So, they decided to go to this expensive restaurant for really.

When they went over there it was so luxury restaurant inside and with very beautiful environment outside full with green grass in front and multicolor flower that were with wonderful combinations about their color that looked like one beautiful carpet.

They got two tables in one side of the restaurant that wall was only glass and they can enjoy all outside beautiful view. The younger man Zeeshan, ordered for all the traditional meal that he knows that was so good.

All tables were covered with white quality textile table – cover, while the chairs were covered with colorful silk, textile and wood of the chair had design in itself while has dark brown color. Three big beautiful Chrystal chandeliers were up.

Restaurant was full with people that all of them looked very happy. Professor started to discuss about those things that they saw for those two days, while they said: In this country United Arab Emirates (UAE) and specific in this very beautiful modern city of Dubai, it is the last word of science about buildings and architecture so many people from around the world have something to learn in this city.

At that time came in line three waiters with one big table like cart with so many dishes in it. They did three times way, back and forth to bring everything on two tables. The professor of architecture lady said with humor. Those our two tables are full with different meal like we are in any wedding. All they laughed.

After lunch they wanted to visit area and to see the tallest tower of this city Burja Khalifa. They went over there and spent so much time around and they liked so much that view for really. The day was going so fast so they said to go next day to the University of this city and after to come around some places of city while in the evening they will go to airport to travel to their country in Ljubljana of Slovenia and Vienna of Austria.

All were happy for this tour in this city suddenly the younger man Zeeshan, said to them let's go to see the "Expo -2020". They shocked they did not speak anything maybe they thought about finance or whatever but when the younger man Zeeshan, said to them: It is very modern building and very interesting things you can see inside. After he said to them do not think another thing just let's go.

They all said: Okay let's go and they were very happy about that. After they visited this "Expo -2020" the leader said loudly: I like to go to cafeteria aside of ocean where we were yesterday in the evening while is our time to pay over there.

All laughed and the younger man Zeeshan, laughed while said: Okay we will go but with one condition: You will pay only to your country when we will come over there, here it is my time or more exact our time, because I am representing my crew, he made them to understand about his employees, lawyer man Nassar, and account lady Adara, of his government - staff. All laughed and were agreed too.

They went to cafeteria and started to discuss about everything that they. have seen in this very beautiful and modern city too. At that time professor Bojana, with smile said to the younger man Zeeshan:

Do you like to go to balcony and to see together the stars, because it is very beautiful night outside tonight. They both got out to balcony while left all the crew that were discussing with enthusiasm with each other.

When they got to balcony, they saw that all the stars were out to the dark sky. The full moon looked that was kissing with its light the water of ocean while was doing so much jealous the white waves, and the white flamingo, that waves were moving with noise and faster that were telling that they were nervous and anxious for love of the silver moon with their water.

While the white flamingos were flying fast and leaving behind the water of ocean without turning their head to see this action of love, they cannot accept that the silver moon to love more the water of ocean than them that were visiting the sky area of the moon every day and night sometimes.

So, their fast flying during this night above the water of ocean and were going so far above the ground were showing their nervous reaction like protest to their longer friend beautiful silver moon. The white flamingos were loyal friends to silver moon but they got shocked suddenly by this new strong love with water of ocean now that silver moon was full.

Really it was one magical view that night. At that time professor Bojana asked the younger man when is the other time that he will come to the Western Balkan and specific to her lovely city Ljubljana of Slovenia, also and to Croatia, while she said: You have one reason now to come to "Lunaria" of Croatia.

Suddenly the answer of the younger man Zeeshan, was so confident and strong: You are right Professor Bojana, really, I have one very strong reason to come in that region of Western Balkan, specific in "Lunaria" of Croatia. I need to see Agneza, I miss so much her, I am interested for her.

Strangely Professor Bojana got shocked by his strict strong and confident answer and said to him as I understood, it is not only interested about her, but maybe it is strong new love.

You are not wrong in your perception Professor Bojana and the younger man Zeeshan, smiled. Professor Bojana tried to hidden her strong jealousy because she still thinking about him and hoped so much something will change for good for her, but this answer cut every ties, of feelings of love by him to her. She said: Lucky girl Agneza.

The younger man Zeeshan, got her hand to his hand with gentle way and said: Better expression will be by you: "Very Lucky Me", about this beautiful smart younger Albanian girl Agneza. Both they laughed while professor Bojana loved his action that got her hand to his hand and was holding strong and she thought, at least and last I won one new wonderful and best friend the younger man Zeeshan.

At that time that the universe heard the statement of love by the younger man Zeeshan, about Agneza to his good friend professor Bojana, something happened to the dark sky in distance showed one liked colorful amount of gas mixer color orange with lily color that was creating one figure like cloud.

Both of them shocked by this phenomenon. But after some minutes this amount of gas came in big form and both of them said with one voice: This is beautiful Nebula star with mixer color orange and lily. This is wonderful view.

The universe honored the true statement of the sincere love of the younger man Zeeshan, for the younger Albanian girl Agneza, while sent out the orange- lily, mixer color, beautiful, Nebula star.

He said: Thank you "Allah" for this beautiful phenomenon. While professor Bojana said: Thank You, God, Thank You, universe for this wonderful view. At that time, she called from the door of the balcony her friends to come to see that phenomenon and to bring her camera. They came all of them and they shocked by this very beautiful view above the water of ocean.

During this beautiful night after love of the silver moon with water of ocean came one very beautiful specter of colors of the orange – lily color Nebula star, above the water of ocean. The younger man Zeeshan, called the waiter that he came fast, he was one younger good-looking boy and he said to him to take picture for all of them like group in front of this beautiful view.

So, they did so many pictures, also he did pictures and with professor Bojana alone, also with his account lady Adara and professor Bojana and others with his lawyer man and all this crew of professors and students too.

Really it was one magnificence night. After that the younger man, made jokes with professor Bojana, while he was risen up the confidence with her like his best friend, and said to her: I promise to you that tomorrow I will give you exact answer when I will come to visit you over there in Western Balkan. She showed happiness and said really you will tell me tomorrow?!

Really, he said I will calculate tonight about all problems that I have during this time of this season of spring time, also I will start and the new project of new town close to desert area and I will tell you for really. Professor Bojana said to him I loved that explanation. I will practice full patience until tomorrow until you to tell me, when you will come to Western Balkan in "Lunaria" of Croatia, and Ljubljana of Slovenia.

Really Professor Bojana was so much happy about this news by him and was speaking with full smile with all others people of her crew. Her happiness did not go without attention by them, but they thought maybe something promised to her the younger man Zeeshan. They were right because professor Bojana did not want to keep secret that news, but said to them: Listen me one fast and flash news:

Tomorrow Prince Zeeshan, will tell me, when he will come again to Western Balkan and to our city Ljubljana, of Slovenia and maybe and to Vienna of Austria but main visit he will have to Croatia for some historic material, she made addition by herself that fact, but did not tell to them really main reason, as very smart and good lady she is.

All professor, and students were happy and all of them strangely said with one voice: uuuuaaau, good news Welcome to our countries. All laughed for this synchronism of voice for really. Really this evening was so wonderful for all.

At that time the younger man Zeeshan, asked his account lady Adara:

Maybe you got so latter those two days for your family and children but she answered with smile and happiness:

I am okay because my mother will support me those three days to take care for my family and specific for my children. I called her and my husband and everything is Okay in my home about my family. They said to me enjoy your time with those guests that is it, and I loved for really that evening tonight.

After time that they spend with happiness to cafeteria aside the ocean, the younger man Zeeshan, with his friend lawyer Nassar, and account lady Adara campaigned their guests to their hotel while they said Good Night, and see all of you next day in the morning.

The younger man Zeeshan, gave the gifts to professor Bojana, so she will establish to her luggage in her room, after he separated his security crew members so some of them will send to their home the lawyer man Nassar, and the account lady Adara, first they send the account lady after the lawyer man.

The younger man Zeeshan, with his loyal friend Emin, leader of security team and two other men were driving to his palace, so left him with one sweet Good Night, greeting, to the palace and were driving to their home.

Strangely, during this time and why was very busy time for Prince Zeeshan, really, he was very happy and very active all the time the smile was decorating his nice face, and his beautiful eyes were in harmony with his beautiful smile, that very white beautiful teeth showed up through it, while doing one nice contract with its face.

When he arrived in his palace, one fresh breeze gave fresh to his face, he entered, to the big hall and was getting fast stairs to go to the second floor, first he did his ritual he entered to the room of two children and hugged and kissed them while, they were sleeping.

He left their room and went to his studio, after some minutes came his wife Leylae, to say welcome to him and when she saw his big smile to his face, she understood that his day was so good anyway she asked him how was your day today with your guests. He smiled and said with full happiness, it was one wonderful day today.

What was specific wonderful today for you she asked again her husband Zeeshan. He answered so much enthusiast, all activities were so good today but wonderful as you want specific was the evening to the cafeteria aside the ocean that we were all of us.

During this evening we enjoyed the most beautiful view while during this dark night with full moon and all bright stars after some minutes showed up in distance while was coming more bigger orange - lily mixer color the most beautiful Nebula star. We did so many pictures I will tell you now while he opened his telephone cellular and opened all the pictures that all crew with their smile with happiness has behind the most beautiful view, created by colorful Nebula star.

His wife Leylae, made one sigh uauauaua, so beautiful I wish to be over there with you this evening, really it is so beautiful magical evening. After he explained to his wife Leylae, about their activity that day while said to her tomorrow we are going to "Zayed" university of city Dubai, and later evening they will travel to their country.

She asked with wondering why they do not stay more days? No answered the younger man Zeeshan, because they are busy in their universities but hey gave me one good idea for those empty land outside the city, they will work for project design for that and will send to my office this project.

She said to her husband really this wonderful job, and you have credit for their welcome for them and campaigning. Really you were so busy this time with two different important group to be in activity every day to different center.

Yes, it is, true replied Prince Zeeshan, to his wife Leylae, while was smiling and was expressing his happiness for his good job. She left after some minutes alone in his office the younger man Zeeshan, that he wanted to see something in computer.

When he saw that no one was around him he opened his telephone to see message or who had called him. He saw greeting with symbols by Agneza. He calculated difference of hours between two their countries and he wrote right away in short way, "Why" this text message only with symbols.

After some minutes while he was reading e-mails in his computer, he heard sound of arrived message to his telephone. He opened telephone mobile and saw text by Agneza that explained:

I know that you are very busy with people from central Europe and Western Balkan this is the reason of this text with symbols I did not want to bother you. He explained to her that he never can get bother by her, after he wrote to her: I will write you – email now in my computer to you not by phone, so see my e-amil in your e-mail site.

He started to write e-mail to Agneza with full happiness, he explained to her about their activity that day, also that he is so much busy this spring time season about, new project of new town close to desert area, that really, he gave news to her before some weeks.

The last paragraph of his writing, was one big surprise for Agneza while he wrote: I will come to see you for your graduation day of your high school. He gave to her this great news that was something secret and he will tell next day to professor Bojana too.

This news shocked the beautiful younger Albanian girl Agneza, that she did not have patience but she called right away to his telephone. He listened her melodious voice why was asking with wondering and full happiness:

Really you will come the day of my graduation of high school in "Lunaria" of Croatia.

His answered was strict and short: Really, I will come for your graduation day I will be your special guest that day and started to laugh. At that time his wife Leylae, came while heard his loudly voice that was not his nature to do that, she thought maybe was any good news. She asked him what is any good news.

Prince Zeeshan, shocked for presence of his wife at that time in his studio, he was so much happy and he did not control himself while was speaking loudly with happiness, also his email was in open page in computer but he did not write yet the name of Agneza in top page. Looked that his intuition was warning him about e-mail to be careful.

His wife Leylae, while was waiting his answer was reading through-mail fast and carefully. Really e-mail was like report for that daily activity so she never thought that this e-mail was for someone very special of her husband Zeeshan.

He smiled to her and said, that one student in Western Balkan wants me to go for the graduation day of high school but Prince Zeeshan did not make specific if was female student or male student. So, he closed his statement while said to her with calm and smile: I laughed with that innocent invitation, while his wife Leylae, said ooo very good.

After his wife Leylae, left the younger man Zeeshan, touched with his hand his head and said: Thank you "Allah" for saving me now from any unpleasant situation. I do not like this time bad situation. After he whispered with himself: It is later for my wife Leylae, turning back to me with her thoughts.

I am in deep love with this younger beautiful Albanian girl Agneza that is living in "Lunaria" of Croatia, and I am very happy for really, she changed my situation.

He finished his e-mail wrote the name of Agneza and sent right away. The younger man Zeeshan, did not tell by telephone and not by e-mail, to Agneza about presents or gifts that he was sending to her to Gentius and to her cousins- friends Armina, Dalmet and Ardita.

He wanted to made one big sweet surprise to them. After he was thinking for answer that he gave to his wife Leylae, but he justified himself that sometimes needed to do that, to give one answer that really it is not right answer, for to save himself by any big problem in that time that he never needed in that time big conflict anyway.

After he prayed:

"Allah" give me light to my life and protect my new beautiful love now that is giving so much happiness for my life. Keep in good health my two children their mother too, my parents and all my brothers and sisters too.

He was seeing from his window the silver moon and all the stars that were giving so much light during this night, while the younger man Zeeshan, was thinking with himself:

How many big changing suddenly came to my life, to my thoughts and to my feelings during this period time since I saw this younger girl Agneza and those people from Western Balkan. How many new ideas and so much inspiration, gave to me those people in Western Balkan with their hard working, if and in difficult environment or financial situation but they were claiming for success in their life.

I am very happy for those three trips that I did in Western Balkan, Montenegro, Croatia, Slovenia and center of Europe, Vienna of Austria. Now I need to consolidate all my thoughts after this crew to travel to Europe and to focus in this, new project of new town close to desert area.

Next day the younger man Zeeshan, prepared himself to go to his office and to spend this last day with his guests, professors and students from Ljubljana of Slovenia and Vienna of Austria.

He went early in office and ordered his secretary Salma, to go to order by telephone some sweet biscuits for those people, some small chocolates and tea and coffee too, let' have their choice what they will drink coffee or tea. Also, he said to her to order one big chocolate cake and one cake with vanilla and fruits to the top. Guests came to the office of the younger man in 10: A.M.

They got beautiful surprise when they saw in office of the younger man Zeeshan, to big table some small white luxury dishes with knifes, and forks while there were two big cakes on the table one chocolate cake and one vanilla cake with a lot mixer fruits on the top.

On table were two big glass tanks with coffee and tea, some porcelain cups and two big glass dishes with biscuits and small chocolates. The younger man said to them, I prepared that table with those sweets, tea and coffee for you in my office. So, you can take what is your preference about sweets and coffee or tea in same time we can do conversation to discuss for some matters, before we to go to "Zayed" University.

All were agreed with prince Zeeshan, also they laughed with happiness while they said to him: we ate breakfast already why you did not tell us not to eat and continuing to laugh. The younger man Zeeshan, laughed and said to them:

To eat two times, it is not bad anyway. So started this beautiful morning in his office with harmony and good conversation. They discussed so many problems, in short way, while professor of architecture promised to the younger man Zeeshan, that they will prepare and finish this project very soon, as it is possible, for empty land, aside the river and around to area that they saw one day before.

After they finished eating biscuits cake and drinking coffee or tea, the younger man said to them get everyone of you those chocolates to eat later during driving. So, they did and were laughing. At 11: 00 A.M. (eleven a clock) all got out of the office and went to parking lot where waiting the secret service team's members of the younger man Zeeshan, and started to drive to go to the "Zayed" University.

When they arrived over there leader of "Zayed" university has organized crew to wait these people. So, they gave one sweet welcome, to the guests from Western Balkan and center, of Europe and invited them inside to one big room to make meeting.

Meeting was so much interesting about education system, about experience of this university also more specific was cooperation with material between those architects of Europe and Western Balkan and architects and professor of this university of city of Dubai.

When the meeting finished, they did some pictures all were glad for this experience and combination of thoughts and ideas. It was middle day after 2:00 P.M. (two a clock) when they left modern building of this university with lovely greetings of leader of this university and small group of professors and students too. When they were out Professor Bojana said to the younger man Zeeshan:

I have one request to you. He saw her straight to her eyes and said what is your request? She replied: My friend told me to please you to send us to one center where are selling folk souvenirs. Native's art figurine or souvenir of this country and to one shopping where are sweet and dry fruits in package. They want to buy for their family like present.

The younger man Zeeshan, laughed and said this is easy to do. I thought what is your request that you were speaking so much serious, while all the other people that were listening in silence all laughed. We will go because we have some times before you to go to take some rest in hotel and to prepare for your trip in the evening.

They went to two shopping centers, with those stores and they bought what they liked for their family's members, relatives and their friends too. During walking, through those stores they saw one small store that was preparing, "Donner" longer sandwich with a lot meat inside.

They liked to eat those for lunch and they will have time to come around they ordered those "Donner" and ate fast inside this store. The younger man did not allow they to pay by themselves he paid for all those Donners. After that they went to hotel, during, this time professor Bojana said to the younger man Zeeshan, I established in my luggage your gifts for your people.

The younger man asked her: Did you have space inside your luggage. Professor Bojana answered of course, because I did not have so much clothes when I came so my clothes I put in my handbag and my luggage has space.

The younger man Zeeshan said to her: Thank You, very much. I hope our very - good friendship to have longer term. Professor Bojana said to him:

I think we will work us together to make more stronger our friendship.

Prince Zeeshan, I want to say to you Thank You, very much by you and your people for wonderful welcome that you gave to us to my people and my friends too, I am very happy.

When they arrived to hotel: They wanted to give their hand to the younger man Zeeshan, and his lawyer Nassar, and account lady Adara too, but he said to them: No, we are coming at 6:00 P. M. (six a clock) here to send you to airport over there we will give hand to each other.

During this time, he saw that professor Bojana smiled while her face started to take a little yellow color and her eyes started to fill with tears but she turned her head to the other side. The younger man Zeeshan, pointed her situation, while thought this is love, she is in love with me. He felt himself something compassionate as sensitive person he is.

At that time all others said to the younger man Zeeshan, Thank You, very much that you are coming with us to airport, we feel that we have family member here. The younger man Zeeshan, said to them, we are going now to our office and in 6:00 P.M. (six a clock) we will come here to send you to airport.

At 6:00. P. M. (six a clock) the younger man Zeeshan, with his lawyer Nassar, and his account lady Adara, came with the secret service team 's members with two cars to hotel to take those people to send to airport. When they gave hand to each other to airport, professor Bojana stayed to the end of line to meet the younger man, Zeeshan.

She met lawyer Nassar, and account lady Adara, said to them Thank You, very much and when she gave hand to the younger man Zeeshan, he hugged her she cannot stop her tears while said to him, all the time when I said Good Bye, to people that I am close or I like, I cannot, stop my tears I am sensitive person.

317

She hugged him and said I am waiting, you to come I wish that this day of graduation of Agneza to be next week while was laughing and her tears were going down to her beautiful white face.

The younger man Zeeshan, laughed and said her (Agneza) day of graduation count that is to the door of airport he used metaphoric expression, and made to laugh professor Bojana, account lady Adara, and lawyer man Nassar, too. He wanted to make calm professor Bojana, because her crying touched his heart, while the account lady Adara, and lawyer Nassar, understood that situation but they never discussed anymore.

When they were entering to airport all of them stayed some minutes while were giving greetings with their hands to the younger man Zeeshan, to account lady Adara, and to lawyer man Nassar, of this city's government.

After that the younger man with his lawyer Nassar, account lady Adara, and his secret service crew's members, with two cars started driving to get out of airport to their city. It was one longer day with activity really, they were three days full activities, so they needed to go right away to their home to take rest and to prepare for next day that will be more quiet day in daily routine office's job.

Driver with the other car sent lawyer Nassar, and account lady Adara, to their home, because was taking time them to go to office to get their car, while the younger man Zeeshan, with his security team's members, continued, driving to go to his huge beautiful palace. It was ne beautiful evening of spring time but the younger man Zeeshan, was so tired by those activities in short time for two important group of people and he was really tired so he needed to take rest to his home.

Really, he felt something empty inside himself when was remembering professor Bojana that was crying. He thought:

I must to be more careful when I am communicating with people, that my action or my behave, not to be misunderstood, I do not want anyone on this Earth planet to have pain by me in life if it is business or love story or family matter.

When the younger man Zeeshan, entered to his palace firstly, he went to the room of his two children he did ritual he hugged and kissed them spent some time with them and after he went to his studio.

Really, he was so much tired that evening but strangely he cannot sleep, he did not feel that he wanted to sleep. He opened his computer and started to read some e-mails that different officials sent to him for different problems that they needed help by local government.

Really, he wanted to wait until these people that were his guests those three days to arrive in their countries and he wanted to see text, by professor Bojana that she and them arrived good. Strangely, he did not understand why he was waiting without patience her e-mail and text – message, but maybe her crying has touched so much his heart.

Maybe in some points he felt himself guilty about her, that gave some hope to her with his lovely and warm gesture. Those thoughts were not leaving quiet the younger man Zeeshan, so he was waiting and wanted to spend time with writing.

During this time his wife Leylae, came to his studio and he got wondering that she did not hear noise that he came inside home. She asked him: How was your day today? He answered to her: My day today was very good but I am so tired by all this activities, but I liked all this activities, for really, because all gave me so much enthusiasm and inspiration. After she asked if he saw the children. The younger man Zeeshan, answered with full smile and said: This is the first duty that I have and I am doing all the time when I am entering in palace.

They are giving to me big amount of oxygen and fresh breath for my life and full happiness, as you know those elements are very important for our life for our existence on this earth planet. I love my children like my life too.

She laughed and said to him: I see that your day today was wonderful because I see how you are expressing your happiness in poetic way, because you are using now so many artistic figures in literature, you are using so much metaphoric expression. After that both of them laughed.

She said to him: I believe that you really have something to write now, right? Her husband Zeeshan, answered to her with smile: Really, I do not need to write tonight, but I am waiting until this people to arrive in their home countries and one of them, that was professor of law, to write me text – message or e-mail that all arrived good.

So, I am waiting until them to arrive over there, so tomorrow I will go latter to my office. This is one occasion that I to campaign you tomorrow to your friends of architects for your new project. She said: Really you are doing that tomorrow. Really, I am doing that why not?

I have time tomorrow because my day tomorrow it is like half off day after those two weeks with those two different groups that came to our city Dubai. I deserve some happy hours during those days now. His wife Leylae, said to him: You are very right. You had heavy activities this time with those two groups. After that, she left him alone in his studio and went to see children in their room.

The younger man Zeeshan, started to read one material in computer about environment. Also, he was seeing in computer so many new modern buildings about new futurist architecture. He was thinking about starting his new project of the new town close to are of desert.

He decided to talk with architects and to start next week preparing of the ground to this area. So, he was reading about companies that have huge tractor so he needed to discuss with them and to start next week dinning ground.

Really, he was so much enthusiast and he was feeling so much fresh himself to start this project while was making this idea so much happy him.

After he was writing that information, for those corporations about heavy machine and tractor he heard sound of his telephone that was telling to him that has text message. He opened, his telephone cellular while he saw the text message by professor Bojana, he felt warm inside his chest and was very happy for her text message.

He was reading the text by professor Bojana. She was giving information that she arrived with her friends in Ljubljana Slovenia, while group of Austria did not give news to her yet. When they will text to her she will give information to him.

He did not have patience but called her right away in his telephone cellular. She answered and got wondering. You did not sleep yet? The younger man Zeeshan, answered: No, I am waiting you to give me information. Thank You, for your text message. I am happy that you arrived good to your home.

Really, I was in tension until to hear by you, because I saw you so much desperate when you were going inside airport. She did not speak. He understood that she was impressed by his question and his taking care for her, after some seconds she said to him:

Thank You, very much for everything and for waiting this later night to get news by me. But I know now that the day of graduation of Agneza is close to the door of airport so I am waiting to see you very soon. I miss you since now. Both of them laughed loudly.

The younger man explained to professor Bojana that he will go later in his office, so they continued to speak longer and free. Their conversation has so much happiness, and humor, that was making more lovely and strong their friendship.

It was going 2:00. A.M (two a clock in the morning), was coming the morning of the other day but both of them did not feel tired and why professor Bojana traveled so many hours that night, and all the day were in activity. The younger man Zeeshan, said to her: You are going to work early in the morning. She replied fast I have my assistant to do my job tomorrow. So, he understood that professor Bojana wanted to continued their beautiful conversation.

Really it was beautiful night for both of them, they did not feel tired and why they were busy all the day.

So that night the younger man Zeeshan, cannot sleep quiet until early in the morning, but he stayed later on bed and got out of the bed at the time that he will go with his wife to the center where working group of architects that she has chosen.

Really, she started to work with them or more exact they were preparing some projects about her idea for another section of this new town close to area of desert. It was going 10:30. A.M., when they got out of their beautiful palace.

The younger man Zeeshan, was campaigning her to this office and wanted to leave her over there but she spoke so much for those projects and made to awake his curiosity to see those projects, so he decided to enter in that studio of architects' women with his wife Leylae.

After he gave greetings to them, he saw some of those projects about some beautiful buildings with not so much height. He liked those projects and congratulated them after left this building while said to his wife Leylae, he will send his security team's members to send her to palace and went out to go to his office. It was middle of the day when he went to his office.

He found over there some of his architects and started meeting with them. they said that they have ready projects for the first section so they can start right away. The younger man Zeeshan, was very happy for this news and called another man that was working to his local government while gave to him all the list of the big corporation that had big machineries and tractors, like "Komatsu".

He said to him to order those, tractors, so they will start dinning of the ground for the first section of the new town. At that time the younger man Zeeshan, got one whisky glass bottle that he had since that were his guests in his office and ordered, his secretary Salma, to bring some glass cups.

He started to fill those glass cups with a little whisky and gave to those architects, some of them were foreign European men, also gave and some small chocolates to them. They cheered for starting new project. It was one beautiful spring time that gave so much glad inside chest of the younger man Zeeshan. He whispered with himself: This spring time brought so much good news and full happiness for me about this project of new town close to desert area.

When his man, coordinator called those chief executive officers of those companies, to come to their office with their people to made contract and to order big machinery and Komatsu, this news was spreading out, all around this city Dubai, with speed cosmic, that will start new project of new town close to desert area of this city.

In this meeting the younger man Zeeshan, called and his all account, persons, and lawyers of his office he said to them to do good organize about everything and to call for one engineer of Geodezi, that needed before to start dining the ground with tractor.

All of them decided, to build some building to sleep workers that will work over there since the beginning until to finish this new town. All were enthusiast while they said let's start with dinning ground after step by step to work with construction corporations and different engineers too.

After those architects collected all their paper and material and left his office, the younger man Zeeshan, started to dream during day about this project that was becoming real in this spring time. Everything is coming good as the older saying: "The good beginning it is half of the job". When everybody left his office, he decided to see his telephone for any news and after to see in his computer of office.

He saw longer text message by Agneza. The text message has so much points of big happiness. She got huge surprise for his gift to her and to her brother Gentius, and their cousins Armina and Dalmet. She was explained that professor Bojana in middle day during break time met Ardita and gave to her all those gifts.

Ardita right away sent pictures to me to Gentius to her brother Dalmet. Gentius is so much happy and he told to our parents and never stopped to say my lovely prince Zeeshan, sent me this gift while our parents laughed and said to him sent greeting and Thank You, to your lovely Prince Zeeshan, by yourself and by us too. Gentius said to them yes, yes, I will do but he is continuing to talk with happiness.

Nobody can stop him today, while is calling time by time and Dalmet,

So, your gifts brought so much happiness to us and to our home too with our parents too. While she was putting some signing of smile in text message. Thank You, very much for everything that you are doing for us. Same happy noise is doing Dalmet with his parents too, for gift that you sent for him and his sister Armina.

The younger man Zeeshan, thought: These younger people are so lovely and very good people, while he felt that his eyes started to fill with tears. After he saw longer text message by Armina too.

Armina was writing: In our Earth planet since are living some very good people like you, I hope that the world will become better place for all. Your generosity with your gifts touched my heart and all of us hearts. Your act gave so much inspiration to us, that in future we to be like you, to think like you for people, and to help people as we can.

Those gifts will be big symbol for us by you, that we never will forget. Those gifts will be like treasure in our memories that we will save for all our life, and we will transmit your action, to others, so we will create one legacy that others to continue your way, in future our way. Thank You, very much for everything you are doing for us. At the end she has written: "God ", Bless You!

He saw another very short text message by Gentius and Dalmet: They were writing: We are together now we will call you tomorrow. Thank you very much for your gifts, we will talk longer tomorrow. After specific Gentius was writing oooo my lovely prince Zeeshan! After, both of them put their name and wrote that their parents said Thank You, to you and are saying Hello, to you.

The younger man Zeeshan, thoughts, when I am going for day of graduation of Agneza, I will give to them big surprise, because I advised, Agneza not to tell to them. Really, I am very happy to be present in her day of graduation of high school. After that, he decided to call professor Bojana and to say Thank You, very much for job well done.

323

He called her, while heard her voice he got enthusiasm, when she started to laugh and said: You got news right, you gave so much happiness to those younger people for really. Her voice was sounds like crystal water in river during spring time. She continued: I did not want to write to you until them to tell you.

Ardita, when I told her and I gave the gifts, she got shocked and was saying with full happiness and big wondering: Really prince Zeeshan, sent those gifts for us, really?, and she was very happy while all university got this news here.

After that happy and friendly conversation with professor Bojana the younger man decided to write to Agneza, to Armina and to Gentius and Dalmet, in telephone cellular of Gentius.

He started to write to Agneza, strangely the words to him came so fast in beautiful way during writing. He was expressing to her his happiness that professor Bojana, did very good job and she show herself like a very good friend.

He was writing to her about his dream that he saw during one night while, he named its dream, "Suddenly White Dream" and wanted this dream to be reality. Also, he was writing that he did not have patience until to meet again her very soon. He wanted to write more but secretary Salma, came to his office and interrupted him, so he sent this part of his text, while was talking with his secretary lady Salma.

After some minutes he heard the sound of telephone cellular that was giving sign of text message was coming. After secretary lady Salma, left his office, he opened his telephone cellular and saw text message by Agneza.

She replied so fast while has written: You are writing to me that you do not have patience until to meet me again soon, while I am saying to you, I wish you to be here tomorrow, while has put sign of smile at the end of this phrase.

The younger man Zeeshan, laughed while he thought, I am very happy and I am acting like very younger boy now, this is really great love for me. He started again to write with full inspiration.

If I will have wings now like Angelo I will fly right away to you, during this very beautiful pink to orange sunset. I will not care and for gases that are creating this color around golden sun, if they are danger for me, because my great love will dismiss those gases and will open new path for me. I will try to escape and to fly far away.

Maybe I will find on my way big crew of different birds that will come from cold weather to immigrate to warm weather of spring time. So, I will not be alone until to arrive to "Lunaria" of Croatia, in your village and to be like bird in front of your window.

I will be happy to enjoy your beautiful face with your magical smile in window and after hand by hand together to enjoy the light of silver moon and all great stars, during beautiful night in front of your garden. During this time to enjoy the fresh air that is coming with wind by mountain of your village, that will noise of the river water to send sound of our love far away.

During this night all around to know about our great love. He sent to Agneza this text and was waiting like teenager her answer. She replied so fast with one figure one big white bird with one letter hanged to his neck while the letter has one figure big red heart. She has written only one short phrase: This white bird is for your "Suddenly White Dream".

The younger man Zeeshan, smiled and said loudly: Agneza loves me she really loves me! After he said: Thank You, "Allah" for this lovely girl like beautiful gift that you brought to me. He thought with himself: Really, I am in love with Agneza and I am very happy now.

After he wrote text to Armina, and to Gentius and Dalmet to telephone of Gentius. When he finished writing to all of them, he was watching from the window the most beautiful sunset of this spring time while he whispered to himself: I think and nature is beautiful and is happy for me and my great love.

While he was seeing in distance some taller trees and "Palma" tree were moving their branches slowly by one easy wind that was coming from blue ocean. The tallest buildings that looked while watching the younger man Zeeshan, and said to him we know you secret great love story with this younger beautiful Albanian girl Agneza in Croatia, so we will tell for you up to the golden sun, silver moon and all stars, if you are putting between us some others tallest beautiful building like our rivals, as you see our head are above the clouds. We have all witnesses around about our tolerance to you, that you put in front of us this snob tallest and beautiful tower, we cannot allow you with other buildings to put our beauty down.

At that time the younger man Zeeshan, was thinking how changed his life with so many amplitudes. He whispered to himself: Maybe "Allah" put me in test how I will survive during this turbulent time in my family, while he created for me that beautiful afternoon of later summer to know Agneza that gave to me suddenly one great love inside my heart and left without sleeping so many nights.

During this time, I forget all pain and sadness that I had but I was thinking for this new love, while I never am nervous when my father is criticizing and advising for my wife and my life. He never can understand, and never can imagine, that in this time, suddenly, I am in love but is seeing me with wondering that I am not nostalgic like before. He saw some months before, that my tears were dried.

Anyway, I need to go now in my palace, I am sure that "Allah" with its power will give good direction to my life and to my new love. After that he prepared to go to his palace while called his loyal friend Emin, leader of the security team and said we need to go now. He came to his office while he asked him that they will go straight to his palace or to another place.

The younger man Zeeshan, said strict: We are going to my palace because really, I feel something tired myself now. I was all night awaked while I was working some material and I was waiting answer by those people, to tell me how they arrived to their countries too.

So, I need to take rest tonight and to be ready for tomorrow in the morning because are coming some people of those corporations of heavy machines and "Comatcu", tractor, that we must to do contract to buy those machineries or to rent whatever and to start dinning of the ground to start new project of new town close to desert area.

When they go out, they found security team's members that were waiting they entered, to car and river started driving to go to the palace of the younger man Zeeshan.

It was one wonderful evening with so many colorful lights during the highway, while advertise of the building were doing more colorful and more complex that panorama of this beautiful and modern city of Dubai.

He went to his palace while said Good Night to his security team's members, he entered inside his huge and luxury palace. He did ritual went first to the room of his two children spent some minutes them kissed them and went right away to his studio.

Really, he was not in mood to work that evening, but he ordered for dinner steak meat, fry's potatoes, white cheese, small dish with rice and orange soda, and said to Aasma, the lady that was working to kitchen I need those dishes in balcony.

He continued to read in computer some e-mails while came his wife Leylae, and asked him how was his day. He answered with full smile. This day today was the most beautiful day that I saw the last time or better specific the last year. She asked again with delicatesse can I know what was so better for you today that you are so much happy and with full smile.

Of course, the younger man Zeeshan, did not give to her direct answer, but he said to her: Really now I am very happy because I will eat to balcony, steak meat, white cheese and fry's potatoes but was funny because when he was saying the word cheese, he did longer word Che-e-ese and made his wife Leylae, to laugh for really.

What to say to her, he cannot tell to her that he was living now in magical beautiful world of great love with that younger beautiful Albanian girl Agneza citizen in Croatia.

He did not want to start again big conflict and to argue about her capriccio behavior before sometimes, that brought that situation, but all the time he was thinking, to be quiet in home to enjoy this love story and why in distance and after "Allah" will decide what way he will follow, who knows? What will happen in future?!

After his wife said to him: I see you are very happy and your face is showing me so much painting all around with "Glad' color situation. She started to speak with artistic figure and something with easy irony she wanted to cover up her jealousy.

At that time the younger man Zeeshan, that understood her game's words said with full smile: Do you want to enjoy my painting with "Glad" color of my face about this situation during my dinner to balcony? It is up to you I am not forcing you because I do not want to change maybe your good mood, with my happiness in different situation.

She laughed and said, I am coming to stay with you during your dinner and if your happiness will make me dizzy to fell down from balcony. The younger man Zeeshan, laughed loudly and said no, no, no, I am not leaving you to fell down from balcony because our children need their mother to grow up and I want our children to have happy life.

Another reason is that beautiful silver moon and beautiful stars will see this scene and will be witness against me and why they are my friend during night. Another reason I cannot justify to our children when they grow up that I allow to happen this bad event.

At that time his wife Leylae, with smart brain reacted fast: So those are your reasons that will not allow me to fell from balcony if I am dizzy by your happiness, you did not count your "Love" for me like important reason?!

The younger man Zeeshan, said short and strict with laughing: My "Love" is ingredient to all of those reasons that I counted for you. Both they laughed loudly for his fast and smart answer that justifies himself.

After the younger man Zeeshan, said to his wife Leylae: Now do you want to enjoy your Prince of this city of Dubai, for dinner to balcony?

She said in bold way: I am coming to enjoy this dinner with my rival in our new two separated projects of new town of extending of our beautiful city of Dubai. He smiled and both of them went to balcony to wait this lady. After some minutes the lady from kitchen came with big beautiful silver ashtray with some dishes on it. She did two ways to bring small Christal dishes with fruit and glass cup with orange liquid. She asked the wife of Prince Zeeshan, what she wanted, but she said:

That she wanted only one big glass with ice tea. They took sit to chairs close to one small circle table in balcony. They were enjoying this very beautiful evening under light of silver moon and so many bright stars, while one fresh breeze was touching their face with delicatesse and were creating to them one fresh breath for really.

The fly lights were creating one beautiful environment in garden with their small phosphor lights, while Gjinkalla were doing all around, one beautiful easy noise, zhu, zhu, zhu, during this beautiful lovely spring evening. Really it was one romantic evening. Strangely the younger man Zeeshan, whispered with himself like pray:" Allah" protect me during this evening, not to start any argue with her jealousy because it is so beautiful evening and I do not want to destroy my happiness. ". When he said "Amen" with loudly voice his wife understood that he was praying before to eat dinner.

Really, Prince Zeeshan, did pray for calm situation that will bring beautiful situation of eating of this dinner too. He started to ask his wife in professional way in serious way, what is going with her project where they were until now, so he did not leave space to her to talk indirect for their situation or for any doubt of her for him for another relationship.

She started to explain with enthusiasm, while he was listening very serious his wife and he was getting wonder for her capability to explain in professional way some details that she learnt by architects, women in that office. He promised to her that for everything that they need as the beginning I will help you and your friends, too.

When she asked him about his project for new town and first section, she said to her they will start next week with dinning ground and after we will start first section of this town. His wife got shocked because she did not know that he will start so fast project of new town close to desert area.

She was seeing very carefully him and suddenly she did not control herself while said: He changed so much and fast never is like before. Who stimulated him so much that is so energize? The younger man Zeeshan, heard her but really, he was focused to cut the steak meat with knife in small parts, and did not listen carefully but he understood that she did not control herself and expressed her wondering.

During this very beautiful quiet lovely spring evening was starting one conversation between two rivals of the new two projects that were spouses and were representing their family in extending of new beautiful environment of their beautiful city of Dubai.

Next day the younger man Zeeshan, went to his office that was campaigning by his secret service team's members. His secretary Salma, gave notice to him for those people that will come to meet him in his office for to sign contract for those heavy machineries and Comatcu tractor.

People came to meet him, after some times with full discussion they decided to sign contract for those heavy machinery, so it was the perfect time in this spring time to start dinning of this ground and same time to start this new beautiful project of this new town close to desert area.

Both sides were very happy for signing this contract and more was happy the younger man Zeeshan, that definitely will start this project of this new town.so this meeting was so "fruit-full", and the day was going so good for the younger man Zeeshan. Afternoon he wanted to go to the beach area. He went over there with his friend Emin, leader of secret service.

Strangely he wanted to sit on the sand close to ocean. They got place two of them together and were watching the blue water of ocean. His friend leader of his security team was watching him with wondering while his boss

Zeeshan, was not talking to him but was in deep thinking while was seeing in distance the blue water of ocean.

He asked his younger boss Zeeshan: What is going on about him?

The younger man Zeeshan, started, to speak like he was in cloud while his voice was coming so low like was coming from large distance. I am thinking so much for myself for my children and for my life. I am thinking, how came this big difficult, situation in my life and most of all I am thinking what will be the direction of my life in future, also I am thinking for my job and for this project.

As you saw me, all this time I was not concentrated in so many problems and matter of my life. I was distracted, I was sad, and I do not want to face again this situation, also something has changed inside me and this situation is scaring me.

The beautiful thing for me now is this new connection with this younger girl Agneza her brother and her cousins too, also with those professors of university of Ljubljana of Slovenia, of course and those professors of Vienna of Austria, but professor Bojana is doing more alive our relationship.

Absolutely my children are my love of my life, but to tell you the true I am now in cross road of my life about my family and about my future. I established the situation in my family but something is empty inside me, while this relation- ship with this e girl Agneza is intriguing me and it is attracting me so much.

it is another issue about her longer study about four years in university of Ljubljana of Slovenia or in Zagreb of Croatia wherever she will decide so it is longer time and so many things will change maybe. This situation is scaring me for this suddenly new love in my life.

His loyal friend said to him: You must to be quiet now to see yourself and your family with time "Allah" will give good direction to your life or to your new love. Take easy, do not get so much desperate. It is very good thing that you will work now with this project of this new town, so you will put so much busy yourself and you will not have time to think for those issues and you will not accept negative thoughts.

I am saying that everything is good around you, since all your people that are in your life now, like your family and this younger girl Agneza are good with health, so you do not need to disturb yourself.

At that time the younger man Zeeshan, said to his friend: You are very right; everyone is good so I need now to focus to this new project to have success. During this conversation the younger man Zeeshan, got support by his very good friend Emin, and his bodyguard – leader too, so he felt himself better that his friend was understanding him and supporting him so much.

The leader of security team Emin, said to his younger boss Zeeshan: Now is time we to go in your palace and I do not want to see you anymore in very deep thoughts, but I want to see you with smile, energize and with happy face.

They left that place close to ocean that evening and started to drive to the palace of the Prince Zeeshan,. His friend left him to his palace's garden and was continuing driving to go to his home while said to his younger boss: I will see you tomorrow in the morning.

During walking through the garden of his palace the younger man Zeeshan, was thinking and whispered: I need to go to see Agneza, I do not feel myself quiet if I am not going to see her soon, I have feeling that someone in my life is missing and is her. I think that I left her (Agneza)over there to the other part of the world alone and this is hurting me, and why she is with her family, but now I think that she is part of me.

I know that everyone is good here, because they all are in front of me and I am seeing them but she is so far away, thousands of miles away and my head with thoughts it is most of the time over there, with some questions: Hos is Agneza? What is doing?, How is doing? Etc.

Definitely I must to go to meet this lovely girl in her village "Lunaria" of Croatia. I have planned for her day of graduation but I do not know that is so far this date. Maybe this project of this new town close to desert area will keep me busy so I will be more concentrated to this new job and my time maybe will fly with speed while I hope not to suffer from negative thoughts. Anyway, I am very happy that I know this younger girl Agneza.

With those thoughts he was entering to his palace and all the time he was controlling his telephone cellular if he had any text message by Agneza or by professor Bojana that was his best friend now or by others.

He was thinking in quiet way: Really these people in Western Balkan gave me so much enthusiasm for my job and my life too. I met over there very good people. They created to me new vision for my life and new vision for my job and future project. They were very well-educated people, so we both sides have benefits by our experience in our different countries and why those countries are practicing different system.

I am very satisfied that he found new good intellectual friends in Western Balkan, in Croatia, Montenegro, and Ljubljana of Slovenia, and in center of Europein Vienna of Austria.

His thoughts were interrupted by voice of his two children that were speaking loudly with happiness. The younger man Zeeshan, felt warm and love inside his chest and his heart for his children and said, they did not sleep yet, I need to play a little bit with them now.

Next day the younger man Zeeshan, went in office got some people that were working in his government and with his security team all together they went to area that will start dinning ground for project of new town close to desert area. Really all were enthusiast and some of them did not know for really specific in whish place will start this project so they were very curious to see.

One friend of the younger man Zeeshan, said with humor let's name this day like "Picnic" like holiday, let's hope that is any restaurant over there. The younger man, Zeeshan, laughed and said it is one small restaurant over there close to my horses' field. His friend said to his younger boss Zeeshan, ooo very good so we will name this day "Holiday" and all the others people laughed with happiness.

When they arrived over there they were seeing with attention while their younger boss Zeeshan, started to explain in general way for this new town and after in specific way in details for the first section that he will put the name of his father, to this section of this new town. They approved it. After he explained for the second and third section.

He explained to them that the second section he will honor name, with his mother name that will have some residence but most of all will have some administrative building office etc., while the third name will be something spiritual like about peace.

All were listening with full attention and after they started to discuss and to make so many questions while the architect was giving answer as he can, but he said to them, this project will be done by one group of architects.

After they were driving to the corner of the desert area, and over there the younger man explained to them that this town will be extended until to dessert area and after over there is another project separated by here about one medical center. All those people said, that is very interesting project. They decided to eat lunch to small restaurant that was close with the field where horses had their shelter. They ordered their meal and started to discuss with happiness about this new project for their city Dubai, that will be extended in future.

The younger man Zeeshan, was listening all of them but really his, mind was flying far away, his thoughts were flying above different rivers, different hills, different mountains, different fields, different villages towns and cities until was arrived to "Lunaria" in front of the window of private houses where was living Agneza with her family.

Really he was very happy that was thinking for her and time by time he was not, concentrated to give answer when someone of this group of people was asking him for different thing.

They were thinking about his that maybe he was focused to his project and was thinking about it, so they accepted the younger man Zeeshan's justifies for not good attention. Some of them never can imagine that the younger man was in deep love and was thinking for this girl Agneza. That secret knows only his secret service team' members.

After lunch all of them entered to their car and started drive to go to their home. They have worked that day in nature. All were discussing for that project. Their younger boss Zeeshan. said to them:

Next week we will start dinning the ground and building shelters for workers that will work in that first section and to the others more later. We will do schedule because some people will be here to lead this project and to control, but this problem we will decide in my office when we will do our meeting before to start this dinning of ground.

Maybe we will do in this way different group, to work over there in different time to make enrollment of the people to these projects, so everybody will do participate during this project's operation.

All were agreed with his idea. One architect said with smile, maybe so many will be part time to this project to see and to control but architects and construction engineer and mechanic engineer needs to be all the time to this area until to finish this project.

So, you need to make hire some new professional people. Very right, your idea I like, I have thought about it but now we are continuing with our people and to see what will be the speed of development of this project after I will hire some new professional people for this area, or those younger employees to work in office and some of current employees to work over there to that area close with desert. Really all were agreed with their boss Zeeshan, and said this is really very good idea.

Later they return to their city. The younger man was going happy to his palace and was very early compare with others days of his job. He thought that was good that he was early in his home so he decided to take his two children and his lovely dog Zoros, and to go out to spend time with his two children that afternoon.

He entered to his palace and called the lady Farrah, that was taking care for him, since he was child, like the other lady Aasma that was working in kitchen too. He told to her to prepare his two children to dress because after one hour he will go out with them. He said to her that he did not want to eat because he ate out with his friends of his office.

He entered to his studio, opened his computer and was reading e-mails, after he opened his telephone cellular, while he saw message from so many people but first, he opened the message that was send Agneza. Her message was only one beautiful picture of Agneza with one open book in her hand and one colorful frame of picture around was with shape of red heart. It was only one short phrase:

"I am waiting you, like hot summer's time is waiting raining"!

The younger man Zeeshan, whispered: Agneza loves me! He felt that all his body got shiver while heat was spreading inside his chest, suddenly the tears were going down to his face. He wrote to her immediately:

If you want for me to come now, I will leave so many jobs, behind I will come but I will not stay so longer over there, maybe one or two days, I can do that for you, but if you will wait sometimes until to the day of your graduation, I will have established all my job and I will come over there to stay maybe one week with you. Agneza answered with writing: I am agreed, better to come the day of graduation so the days that you will stay, I have nothing to do because I finish the school, and I will have vacation. So, we will spend so much time together. The younger man Zeeshan wrote to her: I shall come the day of graduation!

After he opened the message that has sent Professor Bojana, she has sent one picture in her room in her home, that were so many books on the table, one picture in beautiful silver frame, where her the younger man Zeeshan, and her friends to university of Ljubljana of Slovenia.

While in front of the wall was one picture of her and the younger man Zeeshan, in balcony of cafeteria to his city Dubai, while the moon looked in the picture and some stars in dark night. The light that was coming from inside of cafeteria was giving light to their face that were in profile between the door of balcony and the view of the sky with moon and stars in distance.

Really this picture was so beautiful, professor Bojana has done bigger that image, looked so in details. Really this picture got with camera by one friend of Professor Bojana when they were in balcony to see the stars in that evening.

The younger man Zeeshan, said with voice: This is very beautiful picture!

I know that she loves me but she will be my best friend in long run. Who knows what will happened in this life?! Now I am loyal and I am in deep love with Agneza. He wrote to Professor Bojana while was giving to her so much compliment for beautiful picture in very beautiful frame on the wall, that really it was like beautiful creative art, and for the picture with group that she has put on the table.

He was continuing to read all others message by other professors of Ljubljana's university of Slovenia, and Vienna 's university of Austria, and from students from Montenegro, really, he was happy that they wrote to him.

At that time lady brought two his children that she dressed up and they were happy to see their father while he hugged them and kissed them. He closed is computer, also closed his telephone cellular, got children and got out of palace, while the beautiful beige color Zoroz dog was walking behind them while was moving all around his shirt tale.

The younger man Zeeshan, established well his children on the car secured them with belt and his dog Zoros, too and started his driving outside of his huge and very beautiful luxury palace.

It was one very beautiful afternoon. They were going to one park that was close with his area. Strangely one ring of his telephone cellular got his attention. He answered to the telephone but was his loyal friend leader Emin, of security team.

He asked him for tomorrow what time to be to his palace, because they will go next day to the place close to dessert – area. At that time his friend Emin, listened the voice of his two children that were screaming and laughing and playing with Zoros dog. The leader of security team Emin, asked his younger boss Zeeshan:

Where are you now because I heard the voice of your children and some noise around. The younger man Zeeshan, said to him:

I am with my two children and my dog Zoros, to this park close to my area. The leader Emin, said to him: You did not tell me that you are going out with your children. So, you are alone and I am coming right away, alone to stay with you.

He did not wait to listen the answer of his younger boss Zeeshan, and closed his telephone cellular. The younger man Zeeshan, wanted to say to him, not to make tired himself and to come, but his friend closed the telephone to the other side.

The younger man Zeeshan, was very happy when he was seeing his two children so much happy to come around and to play with Zoros dog, behind them were going and some others children that started to love the small beautiful beige color dog Zoros.

So, the small dog Zoros, was running around with is small tale lift up while was moving its tale around while the two children of the younger man Zeeshan, and some the other children were running behind dog Zoros, but they cannot arrive it, because the dog Zoros, was going under different benches and looked that dog Zoros, loved this game.

All children were screaming and laughing were doing big noise with happiness that they did not catch the small beautiful dog Zoros. So, the younger man Zeeshan, and their parents were laughing loudly. After 40 minutes the younger man Zeeshan, saw his loyal friend Emin, the leader of security team that came with full smile close to him.

The younger man Zeeshan, was very happy that he saw his friend that came for him. He started to explain to him that he wanted to tell him not to come but heard that his telephone got closed. The leader of secret service Emin, laughed loudly and said to his younger boss Zeeshan:

I knew that you will say not to come here, for that I closed fast. Both of them laughed. After the leader of security team Emin, said to his younger boss Zeeshan, and best friend too that: I never will live you alone wherever you to go and specific when you are with your children.

The afternoon was going good with happiness and people all around with their children were calmer. When the sunset started to show it beautiful mixer color with pink to orange, that was spreading around the blue sky and why was doing jealous the white clouds that were staying persistent to their position but sunset was determinant, to spread its beautiful mixer color.

At that time the younger man Zeeshan, said to his best friend bodyguard Emin: Let's go to take ice cream with my children too. His friend was agreed. When he got his two children to put in his big car Mercedez – Benc and after that was running the small dog Zoros, he heard some children were calling for dog Zoros.

At that time one small boy started to cry loudly and his mother was running to see what happened. The younger man Zeeshan, saw the boy that was lifting his small hand to direction of his car. He asked his mother what happened with your small son?

The mother of the small boy laughed and said to the younger man Zeeshan: My boy, said to me: They are taking the small dog Zoros, that we were playing. He is crying for the dog. At that time and four more others small children came close to ask for the dog Zoros.

The younger man Zeeshan laughed loudly while he got the Zoros dog in his hand and went to the small boy that was continuing to cry, and put the dog to his hand. He hugged dog and stopped his crying, while his mother said to her son, they will tell me when they will bring for you this dog to play here.

The younger man Zeeshan, kissed the small boy and said to him: I will bring for you the dog Zoros, again for you to play with it. At that time all others children said bring tomorrow, bring tomorrow. The younger man Zeeshan, his bodyguard Emin, and the mother of the small boy laughed loudly. It was wonderful afternoon. While his two children were seeing from window of the car and were waiting their small beautiful beige Zoros dog.

After that they were going to one small store that was selling ice cream. The two children chose the ice cream with so many colors like rainbow and they were very happy. The younger man Zeeshan, and is leader of secret service got only Vanila white ice cream and were continuing their conversation for schedule of the next day.

During driving to his palace, the younger man Zeeshan, said to his friend, now days are longer with light so it is very good we to start this project right away. Definitely next Monday we will start dinning ground with those heavy tractor "Comatcu".

When they arrived to the palace of the prince Zeeshan, his friend said to him good night and was driving to go to his home. Prince Zeeshan, got his two children and Zoros dog and entered to his palace. His wife Leylae, got out to the top of the stairs in second floor, and was waiting with happiness and smiling all of them, their two children her husband Zeeshan, and small Zoros dog.

When they got to the kitchen all of them, her husband Zeeshan, explained to her for all afternoon time that was so wonderful and for new friends that their children found to the park and were playing with happiness all of them with Zoros dog.

After he told to her, about that small boy that was crying for dog, while his mother was not able to stop him and promise of the prince Zeeshan, to him to send dog again over there.

After he told for four others small children that said to him with one voice bring tomorrow dog Zoros dog, was so fast in running and sometimes he was going under the benches and two our children and the other children were not able to caught him.

His wife Leylae, laughed loudly. Prince Zeeshan, said with laughing: Really it was today one wonderful afternoon and so much funny, also my friend Emin, leader of security team came to me to stay with us. When we left park we went to the store, to take ice cream and our two children got ice cream with every kind of color, while prince Zeeshan, smiled his wife Leylae, laughed loudly, he continued explanation: While me and my friend we got only Vanila ice cream. Prince Zeeshan, was seeing his wife Leylae, that was laughing loudly for their children and he thought it is a long time I did not see her like that, she is happy now. I never believed that will come that situation like this now.

Next day the younger man Zeeshan, was waiting his security team's members in front of his palace in the beautiful garden that during spring time has showed multicolor of its flowers around.

The garden looked like one carpet that through the green painting color by green grass were spreading around their different colors the innocent quiet flowers with their petals.

The multicolor flowers looked they did not want to bother so much the green grass that sometimes with its capricious was dealing with some bushes around with more bold green color only for jealousy to cover the beauty of multicolor, flowers.

During the time arrived in front of his palace arrived the security team's members of the younger man Zeeshan, while he entered to their car and the driver started driving to the place close to desert's area.

Over there they found one big group of people with engineers, economists, mechanics person and two big trucks and three big tractor "Comatcu". So, the organize was perfect to start this digging ground after two days.

It was Friday that started weekend early for off day, but the younger man Zeeshan, has decided to start after two days this project Monday, everything to be ready. All were very serious for this project and all specialists were over there, after 30 minutes came and so many people from different Corporations of construction to see.

This project was spread all around this big city of Dubai, and all around the country United Arab Emirates (UAE) within one hour came so many others cars with simple citizens they were happy and curious to see what will happen over there, this day looked like preparation of one big event or big holiday.

All people looked happy and this situation was unexpected for the younger man Zeeshan, he got so much impression and felt his eyes were with tears. He was happy when and others simple citizen gave to him warm congratulation.

He understood that people love him, they came from faraway to see, so they love their leader younger man Zeeshan, and they love their beautiful modern and big city Dubai, that was opening its arm beyond until to the desert area.

That day, all decided definitely the Monday will start digging ground for this new project of this new town. The engineers were so much enthusiast and said to the younger man Zeeshan, this is the great idea that you gave for extended or our city of Dubai. This project will open so many jobs for people and will give so much development to this area that was left behind like dead zone.

All those people, were creating some different groups and were discussing with enthusiasm about this project and some of them were giving some new ideas for that first section of this new town. All looked that wanted to contribute in their lovely city Dubai.

The younger man Zeeshan, thought with himself: I never believed that people will have so much interests for this new town, for this reason now I feel myself so much happy that I created this idea and I am making possible that this new idea for new environment to become reality and people to love it. I am proud for my father that supported me and gave okay and forward for my idea for this project too.

When all people started to leave this place the younger man Zeeshan, stayed with his security team behind and they went to field of horses and spent some times over there with horses and camels, after they were driving to go to their city.

Prince Zeeshan, was so much happy and was speaking so much enthusiast with his friends. He said to them: I am very happy to start this project right away because the days are going fast, looks that spring time will leave soon its place to summer times.

We need to use the time not to waste so much time for nothing.

This weather now will be good and for workers that will work in this section now, because very hot weather has its effect and consequences anyway. They spent all the day to this place so when they entered to their city the younger man Zeeshan, said to their friends that he did not want to go that day to his office already was later afternoon, but he wanted to go to his palace while he explained to them, that he wanted to work that afternoon to his studio in his palace.

They left him in front of his palace and continued their driving to go to their home. The younger man Zeeshan, entered to his palace, asked for two children and lady said that they are with their mother to the garden behind palace, so he went straight, to kitchen got one glass with water and went to balcony. He was waiting over there until children to come inside the palace.

He was seeing in distance to the horizon while whispered that spring time is going so fast and I do not know and not recognize myself anymore. I am thinking so much for my family, but I am thinking more and more for this younger girl Agneza that really, I am in deep love with her.

I think that now I am walking in one tight space between two grey and white shadows, that is clouding my thoughts. So, I need some space and sometimes, until he golden sun to make bright this space and with his heat to disappear those two shadows, while I will clarity about my decision for my life.

I need time now, to know more better myself and to know more better situation that I am now, so after not to have regret for my action whatever that to be. The best thing that I like now for myself, is the big changing that happened to me, and big inspiration that I have now.

Now I am with full hope for big progress in my job in my project and in my life. I see big strength to myself and so much confidence that never I believed before that I will have those to my life.

I was going the very turbulent situation during this period of time about my family and my life but now the situation is calmer and this is effect of those people that I know those last time from Western Balkan and specific Agneza, Gentius, Professor Bojana etc, and more important for this calm situation, it is the time because the time is giving healing to everything and is making the turbulent situation quiet.

Weekend was going so fast, and came the first day of the week Monday. To the place that the tractor "Comatcu", will start their digging of the ground were gathering so much people. When the younger man Zeeshan, arrived over there with his security team's members and others people from his government were over there he got shocked for so many people that were in that morning in that place.

All were waiting like was happening one miracle. The officials of the younger man Zeeshan, came close to him and were waiting him what he will say. There were some other politicians and some others Chief Executive Officer of different Corporations, over there.

Some of family's members of the younger man Zeeshan, were over there too, also so many journalists were over there that all the time were getting pictures and were writing in same times. Came the moment that the big tractor "Comatcu" started its engine, while one engineer and one mechanical person were leading the driver of tractor where to start.

When the tractor started to work and to digging the ground one big noise by applause by hands of people came so strong all around. All were happy for this big and good starting. It was unimaginable big enthusiasms that gave big wondering the younger man, Zeeshan.

All were saying with smile started for really project started for really. At that time the younger man Zeeshan, asked one person to one group people: Why you are saying that started for really this project?!

He smiled and said we did not believe because so many projects are discussing in time but some of them really are happening, but the news for this project came so fast in unexpected way, like light in sunny day and started so fact, so thank you very much for job well done, and gave us so much optimism our dear leader Zeeshan.

After that people in this group gave their hand to the younger man Zeeshan, and did one request to make one picture with him that he approved and so they did some pictures with him.

After started this process the tractor was continuing its job and all workers that will work as the beginning over there got their position all around and others people started to leave this place while where driving in direction of the big city Dubai.

All were happy the journalist Hamad, was seeing the pictures that he got to place and said this beginning will be in history of this new town and this picture is so beautiful. All saw the pictures that he has done before the tractor to start, he got image all around and after the picture of the tractors started its digging of the ground. Also, Cameraman Jassim was register with video-camera starting of this process too.

The younger man Zeeshan, said to Journalist: you did one wonderful job because this will be historic fact of this new town in future for new generation. Journalist Hamad, has got in pictures all the different group of people that were present in that day. The younger man Zeeshan, said to the driver:

I need to go to office so continue to drive to our official building.

When they arrived to the building where were offices of the government, the younger man Zeeshan, went to his office. Strangely this day he was very happy to go to stay during this part of the day to his office alone he was feeling comfortable over there. He was alone in office, while opened the computer and was reading some materials and all e-mails and that different people has sent to him, he was thinking:

This spring time has so longer those days. I think, that is taking so longer for me to go to the Western Balkan's countries. I want the days to go faster. Really, he was in love with this girl Agneza and did not have patience to wait more time until to go over there, but he has so many matters and jobs to follow and specific this new project of this new town.

He whispered with himself: Really, I am in deep love with this girl Agneza. When person is in truly love, the highest mountain looked like soft and beautiful, field to go through, to walk fast and with happiness and never to feel tired.

He, opened his telephone cellular and wrote so fast one text message to Agneza. Tell me exact when is the date of your Graduation 's day- ceremony.

Agneza called him right away she was very happy for his text message with this, question. He was unprepared for her calling by telephone so fast and felt that all his body, got warm and started to speak with high voice, that got attention to other office where secretary lady Salma was. She came so fast. She thought maybe is any problem but when she saw her younger boss Zeeshan, with full smile in his face and his eyes were sparkling lightly, so she understood that he was happy and was not any problem.

Secretary lady Salma, did sign with hand that is Okay, everything and left his office. The younger man Zeeshan, laughed and continued conversation with his lovely younger girl Agneza. Both of them were very happy they were talking together like they were both of them teenager.

Their happiness was spreading all around the office, looked that all the book in bookshelves of the office were curious and jealous for their conversation and for their love story, that looked bold and maybe they did not have through their pages one very beautiful and interesting love story like their office's owner the, younger man Zeeshan.

At that time for his voice shouting high in office the beautiful crystal chandelier above his head started to move with elegance softly, that got attention of the younger man Zeeshan, while he was seeing up to it.

Maybe and beautiful crystal chandelier was curios and have jealousy for this love story and happiness of the younger man Zeeshan, because in its crystal it was a longer time that his smile was not reflected to them.

The very beautiful white lace curtains with very beautiful design in itself, were moving slowly and looked that wind that was coming from outside from blue water of ocean was telling to curtains the secret of this love story of the younger man Zeeshan, with this younger girl Agneza. All the furniture, and supplies in this office got movement and got curious to know the really true of this lover story.

The younger man Zeeshan, did not care for all those furniture and supplies that were moving to know something but was continuing this sweet conversation with his lovely girl Agneza.

So many times, two - three employees came to his office with some documents, but when they saw that he was very happy and was talking loudly in English language, they left their document on the table and made with sign to their younger boss Zeeshan, that they will come more latter. During this time Agneza told to him that four important exams are finishing at June

28, and the day of graduation and dinner for finishing high school will be, in June 30.

During the morning will be ceremony and giving diplomas to students while at the evening that day will have dinner for finishing school and to say Good Bye to each other students that will go in different direction in some will study University and some maybe will go to work. During this dinner will have dance too.

The younger man Zeeshan, told to her that he will be over there at June 29 and he will be present in her ceremony and in this dinner in the evening together with her, also he will stay with her over there one week after.

Really the younger man Zeeshan, did not tell to Agneza, that he did not have patience to see her but covered up with the justifies that he was so much busy and so this time in the end of the June will be perfect time for him to be over there, so he will have time to organize all jobs in his city of Dubai.

After he asked Agneza for her brother Gentius and her two cousins Armina and Dalmet. She answered with happiness that all are good and are waiting you when you will come for my Graduation's day of this school.

Agneza was continuing her speech: My brother Gentius is seeing all the time news in online and in You Tube, and when he is seeing news about you or different video, he is telling to our mother and father and said to them:

Look my lovely Prince Zeeshan, he is my best friend, while our parents are laughing with him. He is doing that conversation and when our cousins are coming to our home for visit. When he does not see any news about you, mother and father are making joke with him and said: Gentius you did not have any news about your lovely Prince Zeeshan, today? …Because he is your best friend.

Gentius in the moment is opening the telephone cellular and is doing search in online, at that moment that he is seeing your picture in news, he is screaming and said to our parents: Look where is my lovely Prince Zeeshan, all the time in news what are you asking for?!

So, during this time of those conversation in our home is so much fun and happiness when we see so much happy Gentius and when he is speaking for you, all his very nice and white face is taking red color and speaking with full enthusiasm. After that statement by Agneza about her brother Gentius the younger man Zeeshan, laughed loudly. So, this afternoon was so much happy time for the younger Zeeshan, with this sweet conversation with his lovely girl Agneza.

When they finished conversation and gave Good Bye to each other the younger man said: Thank You, "Allah" for this happiness that you are bringing to me.

He was thinking so much for Agneza. In his fantasy she was like one fluorescent light that in dark was giving so much sparkle to his life and to his glad situation and to his happiness. With her sweet behavior and her innocent and full love for the younger man Zeeshan she was increasing possibility to him to think, that in future he to be closer with her and to create family with her.

During this progressive situation between the younger man Zeeshan, and this younger girl Agneza the Universe with his extra positive energy, was giving speed to the time that the younger man Zeeshan, to show to Agneza, what was born to his heart during this time.

So many evenings during the dark night that he was praying to the stars for his love, he thought that the stars were giving more bright light, while looked that Halley Comet, got this news from Earth Planet, for this new love by the younger Zeeshan, while during its flying was spreading with its tale this news to all the stars while was flying aside.

With those thoughts the younger man Zeeshan, decided to see the documents that his official people brought to his office, while was reading those he decided to discuss next day with them about those documents. He decided to go in his palace, really, he was tired that day and was so much preoccupied about this day of starting this project while everything is done good.

He called his leader of security team Emin, and said to him that he needs to go to his palace. He left office and went to his car while with his security - team's members was waiting over there. They entered in car and the driver started driving to go to his palace.

When he arrived in palace, gave greeting to his security - team's members and was going to enter to his palace. Really, he felt something difficult breath, during this time. He knew that the situation was quiet and calmer now in his family, but really, he did not feel happiness to tell again to his wife Leylae, about this success of starting this project that day, and specific after the conversation that he had with his lovely girl Agneza.

He whispered with himself: I do not know myself anymore! I feel that I am entering to one very heavy forest with taller trees and I do not find in easy way the path to go through the forest to the other side or to go out of this forest.

I feel that I have lost in this forest, but I will follow the ways of golden sun's rays where are coming that will tell me east, west or north and south after that I will take what direction I will decide. I am confused, about this situation but I love so much my happy situation about this new love.

He entered inside his luxury palace, and did routine action he went to the room of their two children and spent some minutes with them, after entered to his studio and was waiting his wife Leylae, to come because he was sure that she was coming.

What he thought so happened his wife Leylae, came and he started to tell to her about that day how they started this project with first step of digging the ground all around. When she left, he went to another room and wanted to relax to one luxury sofa while was thinking so much. After this full activity day this evening was so much quiet in his home, and he has so much time to think.

Next day he went to office to meet with some other chief executive officers of so many others corporations, so they will discuss for others steps of this project, for starting construction of buildings. He did meet with them and after he understood that he will be very busy with this project, but anyway he never regrets his decision to go to meet Agneza and his promise to her for the Graduation's Day.

Days really after started project were going incredibly, fast and the place of new town was taking image of one big of construction's cantier while was forwarding. The younger man Zeeshan, was very happy that days were going fast, and he was waiting without patience to go to see Agneza.

Looked that his brain was working so hard and his wish and decision to see her was coming stronger and definitely he understood inside of him in his heart and mind that he did not want to lose Agneza.

During this season of spring time, while the field around were taking green color by green grass and multicolor flowers started to show themselves through the field, and so many birds were coming from the north of the Earth planet and were filling the electric line and so many branches of the trees while were chirping and tweeting, all around, the nature was so beautiful.

The breeze was coming from blue water of ocean and was giving fresh air all around while made people to have freely breath and so much happiness, while with full energize to perform their duty in different field, so like them was not exception and the younger man Zeeshan.

The days were going fast like the river's water on hills relieve, during this time the younger man Zeeshan, was continuing his daily job, while time by time he was going with his friends to see progress of the job of the construction of new town close to desert's area.

Really, he was so much energizing during this time also he was waiting with happiness when he will travel to village "Lunaria" of Croatia on Western Balkan. He was waiting this day like big holiday, for his new friend lovely girl Agneza, that with her sweet speech has planted the seed s of love in the heart of the younger man Zeeshan.

Really, he wanted to take her to study University to his country but when he analyzed the situation of his family, he understood that tension was down level but under the lay of this situation the feelings of the two sides, his wife Leylae, and him were very hot to explode in wild way in surface.

During this time that he started this new project of this "New Town" close to desert 's area, the younger man Zeeshan, wanted quiet time and very calm situation. The feelings of hot love were flying to "Lunaria" village of Croatia on the Western Balkan, while the feeling of taking care about everything for his family still stronger to his luxury huge palace.

The love for his children was unconditionally. His behave to his wife Leylae, was respectful but about hot love to her this was matter of discussion of his heart.

He was counting weeks and days now until to go to make happy his girl Agneza for her big day of graduation of high school and to spent one week over there with her with her brother Gentius, her cousins Armina and Dalmet, and some friends that he has found over there he was thinking to visit one day and Ljubljana of Slovenia to meet those professors and his best friend now Professor Bojana.

This trip over there was important that the main point was about Agneza's Graduation - day also and for the other friends too. He understood that knowing new and other people was creating possibility to open different paths of life and to learn different experiences.

During this time, he understood that really, he was in deep love with Agneza but he decided not to make any decisive action, while was thinking, that time and distance sometimes are important factors in relationship between two people. He thought: "Allah" will give good way to happen my "Suddenly White Dream".

Season of spring time slowly was leaving its place to the bright hot summer time, so and the beautiful June month was coming with its multicolor flowers that were greeting with their petals the hot rays of the golden sun under one very clear open blue sky.

The heart of the younger man Zeeshan, was glad for the trip that was coming in future for him. He was very happy all those days. He was smiling all the time with his people in his office. His happiness was spreading all around his palace too, but no one was understanding what was the source of this happiness. Some people were thinking maybe the source of this happiness, is this new project that was forwarding so good.

Whatever was it source of happiness this was influencing so good to all people that surrounding the younger man Zeeshan, in office and in his palace too. With his children he was spending so much time, specific for weekend and was doing them so much happy with different surprises of games.

He was sending his two children and his dog "Zoros", to play with their new friends – other children in park, that this situation turned like ritual. So, all children over there were happy and their parents were happy too while they were playing with Zoros dog around. One beautiful day he told to his friend Emin, leader of the security team that they will travel at the end of the June to Croatia on the Western Balkan. He explained to him that he wanted to be over there for Graduation's Day of Agneza of high school also to spend some times with her.

His best loyal friend Emin asked him: What you have decided to do?!

The younger man Zeeshan, answered straight to him:

The situation with my wife has changed for good, but really, I am in love with this girl Agneza. I did not decide anything now only to present to her Graduation – Day. After the younger man Zeeshan, make sign with his finger up to the sky and said: Only "Allah" know what will be decision in future!

The leader of the security team Emin, said to his younger boss Zeeshan:

I wish your happiness all your life. "Allah" to help and to be with you all the time. Both said in same time:" Amen!"

One evening the younger man Zeeshan, explained to his wife Leylae, for his trip in the end of the June month. He explained to her short strict he needs to go over there first for Graduation's Day of one student that he promised to her and other reasons were job 's matter.

His wife Leylae, started to speak with easy irony with smile: Does has to do this graduation's day with your private life. He answered serious: It is only Graduation's Day, of the high school that is big performer for this student girl that is preparing to study in Ljubljana 's University of Slovenia.

She did not speak anymore but changed topic of the conversation. Really, the younger man Zeeshan, has some principles he did not want to give fake situation to his wife Leylae, so in future whatever to happen, he told to her the reason of this trip.

This matter did not have to do with their religion rights to have more than one wife but has to do with new love that was born during vacant time of their conflict and their families too.

Anyway, situation was going calmer and why the answer of his wife's question was staying in air. So, this conversation created one new situation that the younger man Zeeshan, was staying strict in his principles and his wife Leylae, was accepting compromise and not to fight in wild way, so they choose better way for their family and their two children too. The week was coming that the younger man Zeeshan, with his security team's members will travel to Western Balkan.

He was doing in schedule so good everything that he has planned until he to travel, he was happy for his achievement and progress of this new project of "New Town".

He has so many things what to tell to professors and architects of Ljubljana 's university of Slovenia that he will visit them and to the Vienna's university of Austria that he will talk with telephone and with skype by computer.

So many things changed during this time around so and to the younger man Zeeshan, changed so many things about concepts for life and about vision for future of environment. Everything was in progress in his daily life and his daily job too.

The week that they will travel was in "corner" so he was thinking with enthusiasm for this trip. This trip and this new relationship it was, like one gate that was opening for the younger man Zeeshan, that was entering to one wide unknown but beautiful field of life.

So, in this beautiful green field the younger man Zeeshan, will find the multicolor beautiful flowers with good scent, and maybe some wild plants and bushes that will burn his hand if was touching those.

Anyway, the younger man Zeeshan, was preparing himself to see only beautiful multicolor flowers with good scent for really on this beautiful field of life. He was thinking to spend some days with Agneza and her brother Gentius, together and to visit some beautiful places with them and his security team's members.

He was thinking that during this trip while they will fly with his private jet, up to the sky he wishes that his dream to fly up to the sky too, and the golden sun, silver moon and all stars, to honor and greeting its dream too. So, universe with its positive energy to bless his "Suddenly White Dream" for this younger girl Agneza.

The source of his happiness was this new relationship with this younger girl Agneza. He whispered with himself: Whatever to happen in future, I do not want to think now, important for me is that I am very happy now.

"Allah" will help me and will be with me in this journey!

Came the day that they will travel in June 29 so they will be over there for ceremony and dinner at June 30, of Graduation's Day, of Agneza. Before to fly he called Agneza and told her that they will start flying now, while he heard her cheering with happiness.

During flying with his crew, members of his security team, with his private jet, he was watching calmer with full happiness while, he was seeing the heavy white cloud up to the blue sky: He whispered with himself: My "Suddenly White Dream" it is between those white clouds and the trip is sending me to it! "Allah" bless me! I adore this girl Agneza, I love her. I hope this dream to be reality.

Printed in the United States
by Baker & Taylor Publisher Services